MW01283826

TEXTS IN COMPUTER SCIENCE

Editors
David Gries
Fred B. Schneider

Springer
New York
Berlin
Heidelberg
Barcelona
Hong Kong
London
Milan
Paris
Singapore
Tokyo

TEXTS IN COMPUTER SCIENCE

(continued after index)

Peter Revesz

INTRODUCTION TO CONSTRAINT DATABASES

With 112 Illustrations

 Springer

Peter Revesz
Department of Computer Science and Engineering
University of Nebraska
Lincoln, NE 68588-0115, USA
revesz@cse.unl.edu

Series Editors

David Gries
Department of Computer Science
415 Boyd Graduate Studies Research Center
The University of Georgia
Athens, GA 30602-7404, USA

Fred B. Schneider
Department of Computer Science
Upson Hall
Cornell University
Ithaca, NY 14853-7501, USA

Cover illustration: Cover art by William Clocksin, 2001.

Library of Congress Cataloging-in-Publication Data
Revesz, Peter Z.
    Introduction to constraint databases / Peter Revesz.
        p.   cm. — (Texts in computer science)
    Includes bibliographical references and index.
    ISBN 0-387-98729-0 (alk. paper)
    1. Constraint databases.   I. Title.   II. Series.
QA76.9.C67 R48 2001
005.75—dc21   2001041134

Printed on acid-free paper.

Production managed by Michael Koy; manufacturing supervised by Jacqui Ashri.
Typeset pages prepared using the author's LaTeX 2$_\varepsilon$ files by Integre Technical Publishing Company, Inc., Albuquerque, NM.
Printed and bound by Hamilton Printing Co., Rensselaer, NY.
Printed in the United States of America.

9 8 7 6 5 4 3 2 1

ISBN 0-387-98729-0   SPIN 10707989

Springer-Verlag   New York Berlin Heidelberg
A member of BertelsmannSpringer Science+Business Media GmbH

In memory of Paris C. Kanellakis

Hold Infinity in the palm of your hand,
And Eternity in an hour.

—William Blake, *Auguries of Innocence*

Preface

Purpose and Goals

This textbook provides comprehensive coverage of constraint databases. The primary audience of the book is advanced undergraduate and beginning graduate students. For them the extensive set of exercises at the end of each chapter will be useful. The text and the exercises assume as prerequisite only basic discrete mathematics, linear algebra, and programming knowledge. Many database experts will also find the bibliographic notes after each chapter a valuable reference for further reading. For both students and database experts the sample systems discussed in Chapters 18–20, as well as some slides, are available free from the author's Web page: `http://cse.unl.edu/~revesz`

Topics Coverage and Organization

The dependencies of the chapters are shown in the chart on the next page. The material covered is organized into five broad categories:

- **Models:** The material covered includes data abstraction and the relational data model (Chapter 1), the constraint data model (Chapter 2), several spatiotemporal data models (Chapter 13.1–3), and data storage (Chapter 17).

- **Queries:** Relational algebra and SQL (Chapter 3), Datalog (Chapter 4), Datalog with negation and aggregation (Chapter 5), refinement queries (Chapter 6), and spatiotemporal database queries (Chapter 13.4).

- **Evaluation:** The evaluation issues discussed are safety (Chapter 8), evaluation and quantifier-elimination (Chapter 9), computational complexity

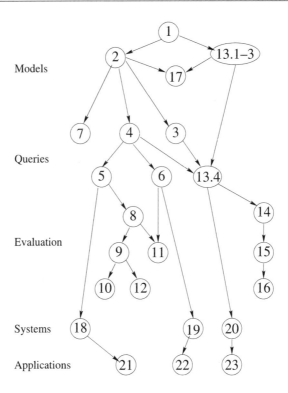

(Chapter 10), certification of safety (Chapter 11), and implementation out-line with data structures and pseudo-codes or key algorithms (Chapter 12). There is also coverage of interoperability among several types of constraint and spatiotemporal databases (Chapter 14), approximation data representation and query evaluation (Chapter 15), and data visualization (Chapter 16).

- **Systems:** The book describes a sample linear constraint database system (Chapter 18), a Boolean constraint database system (Chapter 19), and a spatiotemporal database system (Chapter 20).

- **Applications:** Sample applications are included in three diverse areas: computer vision (Chapter 21), bioinformatics (Chapter 22), and environmental modeling (Chapter 23).

A special strength of the book is that it allows a flexible course design. A good introductory course would cover some chapters from each category. For example, an introductory course focused on linear constraint databases may cover Chapters 1, 2, 3, 4, 5, 8, 18, and 21. An introductory course focused on Boolean constraints may replace the last three of these with Chapters 6, 19, and 22.

The text also allows several types of advanced courses. An advanced course focused on query evaluation may start with a brief review of Chapters 1–5 and then cover Chapters 8, 9, 10, 12, and 17. An advanced course focused on spatiotemporal databases may briefly review Chapters 1–4 and then cover Chapters 13–17, 20, and 23.

Acknowledgments

I would like to thank Berthe Choueiry and Manolis Koubarakis for reviewing almost the entire book, French Roy and James Van Etten for reviewing the specialty chapter on bioinformatics, Franz Mora for reviewing the chapter on environmental modeling. All the chapters except the first five are based on material presented in numerous journals, conferences, and workshops. I thank my coauthors on many of those papers, including the late Paris Kanellakis, my Ph.D. thesis advisor, and Gabriel Kuper, my two coauthors on the original paper on constraint databases. I also thank the following more recent coauthors from whom I learned much: Andras Benczur, Jan Chomicki, Floris Geerts, Gosta Grahne, Alberto Mendelzon, Agnes Novak, Raghu Ramakrishnan, Divesh Srivastava, and Jan Van den Bussche. I also thank the anonymous reviewers of our papers.

The book was used in manuscript form as a textbook for several years at the University of Nebraska. I would like to thank the following students for their comments on the text: Brian Boon, Mengchu Cai, Rui Chen, Yi Chen, Ying Deng, Dinesh Keshwani, Lixin Li, and Min Ouyang. In addition, the following students contributed to the material presented in the book via their programming efforts of the constraint database systems described in Chapters 18–20: Jo-Hag Byon, Pradip Kanjamala, Yiming Li, Yuguo Liu, Prashanth Nandavanam, Andrew Salamon, Yonghui Wang, and Lei Zhang. I also thank Pradeep Gundavarapu and Vijay Eadala for their help in drawing figures or contributing some examples.

I am grateful to the editors at Springer-Verlag, especially Wayne Wheeler and Wayne Yuhasz, for their careful editing and attention to several details in the production of the book. The preparation of this book was supported in part by the U.S. National Science Foundation under grants IRI-9625055 and IRI-9632871, by a Gallup Research Professorship, and by the University of Nebraska-Lincoln.

Finally, I would like to thank Lilla, my wife, for her enthusiasm and patience during the writing of this book.

Lincoln, Nebraska, USA   Peter Revesz
May 2001

Contents

1

Infinite Relational Databases

All good products provide some abstraction for the users. For example, people can drive a car without knowing how its engine works. For the task of driving cars the details of the working of the engine are unimportant. Similarly, *data abstraction* allows people to forget about some details of the data that may be unimportant to them. Good database systems have to provide an abstract view of the actual data stored in the computer.

In this chapter we describe the two highest levels of data abstraction, the *view* and the *logical* levels, used in relational database systems.

1.1 The View Level

The highest level of data abstraction is the *view* level. A view is a way of presenting data to a particular group of users. There are many things that are known about good presentation of data. For example, one has to account for users' preferences for color and layout, size of letters, readability, and so on. Each view also has to be functional for the users. That is, while designing a view for a group of users, one has to keep in mind the tasks they will perform with the data and find a view that facilitates the tasks. These are some of the issues that are studied in the area of *human-computer interaction* in computer science. However, view-level presentation of the data is only partly science; it remains partly art, requiring creativity in design.

For the view-level presentation of complex data, especially spatiotemporal data, the field of *computer graphics* plays an increasingly important part. Computer graphics deals with issues such as realistic display of images and movies. In this book we will not study either human-computer interaction or graphics in

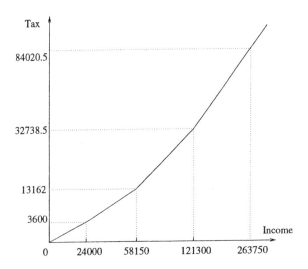

FIGURE 1.1. Income vs. tax chart.

detail. However, we give some examples to illustrate the range of possibilities for view-level presentation of data.

Chart: Charts show continuous curves or discrete bars and can be used to visually illustrate the relationship between two variables. For example, the chart in Figure 1.1 shows the relationship between total income on the x-axis and tax due on the y-axis.

Graph: Suppose that the database contains information about the fastest possible travel times between pairs of cities in the midwest United States. A graph like the one in Figure 1.2 could be a useful view of the data.

Drawing: By drawings we mean simple black-and-white sketches of pictures. An example drawing of a bird is shown in Figure 1.5. Such a drawing can be understood as a set of points on the plane.

Map: The map is a favorite presentation in geographic information systems (GISs) dealing with phenomena about the surface of the earth. The scale of a map can either be huge, like the whole United States, or small, like the blueprint of a house.

For example, Figure 1.3 shows an outline of some city streets. The left side of Figure 1.4 shows a rough approximation of the city of Lincoln, Nebraska, and the right side shows the areas that can be reached by three different radio stations. The three radio stations broadcast to an elliptic, a circular, and a parabolic area.

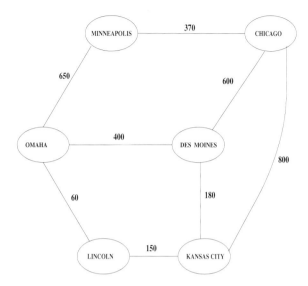

FIGURE 1.2. Fastest connections among cities.

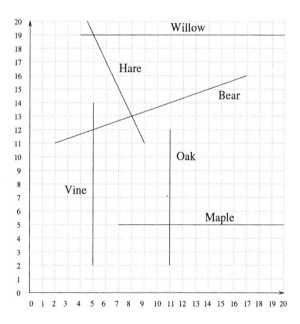

FIGURE 1.3. A street map.

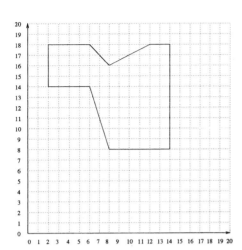 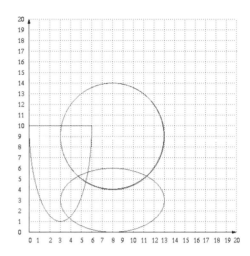

FIGURE 1.4. A town map (left) and radio broadcast areas.

A typical problem in geographic information systems is the *map overlay* problem. This task consists of overlaying several maps on top of each other so that the scales and locations match properly. For example, one would like to see what areas of the city are covered by at least one radio station. The map-overlay problem is complicated by the fact that the scale of different maps may differ. For example, the unit of the city map may be half a kilometer, in the broadcast map it may be one kilometer, and in the street map it may be a hundred yards. In addition, the point of origin in the three maps may also be different.

Video: For moving objects the best presentation is some form of video. This is especially important for *spatiotemporal* objects with a shape that is a spatial extent in either two or three dimensions and that keeps changing over time.

Providing a video or animation of spatiotemporal data is also a challenging problem at the interface of databases and graphics. Animations of spatiotemporal databases are provided within the MLPQ and the PReSTO systems, which are described in Chapters 18 and 20.

1.2   The Logical Level

The second highest level of data abstraction is called the *logical* level. The logical level is the most important level for those who want to query the database. People who query the database write simple programs that are best written and understood when the data is thought of at the logical level. Querying is discussed in Chapters 3, 4, 5, and 7 of this book. In this section we describe the *relational data model* used at the logical level.

The relational data model describes the database as a set of tables. An example with two tables is shown next. Each table has a name and defines a relation. The entry of the top row of a table is called an *attribute name*. The number of attributes of a relation is called its *arity* or *dimension*. We will use arity and dimension interchangeably with a preference for dimension in the case of spatiotemporal relations.

For example, relation *Taxrecord*, which lists for a set of persons their social-security numbers (SSNs), wages, interest incomes, and capital gains, has arity 4. The relation *Taxtable*, which lists for every possible income amount a tax, has arity 2. The ordered set of attributes of a table is called a *relation scheme*. For example, here the scheme of relation *Taxrecord* is (*SSN, Wages, Interest, Capital_Gain*) and that of *Taxtable* is (*Income, Tax*). The set of relation names together with their schemes is called a *database scheme*.

Every entry in a column beneath an attribute name is an attribute value. Each row in a table, except the top row, describes a person, object, concept, or relationship identified by its list of attribute values. For example, the first row of the relation *Taxrecord* describes that the person with the social security number (SSN) 111223333 earned $10,000 in wages, $80 in interest, and had no capital gain.

Each row of a relation is called a *tuple* or *point*. We will also use these two terms interchangeably with a preference for point in the case of spatiotemporal relations.

A row that describes persons, objects, concepts, or relationships is called *an instance* of the scheme. We differentiate between schemes and instances because relation schemes are usually fixed while relation instances may change over time due to database updates.

Taxrecord

SSN	Wages	Interest	Capital_Gain
111223333	10000	80	0
444556666	28000	400	0
777889999	75000	0	5000

Taxtable

Income	Tax
0	0
⋮	
10080	1512
⋮	

In the infinite relational data model a database instance could contain an infinite number of tuples. For example, the *Taxtable* relation contains an infinite number of tuples because we placed no limit on the maximum income and the income amount could be an arbitrarily long decimal number (we did not assume that the figures are rounded).

Note that the preceding instance of *Taxtable* cannot be represented in the finite relational data model, where each table can contain only a finite number of tuples. That can be very cumbersome. For example, the U.S. federal government currently provides a twelve-page tax table for taxpayers. This table only goes up to $100,000 and lists only incomes that are multiples of $50. To accommodate high-income people like Bill Gates, we would need to print an entire library.

Go

City1	Time1	City2	Time2
Omaha	0	Lincoln	60
$\vdots$			
Omaha	0	Lincoln	80
$\vdots$			
Omaha	0	Lincoln	90
$\vdots$			
Omaha	0	Lincoln	110
$\vdots$			
Minneapolis	0	Omaha	650
$\vdots$			
Omaha	660	Lincoln	720
$\vdots$			
Lincoln	60	Kansas_City	210
$\vdots$			
Kansas_City	210	Des_Moines	390
$\vdots$			
Des_Moines	390	Chicago	990
$\vdots$			

The following are a few additional examples of using the infinite relational data model to model data from temporal, spatial, and operational research applications.

Temporal Data: Let us consider again the graph in Figure 1.2 that displays the fastest traveling times among cities. The information presented at the view level can be presented at the logical level in a relation $Go(city1, time1, city2, time2)$ that contains tuples such that if I leave city1 at time1, then I can arrive at city2 at time2.

Not everyone drives at the fastest speed possible. A traveling time that is more than the fastest is also possible. Suppose I can drive from Omaha to Lincoln in 60 minutes. This corresponds to the first tuple in the following table. I can also take a bus from Omaha and arrive at Lincoln in 80 minutes. This corresponds to the second tuple shown in the table. I could also drive from Omaha to Lincoln but stop midway for a 30-minute lunch (see third tuple). Besides lunch, I could also stop for 20 minutes to buy something (see fourth tuple). Further, at time 0, I may still be in Minneapolis and arrive in Omaha 650 minutes later (see fifth tuple). After arriving in Omaha, I could take 10 minutes to drink coffee before driving to Lincoln (see sixth tuple), and so on. It is easy to see that *Go* could contain an infinite number of tuples.

Spatial Data: The streets, broadcast area, and town maps shown in Figures 1.3 and 1.4 describe spatial data. The spatial information here can be represented at

Streets

Name	X	Y
Bear	2	11
⋮	⋮	⋮
Bear	5	12
⋮	⋮	⋮
Bear	8	13
⋮	⋮	⋮
Willow	4	19
⋮	⋮	⋮
Willow	5	19
⋮	⋮	⋮
Willow	20	19

the logical level by a relation *Street(Name, X, Y)* that contains all tuples where the first attribute value is a street name and the last two attribute values specify a location in the plane where the station can broadcast.

Similarly, *Broadcast(Radio, X, Y)* and *Town(Name, X, Y)* are also infinite relations where the first attribute is the radio station number or name of the town, respectively, and the last two attributes specify the extent of these spatial objects.

Operations Research: Suppose a farmer can plant four types of crops, namely, corn, rye, sunflower, and wheat and can use for irrigation only 8000 units of well water and 3000 units of fertilizer. Each acre of corn, rye, sunflower, and wheat needs 30, 25, 5, and 10 units of water, and 15, 8, 10, and 15 units of fertilizer.

The information here can be represented in relation *Crops* in which each tuple represents a possible combination of crops that the farmer could plant. This is also an infinite relation assuming that the farmer can plant any portion of the land with any crop.

Crops

Corn	Rye	Sunflower	Wheat
100	100	10	40
⋮			
160	50	8	8
⋮			
80	150	30	20

Here the farmer would likely want to maximize the profit after selling the crops. This problem is a simple instance of an optimization problem, commonly solved by mathematical programming techniques such as *linear programming*. Such problems are important in *operations research*, an area concerned with planning optimally the work done in companies.

1.3   Abstract Data Types

In all the preceding examples we assumed that the domain of the attributes is a scalar value, that is, string or integer, rational or real number. It is possible to define as the domain of the attributes abstract data types that are sets of points. For example, in the relation *Vertices(Cities)*, the value of the attribute *Cities* is a set of strings. This relation represents all the cities shown in Figure 1.2 in just one tuple.

Vertices

Cities
{*Chicago, Des_Moines, Kansas_City, Lincoln, Minneapolis, Omaha*}

Another possibility is to define an abstract data type that is a set of points in the plane. For example, if there are streets on a map, then the abstract data type can be used to define the extent of the streets. With this abstract data type, the *Streets* relation could be represented as follows:

Streets

Name	Extent
Bear	$\{(2, 11), \ldots, (5, 12), \ldots, (8, 13), \ldots\}$
⋮	⋮
Willow	$\{(4, 19), \ldots, (5, 19), \ldots, (20, 19)\}$

An advantage of abstract data types is that new operations can be defined on them that would be difficult or impossible to define on relations with only scalar data types. For example, on the abstract data type *Extent* in the preceding *Streets* relation, we can define length and intersection as special operators.

Bibliographic Notes

The relational data model was defined by Codd [68] for finite relations. The natural extension to infinite relations was considered by several authors; however,

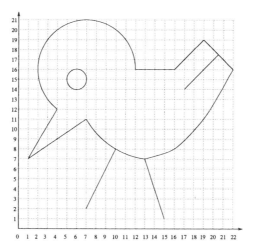

FIGURE 1.5. A bird.

it is allowed in practice only when it is finitely represented as within constraint databases [158], which we discuss in Chapter 2.

Exercises

1. Describe in words three different input relations that contain an infinite number of tuples at the logical level.

2. Find the (x, y) coordinates of at least ten points that belong to the logical level representation of the bird shown in Figure 1.5.

2

Constraint Databases

In Chapter 1 we discussed the two highest levels of data abstraction, that is, the view and the logical levels. It is clear that neither of these levels is suitable for the computer to represent data because they allow an infinite number of tuples or points. In this chapter we describe the *constraint data model* that is used to represent the logical level of data in a concise way.

In Section 2.1 we give a brief overview of the most frequently used types of constraints. In Section 2.2 we describe the constraint data model.

2.1 Constraints

In this section we review the most common types of constraints that are used in constraint databases. Constraints apply to two or more variables. Each variable takes its value from a domain. Common domains are the set of nonnegative integer or natural numbers $\mathcal{N}$, the set of integer numbers $\mathcal{Z}$, the set of rational numbers $\mathcal{Q}$, and the set of real numbers $\mathcal{R}$. Other domains include the set of English words in a dictionary, which we denote as $\mathcal{W}$. We describe arithmetic atomic constraints in Section 2.1.1 and Boolean atomic constraints in Section 2.1.2. We discuss constraint formulas in Section 2.1.3 and the significance of free Boolean algebras in Section 2.1.4.

2.1.1 Arithmetic Atomic Constraints

In the following let u, v be either variables or constants and b and c_i be constants. Let $\pm$ denote $+$ or $-$ and p be a polynomial function over the variables $x_1, \ldots, x_n$ (any valid expression with constants, variables, addition, and multiplication symbols). Let θ be either $\geq$ or $>$. We define the most basic type of constraints, called the *atomic* constraints, over any of the domains $\mathcal{N}$, $\mathcal{Z}$, $\mathcal{Q}$, $\mathcal{R}$ as follows:

Equality:		u	$=$	v
Inequality:		u	$\neq$	v
Lower Bound:		u	θ	b
Upper Bound:		$-u$	θ	b
Order:		u	θ	v
Gap-Order:		$u - v$	θ	b	where $b \geq 0$
Difference:		$u - v$	θ	b
Half-Addition:		$\pm u \pm v$	θ	b	where $b \geq 0$
Addition:		$\pm u \pm v$	θ	b
Linear:	$c_1 x_1 + \ldots + c_n x_n$		θ	b
Polynomial:	$p(x_1, \ldots, x_n)$		θ	b

We call b on the right-hand side of these constraints the *bound*. Note that the bound is restricted to be nonnegative in the case of gap-order and half-addition constraints. We will see the significance of this restriction in Chapter 8. We also call each c_i a *coefficient* in the linear constraint.

In general, if a constraint $\mathcal{C}$ is any of these types of constraints and the domain of the variables is Z or Q we talk of integer $\mathcal{C}$ constraints or rational $\mathcal{C}$ constraints, respectively.

Note that except for equality constraints we did not use the $=$ symbol. This is because we consider each $=$ constraint as the conjunction of two $\geq$ constraints. For example, the linear equation $5x + 7y = 8$ can be expressed as the conjunction of the linear inequality constraints $5x + 7y \geq 8$ and $5x + 7y \leq 8$. This is why we do not consider linear equations as *atomic* constraints. Atomic constraints are supposed to be constraints that cannot be expressed as conjunctions of other simpler constraints. Nevertheless, in this book we will often write constraints with $=$ signs. In each instance, however, the equality constraints should be understood to be conjunctions of two inequality constraints similarly to the preceding example.

We will not insist on always writing the constraints in this form. For example, an upper-bound constraint of the form $-u \geq b$ could be sometimes written as $-b \geq u$. As another example, the gap-order constraint $x - y \geq b$ could sometimes be written as $x \geq y + b$ or $b \leq x - y$ or some other equivalent form. Similarly, the linear equation mentioned earlier could be written as, for example, $y = (-5x + 8)/7$.

The form defined earlier should be considered a standard form for atomic constraints. It is only important to remember that each constraint we use can be expressed as the conjunction of one or more constraints in the standard forms.

The constraints defined earlier have several connections with each other. In general they are increasingly expressive. Hence we find, for example, that each gap-order constraint is also a half-addition constraint. Each half-addition constraint is also an addition constraint, which is a linear constraint. Each linear constraint is also a polynomial constraint.

2.1.2 Boolean Atomic Constraints

In this section we first review Boolean algebras and then we describe Boolean constraints.

A *Boolean algebra B* is a sextuple $\langle \delta, \wedge, \vee, ', 0, 1 \rangle$, where δ is a set called the *domain*; $\wedge, \vee$ are binary functions; $'$ is a unary function; and 0, 1 are two specific elements of δ (called the *zero* and the *identity* element, respectively) such that for any elements x, y, and z in δ the following axioms hold:

$$
\begin{array}{rclcrcl}
x \vee y & = & y \vee x & \quad & x \wedge y & = & y \wedge x \\
x \vee (y \wedge z) & = & (x \vee y) \wedge (x \vee z) & \quad & x \wedge (y \vee z) & = & (x \wedge y) \vee (x \wedge z) \\
x \vee x' & = & 1 & \quad & x \wedge x' & = & 0 \\
x \vee 0 & = & x & \quad & x \wedge 1 & = & x \\
0 & \neq & 1
\end{array}
$$

Note that the definitions and axioms do not completely specify a Boolean algebra. There are many particular examples of domains and meanings of the $\wedge, \vee, '$ functions that satisfy the definitions, including all of the axioms. Therefore, we can talk about specific instances of Boolean algebras, or specific *interpretations* of the elements of the structure.

There is an advantage of grouping the different specific instances that satisfy the definition. This is because even without knowing the specifics of the instance, we may say many interesting things about it just by reasoning from the axioms. In the absence of a specific interpretation, we may talk about an uninterpreted or free algebra.

For any Boolean algebra, we define *Boolean terms* recursively as follows:

1. 0 and 1 are terms.
2. Each element of δ is a term.
3. Each variable is a term.
4. If S and T are terms, then $(S \wedge T)$ and $(S \vee T)$ are terms.
5. If S is a term, then S' is a term.

A *ground Boolean term* is a Boolean term that does not contain variables. A *monotone Boolean term* is a Boolean term that does not contain the complement $'$ operator, except for elements of δ.

For example, if x, y, and z are Boolean variables, then $((x \wedge y)' \vee z')$ is a term, but it is not a monotone Boolean term. On the other hand, $(x \vee y) \wedge (z \vee 0')$ is a monotone Boolean term. Neither of these is a ground term. We sometimes omit the parentheses when they are not necessary within a term. We assume that $'$ has a higher precedence than $\vee$ and $\wedge$. We now define some Boolean atomic constraints. Let T be a term of a Boolean algebra B.

Equality:	T	$=_B$	0
Inequality:	T	$\neq_B$	0
Monotone Equality:	T	$=_B$	0 where T is monotone
Monotone Inequality:	T	$\neq_B$	0 where T is monotone

Some Boolean constraints occur with great frequency and have their own names and symbolic abbreviations. We give some examples. For any terms S, T in any Boolean algebra B:

Precedence: $T \leq_B S$ means $T \wedge S' =_B 0$

Exclusive-Or: $T \oplus_B S$ means $(T \wedge S') \vee (T' \wedge S) =_B 0$

In the following we may use the abbreviation $T =_B S$ for the constraint $T \oplus S =_B 0$. We may also omit the subscript B when it is clear which Boolean algebra we are talking about. Precedence constraints with T a variable and S monotone and monotone inequalities are *order* constraints.

Boolean *upper-bound constraints* are precedence constraints of the form:

$$x_1 \wedge \ldots \wedge x_n \leq_B b$$

where each x_i is a distinct negated or unnegated variable and b is a ground term of the Boolean algebra B. We call a Boolean upper-bound constraint *simple* if there is at most one unnegated variable in it.

The following are some useful facts about the precedence relation. For any elements x, y, z, w in any Boolean algebra B,

$x \leq_B x$	(Reflexivity)
$x \leq_B y$ and $y \leq_B x$ imply $x =_B y$	(Antisymmetry)
$x \leq_B y$ and $y \leq_B z$ imply $x \leq_B z$	(Transitivity)
$0 \leq_B x$	(Zero element)
$(x \wedge y) \leq_B x$	(Augment)
$x \leq_B y$ and $w \leq_B z$ imply $(x \wedge w) \leq_B (y \wedge z)$	(Merge)

Remark 2.1.1   Note the following interesting connection between monotone terms and precedence constraints, which can be proved using the identities. If $g(x_1, \ldots, x_n)$ is a *monotone* Boolean term, then $g(x_1, \ldots, x_n) \leq_B g(y_1, \ldots, y_n)$ whenever $x_i \leq_B y_i$ for each $1 \leq i \leq n$.

Next we give some examples of Boolean algebras.

Example 2.1.1   The specific Boolean algebra B_0 interprets the domain to be the set {*true, false*}, the function $\wedge$ as "and," the function $\vee$ as "or," the function $'$ as "not," the zero element as "false," and the one element as "true." It can be verified that this interpretation satisfies all the axioms; therefore it is a Boolean algebra.

In this Boolean algebra the constraint $x \oplus_{B_0} y$ means that exactly one of x and y is true and the other is false. We may write this Boolean algebra as:

$$B_0 = \langle \{true, false\}, and, or, not, false, true \rangle$$

B_0 is one of the simplest Boolean algebras with only two elements. We now consider a different Boolean algebra that has an infinite number of elements.

Let δ be any of the domains $\mathcal{N}, \mathcal{Z}, \mathcal{Q}, \mathcal{R}$. We call the set of subsets of δ the *powerset of* δ and we write it as $\mathcal{P}(\delta)$. The powerset of δ is a new domain type.

Example 2.1.2   The specific Boolean algebra B_Z interprets the domain to be $\mathcal{P}(\mathcal{Z})$, the function $\wedge$ as set intersection, the function $\vee$ as set union, the function $'$ as complement from $\mathcal{Z}$, the zero element as the empty set, and the one element as $\mathcal{Z}$. It can be verified that this interpretation satisfies all the axioms; therefore it is a Boolean algebra.

In this Boolean algebra the constraint $x \leq_{B_Z} y$ means that x and y are sets of integers such that y contains all the elements of x.

As another example, the constraint $(x' \wedge z) \vee (y \wedge z) \vee (x \wedge y' \wedge z') =_{B_Z} 0$ means that x, y, z are sets of integers such that z is the set difference of x and y, that is, z is the set of elements that are in x but not in y.

We may use the usual set function symbols $\cup$ for union, and $\cap$ for intersection. Then we can write:

$$B_Z = \langle \mathcal{P}(\mathcal{Z}), \cap, \cup, ', \emptyset, \mathcal{Z} \rangle$$

Using the usual set function symbols $\subseteq$ for containment and $\setminus$ for set difference, we may also write the first constraint as $x \subseteq y$ and the second constraint as $x \setminus y = z$.

Similarly to B_Z we can define many other Boolean algebras in which the operators are interpreted as the set operators.

Example 2.1.3   Similarly to B_Z we can specify the Boolean algebra B_W on sets of words. B_W is the same as B_Z except that $\mathcal{Z}$ is replaced by $\mathcal{W}$. More precisely,

$$B_W = \langle \mathcal{P}(\mathcal{W}), \cap, \cup, ', \emptyset, \mathcal{W} \rangle$$

In this Boolean algebra, we can define set containment and set difference similarly to B_Z.

2.1.3   Constraint Formulas

Let $\mathcal{C}$ be any type of constraints discussed earlier. We define constraint formulas recursively as follows:

1. Each atomic constraint of $\mathcal{C}$ is a formula.
2. If F and G are formulas, then $(F \textbf{ and } G)$ and $(F \textbf{ or } G)$ are formulas.
3. If F is a formula, then $(\textbf{not } F)$ is a formula.

A formula that contains only the "and" connective is called a *conjunction*. Similarly a formula that contains only the "or" connective is called a *disjunction*. A formula that contains only "and" and "or" connectives is called a *positive formula*.

Each of the atomic constraints is said to be *satisfiable,* if there is some instantiation of the variables by constants from the domain that makes it true. For example, the constraint $x - y \geq 5$ is satisfiable because the instantiation 9 for x and 3 for y makes the constraint true. A constraint is said to be *valid* if all instantiations make it true. The preceding constraint is not true because, for example, the instantiation 0 for x and 2 for y makes the constraint false.

Let F be a formula. Note that any instantiation of the variables of F makes each atomic constraint either true or false. Therefore, the formula can be evaluated to be true or false. We say that F is satisfiable if there is an instantiation that makes it true, and we say that it is valid if each possible instantiation makes it true.

Let C be any of the types of constraints and let $F(x_1, \ldots, x_n)$ be any C constraint formula with variables $x_1, \ldots, x_n$. If $t = (c_1, \ldots, c_n)$ is a tuple of constants and substituting each x_i by c_i makes F true, then we say that t satisfies F and we write $t \models F$.

Example 2.1.4   Let $F(x_1, x_2)$ be the formula $x_2 = x_1 \times 0.15$ and t be the pair of constants $(10080, 1512)$. Then $t \models F$ because $1512 = 10080 \times 0.15$ is true.

The *complement* of a formula F is the formula F'. We have that $t \models F$ is true if and only if $t \models F'$ is false.

Example 2.1.5   Let $F(x_1, x_2)$ be the formula $x_2 = x_1 \times 0.15$ and t be the pair of constants $(10080, 1512)$. Then F' is $x_2 \neq x_1 \times 0.15$ and $t \models F'$ is false because $1512 \neq 10080 \times 0.15$ is false.

Formulas are often put into *disjunctive normal form*, which means they are disjunctions of conjunctions. Any formula can be put into disjunctive normal form by using the Boolean algebra axioms and some useful identities, called *De Morgan's laws*, which can be derived from them. These laws are:

$$(F \text{ and } G)' = F' \text{ or } G'$$

$$(F \text{ or } G)' = F' \text{ and } G'$$

Example 2.1.6   Consider the formula $((a \text{ or } b) \text{ and } c)'$. Applying the first law we obtain $(a \text{ or } b)' \text{ and } c'$. Applying the second law we obtain $(a' \text{ and } b') \text{ or } c'$, which is already in disjunctive normal form.

In many cases the negation of a C-type atomic constraint is also a C atomic constraint or a conjunction of C-type atomic constraints. In this case we say that C is *closed under negation.* For example, addition, linear, and polynomial constraints are closed under negation. On the other hand, gap-order and positive linear constraints are not closed under negation.

Disjunctive normal forms are important for many reasons. For example, we can use disjunctive normal forms to show that there is a finite number of possible distinct terms that can be expressed in free Boolean algebras with a fixed number of constants and variables.

Lemma 2.1.1   Let B_m be the free Boolean algebra with m constant symbols. Then there are only $2^{2^{m+k}}$ different disjunctive normal forms of terms with the m constant symbols and k variables.

Proof. Let $t(z_1, z_2, \ldots, z_n)$ be any term where the zs are the distinct variable or constant symbols occurring in it. Then the following equation is true:

$$t(z_1, z_2, \ldots, z_n) = (t(0, z_2, \ldots, z_n) \wedge z_1') \vee (t(1, z_2, \ldots, z_n) \wedge z_1)$$

Let us use the convention that z^0 means z' and z^1 means z, and that the zs are ordered from z_1 to z_n. Then we also may write the equation in the previous theorem as $t(z_1, z_2, \ldots, z_n) = \bigvee_{a_1 \in \{0, 1\}} (t(a_1, z_2, \ldots, z_n) \wedge z_1^{a_1})$. By repeatedly using the preceding theorem and the Boolean algebra axioms, it is possible to transform each term into the following disjunctive normal form:

$$t(z_1, \ldots, z_n) = \bigvee_{\overline{a} \in \{0,1\}^n} (t(a_1, \ldots, a_n) \wedge z_1^{a_1} \wedge z_2^{a_2} \wedge \ldots \wedge z_n^{a_n})$$

where $\bigvee_{\overline{a} \in \{0,1\}^n}$ denotes the disjunction of all 0, 1 substitutions for $a_1, \ldots, a_n$. The function determined by $t(z_1, \ldots, z_n)$ depends only on the values of the 2^n expressions $t(a_1, \ldots, a_n)$, where each a_i is either 0 or 1. One can see that each of these 2^n expressions has value either 0 or 1. Hence, it is possible to see that there are 2^{2^n} disjunctive normal forms with n variable and constant symbols.   ■

Let B_m be a free Boolean algebra with m constant symbols. We call the constant symbols the *generators* and all possible conjunctions of the generators the *minterms* of the algebra. Different terms that can be rewritten to the same disjunctive normal form are denoting the same elements of B_m. Hence, all possible distinct elements of the Boolean algebra can be expressed as a disjunction of some minterms. Therefore, by Lemma 2.1.1 there are 2^{2^m} different elements of B_m. Because the constant symbols are uninterpreted in a free Boolean algebra, each free Boolean with m distinct constant symbols has the same number of distinct elements.

Example 2.1.7   Consider the free Boolean algebra B_3 generated by the constant symbols a, b, c. B_3 has 2^3 minterms. These minterms, in descending order of binary superscript values, are:

$$a \wedge b \wedge c,$$
$$a \wedge b \wedge c',$$
$$a \wedge b' \wedge c,$$
$$a \wedge b' \wedge c',$$
$$a' \wedge b \wedge c,$$
$$a' \wedge b \wedge c',$$

$$a' \wedge b' \wedge c,$$
$$a' \wedge b' \wedge c'$$

By Lemma 2.1.1 each element of B_3 can be written in a disjunctive normal form in which each minterm either occurs as a disjunct or does not. Hence there are 2^{2^3} elements of the free Boolean algebra B_3.

2.1.4   Interpretations of Free Boolean Algebras

There are many Boolean algebras in addition to free Boolean algebras that may be interesting to specific database applications. However, it is difficult and unnecessary to consider all of these Boolean algebras separately. The reason for this is that we can generate any Boolean algebra from some free Boolean algebra by an interpretation that includes a specific definition of the Boolean algebra operators $\wedge$, $\vee$, $'$; elements 0 and 1; and a substitution σ for the generators or constant symbols of the free Boolean algebra by elements of the new Boolean algebra.

In the interpretation, the symbols of the free algebra take specific values. For example, if a is symbol, then its specific value will be denoted by $\sigma(a)$. The equality relation is also made more specific in interpreted Boolean algebra, that is, two terms that are equal in the free algebra are also equal in the interpreted algebra, but in the interpreted algebra some terms are equal that are not equal in the free algebra. We denote by $=_{B,\sigma}$ the equality relation in the interpreted algebra B when it is obtained from a free algebra using substitution σ.

Example 2.1.8   Consider the following specific interpretation of the free Boolean in Example 2.1.7. The symbol $\wedge$ is interpreted as set intersection, $\vee$ as set union, $'$ as set difference from $\{1, 2, 3, 4, 5, 6, 7, 8\}$, the element 0 of B_3 as $\emptyset$, and the element 1 of B_3 as the set $\{1, 2, 3, 4, 5, 6, 7, 8\}$. Also,

$$\sigma(a) = \{1, 2, 3, 4\}$$
$$\sigma(b) = \{1, 2, 5, 6\}$$
$$\sigma(c) = \{1, 3, 5, 7\}$$

The interpreted Boolean algebra B is $\langle \delta, \wedge, \vee, ', \emptyset, \{1, 2, 3, 4, 5, 6, 7, 8\} \rangle$ where δ is the powerset of the set $\{1, 2, 3, 4, 5, 6, 7, 8\}$. The minterms in B are all different elements:

$$a \wedge b \wedge c =_{B,\sigma} \quad \{1\}$$
$$a \wedge b \wedge c' =_{B,\sigma} \quad \{2\}$$
$$a \wedge b' \wedge c =_{B,\sigma} \quad \{3\}$$
$$a \wedge b' \wedge c' =_{B,\sigma} \quad \{4\}$$
$$a' \wedge b \wedge c =_{B,\sigma} \quad \{5\}$$

$$a' \wedge b \wedge c' =_{B,\sigma} \ \{6\}$$
$$a' \wedge b' \wedge c =_{B,\sigma} \ \{7\}$$
$$a' \wedge b' \wedge c' =_{B,\sigma} \ \{8\}$$

The free Boolean algebra B_3 under the interpretation (B, σ) became another specific Boolean algebra B with eight different minterms that are not equal to $\emptyset$ and a total of 2^8 elements.

Example 2.1.9   Now let us look at a different interpretation (B, σ_2) for the free Boolean algebra B_3. In this interpretation assume the same meaning for the Boolean algebra operators as in Example 2.1.8, but assume that σ_2 is the following:

$$\sigma_2(a) = \{1\}$$
$$\sigma_2(b) = \{2\}$$
$$\sigma_2(c) = \{3\}$$

In this case some of the minterms are equivalent. In fact,

$$a \wedge b \wedge c =_{B,\sigma_2} \ \emptyset$$
$$a \wedge b \wedge c' =_{B,\sigma_2} \ \emptyset$$
$$a \wedge b' \wedge c =_{B,\sigma_2} \ \emptyset$$
$$a \wedge b' \wedge c' =_{B,\sigma_2} \ \{1\}$$
$$a' \wedge b \wedge c =_{B,\sigma_2} \ \emptyset$$
$$a' \wedge b \wedge c' =_{B,\sigma_2} \ \{2\}$$
$$a' \wedge b' \wedge c =_{B,\sigma_2} \ \{3\}$$
$$a' \wedge b' \wedge c' =_{B,\sigma_2} \ \{4, 5, 6, 7, 8\}$$

Under this interpretation of the constants, only a subalgebra of the Boolean algebra in Example 2.1.8 is generated. This subalgebra has only four different minterms that are not equal to $\emptyset$ and only 2^4 elements.

In *atomless Boolean algebras*, between 0 and any element there is always another element.

Example 2.1.10   Let B_h be the Boolean algebra whose elements are finite unions of half-open intervals over the rational numbers, including the empty set and the set of all rational numbers $Q \cup \{+\infty\}$. In B_h let $\wedge$ mean intersection, $\vee$ mean union, and $'$ mean complement with respect to the set of rational numbers. Let a, b, c be three constants allowed within the terms, and let their interpretation be defined by σ_3 as follows:

$$\sigma_3(a) = [2, 10)$$
$$\sigma_3(b) = [3, 35)$$
$$\sigma_3(c) = [4, 21)$$

The minterms of the free Boolean algebra B_3 under the interpretation (B_h, σ_3) are various elements of B_h. For example, the minterm $a \wedge b \wedge c$ would be the half-open interval $[4, 10)$. It is not an atom because it contains the half-open interval $[5, 8)$, which is also an element of B_h. The Boolean algebra B_h is a well-known example of an atomless Boolean algebra.

2.2   The Constraint Data Model

The constraint data model provides a finite representation of the infinite relational data model. In the constraint data model each attribute is associated with an attribute variable, and the value of the attributes in a relation is specified implicitly using constraints.

A *constraint database* is a finite set of constraint relations. A *constraint relation* is a finite set of constraint tuples, where each *constraint tuple* is a conjunction of atomic constraints using the same set of attribute variables. For simplicity, we abbreviate within constraint tuples the "and"s by commas.

As an example, let us take a look at the constraint relation *Taxtable*.

Taxtable

Income	Tax	
i	t	$0 \leq i,\ i \leq 24000,\ t = 0.15i$
i	t	$24000 < i,\ i \leq 58150,\ t = 3600 + 0.28(i - 24000)$
i	t	$58150 < i,\ i \leq 121300,\ t = 13162 + 0.31(i - 58150)$
i	t	$121300 < i, i \leq 263750, t = 32738.5 + 0.36(i - 121300)$
i	t	$263750 < i,\ t = 84020.5 + 0.396(i - 263750)$

This constraint relation describes the same relation as in Chapter 1. However, the description is different. The constraint relation *Taxtable* uses a variable i as the value of the income and a variable t as the value of the attribute tax. Both variables range over the rational numbers. The first row of relation *Taxrecord* means that a person with income i should pay t amount in tax such that the condition $0 \leq i, i \leq 24000, t = i \times 0.15$ is true. This is an example of a constraint tuple. This constraint tuple expresses that up to \$24,000 each person should pay 15 percent of their income as tax. The rest of the table expresses the current U.S. federal tax rules for single-income taxpayers, assuming income means taxable income.

Note that the entire constraint relation consists of only five constraint tuples although it represents the infinite relation described earlier. The constraints in the table are order constraints and linear equations over the rational numbers.

The *Go* relation can be represented by the following constraint table. Here the assumption is that if the shortest direct path from city1 to city2 is some m minutes, then if we leave city1 at time t_1 we may arrive at city2 at some time t_2 such that $t_2 - t_1 \geq m$.

Go

City1	Time1	City2	Time2	
Omaha	t_1	Lincoln	t_2	$t_2 - t_1 \geq 60$
Omaha	t_1	Minneapolis	t_2	$t_2 - t_1 \geq 650$
Omaha	t_1	Des_Moines	t_2	$t_2 - t_1 \geq 400$
Minneapolis	t_1	Chicago	t_2	$t_2 - t_1 \geq 370$
Des_Moines	t_1	Chicago	t_2	$t_2 - t_1 \geq 600$
Des_Moines	t_1	Kansas_City	t_2	$t_2 - t_1 \geq 180$
Lincoln	t_1	Kansas_City	t_2	$t_2 - t_1 \geq 150$
Kansas_City	t_1	Chicago	t_2	$t_2 - t_1 \geq 800$
Lincoln	t_1	Omaha	t_2	$t_2 - t_1 \geq 60$
Minneapolis	t_1	Omaha	t_2	$t_2 - t_1 \geq 650$
Des_Moines	t_1	Omaha	t_2	$t_2 - t_1 \geq 400$
Chicago	t_1	Minneapolis	t_2	$t_2 - t_1 \geq 370$
Chicago	t_1	Des_Moines	t_2	$t_2 - t_1 \geq 600$
Kansas_City	t_1	Des_Moines	t_2	$t_2 - t_1 \geq 180$
Kansas_City	t_1	Lincoln	t_2	$t_2 - t_1 \geq 150$
Chicago	t_1	Kansas_City	t_2	$t_2 - t_1 \geq 800$

In *Go* we represent each connection between two cities by two constraint tuples. This may seem redundant because we assumed that the traveling time is the same in both directions between any two cities. This assumption may not be true if construction or a traffic jam occurs on only one side of the road. However, the representation can be easily adjusted in these cases.

In the broadcast example, the first radio station broadcasts within a circle with center at location (8, 9), the second in an elliptic area, and the third in a parabolic area that is cut off by a line. The *Broadcast* relation can be expressed as a constraint table with quadratic constraints over the real numbers as shown here.

Broadcast

Radio	X	Y	
1	x	y	$(x - 8)^2 + (y - 9)^2 \leq 25$
2	x	y	$\frac{(x-8)^2}{5^2} + \frac{(y-3)^2}{3^2} \leq 1$
3	x	y	$(y - 1) \geq (x - 3)^2, y \leq 10$

Similarly, the town map can be represented as a set of convex polygons, where each polygon is represented as a conjunction of linear inequalities.

The drawing of the bird in Figure 1.5 can be represented using real polynomial constraints as shown in relation *Bird*.

Bird

X	Y	
x	y	$5x - 3y + 16 = 0, x \geq 1, x \leq 4$
x	y	$2x - 3y + 19 = 0, x \geq 1, x \leq 7$
x	y	$2x - y - 12 = 0, x \geq 7, x \leq 10$
x	y	$3x + y - 46 = 0, x \geq 13, x \leq 15$
x	y	$y = 16, x \geq 12, x \leq 16$
x	y	$y = x, x \geq 16, x \leq 19$
x	y	$x + y - 38 = 0, x \geq 19, x \leq 22$
x	y	$x - y - 3 = 0, x \geq 17, x \leq 20.5$
x	y	$(x - 7)^2 + (y - 16)^2 = 25, x \leq 4$
x	y	$(x - 7)^2 + (y - 16)^2 = 25, x \geq 4, y \geq 16$
x	y	$(x - 6)^2 + (y - 15)^2 = 1$
x	y	$\frac{1}{9}(x - 13)^2 = y - 7, x \geq 7, x \leq 22$

Finally, let us look at the farming example. Here the data can be represented by the following constraint relation using linear inequality constraints over the rational numbers.

Crops

Corn	Rye	Sunflower	Wheat	
x_1	x_2	x_3	x_4	$15x_1 + 8x_2 + 10x_3 + 15x_4 \leq 3000,$ $30x_1 + 25x_2 + 5x_3 + 10x_4 \leq 8000.$

2.3   Data Abstraction

Each data model provides some abstraction about the stored data. We distinguish four levels of data abstraction, namely, the view, logical, constraint, and physical levels. The various levels of data abstraction are linked by translation methods. Let us discuss these briefly.

View Level: This is how users can view their data. For different sets of users different views can be provided by a database. We saw several examples in Chapter 1. We'll see more examples of visualization used in the MLPQ and PReSTO constraint database systems in Chapters 18 and 20.

Logical Level: This describes what data are stored in terms of sets of infinite relations. We saw examples of these in Chapter 1.

Constraint Level: This level describes the data stored using one or more constraint relations. We saw several examples of these in Section 2.2. There is a natural link between the logical and the constraint levels. Let r be the infinite relational model and R be the constraint model of a relation. Then a tuple t is in r if and only if there is a constraint tuple C in R such that after substitution of the constants in t into the variables of C we get a true formula, that is, t satisfies C. We can summarize:

$$t \in r \text{ iff } t \models C \text{ for some } C \in R$$

For example, (10080, 1512) is in the infinite relational model of *Taxtable* because it satisfies the first constraint tuple in the constraint data model, as we saw in Example 2.1.4.

Physical Level: This level corresponds to the way the data is actually stored in a computer system. We will see some examples of this in Chapter 17.

Bibliographic Notes

Constraint databases in the form of sets of constraint facts in logic programming were introduced by Jaffar and Lassez [151]. The constraint data model as defined in Section 2.2 and the discussion on data abstraction is from Kanellakis, Kuper, and Revesz [158, 159]. Boolean algebras are discussed in, for example, Burris and Sankappanavar [46], Halmos [138], Helm et al. [142], and Marriott and Odersky [204].

Exercises

1. Represent the constraint relation *Free* in a relational form assuming that d is an integer.

Free

PERSON	DAY	
Andrew	d	$3 \le d, d \le 6$
Andrew	d	$16 \le d, d \le 26$
Barbara	d	$6 \le d, d \le 18$
Barbara	d	$25 \le d, d \le 30$

2. The postage fee charged for packages is computed based on the weight of the package and the postage rate. The postage rate increases piecewise linearly with the weight of the package. Up to five ounces, the fee is the weight of the package times 0.53, between 5 and 15 ounces the fee is \$2.65 plus 0.45 times the weight over 5 ounces, between 15 and 30 ounces the fee is \$7.15 plus 0.3 times the weight over 15 ounces, and more than 30 ounces the fee is \$11.65 plus 0.25 times the weight over 30 ounces. Find a constraint database representation for relation $Postage(w, f)$ where w is the weight of the package and f is the postage fee required.

3. Using a constraint relation represent the street map shown in Figure 1.3.

4. Using a constraint relation represent the town map shown in Figure 1.4. (**Hint:** Divide the town map into two convex polygons using the line $y = x + 8$ and represent each convex polygon by a separate constraint tuple with a conjunction of linear inequalities.)

5. Using a constraint relation represent the land areas shown in Figure 2.1.

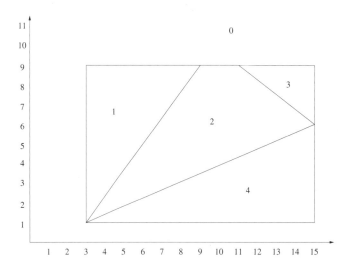

FIGURE 2.1. Land areas.

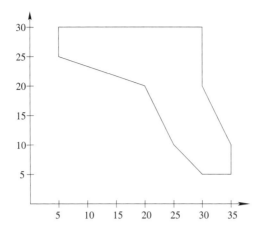

FIGURE 2.2. A map of Florida.

6. Using a constraint relation represent the map of Florida shown in Figure 2.2.

7. Using a constraint relation represent the heart shown in Figure 2.3.

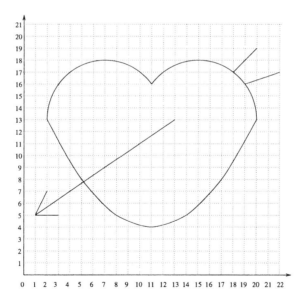

FIGURE 2.3. A heart.

3

Relational Algebra and SQL

In this chapter we will learn about two different query languages for relational databases. The first query language, *relational algebra*, has a small set of well-defined operators that can be composed to form query expressions. It is a *procedural* language, because the sequence of operators and the operators themselves can be evaluated using well-defined procedures. Relational algebra is a useful theoretical language that serves to define more complex languages.

The second language we consider, *Structured Query Language* or SQL, is a practical language that allows a high-level expression of queries. A user of SQL does not need to think procedurally about queries, but can rely, to a significant degree, on the meaning of higher-level keywords provided by SQL. However, most SQL queries can be translated to relational algebra queries, and such translation can elucidate the precise meaning of a SQL query.

3.1 Relational Algebra

Relational algebra is a query language composed of a number of operators described in Section 3.1.1. We give several example relational algebra queries in Section 3.1.2 and discuss relational algebra query composition in Section 3.1.3.

3.1.1 Relational Algebra Operators

Relational algebra is a query language composed of a number of operators, each of which takes in relations as arguments and returns a single relation as result. The following are the main operators in relational algebra.

Intersection: The intersection of two relations A and B, denoted $A \cap B$, is the set of points that belong to both A and B. The intersection operator can be applied only to operands that have the same set and order of attributes.

Union: The union of two relations A and B, denoted $A \cup B$, is the set of points that belong to A or B or both. The union operator can be applied only to operands that have the same set and order of attributes.

Difference: The difference of two relations A and B, denoted $A \setminus B$ is the set of points that belong to A but do not belong to B. The difference operator can be applied only to operands that have the same set and order of attributes.

Product: The product operator applied to an n-dimensional relation A and an m-dimensional relation B, denoted $A \times B$, returns a relation that contains all $(n + m)$-dimensional points whose first n components belong to A and last m components belong to B. The product operator can be applied only to operands that have no common attributes.

Project: This operator is used to reorder the columns of a relation or to eliminate some columns of a relation. The project operator from a relation A is denoted $\Pi_L A$, where L is a list $[l_1, \ldots, l_k]$ that specifies an ordering of a subset of the attributes of A. The project operator creates a new relation that contains in its ith column the column of A corresponding to attribute l_i.

Select: The select operator is used to select from a relation A those points that satisfy a certain logical formula F. The select operator has the form $\sigma_F A$. The logical formula F is a constraint formula, as described in Section 2.1.

Rename: The rename operator, $\rho_{B(X_1/Y_1, \ldots, X_n/Y_n)} A$ for any $n \geq 1$, changes the name of relation A to B and changes the attribute X_i to Y_i. If we only want to change the name of the relation, then the form $\rho_B A$ can be used.

Natural Join: The natural join operator applied to an n-dimensional relation A and an m-dimensional relation B that have k attributes in common is denoted $A \bowtie B$. The natural join operator returns a relation that contains all $(n + m - k)$-dimensional points whose projection onto the attributes of A belong to A and whose projection onto the attributes of B belong to B.

Example 3.1.1 We illustrate these relational algebra operators on spatial relations. Consider the set of points $A(x, y)$ and $B(x, y)$ shown in Figure 3.1. They both have dimension two, hence the operators of intersection, union, and difference can be applied.

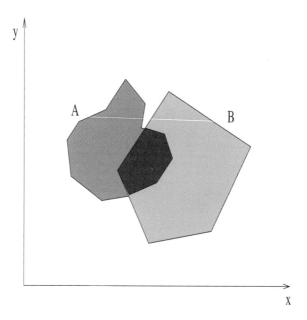

FIGURE 3.1. Two point sets.

- The intersection $A \cap B = C$, where C is shown in Figure 3.2.

- The union $A \cup B = D$, where D is shown in Figure 3.3.

- The difference $A \setminus B = E$, where E is shown in Figure 3.4.

- Let $F(z)$ be a relation that contains all points on the z-axis between $z = 5$ and $z = 15$. Then the product $A(x, y) \times F(z) = G(x, y, z)$, where G is the polyhedron shown in Figure 3.5.

- Consider now $H(x, y, z)$, the polyhedron shown in Figure 3.6. The projection $\Pi_{x,y} H$ is the shaded rectangle in the (x, y) plane, while $\Pi_{y,z} H$ is the shaded rectangle in the (y, z) plane.

- Consider now the rectangular body $I(x, y, z)$ shown in Figure 3.7. The shaded rectangle that lies in the plane defined by the equation $2x + z = 0$ cuts I into two. The selection operation $\sigma_{2x+z \leq 0} I$ returns the part of I that lies below the shaded rectangle.

- Finally, in Figure 3.8 the natural join of the shaded rectangle $J(x, y)$ and the shaded circle $K(y, z)$ is the cylinder $L(x, y, z)$. This is written as $J(x, y) \bowtie K(y, z) = L(x, y, z)$.

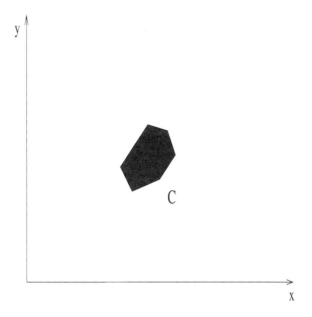

FIGURE 3.2. Intersection of A and B.

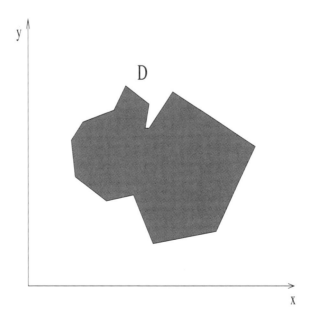

FIGURE 3.3. Union of A and B.

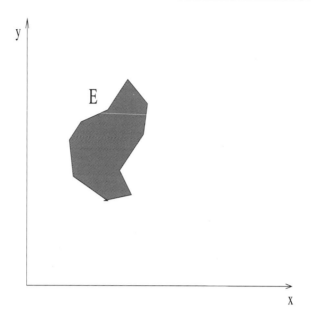

FIGURE 3.4. Difference of A and B.

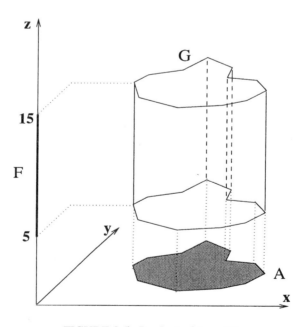

FIGURE 3.5. Product of A and F.

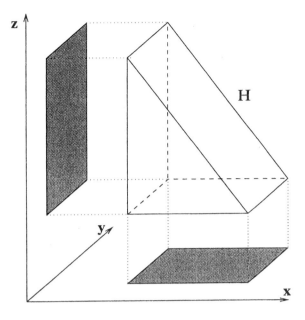

FIGURE 3.6. Projections from H.

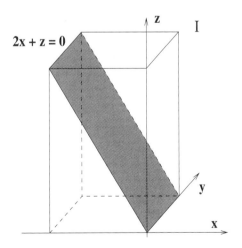

FIGURE 3.7. Select part of I below $2x + z = 0$.

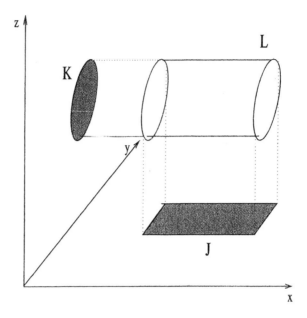

FIGURE 3.8. Natural join of J and K.

3.1.2 Relational Algebra Queries

Because the result of each operation is a relation, the operators can be composed to express queries. In particular, the relational algebra query language is defined recursively as follows:

1. Each relation name R_i is a relational algebra expression. (This will just return the relation R_i as a result.)

2. If e_1 and e_2 are relational algebra expressions that result in relations that have the same set and order of attributes, then $(e_1 \cap e_2)$, $(e_1 \cup e_2)$, and $(e_1 \setminus e_2)$ are also relational algebra expressions.

3. If e_1 and e_2 are relational algebra expressions that result in relations with no common attributes, then $(e_1 \times e_2)$ is also a relational algebra expression.

4. If e_1 and e_2 are relational algebra expressions, then $(e_1 \bowtie e_2)$ is a relational algebra expression.

5. If e_1 is a relational algebra expression, then $\Pi_L(e_1)$, where L is a subset of the attributes of the resulting relation, $\sigma_F(e_1)$, where F is a selection condition, and $\rho_C(e_1)$, where C is a renaming specification, are also relational algebra expressions.

6. No other expressions are relational algebra expressions.

Example 3.1.2   Consider the relations *Taxrecord* and *Taxtable* from Chapter 1. Suppose that a tax accountant wants to find the Social Security number and tax payable by each person in the database. This can be expressed in relational algebra as follows:

$$\Pi_{SSN,Tax}\sigma_{Wages+Interest+Capital\_Gain=Income}\, Taxrecord \times Taxtable$$

This means something like "if there is a tuple t in Taxrecord and a tuple s in Taxtable such that the sum of the last three attribute values of t equals the first attribute value of s, then print out the first attribute value of t and the second attribute value of s."

This query is easy to write if we just think about the unrestricted relations and don't worry about whether *Taxtable* is an infinite relation. Your database system will take care of that. Here is another example.

Example 3.1.3   The following query finds the names of each pair of streets that intersect:

$$\Pi_{Name,Name2}(Streets \bowtie (\rho_{Streets2(Name/Name2)}\, Streets))$$

This query uses two copies of the *Streets* relation with a renaming of the *Name* attribute in the second. The natural join results in tuples where both *Name* and *Name2* appear only when there is a point (x, y) that belongs to both streets.

Example 3.1.4   Assume for now that the point of origin in both the town and the broadcast maps is the same. The following query finds the parts of the town of Lincoln, Nebraska, that are reached by at least one radio station:

$$(\Pi_{X,Y}(\sigma_{Name="Lincoln"}Town)) \cap (\Pi_{X,Y}Broadcast)$$

Here the part before $\cap$ selects the points of the town and the part after $\cap$ selects the points that belong to at least one radio station broadcast area.

3.1.3   The Benefit of Query Composition

Relational algebra provides a nice example of a query language that allows composition of queries. This is an extremely important feature because it satisfies the needs of both data vendors and application vendors.

Data Vendors: Data vendors buy raw data in the form of databases and produce refined data in the form of databases that they sell to other data vendors. In the information market, there is often a long chain of data vendors from raw data to the users. Each data vendor uses queries to transform raw data to the data product. These queries may be secret or patented.

Considering how data vendors work illustrates two important facts. First, queries to databases should yield other databases as the output. Second, because it is usually difficult to translate between different types of databases, for example, from network to relational databases, there is a tendency for one data model to become a common data communication standard. Currently the relational data model provides that standard. Data vendors using other types of databases have to translate their databases to relational databases and vice versa or be cut off from a large part of the information market. Fortunately, translating between constraint and relational databases is easy.

Application Vendors: Application vendors sell libraries of queries to users. Application vendors must guarantee the termination of the queries on each valid database input because no user will wait indefinitely for a query to complete execution. Termination is a minimum requirement; often vendors also need to guarantee the speed and space performance of their queries. The best way to fulfill these guarantee is by using query languages that allow only expression of queries that terminate fast. Query languages like relational algebra and SQL are such languages. Hence these would be preferable to use instead of a general-purpose programming language, where neither termination nor speed is guaranteed.

3.2   SQL

SQL is a popular query language for relational database systems. It is a complex language with many functions and options. The following is only a description of the most important concepts within SQL. A basic SQL query is of the form:

SELECT $a_{i_1}, \ldots, a_{i_l}$
FROM $R_1, R_2, \ldots, R_m$
WHERE $Con_1, \ldots, Con_k$

Here R_i for $1 \leq i \leq m$ are relation names, a_{i_k} for $1 \leq k \leq l$ are attribute names, and Con_js for $1 \leq j \leq k$ are atomic constraints. Suppose the set of attribute names appearing in the relations $R_1, \ldots, R_m$ is $S = \{a_1, \ldots, a_n\}$. The set of attribute names appearing in the SELECT line must be some subset $S_i = \{a_{i_1}, \ldots, a_{i_l}\}$ of S.

Each basic SQL query can be translated to a relational algebra expression involving the project π, select σ, and product $\times$ operators as follows:

$$\pi_{a_{i_1}, \ldots, a_{i_l}} (\sigma_{Con_1}(\ldots (\sigma_{Con_k} (R_1 \times R_2 \times \ldots \times R_m)) \ldots))$$

This is fairly straightforward to understand except that for some historical reason the SQL select statement is translated as the project operator of relational algebra. If one keeps that in mind, it is easy to translate basic SQL queries into relational algebra queries and vice versa.

Another slight difference from relation algebra is that in SQL, when two relations P and R have a common attribute A, SQL automatically renames them $P.A$ and $R.A$, respectively. Because of this automatic renaming, the product operator can also be applied when there are initially some common attributes. Within the

SQL query, the two attributes should be distinguished using the preceding notation.

Example 3.2.1   The tax accountant query in Example 3.1.2 can be expressed in SQL as follows:

SELECT SSN, Tax
FROM Taxrecord, Taxtable
WHERE Wages + Interest + Capital_Gain = Income

In SQL the AS keyword can be used for renaming attribute names in the SELECT clause and relation names in the FROM clause of basic queries. The AS keyword is also useful for making multiple copies of a relation. For example, to rename attribute A by B and to declare S and T to be copies of the relation R in SQL we write:

SELECT A AS B
FROM R AS S, R AS T
WHERE ...

Example 3.2.2   The streets intersection query in Example 3.1.3 can be expressed in SQL by:

SELECT S.NAME, T.NAME
FROM Streets AS S, Streets AS T
WHERE S.X = T.X and S.Y = T.Y

Basic SQL queries can be combined to form bigger queries. There are two important types of combinations in SQL. The first combination is via the set operators *intersect*, *union*, and *minus*, which has the form:

SQL   Query Q_1
　　　 INTERSECT
SQL   Query Q_2

and similarly for the other two set operators, where the set of attribute names in the SELECT lines of Q_1 and Q_2 are the same and in the same order. The second combination allowed is more interesting. It looks as follows:

SELECT   ...
FROM $R'_1, \ldots, R'_{m'}$
WHERE a_i IN   (SELECT b_j
　　　　　　　　　　　　 FROM $R_1, \ldots, R_m$
　　　　　　　　　　　　 WHERE   ...)

In this query, the result of the inner SQL query is a relation with only one attribute b_j. The relation names R_i in the inner and R'_j in the outer basic SQL query may be equal or different. The outer SQL query may contain several attributes in the SELECT line.

Example 3.2.3   The query in Example 3.1.4 can be expressed as the following SQL query:

```
SELECT   X, Y
FROM     Town
WHERE    Name = "Lincoln"
         INTERSECT
SELECT   X, Y
FROM     Broadcast
```

3.2.1   SQL Aggregate Operators

All the SQL queries we have seen so far can be translated to relational algebra. SQL also goes beyond relational algebra in allowing the aggregate operators `Max`, `Min`, `Avg`, and `Sum` within the SELECT line. A basic SQL query with aggregation looks like the following:

```
SELECT   a_{i_1}, ..., a_{i_l}, opt(f(a_1, ..., a_n))
FROM     R_1, R_2, ..., R_m
WHERE    Con_1, ..., Con_k
```

where opt is some composition of *Max*, *Min*, *Avg*, and *Sum* and f is a linear constraint of the form $c_1 a_1 + \ldots + c_n a_n$. The function f is called an *objective function*, a term that is borrowed from operations research.

Example 3.2.4   Mr. Johnson, who lives in Omaha, Nebraska, wants to send three packages to three clients who live in Atlanta, Boston, and Chicago. The weight of each package can be represented in the following relational database table.

Package

Serial No.	From	Destination	Weight
101	Omaha	Chicago	12.6
102	Omaha	Atlanta	27.3
103	Omaha	Boston	37.5

To all destinations within the United States, the postage fee charged for packages can be computed based on the weight of the package and the postage rate associated with the weight. The following *Postage* relation is a logical-level view of this relation.

Postage

Weight	Fee
5	2.65
⋮	⋮
50	16.65

Suppose Mr. Johnson would like to know how much he should pay to send the three packages. This query can be expressed in SQL as follows:

```
SELECT    Sum(Fee)
FROM      Package, Postage
WHERE     Package.Weight = Postage.Weight
```

The following is a more complex example of aggregation constraints.

Example 3.2.5   Let us consider a food production company that has manufacturing plants in four cities A, B, C, and D around the world. The company produces candies, chocolate bars (CB), ice cream (IC), and yogurt. For the production of each item the company needs some amount of sugar (S), milk (M), and chocolate (C). Suppose the relation

Food (*City, Candy, CB, IC, Yogurt, S, M, C, Profit*)

expresses all possible combinations of city names, items produced, and resources used in that city.

There are some natural questions that one may ask about these data. For example, suppose the CEO of the company would like to know the city where the most profitable company plant is located. This query should return the city name associated with the maximum profit found in any of the four cities. Thus, the query can be expressed in SQL as follows:

```
SELECT    City
FROM      Food
WHERE     Profit IN    (SELECT Max(Profit)
                        FROM Food)
```

Suppose that instead of sugar, we can substitute several different types of sugars, such as cane sugar, corn syrup, beets, molasses, and honey. For example, one unit of sugar can be substituted by one unit of cane sugar or four units of beet sugar, etc. The company has already in store some amounts of each type of sweetener and does not want to buy more. Let us assume that relation *Sugar(City, Cane, Beet, Molasses, Honey, S)* describes the possible combinations of city names, number of units of sweeteners of each type, and the total sugar unit equivalents of the sweetener used in that city.

With this additional assumption, we can find the maximum profit in city A by the following SQL query:

```
SELECT    Max(Profit)
FROM      Food, Sugar
WHERE     City = "A" and Food.S = Sugar.S
```

SQL also allows aggregation by groups using, as an additional clause after a basic SQL query, a clause of the following form:

$$\text{GROUP BY } a_{i_1}, \ldots, a_{i_l}$$

where the a_{i_k} for $1 \le k \le l$ are attribute names. This clause partitions the relation that is the result of the basic SQL query (but not the aggregation operator) into groups such that within each group the tuples agree on the values of the attributes $a_{i_1}, \ldots, a_{i_l}$.

As an example, suppose an investor would like to know the maximum amount of total profit that the company can produce in all the cities.

To express this query we need to find the maximum profit for each city first; then we have to find the sum of the maximums of the four cities. We can express this query in SQL with two aggregations and a grouping as follows:

```
SELECT      Sum(Max(Profit))
FROM        Food
GROUP BY    city
```

Bibliographic Notes

Relational algebra was defined by Codd [68]. The SQL query language was developed at IBM in the early 1970s. Both of these languages were defined on finite relations. The extensions of these languages to the case of infinite relations that are finitely represented by constraint databases were considered, for example, by Kanellakis et al. [158, 159, 112] and Revesz [256, 267].

Belussi et al. [24] present an alternative view of constraint relational algebra over spatial relations expressed as constraint relations over attributes (id, x, y), where id is an object identification number and x and y are spatial dimensions. The relational algebra in [24] allows for example containment operators.

The SQL query examples are from Revesz and Li [274]. Additional references on the safety and computational complexity of constraint relational algebra and SQL queries are given in the bibliographic notes of Chapters 8 to 12.

Exercises

1. Assume that *Town* $(name, x, y)$ and *Broadcast* $(radio, x, y)$ are relations describing the areas of each town and radio broadcast area. Write relational algebra expressions for the following:

   (a) Find the areas of the town that are reached by both radio stations KLIN and XOMA.

   (b) Find the areas of the town that are reached by neither radio station KLIN nor XOMA.

   (c) Find the areas of the town that are reached by either radio station KLIN or XOMA but not both.

2. Let *Climate* (x, y, t, f) describe for each location (x, y) at time t the temperature f in Fahrenheit degrees, and let *States* $(name, x, y)$ describe the areas of each state in the United States. Write SQL queries for the following:

(a) Find the maximum temperature in Nebraska between time units 6 and 12.

(b) Find the state with the highest temperature at time 7.

(c) Find the average of the maximum temperatures in all of the states.

(d) Find the average of the maximum temperatures in the southernmost parts of all the states.

3. Let $Oak(x, y)$ and $Pine(x, y)$ describe the locations of oak and pine trees in an area. Suppose a bird hid seeds always exactly midway between an oak and a pine tree. Write a SQL query that finds the locations of the seeds.

4

Datalog Queries

Datalog is a rule-based language that is related to Prolog, which is a popular language for implementing expert systems. Each rule is a statement saying that if some points belong to some relations, then other points must also belong to a defined relation. Each Datalog query contains a Datalog program and an input database.

4.1 Syntax

We divide the set of relation names $\mathcal{R}$ into defined relation names $\mathcal{D}$ and input relation names $\mathcal{I}$. Each Datalog query consists of a finite set of rules of the form:

$$R_0(x_1, \ldots, x_k) :\!\!-\!\!- R_1(x_{1,1}, \ldots, x_{1,k_1}), \ldots, R_n(x_{n,1}, \ldots, x_{n,k_n}). \qquad (4.1)$$

where each R_i is either an input relation name or a defined relation name, and the xs are either variables or constants.

The relation names $R_0, \ldots, R_n$ are not necessarily distinct. They could also be built-in relation names, such as $\leq, +, \times$, which we will write using the usual infix notation. For example, we will write $x + y = z$ instead of $+(x, y, z)$ for the ternary input relation $+$ that contains all tuples (a, b, c) such that a plus b equals c.

The preceding rule is read "R_0 is true if R_1 and ... and R_n are all true." R_0 is called the *head* and $R_1, \ldots, R_n$ is called the *body* of the rule.

Example 4.1.1   The tax accountant from Chapter 1 may use the following query Q_{tax} to find the Social Security number and taxes due for each person:

$$Tax\_Due(s, t) \quad :\!\!-\!\!- \quad Taxrecord(s, w, i, c), Taxtable(inc, t),$$
$$w + i + c = inc.$$

Here *Taxrecord, Taxable* $\in \mathcal{I}$ are input database relations and *Tax_Due* $\in \mathcal{D}$ is the only defined relation.

Example 4.1.2   Suppose that relation *Street* (n, x, y) contains all combinations of street name n and locations (x, y) such that a location belongs to the street. Find the set of streets that are reachable from point (x_0, y_0).

$$Reach(n) \quad :- \quad Street(n, x_0, y_0).$$
$$Reach(n) \quad :- \quad Reach(m), Street(m, x, y), Street(n, x, y).$$

Here *Street* $\in \mathcal{I}$ and *Reach* $\in \mathcal{D}$. The first rule says that street n is reachable if it contains the initial point. The second rule says that if m is reachable and m and n intersect on some point, then n is also reachable.

Next we give several more examples of Datalog queries where the domain of the attributes is scalar values, i.e., $\mathcal{Z}$, $\mathcal{Q}$, $\mathcal{R}$, or $\mathcal{W}$ as defined in Section 2.1.

Example 4.1.3   The following query Q_{travel} defines the *Travel* (x, y, t) relation, which is true if it is possible to travel from city x to city y in time t:

$$Travel\,(x, y, t) \quad :- \quad Go\,(x, 0, y, t).$$
$$Travel\,(x, y, t) \quad :- \quad Travel\,(x, z, t_2), Go\,(z, t_2, y, t).$$

Example 4.1.4   Let relation *Go2* (x, y, c) represent the fact that we can go from city x to city y by a direct route in c units of time. The following query $Q_{travel2}$ defines the travel relation, which is true if it is possible to travel from city x to city y in time t:

$$Travel2\,(x, y, t) \quad :- \quad Go2\,(x, y, c),\ t \geq c.$$
$$Travel2\,(x, y, t) \quad :- \quad Travel2\,(x, z, t_2), Go2\,(z, y, c),\ t \geq t_2 + c.$$

The main difference between this query and that in Example 4.1.3 is that this query puts the constraint in the query while the other puts the constraint in the database.

Example 4.1.5   Suppose a river and its tributaries are subdivided into a set of river segments such that the river flows through each segment in c hours, where c is some constant. Let the input relation *River* (r, x, y) represent the area of segment r and *Flows* (r_1, r_2) that segment r_1 flows into segment r_2. Suppose some pollution spills into the river at location (x_0, y_0) at time t_0. Find which river segments will be affected by the pollution at what times:

$$Polluted\,(r, t) \quad :- \quad River\,(r, x_0, y_0),\ t \geq t_0.$$
$$Polluted\,(r_2, t_2) \quad :- \quad Polluted\,(r_1, t_1), Flows\,(r_1, r_2),\ t_2 \geq t_1 + c.$$

Suppose relation *Town* $(name, x, y)$ describes the areas of towns. Find which town areas will be endangered and at what times:

$$Crosses\,(r, n) \quad\quad :- \quad River\,(r, x, y), Town\,(n, x, y).$$
$$Endangered\,(x, y, t) \quad :- \quad Polluted\,(r, t), Crosses\,(r, n),$$
$$Town\,(n, x, y).$$

Example 4.1.6   Suppose there is a number of dams on a river and its tributaries. The river is subdivided into segments delimited by either a dam or a merge point, i.e., a point where two segments flow into each other. Let relation *Flows* (r_1, r_2) represent that r_1 flows into r_2 and let relation *Merge* (r_1, r_2, r_3) represent that river segments r_1 and r_2 merge and flow into river segment r_3. Let *Dam* (r, c) represent that at the end of river segment r there is a dam with a capacity to hold up to c units of water. Suppose relation *Source* (r, a) records that the beginning of river segment r is a source point of the river and receives a units of water. Find the amount of water flowing in each river segment if the dams are holding water at the maximum of their capacities. For simplicity, we neglect all losses due to evaporation, irrigation, and other uses of water.

$$
\begin{aligned}
\textit{Amount}\,(r, a) \quad &:\!\!-\quad \textit{Source}\,(r, a).\\
\textit{Amount}\,(r_2, a_2) \quad &:\!\!-\quad \textit{Amount}\,(r_1, a_1),\ \textit{Dam}\,(r_1, c),\\
&\qquad\ \textit{Flows}\,(r_1, r_2),\ a_2 = a_1 - c.\\
\textit{Amount}\,(r_3, a_3) \quad &:\!\!-\quad \textit{Amount}\,(r_1, a_1),\ \textit{Amount}\,(r_2, a_2),\\
&\qquad\ \textit{Merge}\,(r_1, r_2, r_3),\ a_3 = a_1 + a_2.
\end{aligned}
$$

In this query, the first rule says that the amount of water flowing in a river segment whose beginning is a source point is the same as the amount of water at the source. The second rule says that the amount of water flowing from one river segment to another is c units less in the second segment than in the first, if the dam has capacity c. Finally, the third rule says that the amount of water after a merge is the sum of the amounts of water in the two branches before the merge.

Example 4.1.7   Three bank accounts initially have the same balance. Only deposits are made to the first account and only withdrawals are taken from the second account, while neither withdrawals nor deposits are made to the third account. Transactions always come in pairs, namely, each time a deposit is made to the first account, a withdrawal is made from the second account. Each deposit is at most $200, and each withdrawal is at least $300. What are the possible values of the three accounts?

Let x, y, z denote the amount in the three accounts respectively:

$$
\begin{aligned}
\textit{Balance}\,(x, y, z) \quad &:\!\!-\quad x = y,\ y = z.\\
\textit{Balance}\,(x', y', z) \quad &:\!\!-\quad \textit{Balance}\,(x, y, z),\ x' - x \geq 0,\\
&\qquad\ x - x' \geq -200,\ y - y' \geq 300.
\end{aligned}
$$

Here the first rule declares the initial balance of the three accounts to be the same. The second rule says that if at some time the current values of the three accounts are x', y', and z, then after a sequence of transactions the new account balances are x, which is less than $x' + 200$ because at most $200 is deposited; y, which is less than $y' - 300$ because at least $300 is withdrawn; and z, which does not change.

Example 4.1.8   For the broadcasting example of Chapter 1 a possible query may be to find every place in the town that can be reached by at least one broadcast station. Problems of this kind are called *map overlay* problems. It is usual in this kind of problem that the scales and the points of origin of the maps to be overlayed are not the same. Suppose that a relation *Parameters* $(ID, Scale, X_0, Y_0)$ records for each map its scale and point of origin.

For example, let us suppose that in the town map each unit corresponds to a half kilometer, in the broadcast map each unit corresponds to one kilometer, and the point of origins are the same for the two maps. Then $(1, 1, 0, 0)$, $(2, 1, 0, 0)$, $(3, 1, 0, 0)$, and $(Lincoln, 0.5, 0, 0)$ would be in the *Parameters* relation, as mentioned earlier.

We can find the points in the town that are covered using the following query Q_{cover}:

$$
\begin{aligned}
Covered\,(x_2, y_2) \quad :- \quad & Broadcast\,(n, x, y),\ Town\,(t, x_2, y_2), \\
& Parameters\,(n, s, blat, blong), \\
& Parameters\,(t, s_2, tlat, tlong), \\
& x_2 = \tfrac{s}{s_2}x + (tlat\text{-}blat), \\
& y_2 = \tfrac{s}{s_2}y + (tlong\text{-}blong).
\end{aligned}
$$

This query at first scales up and shifts every point (x, y) in the broadcast map n to match the scale and point of origin of the town map. Finally, if it corresponds to a point (x_2, y_2) in the town map, then it is added to relation *Covered*.

Example 4.1.9   Suppose that each tuple of relation *Forest* (r, x, y) denotes the area of a wooded region r. Suppose also that nonforest areas are lakes, rocks, and sand. Suppose a fire starts in a region described by relation *Fire* (x, y) and the wind is blowing east. Fire could spread from a wooded region to another wooded region that is d distance to the east of the first. Once a wooded region catches fire it will burn down entirely. Find the areas that could burn down:

$$
\begin{aligned}
Burn\,(x, y) \quad &:- \quad Fire\,(x, y). \\
Burn\,(x_2, y) \quad &:- \quad Burn\,(x, y),\ Forest\,(r, x_2, y),\ x_2 \geq x,\ x_2 - x \leq d. \\
Burn\,(x_2, y_2) \quad &:- \quad Burn\,(x, y),\ Forest\,(r, x, y),\ Forest\,(r, x_2, y_2).
\end{aligned}
$$

Here the first rule simply says that the area where the fire starts will burn down. The second rule says that if some forest location (x_2, y_2) is less than d distance to the east from a burning location (x, y), then (x_2, y_2) will also burn down. The third rule expresses the fact that forests burn down entirely once any part of them catches fire.

Example 4.1.10   In the *subset sum* problem we are given a set of n items with weights $w_0, \ldots, w_{n-1}$ and we have to find whether the items can be partitioned into two disjoint sets such that the sum of the weights in both sets are equal.

Let *Item* be the input relation that contains the tuple (i, w) when the $(i + 1)$th element has weight w. The following Datalog query, $Q_{\text{subsetsum}}$ defines the relation *Sum* (i, x, y), which is true when it is possible to add the elements from

0 to $i - 1$ to either the first or the second set such that as a result x is the total weight of the first and y is the total weight of the second set:

$$Same\_Sum\,(x) \quad :— \quad Sum\,(n, x, x).$$
$$Sum\,(i', x', y) \quad :— \quad Sum\,(i, x, y), \, Item\,(i, w), \, i' = i + 1, \, x' = x + w.$$
$$Sum\,(i', x, y') \quad :— \quad Sum\,(i, x, y), \, Item\,(i, w), \, i' = i + 1, \, y' = y + w.$$
$$Sum\,(0, 0, 0).$$

The last line of the query defines the case when no item has yet been added to either set. The second and third lines define recursively the addition of a new item to either the first or the second set, and the top line expresses that if all items can be added to one of the two sets and the total weight of the two sets is the same, then an equal partition is possible.

In the preceding queries we assumed that each variable is ranging over the same domain. That does not need to always be true, as the following example shows.

Example 4.1.11   Suppose a piece of land has a right triangle shape with width a and height b. Divide the land into n pieces.

Let the input relation $Divide\,(a, b, n)$ represent the parameters of the problem. Imagine the triangle to be located such that its corner vertices are at locations $(0, 0)$, $(a, 0)$, and (a, b). If we cut the land parallel to the y-axis the first cut should be at a location that cuts off $1/n$ of the area. Similarly, the ith cut should be at a location that would cut off i/n of the area. The following query finds where to cut the land:

$$Cut\,(x) \quad :— \quad Divide\,(a, b, n), \, 1 \le i, \, i \le n, \, \tfrac{i}{n}a^2 = x^2.$$

Here the total area of the triangle is $(ab)/2$. If we cut at location x, then the area cut off will be $(x^2 b)/2a$. Hence the ith cut is taking away i/x of the land. For Cut to contain only the x locations where to divide the land we need i and n to be integers and the other variables to be real numbers.

Example 4.1.12   Express the relations $Sum\,(x, y, z)$, that is true if the sum of x and y is z, and $Mult\,(x, y, z)$, that is true if x times y is z, where x, y, and z are integers, using addition constraints:

$$Inc\,(x1, x) \quad :— \quad x1 - x \ge 1, \, x - x1 \ge -1.$$

$$Sum\,(x1, y, z1) \quad :— \quad Sum\,(x, y, z), \, Inc\,(x1, x), \, Inc\,(z1, z).$$
$$Sum\,(x, y1, z1) \quad :— \quad Sum\,(x, y, z), \, Inc\,(y1, y), \, Inc\,(z1, z).$$
$$Sum\,(0, 0, 0).$$
$$Sum\,(x, y, z) \quad :— \quad Sum\,(x1, y, z1), \, Inc\,(x1, x), \, Inc\,(z1, z).$$
$$Sum\,(x, y, z) \quad :— \quad Sum\,(x, y1, z1), \, Inc\,(y1, y), \, Inc\,(z1, z).$$

$$Mult\,(x1, y, z2) \quad :\!- \quad Mult\,(x, y, z),\ Sum\,(y, z, z2),\ Inc\,(x1, x).$$
$$Mult\,(x, y1, z2) \quad :\!- \quad Mult\,(x, y, z),\ Sum\,(x, z, z2),\ Inc\,(y1, y).$$
$$Mult\,(0, 0, 0).$$
$$Mult\,(x, y, z) \quad :\!- \quad Mult\,(x1, y, z2),\ Sum\,(y, z, z2),\ Inc\,(x1, x).$$
$$Mult\,(x, y, z) \quad :\!- \quad Mult\,(x, y1, z2),\ Sum\,(x, z, z2),\ Inc\,(y1, y).$$

4.2   Datalog with Sets

In this section we assume that the domain of each attribute is a set. With this assumption, we can represent an undirected graph like the one in Figure 1.2 as relation *Vertices* shown in Section 1.3, and a relation *Edge* (X_1, X_2), which contains a pair of singleton sets of city names if and only if there is an edge between them. For example, *Edge* ({*Lincoln*}, {*Omaha*}) would be one tuple in the second relation.

A Hamiltonian cycle in an undirected graph is a path that starts and ends with the same vertex and goes through each vertex exactly once. The next example shows that the Hamiltonian cycle problem can be expressed using Datalog with sets.

Example 4.2.1   Assume that *Start* (X) is an input relation where X is a singleton set containing the name of the starting vertex of the cycle. To find a Hamiltonian cycle, we try to find a path always going from the last vertex seen to an unvisited vertex. We always stay in set A, the set of vertices not yet visited:

$$Path\,(X_1, B) \quad :\!- \quad Vertices\,(A),\ Start\,(X_1),$$
$$X_1 \subseteq A,\ B = A \setminus X_1.$$

$$Path\,(X_1, B) \quad :\!- \quad Path\,(X_2, A),\ Edge\,(X_2, X_1),$$
$$X_1 \subseteq A,\ B = A \setminus X_1.$$

$$Hamiltonian\,(X_1) \quad :\!- \quad Path\,(X_2, \emptyset),\ Edge\,(X_2, X_1),\ Start\,(X_1).$$

Let us see how the query $Q_{\text{hamiltonian}}$ works. The relation *Path* (X_1, A) is true if and only if between the start vertex and vertex X_1 there is a path that traverses all vertices except those that are in A. The first rule is the initialization, saying that when we start from some start vertex X_1, then all vertices except X_1 will still be unvisited.

The second rule says that if there is a path from the start vertex to some vertex X_2 and there is an edge from vertex X_2 to X_1 and X_1 was not yet visited, then *Path* (X_1, B) will be true where $B = A \setminus X_1$. Finally, the third rule says that if there is a path from the start vertex X_1 to some vertex X_2 such that all vertices were visited and there is an edge from X_2 to X_1, then there is a Hamiltonian cycle in the graph. The relation *Hamiltonian* will contain the start vertex if there is a Hamiltonian cycle in the input graph.

4.3   Datalog with Boolean Constraints

In this section we assume that some of the variables range over elements of a free Boolean algebra. We give some example queries that use Boolean equality constraints.

Example 4.3.1   Consider the problem of finding the parity of n bits given in the relation $Parity(i, c_i)$, where i is an integer and each c_i is a distinct generator (constant symbol) in the free Boolean algebra B_n. Assuming we also have the input relation $Last(n)$, the following Datalog query Q could be used:

$$Parity(1, x) \quad :— \quad Input(1, z).$$
$$Parity(i', x) \quad :— \quad Parity(i, y), \; Input(i', z), \; i' = i + 1, \; x =_{B_n} y \oplus z.$$
$$Paritybit(x) \quad :— \quad Parity(n, x), \; Last(n).$$

This Datalog program contains Boolean equality constraints.

Example 4.3.2   Let the constant c describe the set of computer science majors, m mathematics majors, and a, d, s the students who took an abstract algebra, database systems, or software engineering class at a university. We assume that B is any free Boolean algebra that includes the constants $\{a, c, d, e, s\}$.

Suppose that those eligible for a mathematics minor must be non-mathematics majors and have taken an abstract algebra class, among other requirements. Similarly, those eligible for a computer science minor must be noncomputer science students and have taken either a database systems or software engineering class, among other requirements. These can be expressed using the following constraint tuples:

$$Math\_Minor(x) \quad :— \quad x \leq_B m' \wedge a.$$
$$CS\_Minor(x) \quad :— \quad x \leq_B c' \wedge (d \vee s).$$

Suppose further that those who can apply to the computer science master's program must be either computer science majors or eligible for a computer science minor, among other requirements. Note that if x are the students eligible for a computer science minor, then y, the students who can apply, is expressible as $y \leq_B c \vee x$. This constraint can be rewritten as $x' \wedge y \leq_B c$. Hence this information can be expressed by the rule:

$$Can\_Apply\_CS\_MS(y) \quad :— \quad CS\_Minor(x), \; x' \wedge y \leq_B c.$$

The two preceding constraint tuples form an input database, and the rule is a Datalog program. Note that both contain only simple Boolean upper-bound constraints.

4.4   Datalog with Abstract Data Types

The domain of each abstract data type ranges over some set $\mathcal{S}$. For example, in the *Street* example of Section 1.3, the *Extent* attribute was an abstract data type that ranged over sets of points in the plane, i.e., over $\mathcal{R}^2$ where $\mathcal{R}$ is the set of real numbers. With each abstract data type only certain operations are allowed and can be used within a query. For an abstract data type that ranges over points in the plane, all the basic set operations, that is, equality ($=$), containment $\subseteq$, intersection $\cap$, and union $\cup$, can be allowed.

Example 4.4.1 First let's see how the query in Example 4.1.2 can be rewritten using abstract data types as in Section 1.3:

$$Reach\,(n) \quad :- \quad Street\,(n, Extent), \; \{(x_0, y_0)\} \subseteq Extent.$$
$$Reach\,(n) \quad :- \quad Reach\,(m), \; Street\,(m, S1), \; Street\,(n, S2),$$
$$S1 \cap S2 \neq \emptyset.$$

In this case the first rule declares that any street is reachable that contains the point (x_0, y_0). The second rule asserts that if street m is reachable and intersects street n, then street n is also reachable.

It is worthwhile to compare Example 4.1.2 and Example 4.4.1. These two examples express the same query in different ways. The first query uses more attributes, but it avoids using set constraints. Hence, in this case, the use of abstract data types does not show a clear advantage. Next we see an example where abstract data types provide a clear improvement.

Example 4.4.2 Suppose the input relation *Mobile_Phone* (u, A) describes which person can use a mobile phone to call anyone within area A, where A is an area of the plane. Let's also suppose that the constant *NE* describes the land area of the state of Nebraska. We can find the set of mobile phone users who call only within Nebraska by the following query:

$$NE\_Mobile\_Phone\_User(u) \quad :- \quad Mobile\_Phone\,(u, A),$$
$$A \subseteq NE.$$

We could have used *Mobile_Phone_Area* $(Name, x, y)$ as a relation to describe each person's mobile phone area and *State* $(Name, x, y)$ to describe each state's area similarly to the Town example in Chapter 1. However, then we would not be able to express the query as a simple one-line rule. We could express it using Datalog with negation (see Chapter 5), although it would not be simple. Hence in this case the use of abstract data types shows a clear improvement in simplicity of expression.

Example 4.4.3 As another example, we can find all pairs of persons who can talk with each other and who can send a message to each other with the following Datalog program:

$$Can\_Send\_Message\,(u, v) \quad :- \quad Can\_Send\_Message\,(u, w),$$
$$Can\_Talk\,(w, v).$$

$$Can\_Send\_Message\,(u, v) \quad :- \quad Can\_Talk\,(u, v).$$

$$Can\_Talk\,(u, v) \quad :\!\!- \quad Mobile\_Phone\,(u, A),$$
$$Mobile\_Phone\,(v, B),$$
$$A \cap B \neq \emptyset.$$

The following is another example of Datalog with abstract data types.

Example 4.4.4   Consider the relation $Range\,(x, R)$ stating that animal x can be found within range R in a national park. Suppose that each x is a string and each R is a set of points.

Suppose that animal $deer12$ is infected with a virus that spreads by contact with other animals. The following Datalog program defines the set of animals that are in danger of being infected by the first infected animal:

$$Infection\_Area\,(R) \quad :\!\!- \quad Range\,('deer12', R).$$

$$Infection\_Area\,(R) \quad :\!\!- \quad Infection\_Area\,(R1),\ Range\,(x, R2),$$
$$R1 \cap R2 \neq \emptyset,\ R1 \cup R2 = R.$$

$$In\_Danger\,(A) \quad :\!\!- \quad Infection\_Area\,(R1),\ Range\,(A, R2),$$
$$R1 \cap R2 \neq \emptyset.$$

4.5   Semantics

The proof-based semantics of Datalog queries views the input database as a set of axioms and the rules of the query as a set of inference rules to prove that specific tuples are in some defined relation. We will define this more precisely shortly.

We call an *instantiation* of a rule, the substitution of each variable in it by constants from the proper domain. (For example, the domain may be the set of character strings, the set of integers, or the set of rational numbers.)

Let Q be a query, I an input database, $a_1, \ldots, a_k$ constants, and R a relation name. We say that $R(a_1, \ldots, a_k)$ has a proof using Q and I, written as $\vdash_{Q,I} R(a_1, \ldots, a_k)$, iff

$R \in \mathcal{I}$ represents the relation r and $(a_1, \ldots, a_k) \in r$ or
$R \in \mathcal{D}$ and for some rule in Q there is an instantiation

$$R(a_1, \ldots, a_k) :\!\!- R_1(a_{1,1}, \ldots, a_{1,k_1}), \ldots, R_n(a_{n,1}, \ldots, a_{n,k_n}).$$

where $\vdash_{Q,I} R_i(a_{i,1}, \ldots, a_{i,k_i})$ for each $1 \leq i \leq n$.

The *proof-based* semantics of Datalog queries is the following. Each Datalog query Q is a function that, on any input database I, returns for each relation name R the relation $\{(a_1, \ldots, a_k) \quad \vdash_{Q,I} R(a_1, \ldots, a_k)\}$.

When the query and the input database are obvious, we will write $\vdash$ without any subscript.

Example 4.5.1   Let us prove using the query in Example 4.1.2 that from point $(5, 2)$ we can reach Willow Street.

We apply the first rule with the instantiation $n/Vine$, $x_0/5$, $y_0/2$ to get:

Reach (*Vine*) :— *Street* (*Vine*, 5, 2).

Because point (5, 2) is the south end of Vine Street, the rule body is true. Hence we have:

⊢ *Reach* (*Vine*)

We apply the second rule with $n/Bear$, $m/Vine$, $x/5$, $y/12$ to get:

Reach (*Bear*) :— *Reach* (*Vine*), *Street* (*Vine*, 5, 12), *Street* (*Bear*, 5, 12).

Because point (5, 12) is the intersection point of Bear and Vine Streets, the rule body is true. Hence:

⊢ *Reach* (*Bear*)

We apply the second rule with $n/Hare$, $m/Bear$, $x/8$, $y/13$ to get:

Reach (*Hare*)   :—   *Reach* (*Bear*), *Street* (*Bear*, 8, 13),
                          Street (*Hare*, 8, 13).

Because point (8, 13) is the intersection point of Bear and Hare Streets, the rule body is true. Hence:

⊢ *Reach* (*Hare*)

We apply the second rule with $n/Willow$, $m/Hare$, $x/5$, $y/18$ to get:

Reach (*Willow*)   :—   *Reach* (*Hare*), *Street* (*Hare*, 5, 18),
                            Street (*Willow*, 5, 18).

Because point (5, 18) is the intersection point of Hare and Willow Streets, the rule body is true. Hence:

⊢ *Reach* (*Willow*)

Example 4.5.2   Let us prove using the query in Example 4.1.3 and the input instance of *Go* from Chapter 1 that one can travel from Omaha to Chicago in 990 minutes. We show only the derived tuples without mentioning the instantiations used:

⊢ *Go* (*Omaha*, 0, *Lincoln*, 60)	by the first displayed tuple
⊢ *Go* (*Lincoln*, 60, *Kansas_City*, 210)	by the seventh tuple
⊢ *Go* (*Kansas_City*, 210, *Des_Moines*, 390)	by the eighth tuple
⊢ *Go* (*Des_Moines*, 390, *Chicago*, 990)	by the ninth tuple
⊢ *Travel* (*Omaha*, *Lincoln*, 60)	by the first rule
⊢ *Travel* (*Omaha*, *Kansas_City*, 210)	by the second rule
⊢ *Travel* (*Omaha*, *Des_Moines*, 390)	by the second rule
⊢ *Travel* (*Omaha*, *Chicago*, 990)	by the second rule

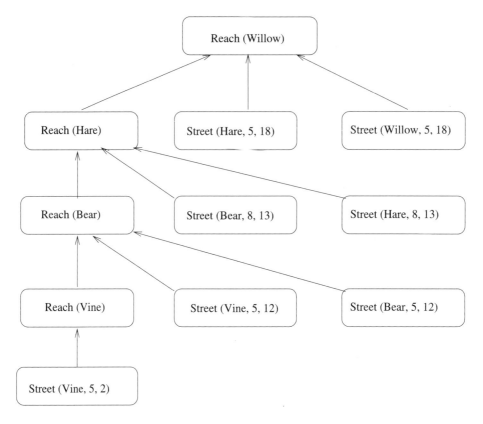

FIGURE 4.1. A proof tree for reaching Willow Street.

4.5.1   Proof Trees

It is easy to draw any proof as a tree in which each internal node is the head of an instantiated rule, and its children are the instantiated relations in the body of the rule. For example, the proof that one can reach Willow Street from the original location (5, 2) can be visualized by the proof tree in Figure 4.1.

In many applications, a user will be interested not only in the set of provable tuples, but also in the reason why they are true. Such users may want to have a proof tree displayed for specific tuples in the output database.

Fortunately, it is easy to add more meaning to Datalog queries. We can require that when adding to the current database a new derived tuple, it should be affixed with the rule number and the instantiation of the rule that was used in the last step of its derivation. (Note that if a derived tuple is not new but already exists in the database, then the affix stays the same and the later derivation is ignored.) This way we can reconstruct a proof tree for any tuple in the output.

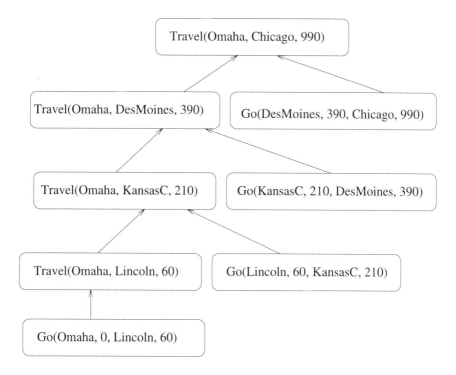

FIGURE 4.2. A proof tree for traveling from Omaha to Chicago.

A proof tree is convenient if one would like to find the actual path to be taken from location (5, 2) to Willow Street and not just to know that there exists some path. For this purpose, it is sufficient to look at the leftmost branch of the proof tree in Figure 4.1. As we read this branch from the leaf to the root node, the instantiated attribute of relation *Reach* is always the next street to reach.

Another example of a proof tree is shown in Figure 4.2. This proof tree summarizes the proof given in Example 4.5.2. A user looking for a path from Omaha to Chicago that takes only 990 minutes nees to look only at the leftmost branch. There, the second instantiated attribute of relation *Travel* is always the next city to go to.

Finally, let us prove using the query in Example 4.2.1 that there is a Hamiltonian cycle in the graph of Figure 1.2 using as the input database relation *Vertices* from Section 1.3 and *Chicago* as the start vertex. This can be done using the proof tree in Figure 4.3. The proof tree uses only the first letters of the cities instead of their full names. The Hamiltonian cycle can be read off from the leftmost branch of the proof tree from the leaf to the root node as the first argument of the *Path* relation in sequence.

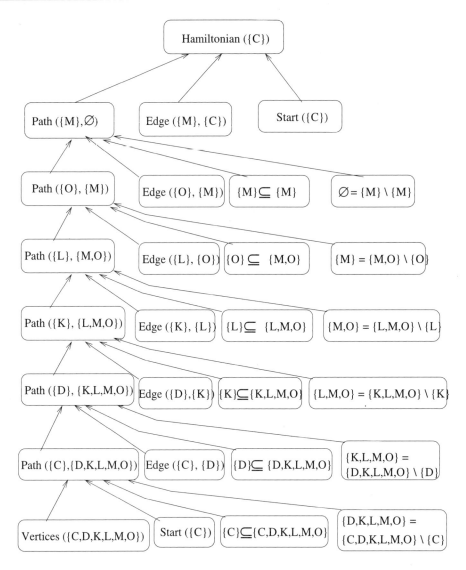

FIGURE 4.3. A proof tree for a Hamiltonian cycle.

4.5.2   Least Fixpoint

There is an alternative description of the semantics of Datalog queries that can be explained as follows.

Let Q be any Datalog query. We call an *interpretation* of Q any assignment r_i of a finite or infinite number of tuples over $\delta^{\alpha(R_i)}$ to each R_i that occurs in Q, where δ is the domain of the attribute variables and $\alpha(R_i)$ is the arity of relation R_i.

The *immediate consequence operator* of a Datalog query Q, denoted T_Q, is a mapping from interpretations to interpretations as follows. For each interpretation db that assigns to $R, R_1, R_2, \ldots$ the relations $r, r_1, r_2, \ldots$ we say that $R(a_1, \ldots, a_k) \in T_Q(db)$, iff

$R \in \mathcal{I}$ and $(a_1, \ldots, a_k) \in r$ or
$R \in \mathcal{D}$ and for some rule in Q there is an instantiation

$$R(a_1, \ldots, a_k) :\!\!- R_1(a_{1,1}, \ldots, a_{1,k_1}), \ldots, R_n(a_{n,1}, \ldots, a_{n,k_n}).$$

where $R_i(a_{i,1}, \ldots, a_{i,k_i}) \in r_i$ for each $1 \le i \le n$.

Each input database I is an interpretation that assigns a finite or infinite relation to each $R \in \mathcal{I}$ and the empty set to each $R \in \mathcal{D}$. Let

$$T_Q^0(I) = T_Q(I)$$

Also let

$$T_Q^{i+1}(I) = T_Q^i(I) \cup T_Q(T_Q^i(I))$$

We call the *least fixpoint semantics* of Q on I, denoted $lfp(Q(I))$, the interpretation $\bigcup_i T_Q^i(I)$.

Note: Any interpretation J is called a *fixpoint* of a query Q iff $J = T_Q(J)$. There could be many fixpoints of a query. The interpretation $\bigcup_i T_Q^i(I)$ is a fixpoint that is distinguished from other fixpoints in that it is a subset of any other fixpoint that the query may have. That is why it is called the least fixpoint.

The proof-based and the least fixpoint semantics are equivalent, as shown in the following theorem.

Theorem 4.5.1

$$\{(a_1, \ldots, a_k) : \ \vdash_{Q,I} R(a_1, \ldots, a_k)\} =$$
$$\{(a_1, \ldots, a_k) : \ R(a_1, \ldots, a_k) \in \bigcup_i T_Q^i(I)\} \qquad \blacksquare$$

4.6   Recursive Datalog Queries

We define a binary relation *depends_on* on $\mathcal{R}$ as follows: *depends_on* (H, B) is true if for $H, B \in \mathcal{R}$ there is a rule such that H occurs in the head and B occurs in the body of the rule. For each query the *depends_on* relation can be easily illustrated by a directed graph.

We call a query *recursive* if the graph of the *depends_on* relation does not contain a cycle. Otherwise we call the query *nonrecursive*. For example, Q_{tax} is a nonrecursive and Q_{travel} is a recursive query.

Bibliographic Notes

Datalog queries and logic programming are closely tied together, and their history (without constraints) is reviewed in several textbooks including the ones by Abiteboul et al. [1], O'Neil [223], Ramakrishnan [243], Silberschatz et al. [288], and Ullman [310]. Datalog with nested sets is discussed by Vadaparty [311].

Constraint logic programs were defined by Jaffar and Lassez [151] and discussed in the textbooks by Marriott and Stuckey [205] and Van Hentenryck [317] and in Benhamou and Colmerauer [32]. Datalog with constraint queries was studied by Kanellakis, Kuper, and Revesz [158, 159], and Kuper et al. [194] is a recent edited book on the subject. One of the most interesting issues in both cases is the evaluation methods used, which are discussed in Chapter 9. The types of constraints used affect the termination of the evaluation methods as described in Chapter 8.

The Hamiltonian cycle example is from [262] and the travel example is from [267]. The other example Datalog queries and proof trees are new. The first four questions of Exercise 6 are based on Chomicki and Revesz [62].

Exercises

1. Find every city within 500 minutes of Omaha. Assume that we know the minimum traveling time on each direct route connection between cities.

2. A sales agency has offices in 30 major cities in the continental United States. Find all cities where the agency can ship goods within 500 minutes. Assume that we know the minimum traveling time on each direct route connection between cities and the cities where the agency is located.

3. Assume that you want to design a database of flight schedules where flights are represented by numbers 1,2,3, etc. Relation *Flights* lists for each flight an origin and a destination city and information on the time of arrival and the time of departure measured in minutes past 12 midnight. Relation *Airport* lists the minimum delay in transit at airports in various cities. Find all pairs of cities between which travel is possible.

Flights

No	Orig	Dest	Depart	Arrive
1	Atlanta	Chicago	870	925
2	Atlanta	Denver	830	940
3	Boston	Atlanta	690	800
4	Boston	Chicago	545	645
5	Chicago	Atlanta	710	765
6	Chicago	Denver	660	780

Airport

Name	Arrive	Depart	
Atlanta	t_1	t_2	$t_2 - t_1 \geq 60$
Boston	t_1	t_2	$t_2 - t_1 \geq 50$
Chicago	t_1	t_2	$t_2 - t_1 \geq 45$
Denver	t_1	t_2	$t_2 - t_1 \geq 70$

4. In a garden there are two types of flowers: tulips and daffodils. We know the location of these flowers with respect to the southwest corner of the garden. In the garden there are several hives of bees and wasps. We know the area where each hive of bees and wasps collects pollen from flowers. For example, the first hive of bees visits flowers in the rectangular area 50 to 200 meters east and 100 to 350 meters north from the southwest corner of the garden. Bees visit both tulips and daffodils, while wasps visit only daffodils. Both insects may carry pollen from one flower to another. Suppose there is a special strain of daffodils at location 2 meters east and 3 meters north from the southwest corner. Find all daffodils that may be pollinated by this flower.

5. Write a query that tests whether propositional formulas are true. (In this exercise you have to define a representation for the input database propositional formulas.)

6. Express in Datalog the following queries assuming we have a land area relation similar to the one in Exercise 2.5:

   (a) Find the edges between any pair of regions.

   (b) Find the boundary of each region.

   (c) Find the vertices of each region.

   (d) Find the endpoints of each edge for each region.

   (e) Find the length of the boundary of each region.

   (f) Find the area of each inside region.

5

Aggregation and Negation Queries

Aggregate operators are operators that take in a set of values and return a single value. Negation of a relation with arity k returns a constraint representation of the complement of the relation. That is, if δ is the domain, then those tuples in δ^k that do not belong to the relation should be returned.

Both aggregation and negation require that the entire relation be completely known. Therefore we apply these only to input relations, although the input relations to these operators could be relations that were defined earlier in Datalog queries and already completely computed in some way. This is called the *stratified composition* of queries.

First we describe some common aggregate operators and negation in constraint databases, then we will discuss the composition of Datalog queries.

5.1 Set Grouping

The set grouping operator has the syntax:

$$R_0(y_1, \ldots, y_m) \quad :\!\!- \quad R(x_1, \ldots, x_n).$$

where each y_i is either x_j or $\langle x_j \rangle$ for $1 \le i \le m$ and $1 \le j \le n$.

This operator is restricted to cases where at least the (column of) attributes referred to by the regular variables in the head are constants. This operator first groups all the tuples in R into groups where these variables have the same values. Then for each group it takes the union of the column of attributes referred to by $\langle \rangle$ bracketed variables in the head.

For example, let *Can_Send_Message* (x, y) be true if person x can send a message to person y using mobile phones as in Example 4.4.3. Suppose we want to find for each person x the set of persons that x can reach. We can do that using a set grouping operator as follows:

$$Reach\,(x, \langle y \rangle) \quad :\!\!- \quad Can\_Send\_Message\,(x, y).$$

To find the set of mobile phone users, we can use:

$$Mobile\_Phone\_Users\,(\langle x \rangle) \quad :\!\!- \quad Mobile\_Phone\,(x, A).$$

Set grouping operators can be also applied to a column of intentional set constants. For example, to find the areas with at least one mobile phone user we can use:

$$Areas\_with\_Mobile\_Phones\,(\langle A \rangle) \quad :\!\!- \quad Mobile\_Phone\,(x, A).$$

5.2   Average, Count, Sum

These aggregate operators are like the set grouping operators. In fact, the syntax is similar to the set grouping operator, with each $\langle\rangle$ bracketed variable in the head preceded by one key word: *avg*, *count*, or *sum*. For these aggregate operators, the column of attributes referred to by bracketed variables in the head must also be constants.

For example, the following query finds for each person x the number of persons that x can reach:

$$Reach\,(x, count\langle y \rangle) \quad :\!\!- \quad Can\_Send\_Message\,(x, y).$$

As another example, let's consider $NE\_Mobile\_Phone\_User\,(x)$, which describes the mobile phone users in the state of Nebraska, as in Example 4.4.2, as an input relation. Then the following query $Q_{\text{number}\_NE\_\text{Users}}$ finds the number of mobile phone users in Nebraska:

$$Number\_NE\_Users\,(count\langle x \rangle) \quad :\!\!- \quad NE\_Mobile\_Phone\_User\,(x).$$

5.3   Area and Volume

The *area* aggregate operator works on relations that represent maps. In each such relation we assume that the two distinguished attributes, called the *spatial attributes*, are rational variables x, y on which we place linear constraints. The other attributes, called the *nonspatial attributes*, are constants. The relation describes which attributes hold for regions of the plane.

For example, the *Town* relation in Chapter 1 represents maps as we described earlier. In the *Town* relation the second and third attributes are the spatial attributes and the first attribute is the only nonspatial attribute.

The syntax of the area operator is similar to the other aggregate operators, but we will have $area\langle x, y \rangle$ in the head because area is a two-argument operator unlike average, count, and sum. For example, to find the total area of each town, we can write the following:

$$Town\_Area\,(t, area\langle x, y\rangle) \quad :- \quad Town\,(t, x, y).$$

The *volume* aggregate operator is like the area aggregate operator except that it takes three variables as arguments.

In many geographic applications it is useful to find total area statistics for each band region of a map. Therefore in the area aggregate operator we allow the following constant parameters as an optional argument: x_0, d, and n. With these parameters present, the area operator will find the total area now in each band. That is, it will return two more attributes following the area attribute. Namely, it will return $x_0 + id$ and $x_0 + (i + 1)d$ for each $0 \leq i \leq n$, and the total area value will be only the total area where $x_0 + id \leq x \leq x_0 + (i + 1)d$. For example, the following query returns for each 1-unit-wide x band the total area of each town, where the left side of the first band will be 2 and there are 12 bands:

$$Town\_Area\,(t, area\langle x, 2, 1, 12, y\rangle) \quad :- \quad Town\,(t, x, y).$$

We also allow similar optional constant parameters after the y argument. In this case, the total area statistics will be returned for each little square or rectangular region of the map.

5.4   Minimum and Maximum

The *minimum* and *maximum* aggregate operators work on relations within which all attributes occurring in the head outside of the $\langle\rangle$ brackets are constants while attributes occurring within the brackets can be variables constrained by linear constraints.

The syntax of the minimum and maximum operators differs from the syntax of the average, count, and sum operators only in that the argument of max can be a linear function, called the *objective* function. That is, the argument list will be $\langle c_1 x_1 + \cdots + c_n x_n\rangle$ where $x_1, \ldots, x_n$ occur in the input relation.

Example 5.4.1   Suppose the farmer in Chapter 1 wants to find the maximum profit possible given that each acre of corn, rye, sunflower, and wheat yields a profit of 30, 25, 8, and 15, respectively.

The following query Q_{profit} can calculate the maximum profit possible for any of the planting options:

$$Profit\,(\max\langle 30x_1 + 25x_2 + 8x_3 + 15x_3\rangle) \quad :- \quad Crops\,(x_1, x_2, x_3, x_4).$$

As another example, the following query Q_{edge} finds the minimum time between each pair of towns connected by a single edge:

$$Edge\,(x, y, \min\langle t\rangle) \quad :- \quad Go\,(x, 0, y, t).$$

5.5   Negation

The negation operator has the following syntax:

$$R_0(x_1, \ldots, x_k) \quad :\!\!- \quad not\ R(x_1, \ldots, x_k).$$

R could be a relation with linear constraints over the rationals or polynomial constraints over the reals. R could also be a relation with $=$, $\neq$, $<$, and $\leq$ constraints over the integers. In all of these cases it is possible to find a constraint representation of the complement of R. The constraint representation will contain the same type of constraints as the input relation. (For example, if R is a relation with polynomial constraints over the reals, then R_0 will also be a relation with polynomial constraints over the reals.) This is called a *closed-form* representation.

As an example, suppose that relation *Covered*(x, y) describes the areas reached by at least one radio station as in Example 4.1.8. Then the areas that are not reached by any radio station or that are not within the town can be found by the following query $Q_{\text{not\_cover}}$:

$$Not\_Covered(x, y) \quad :\!\!- \quad not\ Covered(x, y).$$

5.6   Stratified Datalog Queries

Let us suppose that we want to find the fastest possible travel time between any pair of cities. This can be done by first evaluating Q_{travel} and then finding the minimum travel times by the following query Q_{fastest}, which assumes *Travel* as an input relation:

$$Fastest(x, y, \min\langle t \rangle) \quad :\!\!- \quad Travel(x, y, t).$$

The composition of the Q_{fastest} and Q_{travel} queries is a new query that we write as $Q_{\text{fastest}}(Q_{\text{travel}}())$. The composite query takes as input the relation *Could_Go* and returns relations *Could_Go*, *Travel*, and *Fastest*.

Each part of a composite query is called one level, or *stratum*. A composite query is called a *stratified Datalog* query. Here Q_{travel} is the first and Q_{fastest} is the second stratum of the composite query.

As another example, the Q_{cover} query in Example 4.1.8 took as input relations *Town* and *Broadcast*, while query $Q_{\text{not\_cover}}$ took as input the relation Q_{cover}. We write the composition of these two queries as $Q_{\text{not\_cover}}(Q_{\text{cover}}())$.

We call a stratified Datalog query nonrecursive if each of its component queries is nonrecursive. Otherwise, we call it a recursive query. For example, the composite query $Q_{\text{fastest}}(Q_{\text{travel}}())$ is recursive because Q_{travel} is itself recursive. However, $Q_{\text{not\_cover}}(Q_{\text{cover}}())$ is nonrecursive, because neither Q_{cover} nor $Q_{\text{not\_cover}}$ is a recursive query.

Finally, let us see a stratified Datalog query that uses set constants.

Example 5.6.1   Let's call $Q_{\text{mobile\_phone\_users}}$ and Q_{reach}, respectively, the queries that define relations *Mobile_Phone_Users* and *Reach* as shown in Section 5.1. Let's call the following query Q_{Alice}:

$$\textit{Alice\_Cannot\_Reach}\,(Z) \quad :\!— \quad \textit{Mobile\_Phone\_Users}\,(X),$$
$$\textit{Reach}\,(\text{``Alice''}, Y),$$
$$Z = X \setminus Y.$$

The stratified Datalog query $Q_{\text{Alice}}(Q_{\text{mobile\_phone\_users}}(Q_{\text{reach}}()))$ finds the set of people to whom Alice cannot send a message.

Bibliographic Notes

Stratified Datalog queries have been studied extensively by many authors, and detailed descriptions can be found in Abiteboul et al. [1], Ramakrishnan [243], Revesz [264], and Ullman [310]. Datalog can be extended with other types of negation and aggregation, for example, well-founded negation and aggregation [299, 315, 316] and inflationary negation [173].

The presentation of the stratified composition of queries is a simplification of the usual presentation in that it does not require the finding of "natural stratifications" among alternatives but rather forces the user to choose a stratification. The biggest advantage of this is the sharp distinction between Datalog queries and aggregation and negation queries; it also reveals the close connection between aggregation and negation. The maximum and minimum operators are also easily seen as cases of linear programming. We review that in more detail in the bibliographic notes in Chapter 8.

Exercises

1. Write a query that finds all parts of the town that are reached by two broadcast stations but not by three.

2. Suppose relation *Postage* (w, f) describes the postage fee f required for a package with weight w. Mr. Johnson, who lives in Omaha, Nebraska, wants to send three packages to three clients who live in Atlanta, Boston, and Chicago. He wants to know the total amount he should pay for his packages. The weight of each package can be represented in the following relational database table.

Package

No.	From	To	Weight
101	Omaha	Chicago	12.6
102	Omaha	Atlanta	27.3
103	Omaha	Boston	37.5

Write a Datalog query with linear constraints that finds the total postage fee required.

3. Suppose a farmer can harvest 1125, 500, and 250 pounds of asparagus from locations 1, 2, and 3, respectively. The asparagus can be shipped to two cool rooms, which can store 1250 and 950 pounds, respectively.

   The average cost of transporting asparagus from location 1 to cool rooms 1 and 2 is 0.03 and 0.07 dollars per pound, respectively. The average cost of transporting asparagus from location 2 to cool rooms 1 and 2 is 0.05 and 0.03 dollars per pound, respectively. The average cost of transporting asparagus from location 3 to cool rooms 1 and 2 is 0.08 and 0.10 dollars per pound.

   The farmer would like to buy some extra land adjacent to one of the three locations that will yield an extra 325 pounds of asparagus.

   Write a Datalog query that finds where the farmer should buy extra land and how many pounds of asparagus should be shipped from which location to which cool room for the maximum profit.

4. Write a Datalog query with aggregation query that finds the area of each inside region assuming we have a land area relation similar to Exercise 2.5. Compare the answer to the solution of the last question of Exercise 4.6.

6

Constraint Automata

Constraint automata are used to control the operation of systems based on conditions that are described using constraints on variables. Section 6.1 presents a concrete definition and gives several examples of constraint automata.

A constraint automaton can be simplified using *reduction rules* that redraw constraint automata into equivalent constraint automata. Section 6.2 presents some reduction rules.

An important problem for constraint automata is to find the set of *reachable configurations*, which is the set of states and state values that a constraint automaton can enter. Section 6.3 presents a method of analyzing the reachable configurations of constraint automata by expressing the constraint automata in Datalog with constraints.

6.1 Definition of Constraint Automata

A constraint automaton consists of a set of states, a set of state variables, transitions between states, an initial state, and the domain and initial values of the state variables. Each transition consists of a set of constraints, called the *guard* constraints, followed by a set of assignment statements. The guard constraints of a constraint automaton can contain relations. In constraint automata the guards are followed by question marks, and the assignment statements are shown using the symbol :=.

A constraint automaton can move from one state to another if there is a transition whose guard constraints are satisfied by the current values of the state variables. The transitions of a constraint automaton may contain variables in addition to the state variables. These variables are said to be *existentially quantified* variables. Their meaning is that some values for these variables can be found such that the guard constraints are satisfied.

A constraint automaton can interact with its environment by sensing the current value of a variable. This is expressed by a *read* (*x*) command on a transition between states, where *x* is any variable. This command updates the value of *x* to a new value. The read command can appear either before or after the guard constraints.

The following is an example of a constraint automaton with a single state.

Example 6.1.1   While visiting some countries, a tourist who has dollars, euros, and yens always exchanges these at the rate of one dollar equals two euros, which equals three hundred yens. Each exchange is a multiple of 100 dollars, 200 euros, or 30,000 yens and has a commission charge of 1 percent.

Let *d* be the total amount of dollars the tourist has spent on anything except commissions plus the amount that remains in his wallet. Let *e* and *y* be defined similarly. We are interested in the possible values of *d*, *e*, and *y* at any time during the trip. The constraint automaton that defines the possible values of *d*, *e* and *y* is shown in Figure 6.1.

Each constraint automaton can be drawn as a graph in which each vertex represents a state and each directed edge represents a transition. There is only one state and three state variables, *d*, *e*, and *y*.

The following two examples show the use of read commands.

Example 6.1.2   A hotel elevator can move from the lobby up to the restaurant or down to the underground parking garage. The elevator can sense the number of people waiting

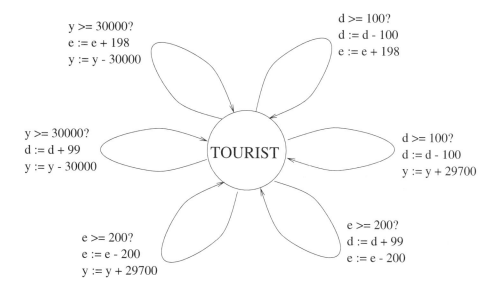

FIGURE 6.1. The tourist's currency constraint automaton.

in front of the elevator on each floor, the up and down signals pushed in the lobby, and the floor request signals pushed within the elevator. (There are no up and down signals in the restaurant or the parking garage.)

The elevator does not always go all the way up and down. Instead it operates as follows. If while going from the parking garage to the lobby it senses no request for the restaurant either within the elevator or in the lobby and there are more people in the lobby than in the restaurant, then it will go down again after reaching the lobby. Otherwise, it will go up to the restaurant.

Similarly, if while going from the restaurant to the lobby it senses no request for the parking garage either within the elevator or in the lobby and there are more people in the lobby than in the parking garage, then it will go up again after reaching the lobby. Otherwise, it will go down to the parking garage.

This hotel elevator system can be described by the constraint automaton shown in Figure 6.2. The constraint automaton has three states, each corresponding to and named after a possible position of the elevator. Each state has the following variables:

- x, y, and z, which describe the number of people sensed to be waiting for the elevator in the lobby, in the parking garage, and in the restaurant, respectively;

- d, which shows whether the next move of the elevator will be down;

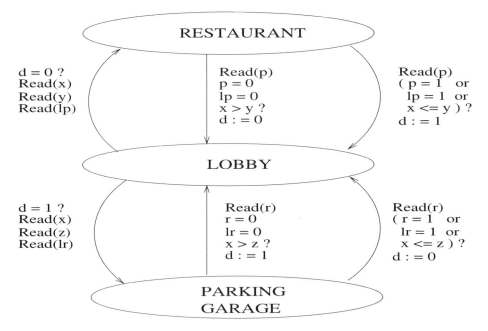

FIGURE 6.2. The hotel elevator system.

- p and r, which show whether anyone in the elevator requested the parking garage or the restaurant, respectively; and

- lp and lr, which show whether anyone in the lobby pushed the down or the up button.

Each of the last five variables is 1 when the answer is yes and 0 when it is no.

Example 6.1.3   A ferry takes passengers across a river between shores A and B. The ferry also stops occasionally at an island C, which is visited by few passengers. The ferry visits the island according to the following rules. (1) If there is any passenger waiting to stop at C, then visit C on the third crossing since the last visit. (2) If there are at least ten passengers who are waiting to stop at C, then the ferry may visit C earlier, but never on two subsequent crossings.

Assume that we know how many new passengers who want to go to island C board the ferry in each hour. Find all possible combinations of location and number of passengers waiting in the ferry for one or two crossings.

The constraint automaton is shown in Figure 6.3. There are three states for the three possible locations of the ferry. The state variables are n, the number of crossings since the last visit to C; variables x_0 and x_1, the number of passengers

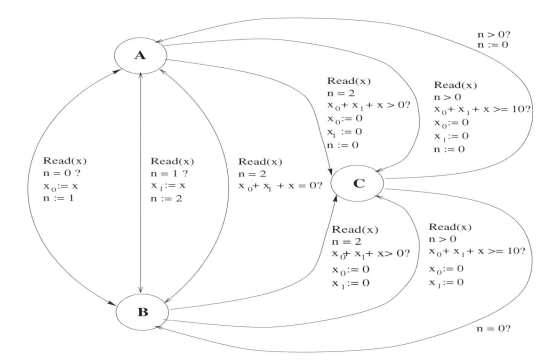

FIGURE 6.3. The ferry system.

waiting to visit C since $t = 0$ and $t = 1$, respectively; and x, the number of passengers freshly boarding with tickets to the island.

Drawing a constraint automata can be a good way to design a control system. The next is a real-life example of a complex design.

Example 6.1.4   A subway train speed regulation system is defined as follows. Each train detects beacons that are placed along the track and receives a "second" signal from a central clock.

Let b and s be counter variables for the number of beacons and second signals received. Further, let d be a counter variable that describes how long the train is applying its brake. The goal of the speed regulation system is to keep $\mid b - s \mid$ small while the train is running.

The speed of the train is adjusted as follows. When $s + 10 \le b$, then the train notices it is early and applies the brake as long as $b > s$. Continuously braking causes the train to stop before encountering 10 beacons.

When $b + 10 \le s$ the train is late and will be considered late as long as $b < s$. As long as any train is late, the central clock will not emit the second signal.

The subway speed regulation system can be drawn as a constraint automaton shown in Figure 6.4, where $x + +$ and $x - -$ are abbreviations for $x := x + 1$ and $x := x - 1$, respectively, for any variable x.

The following is an example constraint automaton with existentially quantified variables.

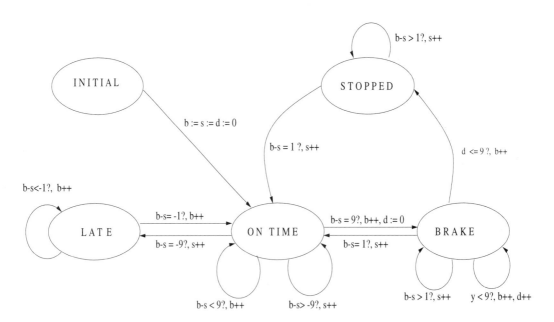

FIGURE 6.4. The subway train control system.

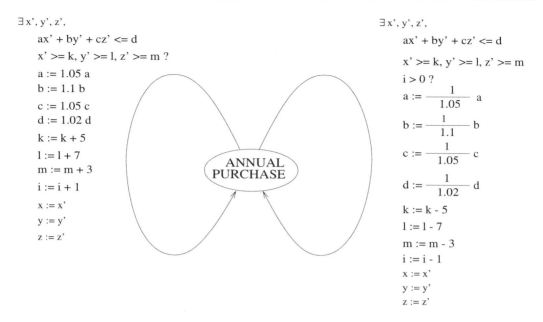

FIGURE 6.5. The annual purchase constraint automaton.

Example 6.1.5   A business needs to annually purchase three resources x, y, and z. Currently the price of these resources are a, b, and c, respectively, and the purchase budget is d. The business needs at least k, l, and m of these items, respectively.

Each year we have either an inflation or a deflation. During an inflationary year, a and c increase 5%, b increases 10%, and d increases 2%, while k, m, and l increase 5%, 7%, and 3%, respectively. Each deflationary year cancels the effect of a previous inflationary year, and the prices and limits decrease to regain their previous values. Assume that the number of inflationary years is always more than the number of deflationary years.

This problem can be represented using the constraint automaton shown in Figure 6.5.

The following is an example of a constraint automaton in which the guards contain relations.

Example 6.1.6   A cafeteria has three queues where choices for salad, main dishes, and drinks can be made. A customer has a coupon for $10. He first picks a selection. His selection must include a main dish and a salad, but drink may be skipped if the salad costs more than $3. If the total cost of the selection is less than $8 then he may go back to make a new choice for salad or drink.

Let *salad*, *main*, and *drink* be three binary relations in which the first argument is the name of a salad, main dish, or drink and the second argument is its price. The constraint automaton in Figure 6.6 expresses this problem.

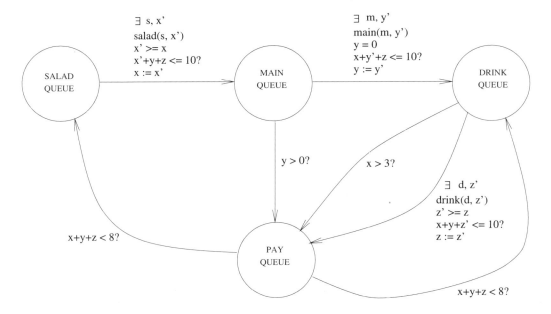

FIGURE 6.6. The cafeteria constraint automaton.

An interesting special case of constraint automata has only one state and one transition, which updates the values of the state variables such that each variable is a linear combination of the others. The following is an example.

Example 6.1.7   On a certain planet water can occur in the form of clouds, rain, streams, and ocean. We know that each year one-sixtieth of the ocean becomes clouds, one-half of the clouds becomes rain, one-third of the rain becomes clouds, one-third of the rain becomes streams, and one-third of the rain becomes ocean. One-sixth of the streams becomes clouds and one-sixth becomes ocean.

The water cycle on this planet can be represented by the constraint automaton shown in Figure 6.7, where c, r, s, and o represent the amount of water in the four forms before and c', r', s', and o' represent them after a transition. Given an initial amount of water in the four forms, an interesting problem would be to find whether the proportion of water in the different forms ever stabilizes.

6.2   Simplifications of Constraint Automata

Drawing a constraint automaton can be a good start in solving a problem. However, the first drawing may be more complex than necessary and may need to be simplified. The following example illustrates the simplification process.

A correct design of the constraint automaton in Figure 6.4 would mean that $b - s$ is at least some constant c_1 and at most some constant c_2. The value of

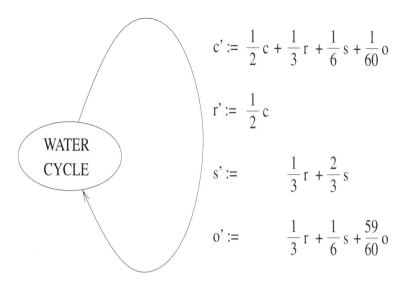

$$c' := \frac{1}{2}c + \frac{1}{3}r + \frac{1}{6}s + \frac{1}{60}0$$

$$r' := \frac{1}{2}c$$

$$s' := \frac{1}{3}r + \frac{2}{3}s$$

$$0' := \frac{1}{3}r + \frac{1}{6}s + \frac{59}{60}0$$

FIGURE 6.7. The water cycle constraint automaton.

$b - s$ may be unbounded in case of an incorrect design. To test the correctness of the constraint automaton, let's rewrite it using variable x instead of the value $(b - s) - 20$ and variable y instead of d. This change of variables yields the automaton shown in Figure 6.8.

Now we can make some observations of equivalences between automata. We call these equivalences *reduction rules*. Reduction rules allow us to either rewrite complex constraints into simpler ones (like rules 1 and 2 in the following) or eliminate some transitions from the constraint automaton (like rule 3 in the following).

1. **Moving increment after self-loop:** This reduction rule is shown in Figure 6.9. This rule can be applied when no other arcs are ending at state S. This rule says that if there is only one self-loop at S and it can decrement repeatedly a variable while it is greater than c, then the $x++$ before it can be brought after it, if we replace c by $c - 1$ in the guard condition of the self-loop. It is easy to see that in state S for each possible configuration before this reduction there will be a corresponding configuration with the same values except that x is one smaller. The set of possible configurations in the other states is not changed by this reduction rule. We give an example of the use of this reduction rule later.

2. **Elimination of increment/decrement from self-loops:** This reduction rule is shown in Figure 6.10. There are two variations of this rule shown on the top and bottom, depending on whether the variable is incremented or decremented. The top variation says that if a variable is decremented one or

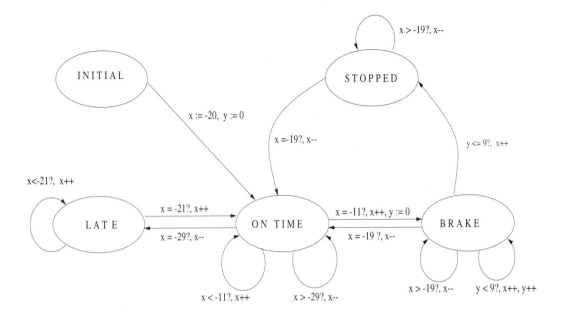

FIGURE 6.8. The subway system after changing variables.

more times using a self-loop until a guard condition $x > c$ is satisfied, then the repetition is equivalent to a self-loop, which just picks some value x' greater than or equal to c and less than the initial value of x and assigns x' to x. The bottom variation is explained similarly. Note that both reduction rules eliminate the need to repeatedly execute the transition. That is, any repetition of the transitions on the left-hand side is equivalent to a single execution of the transition on the right-hand side.

3. **Elimination of increment/decrement from a pair of self-loops:** This reduction rule is shown in Figure 6.11. This rule can be applied when $c_1 < a$ and $b < c_2$ and no other arcs end at S. Clearly, the repetitions of the double increment loop alone will keep $y - x = (b - a)$ because both y and

FIGURE 6.9. Moving increment after self-loop.

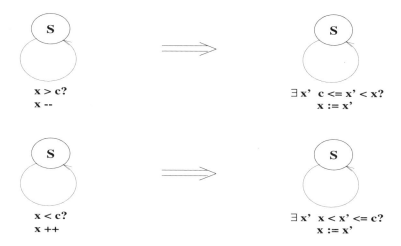

FIGURE 6.10. Elimination of increment/decrement from self-loops.

x are incremented by the same amount. The incrementing applies between $c_2 \geq y \geq b$. However, the double increment loop may be interleaved with one or more single decrement rules that can decrease x to c_1. The net effect will be that the condition $x' \geq c_1$, $c_2 \geq y' \geq b$, $y' - x' \geq (b - a)$ must be true after any sequence of the two self-loop transitions.

Now let's see how these reduction rules can be applied to the constraint automaton in Figure 6.8. Applying the first rule brings $x + +$ after the self-loop over state *Stopped*. Then it is trivial to note that "increment x, test whether it is -19 and if yes decrement x" is the same as "test whether $x = -20$." Hence we can further simplify the constraint automaton as shown in the top of Figure 6.12.

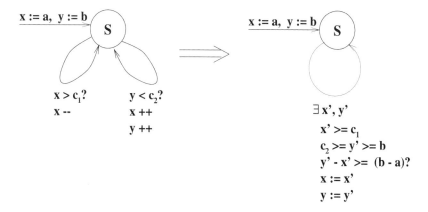

FIGURE 6.11. Elimination of increment/decrement from pairs of self-loops.

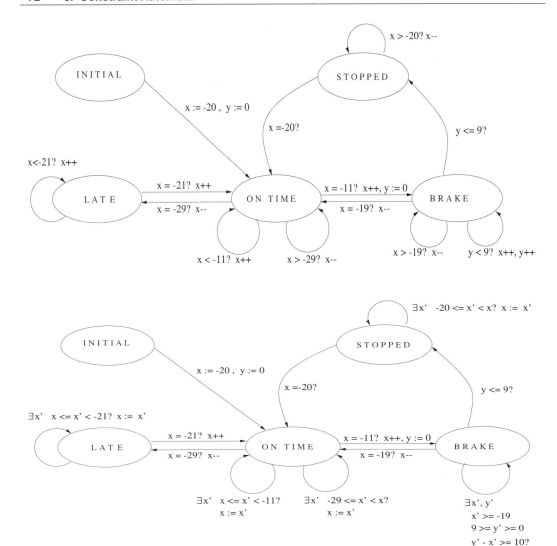

FIGURE 6.12. The subway system after rules 1 (top) and 1 to 3 (bottom).

After applying the second rule with the self-loops over the states *Late, On-time,* and *Stopped* and the third rule over the state *Brake* we obtain the constraint automaton shown in the bottom of Figure 6.12.

6.3 Analysis of Reachable Configurations

Each combination of a state name with values for the state variables is a *configuration*. It is often important to know the set of configurations to which a constraint automaton may move. This set is called the set of *reachable* configurations.

The set of reachable configurations can be found by translating the constraint automaton into a Datalog query. The Datalog query will use a separate relation to represent each state. Each relation will have the set of state variables as its attributes. Each transition of the constraint automaton will be translated to a Datalog rule. We give a few examples of translations.

Analysis of Example 6.1.1   We can translate the constraint automaton of Example 6.1.1 into Datalog as follows. Note that the assignment statements are expressed in Datalog by introducing new variables (d', e', y') and using these within the arguments of the defined relation:

$$
\begin{aligned}
T(d', e', y) &:\!- \quad T(d, e, y), \quad d \geq 100, \quad d' = d - 100, \quad e' = e + 198. \\
T(d', e, y') &:\!- \quad T(d, e, y), \quad d \geq 100, \quad d' = d - 100, \quad y' = y + 29700. \\
T(d', e', y) &:\!- \quad T(d, e, y), \quad e \geq 200, \quad d' = d + 99, \quad e' = e - 200. \\
T(d, e', y') &:\!- \quad T(d, e, y), \quad e \geq 200, \quad e' = e - 200, \quad y' = y + 29700. \\
T(d', e, y') &:\!- \quad T(d, e, y), \quad y \geq 30000, \quad d' = d + 99, \quad y' = y - 30000. \\
T(d, e', y') &:\!- \quad T(d, e, y), \quad y \geq 30000, \quad e' = e + 198, \quad y' = y - 30000.
\end{aligned}
$$

Analysis of Example 6.1.2   Let us assume that in Example 6.1.2 the number of people waiting in the parking garage grows by at least one between each reading until the elevator goes down to the parking garage. Similarly, the number of people waiting in the restaurant grows by at least two between each reading.

We also assume that the elevator is initially empty and at the lobby. Initially, the elevator will go down if there are more people waiting at the parking garage than at the restaurant. Otherwise it will go up. We can express the set of possible configurations of the constraint automaton using Datalog as follows:

$$
\begin{aligned}
R(x', y', z, p, r, lp', lr, d) \quad &:\!- \quad L(x, y, z, p, r, lp, lr, d), d = 0, \\
&\qquad\quad y' - y \geq 1.
\end{aligned}
$$

$$
\begin{aligned}
L(x, y, z, p', r, lp, lr, 0) \quad &:\!- \quad R(x, y, z, p, r, lp, lr, d), p' = 0, \\
&\qquad\quad lp = 0, x > y. \\
L(x, y, z, p', r, lp, lr, 1) \quad &:\!- \quad R(x, y, z, p, r, lp, lr, d), p' = 1. \\
L(x, y, z, p', r, lp, lr, 1) \quad &:\!- \quad R(x, y, z, p, r, lp, lr, d), lp = 1. \\
L(x, y, z, p', r, lp, lr, 1) \quad &:\!- \quad R(x, y, z, p, r, lp, lr, d), x \leq y.
\end{aligned}
$$

$$
\begin{aligned}
L(x, y, z, 0, 0, lp, lr, 1) \quad &:\!- \quad 0 \leq lp \leq 1, 0 \leq lr \leq 1, y > z. \\
L(x, y, z, 0, 0, lp, lr, 0) \quad &:\!- \quad 0 \leq lp \leq 1, 0 \leq lr \leq 1, y \leq z.
\end{aligned}
$$

$$L(x, y, z, p, r', lp, lr, 1) \quad :\!\!- \quad P(x, y, z, p, r, lp, lr, d), r' = 0,$$
$$lr = 0, x > z.$$
$$L(x, y, z, p, r', lp, lr, 0) \quad :\!\!- \quad P(x, y, z, p, r, lp, lr, d), r' = 1.$$
$$L(x, y, z, p, r', lp, lr, 0) \quad :\!\!- \quad P(x, y, z, p, r, lp, lr, d), lr = 1.$$
$$L(x, y, z, p, r', lp, lr, 0) \quad :\!\!- \quad P(x, y, z, p, r, lp, lr, d), x \le z.$$

$$P(x', y, z', p, r, lp, lr', d) \quad :\!\!- \quad L(x, y, z, p, r, lp, lr, d), d = 1,$$
$$z' - z \ge 2.$$

In this Datalog program the two middle rules express the initial state when the automaton starts from the lobby. Because the elevator is empty, there is no one to push the buttons inside. Hence p and r must be 0 initially.

Analysis of Example 6.1.3 Let us assume that the number of newly boarding passengers to the island is always between 0 and 5 inclusive. Then we can express the set of possible configurations of the constraint automaton of Example 6.1.3 using Datalog as follows:

$$A(0, x_0, x_1, x).$$
$$A(1, x', x_1, x') \quad :\!\!- \quad B(0, x_0, x_1, x), 0 \le x' \le 5.$$
$$A(2, x_0, x', x') \quad :\!\!- \quad B(1, x_0, x_1, x), 0 \le x' \le 5.$$
$$A(2, 0, 0, x') \quad :\!\!- \quad B(2, 0, 0, 0), 0 \le x' \le 5.$$
$$A(0, x_0, x_1, x) \quad :\!\!- \quad C(n, x_0, x_1, x), n > 0.$$

$$B(1, x', x_1, x') \quad :\!\!- \quad A(0, x_0, x_1, x), 0 \le x' \le 5.$$
$$B(2, x_0, x', x') \quad :\!\!- \quad A(1, x_0, x_1, x), 0 \le x' \le 5.$$
$$B(2, 0, 0, x') \quad :\!\!- \quad A(2, 0, 0, 0), 0 \le x' \le 5.$$
$$B(0, x_0, x_1, x) \quad :\!\!- \quad C(0, x_0, x_1, x).$$

$$C(0, 0, 0, x') \quad :\!\!- \quad A(2, x_0, x_1, x), 0 \le x' \le 5, \ x_0 + x_1 + x' > 0.$$
$$C(0, 0, 0, x') \quad :\!\!- \quad A(n, x_0, x_1, x), 0 \le x' \le 5, \ n > 0,$$
$$x_0 + x_1 + x' \ge 10.$$
$$C(2, 0, 0, x') \quad :\!\!- \quad B(2, x_0, x_1, x), 0 \le x' \le 5, \ x_0 + x_1 + x' > 0.$$
$$C(n, 0, 0, x') \quad :\!\!- \quad B(n, x_0, x_1, x), 0 \le x' \le 5, \ n > 0,$$
$$x_0 + x_1 + x' \ge 10.$$

Analysis of Example 6.1.4 We saw in Section 6.2 that the constraint automaton of Example 6.1.4 can be simplified to the one shown in Figure 6.12. The set of reachable configurations of the constraint automaton shown in Figure 6.12 can be expressed in Datalog as follows:

Initial $(-20, 0)$.

$$Ontime\,(x, y) \quad :— \quad Initial\,(x, y).$$
$$Ontime\,(-20, y) \quad :— \quad Late\,(-21, y).$$
$$Ontime\,(-20, y) \quad :— \quad Brake\,(-20, y).$$
$$Ontime\,(-20, y) \quad :— \quad Stopped\,(-20, y).$$
$$Ontime\,(x', y) \quad :— \quad Ontime\,(x, y),\ x \leq x' < -11.$$
$$Ontime\,(x', y) \quad :— \quad Ontime\,(x, y),\ -29 \leq x' < x.$$

$$Stopped\,(x', y) \quad :— \quad Stopped\,(x, y),\ -20 \leq x' < x.$$
$$Stopped\,(x, y) \quad :— \quad Brake\,(x, y),\ y \leq 9.$$

$$Brake\,(-10, 0) \quad :— \quad Ontime\,(-11, y).$$
$$Brake\,(x', y') \quad :— \quad Brake\,(x, y),\ x' \geq -19,\ 9 \geq y' \geq 0,$$
$$y' - x' \geq 10.$$

$$Late\,(-30, y) \quad :— \quad Ontime\,(-29, y).$$
$$Late\,(x', y) \quad :— \quad Late\,(x, y),\ x \leq x' \leq -21.$$

Analysis of Example 6.1.5   The set of reachable configurations of the constraint automaton shown in Figure 6.5 can be expressed in Datalog as follows. The first rule represents the inflationary years; the second rule represents the deflationary years:

$$Purchase\,(i', x',\quad y', z', a', b', c', d', k', l', m') :—$$
$$Purchase\,(i, x, y, z, a, b, c, d, k, l, m),$$
$$ax' + by' + cz' \leq d,\ x' \geq k,\ y' \geq l,\ z' \geq m,$$
$$a' = 1.05a,\ b' = 1.1b,\ c' = 1.05c,\ d' = 1.02d,$$
$$k' = k + 5,\ l' = l + 7,\ m' = m + 3,\ i' = i + 1.$$

$$Purchase\,(i', x',\quad y', z', a', b', c', d', k', l', m') :—$$
$$Purchase\,(i, x, y, z, a, b, c, d, k, l, m),$$
$$ax' + by' + cz' \leq d,\ x' \geq k,\ y' \geq l,\ z' \geq m,\ i > 0$$
$$a' = \tfrac{1}{1.05}a,\ b' = \tfrac{1}{1.1}b,\ c' = \tfrac{1}{1.05}c,\ d' = \tfrac{1}{1.02}d,$$
$$k' = k - 5,\ l' = l - 7,\ m' = m - 3,\ i' = i - 1.$$

Analysis of Example 6.1.6   Assume that in Example 6.1.6 each main dish costs between five and nine dollars, and each salad and drink costs between two and four dollars. The set of reachable configurations of the constraint automaton shown in Figure 6.6 can be expressed in Datalog as follows:

$$Drink\_Queue\,(x, y', z) \quad :— \quad Main\_Queue\,(x, y, z),\ 5 \leq y' \leq 9,$$
$$y = 0,\ x + y' + z \leq 10.$$
$$Drink\_Queue\,(x, y, z) \quad :— \quad Pay\_Queue\,(x, y, z),\ x + y + z < 8.$$
$$Main\_Queue\,(x', y, z) \quad :— \quad Salad\_Queue\,(x, y, z),\ 2 \leq x' \leq 4,$$
$$x' \geq x,\ x' + y + z \leq 10.$$

$$Pay\_Queue\,(x, y, z') \quad :- \quad Drink\_Queue\,(x, y, z),\ 2 \le z' \le 4,$$
$$z' \ge z,\ x + y + z' \le 10.$$
$$Pay\_Queue\,(x, y, z) \quad :- \quad Drink\_Queue\,(x, y, z),\ x > 3.$$

$$Pay\_Queue\,(x, y, z) \quad :- \quad Main\_Queue\,(x, y, z),\ y > 0.$$

$$Salad\_Queue\,(x, y, z) \quad :- \quad Pay\_Queue\,(x, y, z),\ x + y + z < 8.$$
$$Salad\_Queue\,(0, 0, 0).$$

Analysis of Example 6.1.7   Let the initial proportion of cloud, rain, stream, and ocean be 20, 20, 30, and 30 %. Then all possible end-of-year proportions of the four forms of water can be expressed by the following Datalog query:

$$Water\,(0.2, 0.2, 0.3, 0.3).$$

$$Water\,(c', r', s', o') \quad :- \quad Water\,(c, r, s, o),$$
$$c' = \tfrac{1}{2}c + \tfrac{1}{3}r + \tfrac{1}{6}s + \tfrac{1}{60}o,$$
$$r' = \tfrac{1}{2}c,$$
$$s' = \tfrac{1}{3}r + \tfrac{2}{3}s,$$
$$o' = \tfrac{1}{3}r + \tfrac{1}{6}s + \tfrac{59}{60}o.$$

As these examples illustrate, Datalog with constraints can be used to define the set of reachable configurations of constraint automata. In some cases this is helpful because the Datalog with constraints program can be evaluated. In some cases the evaluation may not terminate. Chapter 8 discusses when and Chapter 9 how Datalog with constraints can be evaluated. An advanced example of constraint automata can be found in Chapter 22.

Bibliographic Notes

Many cases of constraint automata have been studied by various authors. Constraint automata with increment and decrement by one operators and comparison operators as guard constraints have been called *counter machines* and were studied by Minsky [213, 214], who showed that they have the same expressive power as Turing machines. Floyd and Beigel [97] is an introduction to automata theory that covers counter machines.

More complex guard constraints have been allowed in later extensions of counter machines and applied to the design of control systems in Boigelot and Wolper [39], Fribourg and Olson [105], Fribourg and Richardson [106], Halbwachs [137], and Kerbrat [170]. Boigelot et al. [38], Cobham [67], and Wolper and Boigelot [330] study automata and Presburger definability. Alur and Dill [13] consider timed automata, which is subsumed by constraint automata.

The problem description of the subway train control system in Example 6.1.4 is from [137]. The reduction rules and simplifications applied to this constraint automaton, Example 6.1.6, and Exercise 7 are from Revesz [270].

Fribourg and Richardson [106] presented another simplification method that gives an approximation of the reachable configurations for Example 6.1.4. Another approximation method in analyzing automata with linear constraints is presented in Kerbrat [170].

Translations of constraint automata into constraint logic programming or constraint Datalog queries are presented by Fribourg and Richardson [106], Delzanno and Podelski [78], and Revesz [263, 270].

Constraint automata with comparison guard constraints and the update of state variables by addition of constants to them are called *Petri nets* or *vector addition systems*. Example 6.1.1 is an example of a Petri net. The reachable configuration problem has been studied extensively in Petri nets and vector addition systems. More details about these are given in the bibliographic notes of Chapter 11.

The problem of verifying the correctness of counter machines and related systems without a full constraint evaluation of the set of possible states is called *symbolic model checking*. McMillan [209] and Clarke et al. [66] are books on symbolic model checking, and Alur et al. [12] is a survey. Other works on model checking include Alur et al. [11, 14], Cimatti et al. [65], Comuzzi and Hart [71], Graf and Saidi [115], and Lowry and Subramaniam [203]. A model checking system called HyTech is presented in Henzinger et al. [143].

Exercises

1. Can you find any potential problems with the hotel elevator system? If yes, can you correct it?

2. Suppose that in Example 6.1.3 the ferry can carry both cars and people. Suppose each car takes up as much space as three people. Modify the constraint automaton in Figure 6.3 to reflect this change.

3. Suppose that in Example 6.1.6 instead of replacing the salad or drink with one of a higher value, one can choose a second salad or drink of the same type, provided the total cost is at most ten dollars. Modify the constraint automaton in Figure 6.6 to reflect this change.

4. A thermostat operates the following way. It can sense m, the measured temperature in the room; r, the requested temperature; and s, a switch that can be set to heat, off, or cool (assume that these are indicated by the values one, zero, and minus one, respectively). If r is more than three degrees above m and s is on "heat," then the system starts heating and will continue to heat until m is greater than or equal to r. If r is more than 2 degrees below m and s is on "cool," then the system starts cooling and will continue to cool until m is less than or equal to r. When the system is neither heating nor cooling, it will rest in a wait state.

   (a) Draw a constraint automaton for the thermostat.

   (b) Assume that while the thermostat is heating, the temperature rises at least two degrees between each pair of readings. While the thermostat is cooling, the temperature decreases at least one degree between each pair of readings. Also assume that initially the thermostat is in the wait state, s is zero, and r and m could be anything. Using Datalog, express the set of reachable configurations of the constraint automaton you drew.

5. Draw a constraint automaton for the subset-sum problem discussed in Example 4.1.10.

6. Find a variation of the reduction rule shown in Figure 6.11, for example, when x is incremented in the single-variable self-loop and x and y are both decremented in the double-variable self-loop.

7. A person with $500 cash, a checking account with balance $3000, and a credit card with balance minus $100 can make the following transactions: pay cash, write a check, or make charges on the credit card to buy something, deposit cash into the checking account, write a check to pay the credit card, withdraw money from the checking account using an ATM machine, or get a cash advance from the credit card. On all these transactions the checking account balance must remain positive and the credit card balance must stay above the credit limit of minus $1000. Each month this person gets $1000 in cash, pays from the checking account mortgage of $600, and charges on the credit card at least $500.

   (a) Draw a constraint automaton that describes the possible values for the cash x, the checking account balance y, and the credit card balance z of this person, for each month m.

   (b) Simplify the constraint automaton as much as possible.

   (c) Express the set of reachable configurations using Datalog.

8. There are people who are employed (by others), unemployed, and self-employed. Each year one-eighth of the employed become unemployed and the same number become self-employed. Also, one-third of the unemployed are hired as new employees and the same number become self-employed by opening a business. One-fourth of the self-employed are hired, and become employed and one-eighth become unemployed. Draw a constraint automaton that counts the number of employed, unemployed, and self-employed persons.

9. Persons in a country are rich, middle class, or poor. Each year one in thirty middle-class and one in fifty poor persons become rich. Also one in ten rich and one in twenty poor become middle class. Further, one percent of the rich and one in sixty middle-class persons become poor. Draw a constraint automaton that counts the number of rich, middle-class, and poor persons.

7

Refinement Queries

In many applications, our information about the world is incomplete. For example, we may know about a group of persons some information about their ages, such as that one person's age is greater or less than forty or one person is older than another, without knowing their precise ages. Section 7.1 describes the *universal object relation*, or UOR, model for representing incomplete information.

The UOR requires different assumptions about the database than the assumptions made in earlier chapters. Section 7.2 describes the closed, open, and possible world assumptions. The UOR satisfies the possible world assumption.

Refinement queries add (conjoin) new constraints to the UOR. Each constraint added eliminates some of the possibilities or ambiguities from the UOR. For example, as we add more constraints about the ages of the group of persons, we may get more precise knowledge about their ages. In the limit, this will approach the state where there is only one solution of the UOR, and then we obtain the exact age of each person. Sections 7.3, 7.4, and 7.6 describe the syntax, the semantics, and the evaluation of refinement queries. Section 7.5 describes projection queries from the UOR.

7.1 The Universal Object Relation Data Model

Our incomplete information can be described using constraint objects and a special relation called a *universal object relation*, or UOR. Each constraint *object* is composed of a unique object identifier (oid) and a set of attributes. For example, each person in a set of persons with different names can be represented by an object, with oid equal to the name of the person and an age attribute variable. The UOR contains all known constraints about all objects and their attribute variables.

For example, suppose we represent the persons Alice, Brian, and Tom as constraint objects with oids equal to their names and the constraint attribute y representing their ages. If we know that Alice is three years older than Brian, the total age of the three persons is less than 60, and Tom is the youngest, then this information can be represented by the following UOR:

UOR

Alice_Age	Brian_Age	Tom_Age	
Alice.y	Brian.y	Tom.y	$Alice.y = Brian.y + 3$ $Alice.y + Brian.y + Tom.y \leq 60$ $Tom.y \leq Alice.y$ $Tom.y \leq Brian.y$

The UOR is a constraint relation like the ones we saw earlier, except that instead of regular variables it contains attribute variables of constraint objects. All substitutions of nonnegative integer constants for the three attribute variables that satisfy the constraint are possible age combinations for the three persons.

7.2   Closed, Open, and Possible Worlds

There are three types of assumptions that are commonly made about the validity of the data stored in a database relation:

- **Closed world assumption:** This means that every tuple in the relation is true, and every tuple outside the relation is false. For example, the *Crops* relation satisfies the closed world assumption because every possible combination of planting is within the relation, and what is not a possible combination is left out.

- **Open world assumption:** This means that every tuple in the relation is true, and every tuple outside the relation is either true or false. For example, the *Go* relation satisfies the open world assumption. Every tuple within this relation is a possible travel between two cities, but there are travel possibilities that are not in the relation. Another example, comprises the following relations *Firesource* and *Flammable*:

Firesource
Object
Cigarette
Fireplace

Flammable
Object
Gasoline
Spray can
Wood

The open world assumption holds for these relations because the objects they contain are indeed normally fire sources and flammable, respectively. However, the closed world assumption fails because there are other fire sources, for example, a stove top or a match, which are not in the first relation, and other flammable objects, such as coal and gas, which are not in the second object.

- **Possible world assumption:** This means that every tuple in the relation is possibly true, and every tuple outside the relation is false. This is meaningful, for example, for the UOR relation of Section 7.1. For example, the UOR in Section 7.1 contains many solutions including $Alice.y = 23$, $Brian.y = 20$, $Tom.y = 15$ and $Alice.y = 28$, $Brian.y = 25$, $Tom.y = 5$. That means that both of these are possible at this time. None of the possible solutions can be excluded until more information is learned that contradicts them.

It is important to know exactly what assumptions we can make about the input database relations.

For example, it would not make sense to try to write a query to find the maximum profit the farmer could earn without the closed world assumption in the *Crops* relation. If the closed world assumption does not hold, then any query may fail when the planting combination that yields the maximum profit is not in the *Crops* relation. The closed world assumption in this case is warranted and helpful.

On the other hand, it would be unwarranted to assume the closed world assumption in the case of the *Firesource* and *Flammable* relations. One may write a query that says "x won't burn y if x is not a fire source or y is not flammable." Under the closed world assumption, everything not listed in *Firesource* is not a fire source, and everything not listed in *Flammable* is not flammable. Hence this query would derive wrong conclusions, for example, that a stove top will not burn a spray can.

Most useful queries preserve the condition of the database. Sometimes a query fails to do that. Suppose we list enough objects in the *Firesource* and *Flammable* relations and they satisfy the closed world assumption. Then the query "x won't burn y if x is not a fire source" will not derive the true tuple that a cigarette will not burn a steel knife. Hence the output relation *Won't_Burn* will not satisfy the closed world assumption.

In every query, the assumptions that we can make about the output relations depend on the assumptions that hold about the input relations. Also some queries are meaningful to apply only under some assumptions and not under others. Therefore, it is important to know what assumptions we can make about the input database relations.

7.3 Syntax

Each refinement query consists of a finite set of rules of the form

$$\phi(y_1, \ldots, y_k) :\!\!- R_1(x_{1,1}, \ldots, x_{1,k_1}), \ldots, R_n(x_{n,1}, \ldots, x_{n,k_n}).$$

where ϕ is a constraint formula of attribute variables, each R_i is an input relation, and the xs are either oids or variables ranging over oids and the ys are attribute variables. The formula may contain conjunction, disjunction, implication ($\rightarrow$), and atomic constraints that may be any type we saw in Chapter 4. The R_is contain only a finite number of tuples of oids. They do not contain constraints. We call ϕ the *rule head* and the R_is together the *rule body*.

We refer to the value of attribute A of an object with oid O by the syntax $O.A$. We give a few examples.

Example 7.3.1   Suppose that Alfred, Alice, Bernard, Bernice, Carl, Donald, Denise, Edward, Elise, Fred, Felice, Gerald, and Harold are persons in an extended family. We know that Alfred is not yet 70, and Harold is already in school (i.e., 5 years or older). Gerald was born just last month. Elise is more than 4 years older than Fred, and Bernard is more than 25 years older than Edward.

This incomplete information can be represented by one object for each person with the oid equal to the name of the person and an attribute variable y representing the person's age. The UOR in this case would be the following (where comma means logical and):

$$Alfred.y < 70,$$
$$Gerald.y = 0,$$
$$Harold.y \geq 5,$$
$$Bernard.y - Edward.y > 25,$$
$$Elise.y - Fred.y > 4$$

Finally, suppose we learn that no siblings are twins or were born in the same year and that between parents and their children there is at least 18 years difference. We also know that each person's age is nonnegative. This information can be expressed by the following refinement rules:

$$x.y < z.y \qquad :\!\!- \quad Sibling\,(x, z).$$

$$z.y - x.y \geq 18 \quad :\!\!- \quad Parent\,(x, z).$$

$$x.y \geq 0 \qquad :\!\!- \quad Person\,(x).$$

where we assume that relations *Parent* (x, y), *Person* (w), and *Sibling* (z, u) contain object oids such that x is a child of y, z is a younger sibling of u, and w is a person.

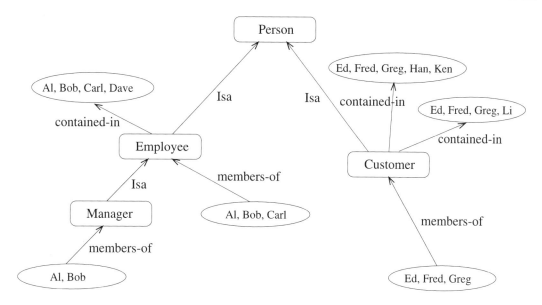

FIGURE 7.1. The inheritance hierarchy.

Example 7.3.2   Suppose that Customer, Employee, Manager, and Person are classes in a class hierarchy shown in Figure 7.1. We know about each class that it is a subset or superset of other classes. We also know the elements of some lower and upper bounds of these classes. The lower bound tells which persons must be in the class, while the upper bound tells which persons may be in the class. Any set in between the two is a possible solution. For example, the given constraint for the Employee class allows two possible solutions, one is {*Al*, *Bob*, *Carl*} the other is {*Al*, *Bob*, *Carl*, *Dave*}.

We can represent all this information by creating four objects with oids Person, Employee, Manager, and Customer. Each of these objects has one attribute variable *S* representing the set of members of the class with the same name as the oid. The UOR will be the conjunction of the following:

$$\{Al, Bob, Carl\} \subseteq Employee.S$$
$$Employee.S \subseteq \{Al, Bob, Carl, Dave\}$$
$$\{Al, Bob\} \subseteq Manager.S$$
$$\{Ed, Fred, Greg\} \subseteq Customer.S$$
$$Customer.S \subseteq \{Ed, Fred, Greg, Li\}$$
$$Customer.S \subseteq \{Ed, Fred, Greg, Han, Ken\}$$

It is intuitive that the upper bound of a superclass is also an upper bound of its subclasses, and the lower bound of a subclass is also a lower bound of its superclass. This can be expressed using the following refinement rule:

$$x.S \subseteq y.S \quad :\!\!- \quad Isa\,(x, y).$$

where relation $Isa\,(x, y)$ records which object x is a subclass of which other object y.

Example 7.3.3 A classical syllogism is a valid deductive rule involving the binary relations *All*, *No*, *Some*, and *Somenot* whose arguments are oids of objects that represent sets. We assume that each object has an attribute S ranging over sets of strings representing possible members of these sets. Then the following refinement rules define the implications of the four relations:

$$x.S \subseteq y.S \qquad :\!\!- \quad All\,(x, y).$$

$$x.S \cap y.S = \emptyset \quad :\!\!- \quad No(x, y).$$

$$x.S \cap y.S \neq \emptyset \quad :\!\!- \quad Some\,(x, y).$$

$$x.S \not\subseteq y.S \qquad :\!\!- \quad Somenot\,(x, y).$$

Sometimes our initial UOR is empty and the information needs to be represented by rules whose rule bodies may also be empty. This means that the left-hand side of these rules should be added to the UOR. The following is an example.

Example 7.3.4 In many numerical cryptographic problems, we have to find out which digit value each letter represents in a summation or multiplication. For example, in the *send + more = money* problem we need to find for each letter a different digit value from 0 to 9 such that the resulting numbers satisfy the summation. Here we show the summation, including the carry-in and carry-out variables:

```
c1 c2 c3 c4 c5
    s  e  n  d
 +  m  o  r  e
--------------
 m  o  n  e  y
    c1 c2 c3 c4
```

Let each letter digit be represented by a constraint object with an oid, which we take to be equal to the letter itself, and an attribute n denoting its digit value. Similarly, let each carry-in and carry-out be represented by a constraint object with an oid, equal to character string ci, and an attribute n denoting its digit value. Let relations *Letter* and *Carry* contain the oids of these two objects. The following refinement rules express that each letter has a different digit value:

$$1 \leq x.n \leq 9 \quad :\!\!- \quad Letter\,(x).$$

$$x.n \neq y.n \qquad :\!\!- \quad Letter\,(x), Letter\,(y), x \neq y.$$

Implicit in this problem is that no number starts with a 0 digit, hence m, which is the carry-out in the leftmost column, must be 1. We also have to note that in the rightmost column the carry-in c_5 must be 0. This can be expressed by the following refinement rules:

$$c1.n = m.n \quad :\!\!- \quad .$$

$$c5.n = 0 \quad :\!\!- \quad .$$

In this problem there are some constraints among the variables in each column of the summation. In particular, let relation *Column* (i, x, y, z, o) contain all quintets of carry-in i, input digits x and y, output digit z, and carry-out o. The following refinement query expresses the constraint that holds among these objects:

$$i.n + x.n + y.n = z.n + 10 \times o.n :\!\!- Column\,(i, x, y, z, o).$$

Example 7.3.5 A department needs to select a team of students to participate in a programming contest. The selection must satisfy a number of requirements on a team object with oid T and attribute variable S representing the members of the team. We state each requirement separately and express it by a refinement rule.

The students eligible to participate are Jenny, David, Pat, Mark, Tom, Lilly, and Bob. This is expressed as:

$$T.S \subseteq \{\text{``Jenny''}, \text{``David''}, \text{``Pat''}, \text{``Mark''}, \text{``Tom''}, \text{``Lilly''}, \text{``Bob''}\} :\!\!- .$$

If Bob is selected, then David must be selected:

$$\text{``Bob''} \in T.S \to \text{``David''} \in T.S :\!\!- .$$

If both David and Pat are selected, then Mark cannot be selected:

$$\{\text{``David''}, \text{``Pat''}\} \subseteq T.S \to \text{``Mark''} \notin T.S :\!\!- .$$

If both Jenny and Tom are selected, then Bob cannot be selected:

$$\{\text{``Jenny''}, \text{``Tom''}\} \subseteq T.S \to \text{``Bob''} \notin T.S :\!\!- .$$

If Pat is selected, then either Lilly or Tom must be selected:

$$\text{``Pat''} \in T.S \to (\text{``Lilly''} \in T.S \vee \text{``Tom''} \notin T.S) :\!\!- .$$

Either Jenny or Lilly must be selected, but Jenny and Lilly cannot be both selected:

$$(\text{``Jenny''} \in T.S, \text{``Lilly''} \notin T.S) \vee (\text{``Jenny''} \notin T.S, \text{``Lilly''} \in T.S) :\!\!- .$$

It makes sense to associate certain attributes with a set of objects instead of a single object. For example, the distance between a pair of cities is associated with a composition of the two cities. In general, if a and b are object oids, then $a \times b$ is an object oid for a composite object. The following is an example of the use of this feature.

Example 7.3.6   Suppose that each city is represented by an object with attribute variables x for the longitude and y for the latitude of its location. Pairs of cities are composite objects with attribute variable d for the distance between them. We also define input relations *city* (c), which is true if c is the oid of a city object, and *road* (a, b), which is true if a and b are oids of city objects connected by a direct road. We can assume that the road between two cities follows a straight line. Then the following refinement query finds the distance between pairs of cities:

$$(a \times b).d = \sqrt{(a.x - b.x)^2 + (a.y - b.y)^2} :\!\!-\, road\,(a, b).$$

$$(a \times b).d \leq (a \times c).d + (c \times b).d :\!\!-\, city\,(a), \; city\,(b), \; city\,(c).$$

The first rule states that the distance is equal to the Eucledian distance between two cities with a direct road connection. The second rule is useful for pairs of cities between which there is no direct road connection, but only connections that go through other cities. For all cities a, b, and c the distance between a and b is defined to be always smaller than or equal to the sum of the distances between a and c and between c and b.

7.4 Semantics

The semantics of refinement rules is that for any instantiation, if the body is true, then the head is added (i.e, conjoined with a logical **and**) to the UOR.

Evaluation of Example 7.3.1:   Suppose we learn that Alfred and Alice have children Bernard, Carl, and Donald in this order. Bernard and Bernice have child Edward. Donald and Denise have children Elise and Fred. Edward and Elise have child Gerald. Fred and Felice have child Harold (see Figure 7.2 where husband-wife pairs are connected by the symbol ∞).
In this case the *Sibling* relation is:

Sibling

Younger	Older
Carl	Bernard
Donald	Carl
Fred	Elise

The evaluation of the first rule adds to the UOR the following constraints:

$Carl.y < Bernard.y$

$Donald.y < Carl.y$

$Fred.y < Elise.y$

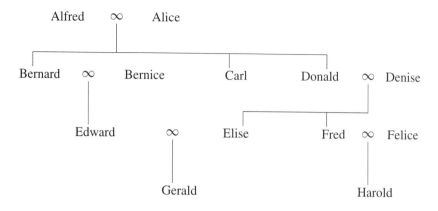

FIGURE 7.2. Alfred and Alice's family.

The *Parent* relation is:

Parent

Child	Parent
Bernard	Alfred
Bernard	Alice
Carl	Alfred
Carl	Alice
Donald	Alfred
Donald	Alice
Edward	Bernard
Edward	Bernice
Elise	Donald
Elise	Denise
Fred	Donald
Fred	Denise
Gerald	Edward
Gerald	Elise
Harold	Fred
Harold	Felice

The evaluation of the second refinement rule adds to the UOR the following constraints:

$$Alfred.y - Bernard.y \geq 18$$
$$Alice.y - Bernard.y \geq 18$$
$$Alfred.y - Carl.y \geq 18$$
$$Alice.y - Carl.y \geq 18$$
$$Alfred.y - Donald.y \geq 18$$
$$Alice.y - Donald.y \geq 18$$
$$Bernard.y - Edward.y \geq 18$$
$$Bernice.y - Edward.y \geq 18$$
$$Donald.y - Elise.y \geq 18$$
$$Denise.y - Elise.y \geq 18$$
$$Donald.y - Fred.y \geq 18$$
$$Denise.y - Fred.y \geq 18$$
$$Edward.y - Gerald.y \geq 18$$
$$Elise.y - Gerald.y \geq 18$$
$$Fred.y - Harold.y \geq 18$$
$$Felice.y - Harold.y \geq 18$$

Finally, the *Person* relation contains the oids of all the family members. The evaluation of the third rule will add to the UOR the following constraints:

$$Alfred.y \geq 0$$
$$Alice.y \geq 0$$
$$Bernard.y \geq 0$$
$$Bernice.y \geq 0$$
$$Carl.y \geq 0$$
$$Donald.y \geq 0$$
$$Denise.y \geq 0$$
$$Edward.y \geq 0$$
$$Elise.y \geq 0$$
$$Fred.y \geq 0$$
$$Felice.y \geq 0$$

The final UOR will be the conjunction of the original UOR and all of the preceding constraints. The UOR may be simplified by rewriting it into logically equivalent but simpler forms. For example, the constraint *Fred.y* $<$ *Elise.y* generated during the evaluation of the second rule can be dropped because of the presence of the stronger constraint $Elise.y - Fred.y > 4$ in the original UOR.

Evaluation of Example 7.3.2:   The information about which class is a subclass of another class can be represented by the following relation:

Isa

Subclass	Class
Employee	Person
Customer	Person
Manager	Employee

There is only one refinement rule in Example 7.3.2. The body of this rule can be satisfied by the instantiation of x by *Employee* and z by *Person*. Therefore, the constraint $Employee.S \subseteq Person.S$ will be added to the UOR. The instantiation *Customer* and *Person* for x and z also makes the body true. Hence $Customer.S \subseteq Person.S$ will also be added. Finally, the instantiation $Manager.S \subseteq Employee.S$ also makes the body true. Hence $Manager.S \subseteq Employee.S$ will also be added to the UOR. Because only these three instantiations make the body of the refinement rule true, the final UOR will be:

$$\{Al, Bob, Carl\} \subseteq Employee.S$$
$$Employee.S \subseteq \{Al, Bob, Carl, Dave\}$$
$$\{Al, Bob\} \subseteq Manager.S$$
$$\{Ed, Fred, Greg\} \subseteq Customer.S$$
$$Customer.S \subseteq \{Ed, Fred, Greg, Li\}$$
$$Customer.S \subseteq \{Ed, Fred, Greg, Han, Ken\}$$
$$Employee.S \subseteq Person.S$$
$$Customer.S \subseteq Person.S$$
$$Manager.S \subseteq Employee.S$$

Evaluation of Example 7.3.3:   Suppose we represent the class of people who are allowed to drive, drive sometimes, drink alcoholic beverages sometimes, have a license, and have passed a driver's license test by five objects with oids A, D, I, L, and P. Suppose also that we learn the following facts about these objects (see Figure 7.3):

1. All persons must pass a test before getting a driver's license.
2. All persons allowed to drive must have a license.
3. No one drives without having passed the test.

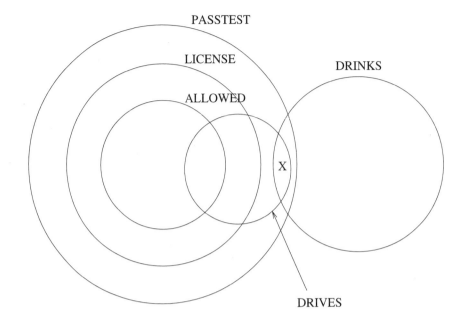

FIGURE 7.3. Drivers and drinkers.

4. No one who drinks has a license.

5. Some person X both drives and drinks.

We can represent these constraints as an input database that contains the tuples $All(L, P)$, $All(A, L)$, $All(D, P)$, $No(L, I)$, and $Some(D, I)$. After the evaluation of the refinement rules with this input database we obtain the following UOR:

$$L.S \subseteq P.S$$
$$A.S \subseteq L.S$$
$$D.S \subseteq P.S$$
$$I.S \cap L.S = \emptyset$$
$$D.S \cap I.S \neq \emptyset$$

Evaluation of Example 7.3.5: The UOR in this case will be the conjunction of the refinement rule heads. The UOR will define all possible teams that may be sent to the programming contest.

Evaluation of Example 7.3.6: Suppose we are given as objects the cities in the map shown in Figure 1.2 with the x and y coordinates of the cities defined such that the distance between cities with a direct connection is exactly the distance shown in the labels of the connecting edges. Then the evaluation of the first refinement rule will generate sixteen constraints to be added to the UOR, including the following:

$$(Omaha \times Lincoln).d = 60$$
$$(Lincoln \times KansasCity).d = 150$$

The evaluation of the second refinement rule will generate $6^3 = 216$ constraints to be added to the UOR, including:

$$(Omaha \times KansasCity).d \leq 210$$

where the variable a is substituted by *Omaha*, variable b by *KansasCity*, and c by *Lincoln*.

7.5 Projection Queries

Refinement queries yield a UOR that may contain a huge formula with one variable $O.A$ for each object O having an attribute A. Most users will not want to read the entire UOR and try to understand it. Instead, to obtain a meaningful result, a user may want to concentrate on a small subset of the variables and ask a refinement query system to display only the known or implied relationships among them and eliminate any other variables.

For this, a user may use *projection* queries of the following form:

SELECT $y_1, \ldots, y_k$
FROM UOR

where the ys are attribute variables. Next we give some examples.

Projection from the UOR in Example 7.3.1:   In this example a user may want to know only the age of Donald. Our best information based on the UOR can be found by the projection query:

SELECT *Donald.y*
FROM UOR

A refinement query system in this case would return the following formula as the answer:

$$47 \leq Donald.y, \quad Donald.y \leq 49$$

This would mean that according to our current knowledge Donald's age is somewhere between 47 and 49, inclusively.

Projection from the UOR in Example 7.3.3:   A user may wish to know in Example 7.3.3 the relationship between people who have passed a driver's license test and those who have been caught driving drunk. The information needed can be found by the projection query:

SELECT $C.S$, $P.S$
FROM UOR

A refinement query system in this case would return the answer:

$$C.S \cap P.S \neq \emptyset$$

which means that there is someone caught driving drunk who has passed the driver's license test.

Projection from the UOR in Example 7.3.6:   A user may wish to know in Example 7.3.6 the distance between Omaha and Chicago. The information can be found by the following:

SELECT $(Omaha \times Chicago).d$
FROM UOR

A refinement query system in this case would return the answer:

$$(Omaha \times Chicago).d \leq 990$$

which means that currently the shortest known distance between the two cities is 990 miles.

7.6   Evaluation of Refinement Queries

Refinement queries are evaluated similarly to Datalog rules, except that whenever the rule body is true, instead of adding a tuple in the head to the database, we add a constraint in the head to the UOR. The refinement query evaluation algorithm can be described as follows:

Algorithm Eval Refinement Query(Q,D,C)

input: Refinement query Q, input database D and UOR C
output: The refined UOR

for each refinement rule of Q **do**
　　for each instantiation that makes the body true **do**
　　　　add instantiated head to C
　　end-for
end-for

if C is satisfiable **then**
    return(C)
else
    return(``False'')

Bibliographic Notes

Incomplete information has a long history in relational databases starting with traditional work on null values (researchers often use the term indefinite information interchangeably). Van der Meyden [314] is a recent survey on this topic. The earliest paper on null values that is related to constraint databases is by Imielinski and Lipski [148, 149]. Imielinski and Lipski study *marked null* using equality and inequality constraints. The computational complexity of queries and updates in the framework of Imielinski and Lipski was later studied by Abiteboul et al. [2, 3] and Grahne [116].

Incomplete information was also studied early on by deductive database researchers [251, 252] and by researchers working on knowledge representation [202].

More recently, Koubarakis [178, 181, 180, 182] presented a framework of indefinite constraint databases that unifies the constraint data model of Chapter 2 and the work on marked nulls by Imielinski and Lipski [149]. This is the most expressive framework based on the relational model that is able to represent infinite and indefinite information using constraints. Another interesting recent paper on indefinite information with order constraints over the rational numbers is by van der Meyden [313, 314].

Closed, open, and possible world relational databases are considered by Reiter [253], by Imielinski and Lipski [148, 149], by Abiteboul et al. [1, 2, 3], and by Grahne [116].

The constraint object data model of Section 7.1 is from Srivastava, Ramakrishnan, and Revesz [293]. The definition of refinement queries presented in this chapter is an improvement of the one in [293]. Saraswat [280] uses a constraint store, which is similar to the UOR, and another refinement query language for concurrent logic programming. Constraint objects have also been studied by Brodsky and Kornatzky [42], who present different queries with constraint objects and by Warmer and Kleppe [323].

Examples 7.3.1, 7.3.2, and 7.3.5 are modified from Revesz [257, 258, 267]. The other examples are new. A refinement query system was implemented in Gundavarapu [129]. Di Deo and Boulanger [81] present an object-oriented approach to build constraint objects.

Exercises

1. Using a UOR represent the latitude and longitude locations of the towns of Chicago, Lincoln, and Omaha when we know only that Lincoln is 60 miles to the west of Omaha and Chicago is at least 200 miles north of both Lincoln and Omaha.

2. Each constraint object represents a person with an appointment with Mr. Brown. Each object has an oid and attributes b and e for the beginning and ending times of the person's appointment. Relation *Duration* (x, t) is true if x has an appointment that lasts at least t minutes. Relations *After* (x, t) or *Before* (x, t) are true if x's appointment takes place entirely after or before time t, respectively. Relations *Follow* (x, y) or *Precede* (x, y) are true if x's appointment is after or before y's appointment, respectively. We know that each person's appointment lasts at least one hour and that no two persons meet at the same time. Write a refinement query for the appointment schedule of Mr. Brown.

3. Each constraint object represents one of a set of cars parking next to each other in some unknown order on one side of a street with an oid and an attribute for its location. Relation *Next* (x, y) or *Next* (y, x) is true if x is parking next to y. Relation *Gap* (x, y, z) or *Gap* (y, x, z) is true if there are at least z number of cars parking between x and y. Write a refinement query for the parking locations of the cars.

4. Each constraint object represents a person with oid and attributes for height and weight. Relation *Taller* (x, y) is true if x is taller than y. Relation *Heavier* (x, y) is true if x is heavier than y. Write a refinement query for the height and weight of the persons.

5. Each constraint object represents a person sitting in a movie theater with an oid and attributes for the row and column locations. Relation *Behind* (x, y, z) is true if x is sitting behind y with z seats between them. Relation *Right* (x, y, z) is true if x is sitting to the right of y with z seats between them. Relation *Same_Row* (x, y) is true if x and y are sitting in the same row. Relation *Same_Column* (x, y) is true if x and y are sitting in the same column. Write a refinement query for the row and column locations of the persons.

6. Each constraint object represents a city on a map with an oid and attributes for the longitude and latitude of its location. Relation *East* (x, y, z) is true if x is to the east of y with z miles between them. Relation *South* (x, y, z) is true if x is to the south of y with z miles between them. Relation *Same_Latitude* (x, y) is true if x and y are located at the same latitude. Relation *Same_Longitude* (x, y) is true if x and y are located at the same longitude. Write a refinement query for the row and column locations of the cities. (**Hint:** Use Eucledian distance measure for measuring distance between cities on a map.)

7. We know about a set of events some information recorded in the relations:

   - *Before* (x, y), which is true if event x ended before event y
   - *Overlap* (x, y), which is true if events x and y overlap in time
   - *Not_Overlap* (x, y), which is true if events x and y do not overlap in time.

   Write a refinement query for the duration of the events. (**Hint:** Consider objects defining events with an oid and attributes for the beginning and ending instances.)

8. A computer science department consists of six professors: Andersen, Brown, Clark, Davis, Edmonds, and Fagin. The professors' offices are located in a row of rooms, which are numbered consequtively 101, 102, 103, 104, 105, and 106, with each professor having a different office. Each professor is teaching exactly one course this semester. The courses offered are artificial intelligence, databases, graphics, hardware, software, and theory. We know the following information:

   (a) Anderson's office is room 102 and Fagin's is room 105.
   (b) Brown has the office in room 103 and teaches databases.
   (c) Clark teaches software and his office is not room 101.
   (d) Davis teaches theory and his only neighbor teaches graphics.
   (e) The professor who teaches hardware has the office in room 104.

   Write a refinement query for the office room numbers and the subjects taught by each professor.

9. Write refinement rules that reflect the following information about a certain group of musicians:

   (a) Lilla plays the piano.
   (b) Bob and Peter play the flute.
   (c) Only Bob, Jenny, Peter, and Tom could possibly play the trumpet.
   (d) All organ players are also piano players.
   (e) All trumpet players are also flute players.
   (f) All piano players are also drummers.
   (g) All violin players are also guitar and piano players.
   (h) Some person can play both the flute and the guitar.
   (i) Some person can play both the drum and the piano.
   (j) Some person can play the trumpet and either the violin or the organ.

10. Suppose that the objects in a problem are the departments at a university, and that each object has a single attribute *offers* that describes the courses that it offers. Assume that the database also contains the unary relations *Object* and *Course*. Express the following using refinement rules:

(a) The computer science department offers some course other than the courses 410, 413, 428, and 479.

(b) Not all database and information retrieval courses, i.e., courses 410, 412, and 413, are offered by the computer science department.

(c) The business management department teaches 412.

(d) Each course is offered by only one department. (**Hint:** Assume that the $\neq$ between oids is an input relation.)

11. A number of pigeons are sitting on a telephone line between two poles. The pigeons are numbered according to the order of their location from left to right. We know that the third pigeon is located more than 29 inches from the pole on the left. The fifth pigeon is located between 47 and 54 inches and the seventh pigeon is located more than 72 inches from the same pole. We also know that between any two pigeons there is exactly 10 inches:

(a) Write a refinement query for the location of the pigeons.

(b) Write a projection query to find the location of the fourth pigeon.

(c) Evaluate the projection query.

12. After the refinement rules are applied, find the set of possible ages for each member of the family in Figure 7.2.

13. After the refinement rules are applied, find the set of possible members for each class of the inheritance hierarchy in Figure 7.1.

14. Solve the *send* + *more* = *money* cryptographic problem.

15. Solve the *fall* + *wind* = *cools* cryptographic problem.

16. Solve the *gale* + *neal* = *elsa* cryptographic problem.

17. Express and then evaluate the following projection query for Example 7.3.2: Find the set of managers.

18. Complete the evaluation of the possible team members for Example 7.3.5.

19. Write Datalog queries for the following examples and compare them with the refinement queries presented in this chapter:

(a) Example 7.3.1.

(b) Example 7.3.2.

(c) Example 7.3.3.

(d) Example 7.3.5.

(**Hint:** For your queries you may define additional input relations that help order the children, classes, and conditions to be satisfied.)

Safe Query Languages

Any programmer knows that programs may fall into infinite loops and never terminate. Datalog with constraint programs may have the same problem. When providing library programs for naive users, we need to guarantee that our programs terminate and give a meaningful answer each time they are called and for any possible valid database input. This guarantee is what we call *safety*.

In Section 8.1 we describe different degrees of safety. Sometimes the guarantee is conditioned on the type of database input. It is important that users be warned of what is guaranteed by the program, what is not, and on what condition. The simpler these are to explain the better. A user may still continue to use an unsafe program after receiving a warning from the system but without false expectations. That is the purpose of this chapter.

In this chapter we restrict the syntax of the query language. This is a simple approach to use and explain to a user. Therefore, it is the preferred approach whenever it is possible to use.

8.1 Safety Levels

We say that a program is *safe* if its semantics can be at least partially checked or computed on any valid database input. Obviously only safe programs are useful for applications. We distinguish five levels of safe programs, as shown in Figure 8.1.

1. **Closed-Form.** When the semantics of a program can be computed such that the output database contains the same type of constraints as the input database, then the program is said to be *closed-form safe*. Queries that

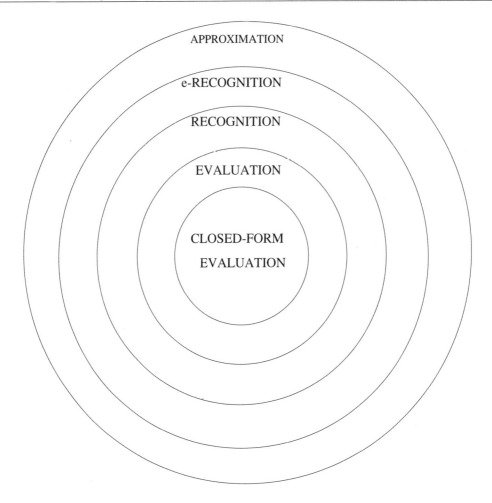

FIGURE 8.1. The safety hierarchy.

take databases without contraints to databases without constraints are also closed-form safe.

2. **Evaluation.** When the semantics of a program can be computed but the output could contain more complex constraints than the input, then the program is *evaluation safe*. For example, suppose an input relation *Line* (x, y) contains only the line $y = 2x$. Then the output of the following program:

$$Slope (x, y) \quad :— \quad Slope (x, z), \; Line (z, y).$$
$$Slope (x, y) \quad :— \quad Line (x, y).$$

is the relation *Slope* (x, y) that contains all the lines $y = 2^k x$ for each integer $k > 0$. Although this program is evaluation safe, the output, which contains an exponentiation constraint, is more complex than the input, which contains only a multiplication constraint.

3. **Recognition.** When any tuple of constants can be tested to be in the semantics of a program, then the program is *recognition safe*.

4. ϵ-**Recognition.** When for any tuple of rational numbers $(a_1, \ldots, a_k)$ and small positive rational number ϵ, it can be tested whether there is a tuple $(b_1, \ldots, b_k)$ in the semantics of the program such that $| a_i - b_i | < \epsilon$; then the program is ϵ-*recognition safe*.

5. **Approximation.** When the semantics of a program can be approximated by a lower and an upper bound, many individual tuples can be said to be definitely in or not in the semantics of the program, but for some tuples we will not be able to get a definite answer.

It is obvious that these are increasingly broader classes of safe programs. For example, any closed-form safe program is also evaluation safe.

Nevertheless, there are many programs that do not meet any of the five safety conditions. We call these programs *unsafe*. Imagine you are given a library of unsafe programs. If you tried to execute a program from that library on your database, then the execution may never return any answer.

On the other hand, if your library contained only safe programs, then at least you could always get an answer to the question whether a particular tuple or some other tuple very close to it is in the semantics of the query.

If your library contained only closed-form safe programs, then you would be assured to get a database as output that uses the same type of constraints as your input database. Therefore, after creating the output database you could execute another query from the library and you would be still guaranteed an output database in the same form. In fact, you could execute any composition of programs on the input database and get an output database as described in Section 3.1.2.

Obviously, it is important to provide for constraint database users only libraries of safe programs. But how can a programmer guarantee that a program is safe before adding it to the library? That is a difficult task in general, not only for Datalog programs but in any programming language. However, it is known that Datalog programs are always safe when executed on certain types of constraint databases.

8.2 Restriction

By restricting the allowed type of constraints we may obtain a query language in which every program is terminating on every input database. The advantage is that it is easy to check whether all the constraints used are of the allowed type. The disadvantage is that the expressiveness of the language is limited, hence it would be difficult to express many useful queries.

Domain	Constraint	Datalog	Max Min (Q)	Area Vol (Q)	Negation
Q, Z	equality, inequality	any	any		any
Q	order	any	any	any	any
Q, Z	lower bound, upper bound gap-order, positive linear	any	any	any	any^e unary
Q, Z	lower bound, upper bound gap-order, negative linear	any	any	any	any^e unary
Q, Z	lower bound, upper bound half-addition	any	any	any	any^e unary
Q, Z	difference	any^a	any	any	any
Q, Z	addition	any^a	any	any	any
Q, Z	linear	nonrecursive	any	any	any
R	polynomial	nonrecursive			any
B	equality	any			
B^{aless}	equality, inequality	any			
B	order				

FIGURE 8.2. Restrictions that guarantee safety.

Figure 8.2 summarizes some restrictions that guarantee safety in evaluating Datalog, maximum, minimum, area, volume, and negation queries. In the figure superscript *aless* means atomless, *e* means evaluation safe, and superscript *a* means approximation safe. The negation of a gap-order constraint is not always a gap-order constraint because the bound may become negative by the negation. The negation of a positive linear constraint is a negative linear constraint and vice versa. We can use Figure 8.2 to show that the following queries are safe.

Example 4.1.3: This example used a (half)-addition constraint within each constraint tuple to record the possible travel times between a pair of cities. Therefore, Q_{travel} must be a safe query by Figure 8.2.

Example 4.1.9: This Datalog program contains only a single addition constraint. Hence if the input relations *Fire* and *Forest* also contain only addition constraints, then the query is approximation safe by Figure 8.2.

Example 4.2.1:   This query used only Boolean equality constraints. Therefore it is a safe query.

Example 4.4.2:   Here we used the constraint $A \cap B \neq \emptyset$, which is a monotone Boolean inequality constraint. Because this is the only constraint used, it is a safe query by Figure 8.2.

Example 6.1.3:   This Datalog query about the ferry system contains only positive linear constraints. Hence it is safe.

In the restriction approach we simply check what is the domain, the type of constraints, and the type of the query used. If library queries are labeled as being recursive or nonrecursive and both queries and input databases are labeled as the type of constraints used and their domains, then users can do this type of safety checking themselves.

Alternatively, one or more of the restricted constraint query languages can be provided within a system. That is similar to relational database systems that provide safe languages like SQL for users instead of the complete power of high-level programming languages. Users of these systems do not have to be concerned with safety issues, although they may find the expressiveness of the query languages too limited. There is always a trade-off between more safety and less flexibility.

8.3   Safe Aggregation and Negation Queries

Aggregation and negation are safe in the cases listed in Figure 8.2. Note that the negation of a half-addition constraint may not be a half-addition constraint, although it is always a linear constraint. Therefore, relations with only half-addition constraints are evaluation safe—the output of the negation will be a general linear constraint relation—but not closed-form evaluation safe.

There are techniques to test and certify that a stratified query in which Datalog with half-addition constraint queries and negation queries alternate is safe. Note that each half-addition constraint in which at least one of the variables becomes a constant, is equivalent to an order constraint. The certification method essentially verifies that in each half-addition constraint in the output relation at least one variable becomes constant. Because order constraint relations can be negated, the stratified Datalog query is therefore also evaluable. Chapter 11 describes several certification methods.

8.4   Safe Refinement and Projection Queries

Refinement queries are always safe because they can be evaluated only by adding constraints to the UOR. Projection queries are also evaluable whenever the UOR contains only addition, linear, or polynomial constraints.

However, we should not take for granted that projection queries are always evaluable. For example, when the UOR contains integer polynomial constraints, the projection may not be safe and evaluable.

Bibliographic Notes

The restrictions of Datalog with only inequality, rational order, or Boolean term equations was shown to be safe by Kanellakis, Kuper, and Revesz [158]. The restrictions of Datalog with integer or rational gap-order constraints was shown to be safe by Revesz [257]. This was extended to half-addition constraints in Revesz [266], which also showed that the restrictions with only positive and only negative linear inequality constraints are safe. Kreutzer [186, 187] is a recent work on the fixed-point evaluation of Datalog with linear constraints. The restriction with $\subseteq$ and monotone Boolean term inequation constraints is shown to be safe in Revesz [265].

That nonrecursive Datalog queries with rational linear inequality constraints are safe follows from the general evaluation strategy described in [158], which reduces the evaluation to existential quantifier elimination in the theory of rational linear inequality constraints. The first quantifier elimination algorithm for this case was given by Fourier [99]. Nonrecursive Datalog queries with real polynomial constraints are handled similarly by quantifier elimination in the theory of real polynomial inequality constraints. The first quantifier elimination algorithm for this case was given by Tarski [303]. In both cases, computationally more efficient quantifier elimination algorithms have been developed by other authors. For a review of these see Revesz [264].

Toman [305] shows that any type of restriction satisfying certain (sufficient but not necessary) conditions yields a closed-form evaluation safe Datalog query. Sufficient termination conditions under the assumption of top-down evaluation in constraint logic programs is studied in Aiken et al. [9], Colussi et al. [70], Giacobazzi et al. [109], and Heintze and Jaffar [141]. Safety of other constraint Datalog queries using a nonstandard semantics (i.e., different from the one described in Chapter 4) is studied by Grumbach and Kuper [120].

The approximate evaluation of Datalog with difference constraints was studied by Revesz [268].

That projection is safe in the cases shown in Figure 8.2 follows again from the quantifier elimination methods listed earlier. The result that quantifier elimination in the existential theory of integer polynomial constraints is unsafe follows from the undecidability result of the same theory by Matiyasevich [207], which improves an undecidability result for the whole theory by Gödel.

The minimum and maximum aggregate operators are safe for the case of linear inequality constraints and are used in several systems, including CCUBE [44] and MLPQ [274]. These operators are not generally evaluable for polynomial constraints. The safety of aggregation operators is studied in Benedikt and L. Libkin [31], Chomicki et al. [57, 59], and Kuper [193]. However, in many cases they are evaluable. For example, commercial systems like *Mathematica* or *Maple* can evaluate many queries involving polynomial constraints.

Exercises

1. Prove that the following queries are safe:

   (a) Example 4.1.1 about the taxes due.

   (b) Example 4.1.8 about the broadcast areas of radio stations.

   (c) Example 6.1.2 about the elevator system.

   (d) Example 6.1.4 about the subway train control system.

   (e) Example 6.1.6 about the cafeteria.

2. Is the query that you wrote for the following exercises safe? Why or why not?

   (a) Exercise 6.4 about the thermostat.

   (b) Exercise 6.8 about employment.

   (c) Exercise 6.9 about the wealth of people.

3. Prove that the following queries in Chapter 5 are safe:

   (a) The Q_{profit} query.

   (b) The Q_{edge} query.

   (c) The Q_{not_cover} query.

   (d) The $Q_{fastest}$ query.

   (e) The Q_{Alice} query.

9

Evaluation of Queries

Our notion of queries is as abstract as our notion of databases. Therefore, we may talk about different levels of query abstraction, just as we talked about different levels of data abstraction. In the previous chapters we usually thought of queries as functions from (possibly) infinite relational databases to (possibly) infinite relational databases as shown in Figure 9.1. This is the logical level of query abstraction. This level was enough to write good queries. However, in this chapter we consider queries at the constraint level. At the constraint level, queries can be thought of as functions from finite constraint databases to finite constraint databases, as shown in Figure 9.2.

In Section 9.1 we describe quantifier elimination algorithms. In Sections 9.2, 9.3, and 9.4, we describe the evaluation of relational algebra, SQL, and Datalog queries, respectively.

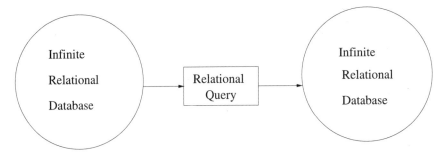

FIGURE 9.1. Queries in the relational data model.

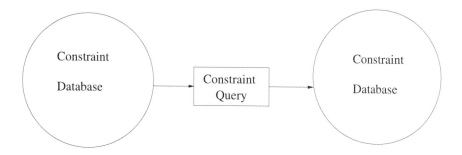

FIGURE 9.2. Queries in the constraint data model.

9.1 Quantifier Elimination and Satisfiability

In Chapter 2 we defined constraint tuples as conjunctions of atomic constraints. Suppose now that S is a constraint tuple over the variables $x, y_1, \ldots, y_n$ ranging over some domain D. Then S defines an infinite relation r that is a subset of D^{n+1}. If we project out from r all the variables except x, that is, if we drop the x attribute column, then we get a new relation r'.

The goal of *existential quantifier elimination* is to find a finite constraint representation of r' that uses only the variables $y_1, \ldots, y_n$. If there is such a finite constraint representation S' then we write $S' = \exists x S$, where the $\exists$ symbol is read as "exists" and it is referred to as the "existential quantifier." The notation reminds us that for each tuple t' in r' there exists in r a tuple t that is the same as t' on the y attributes and has some x value in it.

If for any x and S over some type of constraints there is always an S' over the same type of constraints such that $S' = \exists x S$, then we say that existential quantifier elimination is closed for that type of constraint. The next few theorems give examples of closed quantifier elimination algorithms in various cases of constraints.

Theorem 9.1.1   Existential quantifier elimination is closed for conjunctions of any infinite domain equality and inequality constraints where each constant in the conjunction is an element of D that is a nonempty finite subset of the domain for any fixed D.

Proof. Let S be any conjunction of equality and inequality constraints over x and some other variables as required. Without loss of generality we can assume that each constraint that contains x has x on the left-hand side. We show that $S' = \exists x S$ can be written as required.

S' will be the conjunction of all the constraints in S that do not contain the variable x and all the constraints that can be derived from a pair of constraints in S using the following rule. If $x\theta_1 u$ and $x\theta_2 v$ are in S for any pair u, v of variables or constants and at least one of θ_1 and θ_2 is $=$ then add to S' the constraint $u\theta_3 v$ where if θ_1 and θ_2 are both $=$ then θ_3 is also $=$ else it is $\neq$. By this rule, we add to

S' only equality and inequality constraints that use only constants from D. This proves syntactic closure.

Now we prove the soundness of the quantifier elimination. It can be seen that for any instantiation if the two constraints in S are both true, then the constraint added to S' is also true. Hence if S is true, then S' must be true for any instantiation of x and the other variables.

For the other direction, suppose that S' is true for some instantiation of all the variables except x. Then make the same instantiation into S. Suppose that S contains a list of equality constraints $x = u_1$, $x = u_2, \ldots$, and a list of inequality constraints $x \neq v_1$, $x \neq v_2, \ldots$ in which x occurs.

Because S' is true, after the instantiation of S all the u_is must be the same constant c. Otherwise we would have two different constants c_1 and c_2 equal to x and by our rule we would have derived $c_1 = c_2$, which is false and therefore a contradiction to S' being true. Further, no constant among the vs can be c. Therefore if there is any equality constraint, then we could let $x = c$, and that would make S true. Otherwise, we can choose any constant for x that is different from all the vs. Because the domain is infinite, we can do that. Then again, S must be true. ∎

Theorem 9.1.2   Existential quantifier elimination is closed for conjunctions of rational order constraints where each constant in the conjunction is an element of a nonempty set $D \subset \mathcal{R}$.

Proof. Let S be any conjunction of order constraints over x and some other variables as required. We show that $S' = \exists x\, S$ can be written as a conjunction of order constraints over only the other variables and using only constants from D.

S' will be the conjunction of all the constraints in S that do not contain the variable x and all the constraints that can be derived from a pair of constraints in S using transitivity. That is, if $u\theta_1 x$ and $x\theta_2 v$ are in S for any pair u, v of variables or constants, then add to S' the constraint $u\theta_3 v$ where if θ_1 and θ_2 are both $\geq$ then θ_3 is also $\geq$ else it is $>$. By using transitivity we add to S' only order constraints that use only constants from D. This proves syntactic closure.

Now we prove the soundness of the quantifier elimination. It can be seen that for any instantiation if the two constraints in S are both true, then the constraint added to S' is also true. Hence if S is true, then S' must be true for any instantiation of x and the other variables.

For the other direction, suppose that S' is true for some instantiation of all the variables except x. Then make the same instantiation into S. Suppose that S contains a list of upper bound constraints $u_1 \geq x$, $u_2 \geq x, \ldots$ and a list of lower bound constraints $x \geq v_1$, $x \geq v_2, \ldots$ in which x occurs.

Suppose that after the instantiation the largest lower bound of x is c and the smallest upper bound of x is d. Then by transitivity we must have added a constraint to S', which after instantiation is $d \geq c$. Because S' is true, we can find a value between c and d inclusively for x that will make S also true. ∎

Theorem 9.1.3   Existential quantifier elimination is closed for conjunctions of integer and rational gap-order, lower bound and upper bound constraints where each lower bound and upper bound constraint has a minimum bound of l, and all constants occurring in the conjunction are integers or rational numbers with denominator p for any fixed $l \leq 0$ and $p > 0$.

Proof. Let S be any conjunction of gap-order, lower bound, and upper bound constraints over x and some other variables such that each bound is $\geq l$. We show that $S' = \exists x S$ can be written as a conjunction of gap-order, lower bound, and upper bound constraints over only the other variables such that each bound is $\geq l$.

S' will be the conjunction of all the constraints in S that do not contain the variable x and all the constraints that can be derived by taking the sum of any pair of constraints in S with opposite signs for x. This can happen in three different ways:

Case I: There are two gap-order constraints of the form $x - y \geq a$ and $z - x \geq b$, respectively. Their sum will be $z - y \geq a + b$. Because a and b are nonnegative, their sum will be nonnegative; hence the new constraint is a gap-order constraint.

Case II: There is a gap-order constraint of the form $x - y \geq a$ and an upper bound constraint of the form $-x \geq b$. Their sum will be $-y \geq a + b$.

Case III: There is a gap-order constraint of the form $y - x \geq a$ and a lower bound constraint of the form $x \geq b$. Their sum will be $y \geq a + b$.

Note that $a + b$ is an integer if a and b are integers, and it is a rational with denominator p if a and b are rationals with denominator p. In addition, in each case, $a + b \geq b$ because $a \geq 0$. This proves that if all bounds were greater than l before the shortcut, then all bounds will still be greater than l after the shortcut. This shows that the quantifier elimination is closed for any fixed l.

Now we prove the soundness of the quantifier elimination. For any instantiation, if two constraints are both true, then their sum also must be a true constraint. Hence if S is true, then S' must be true for any instantiation of x and the other variables.

For the other direction, suppose that S' is true for some instantiation of all the variables except x. Then make the same instantiation into S. After the instantiation, x will be the only remaining variable in S. Wherever x occurs positively, the constraint implies a lower bound for x, and wherever x occurs negatively the constraint implies an upper bound for x.

Suppose that the largest lower bound c is implied by some constraint f and the smallest upper bound d is implied by some constraint g. Because the sum of f and g under the current instantiation is equivalent to $d \geq c$ and is in S', which is true, we can find a value between c and d inclusively for x that will make S also true. ■

We can extend Theorem 9.1.3 in two different ways. The first extension replaces gap-order constraints with half-addition constraints.

Theorem 9.1.4 Existential quantifier elimination is closed for conjunctions of integer and rational half-addition, lower bound, and upper bound constraints where all bounds in the half-addition constraints are integers or rational numbers with denominator p and all bounds in the lower and upper bound constraints are integers or rationals with denominator $2p$ and greater than l for any fixed $l \leq 0$ and $p > 0$.

Proof. Let S be any conjunction of half-addition, lower bound, and upper bound constraints over x and some other variables. We show that $S' = \exists x S$ can be written as a similar conjunction of constraints over only the other variables.

S' will be the conjunction of all the constraints in S that do not contain the variable x and all the constraints that can be derived from any pair of constraints in S that have opposite signs for x. There are the following cases:

Cases I–III: Similar to Cases I–III of Theorem 9.1.3.

Case IV: There are two half-addition constraints of the form $x + y \geq a$ and $z - x \geq b$ where $z \neq y$. Their sum will be $y + z \geq a + b$. In this case, if a and b are nonnegative integers or rational numbers with denominator p then so is $a + b$.

Case V: There are two half-addition constraints of the form $x + y \geq a$ and $y - x \geq b$. Their sum will be $2y \geq a + b$.

We can write the new constraint as the lower bound constraint $y \geq (a + b)/2$ in the case of rational numbers and as $y \geq floor((a + b)/2)$ in the case of integers, where the floor function takes the smallest integer value that is greater than or equal to any given rational value. Because a and b are rational numbers with p as the denominator, the new bound $(a + b)/2$ can be written as a rational with denominator $2p$ as required.

Case VI: There are two half-addition constraints of the form $x - y \geq a$ and $-x - z \geq b$ where $z \neq y$. Their sum will be $-y - z \geq a + b$. In this case the proof is similar to Case IV.

Case VII: There are two half-addition constraints of the form $x - y \geq a$ and $-x - y \geq b$. Their sum will be $-2y \geq a + b$. In this case the proof is similar to Case V.

Case VIII: There are two constraints of the form $x + y \geq a$ and $-x \geq b$. Their sum will be $y \geq a + b$. In this case, if a and b are nonnegative integers or rational numbers with denominators p and $2p$, respectively, then $a + b$ is also an integer or a rational number with denominator $2p$.

Case IX: There are two constraints of the form $-x - y \geq a$ and $x \geq b$. Their sum will be $-y \geq a + b$. In this case, if a and b are nonnegative integers or rational numbers with denominators p and $2p$, respectively, then $a + b$ is also an integer or a rational number with denominator $2p$.

We can prove the logical equivalence of $\exists S$ and S' similarly to the proof in Theorem 9.1.3. ∎

We say that the *arity* of a linear constraint is the number of variables with nonzero coefficients. We say that a linear constraint is in *normal form* if all of its coefficients are nonzero integers. Clearly, every linear constraint can be put into normal form. We call *positive* those linear constraints in which all coefficients are nonnegative.

Note that each lower bound constraint can be expressed as a 1-arity positive normal linear constraint. The second extension of Theorem 9.1.3 replaces lower bound constraints with positive linear constraints.

Theorem 9.1.5 Existential quantifier elimination is closed for conjunctions of integer or rational gap-order, upper bound and positive normal linear constraints where each upper bound constraint has a minimum bound of l, each positive normal linear constraint has a maximum arity m, a maximum sum of coefficients s, and a minimum bound $l + (m - k)sl$ where k is its arity and all constants occurring in the conjunction are integers or rational numbers with denominator p for any fixed $l \leq 0$ and $m, p, s > 0$.

Proof. Let S be any conjunction of gap-order, upper bound, and positive normal linear constraints over x and some other variables as required. We show that $S' = \exists x S$ can be written as a similar conjunction of constraints over only the other variables.

S' will be the conjunction of all the constraints in S that do not contain the variable x and all the constraints that can be derived from any pair of constraints in S with opposite signs for x. This can happen in five different ways:

Cases I–II: These are similar to Cases I–II of Theorem 9.1.3. These clearly preserve the required form.

For Cases III–V, assume that one of the constraints is a k-arity positive normal linear constraint of the form

$$c_0 x + c_1 y_1 + \cdots + c_{k-1} y_{k-1} \theta_2 a$$

Case III: The second constraint is an upper bound constraint of the form $-x \theta_1 b$. Multiplying the second constraint by c_0 and adding it to the first yields:

$$c_1 y_1 + \cdots + c_{k-1} y_{k-1} \theta_3 a + c_0 b$$

where θ_3 is $\geq$ if θ_1 and θ_2 are both $\geq$ and $>$ otherwise.

The new constraint is the same as the positive normal linear constraint except that the term $c_0 x$ is deleted and the bound changed from a to $a + c_0 b$. This decreases its arity by one and the sum of its coefficients by $c_0 > 0$. Hence its arity is $\leq m$, and the sum of its coefficients is $\leq s$.

We know that $b \geq l$. Multiplying by $c_0 > 0$ we get $c_0 b \geq c_0 l$. We also know that $c_0 \leq s$. Multiplying by $l \leq 0$ we get $c_0 l \geq sl$. Hence $c_0 b \geq sl$. Because $a \geq l + (m - k)sl$, we have $a + c_0 b \geq l + (m - k)sl + sl = l + (m - k + 1)sl = l + (m - (k - 1))sl = l + (m - k')sl$ where $k' = k - 1$ is the arity of the new constraint.

Case IV: The second constraint is a gap-order constraint of the form $z - x \theta_1 b$ where z is different from each y_i for $1 \leq i \leq k - 1$. Multiplying the second constraint by c_0 and adding it to the first yields:

$$c_0 z + c_1 y_1 + \cdots + c_{k-1} y_{k-1} \theta_3 a + c_0 b$$

where θ_3 is $\geq$ if θ_1 and θ_2 are both $\geq$ and $>$ otherwise.

The new constraint is the same as the positive normal linear constraint except the variable x is replaced by z and the bound changed from a to $a + c_0 b$. Hence its arity and sum of coefficients are the same. Hence its arity is $\leq m$, and the sum of its coefficients is $\leq s$. Further, $a + c_0 b \geq a$ because $b \geq 0$ and $c_0 > 0$. Therefore its bound is also $\geq l + (m - k)sl$ as required.

Case V: The second constraint is a gap-order constraint of the form $y_i - x \theta_1 b$ where $1 \leq i \leq k - 1$. Multiplying the second constraint by c_0 and adding it to the first yields:

$$c_1 y_1 + \cdots + (c_0 + c_i) y_i + \cdots + c_{k-1} y_{k-1} \theta_3 a + c_0 b$$

where θ_3 is $\geq$ if θ_1 and θ_2 are both $\geq$ and $>$ otherwise.

The new constraint is still a positive normal linear constraint because the sum of c_0 and c_i is a positive integer and the other coefficients did not change. The arity decreased by one and the sum of the coefficients stayed the same. Hence its arity is $\leq m$, and the sum of its coefficients is $\leq s$. Further, $a + c_0 b \geq a$ because $b \geq 0$ and $c_0 > 0$. Also, $sl \leq 0$ because $s > 0$ and $l \leq 0$. Because $a \geq l + (m - k)sl$ we have $a + c_0 b \geq l + (m - k)sl \geq l + (m - k)sl + sl = l + (m - k')sl$ where $k' = k - 1$ is the arity of the new constraint.

Finally, note that in Cases III–V if a, b are rationals with common denominator p then the new bound $a + c_0 b$ can be also expressed as a quotient of some integer and p because c_0 is an integer. Therefore the closed form is preserved.

We can prove the logical equivalence of $\exists S$ and S' similarly to the proof in Theorem 9.1.3. ∎

The following is similar to Theorem 9.1.5.

Theorem 9.1.6   Existential quantifier elimination is closed for conjunctions of integer or rational gap-order, lower bound, and negative normal linear constraints where each lower bound constraint has a minimum bound of l, each negative normal linear constraint has a maximum arity m, a maximum sum of coefficients $-s$, and a minimum bound $l - (m - k)sl$ where k is its arity, and all constants occurring in the conjunction are integers or rational numbers with denominator p for any fixed $l \leq 0$, $s < 0$, and $m, p > 0$.   ■

The following theorem is about linear constraints. We only prove it for the case of the rationals; we omit the proof for the case of the integers.

Theorem 9.1.7   Existential quantifier elimination is closed for rational linear inequality constraints.

Proof. Without loss of generality assume that the conjunction S of linear inequality constraints is a set of linear inequalities that do not contain x and a set of k linear inequalities of the form:

$$x + c_{1,1}y_1 + \ldots + c_{1,n}y_n \quad \geq \quad b_1$$
$$\vdots$$
$$x + c_{k,1}y_1 + \ldots + c_{k,n}y_n \quad \geq \quad b_k$$

that contain x with a coefficient of one, and a set of $m - k$ linear inequalities of the form:

$$-x + c_{k+1,1}y_1 + \cdots + c_{k+1,n}y_n \quad \geq \quad b_{k+1}$$
$$\vdots$$
$$-x + c_{m,1}y_1 + \cdots + c_{m,n}y_n \quad \geq \quad b_m$$

that contain x with a coefficient of minus one. Then $S' = \exists S$ will be the conjunctions of all the constraints in S that do not contain x and the $k \times (m-k)$ constraints that we can obtain by adding one of the k constraints in the first displayed set to one of the $m - k$ constraints in the second displayed set. This preserves syntactical closed form.

We can prove the logical equivalence of $\exists S$ and S' similarly to the proof in Theorem 9.1.3.   ■

The following theorem about polynomial constraints requires a more difficult proof, which we omit here.

Theorem 9.1.8   Existential quantifier elimination is closed for real polynomial inequality constraints.   ■

Next we consider free Boolean algebras. First we show the following.

Lemma 9.1.1   Conjunctions of Boolean minterm equality constraints are equivalent to conjunctions of Boolean equality constraints.

Proof. Because each minterm equality constraint is also an equality constraint, one direction of the lemma is obvious. We show that each conjunction of Boolean equality constraints can be expressed as a conjunction of Boolean minterm equality constraints as follows. Let the conjunction of Boolean equality constraints be of the form

$$f_1 =_B 0 \text{ and } \ldots \text{ and } f_l =_B 0$$

where f_i is a Boolean term for each $1 \leq i \leq l$. For each i we can put f_i into disjunctive normal form, that is, in the form:

$$d_{i,1} \vee d_{i,2} \vee \ldots \vee d_{i,k_i} =_B 0$$

where each $d_{i,j}$ is a minterm of the Boolean algebra B. This is equivalent to:

$$d_{i,1} =_B 0 \text{ and } d_{i,2} =_B 0 \text{ and } \ldots \text{ and } d_{i,k_i} =_B 0$$

This proves the lemma.   ∎

Theorem 9.1.9   Existential quantifier elimination is closed for conjunctions of Boolean equality constraints.

Proof. By Lemma 9.1.1 we can rewrite the conjunction of equality constraints into a conjunction of minterm equality constraints.

Let S be any conjunction of Boolean minterm equality constraints over x and some other variables. We show that $S' = \exists x\, S$ can be written as a similar conjunction of constraints over only the other variables.

S' will be the conjunction of all the constraints in S that can be derived from any pair of constraints in S such that the first constraint has the form:

$$x' \wedge y_1 \wedge \ldots \wedge y_n =_B 0$$

and the second constraint has the form:

$$x \wedge z_1 \wedge \ldots \wedge z_m =_B 0$$

where the ys and zs are not necessarily distinct negated or unnegated Boolean algebra variables and constants. Here the first constraint is equivalent to $y_1 \wedge \ldots \wedge y_n \leq_B x$, and the second constraint is equivalent to: $x \leq_B (z_1 \wedge \ldots \wedge z_m)'$. Hence by transitivity, we can derive $y_1 \wedge \ldots \wedge y_n \leq_B (z_1 \wedge \ldots \wedge z_m)'$, which is equivalent to:

$$y_1 \wedge \ldots y_n \wedge z_1 \wedge \ldots z_m =_B 0$$

This is also a Boolean minterm equality constraint. Therefore this preserves syntactic closed form.

We can prove the logical equivalence of $\exists S$ and S' similarly to the proof in Theorem 9.1.3.   ∎

The quantifier elimination method in Theorem 9.1.9 is only for equality constraints. In the case of *atomless* Boolean algebras, we can extend the quantifier elimination to both equality and inequality constraints.

Lemma 9.1.2   Each conjunction of Boolean equality and inequality constraints is equivalent to a disjunction of conjunctions of Boolean minterm equality and inequality constraints.

Proof. Take any conjunction of $C = E \wedge I$, where E is a conjunction of Boolean equality and I is a conjunction of Boolean inequality constraints. We can use Lemma 9.1.1 to rewrite E into a conjunction of minterm equality constraints E'. Let I be of the form

$$f_1 \neq_B 0 \text{ and } \ldots \text{ and } f_l \neq_B 0 \tag{9.1}$$

where f_i is a Boolean term for each $1 \leq i \leq l$. For each i we can put f_i into disjunctive normal form, that is, in the form:

$$d_{i,1} \vee d_{i,2} \vee \ldots \vee d_{i,k_i} \neq_B 0$$

where each $d_{i,j}$ is a minterm of the Boolean algebra B. Because the disjunction of minterms is nonzero if only one of them is nonzero, the preceding is equivalent to:

$$d_{i,1} \neq_B 0 \text{ or } d_{i,2} \neq_B 0 \text{ or } \ldots \text{ or } d_{i,k_i} \neq_B 0$$

When we substitute into (9.1) the preceding for each i, then we get a conjunction of disjunctions. We can rewrite the formula using the distributivity axioms into a disjunction of conjunctions of minterm inequality constraints. Finally, we can add to each disjunct E' to obtain a disjunction of conjunctions of minterm equality and inequality constraints that is equivalent to C.   ∎

Now we consider quantifier elimination in atomless Boolean algebras.

Theorem 9.1.10   Existential quantifier elimination is closed for conjunctions of Boolean equality and inequality constraints in atomless Boolean algebras.

Proof. By Lemma 9.1.2 we may assume that we have only minterm equality and inequality constraints.

Let S be any conjunction of Boolean minterm equality and inequality constraints over x and some other variables. We show that $S' = \exists x\, S$ can be written as a similar conjunction of constraints over only the other variables.

First we derive constraints as in Theorem 9.1.9. Then we check whether there is any minterm such that $m \neq_B 0$ and $m =_B 0$ are both in the conjunction. If not, then we drop from each minterm x or x'.   ∎

Next we consider Boolean order constraints.

Theorem 9.1.11   Existential quantifier elimination is closed for conjunctions of Boolean order constraints.

Proof. Let S be any conjunction of Boolean order constraints over x and some other variables. We show that $S' = \exists x\, S$ can be written as a similar conjunction of constraints over only the other variables.

S' will be the conjunction of all the constraints in S that do not contain the variable x and all the constraints that can be derived from any pair of constraints in S using the following cases:

Case I: We have two Boolean order constraints. The first is of the form $f \geq_B x$, which is equivalent to:

$$x \wedge f' =_B 0 \tag{9.2}$$

and the second is of the form $g \geq_B y$, which is equivalent to $y \wedge g' =_B 0$. Using Lemma 9.1.1 and breaking up the disjunctions, the latter is also equivalent to:

$$x \wedge y \wedge g'_x(1) =_B 0 \text{ and } x' \wedge y \wedge g'_x(0) =_B 0 \tag{9.3}$$

As in Theorem 9.1.9, from (9.2) and the second part of (9.3) we can derive $f' \wedge g'_x(0) \wedge y =_B 0$, which is equivalent to:

$$f \vee g_x(0) \geq_B y \tag{9.4}$$

The closed form is preserved because (9.4) is a Boolean order constraint.

Case II: We have in the conjunction a constraint $g(x, v_1, \ldots, v_n) >_B 0$ and a set of Boolean order constraints where the ith-order constraint has the form:

$$f_i \geq_B x \tag{9.5}$$

Let u be $\bigwedge_i f_i$. Then the derived constraint will be $g(u, v_1, \ldots, v_n) >_B 0$, i.e., x is replaced by u. Because all the f_i are monotone, u is monotone. Because g and u are monotone, the left-hand side of the derived constraint will also be monotone. This shows syntactical closed form.

Now we prove the soundness of the quantifier elimination. For Case I the soundness can be proven similarly to Theorem 9.1.9.

Case II First Direction: Suppose that S is true. Then by the merge of the formulas (9.5), $u \geq_B x$ is true. Further, for any $g(x, v_1, \ldots, v_n) >_B 0$ constraint in S, the preceding and our observation in Remark 2.1.1 imply that the condition $g(u, v_1, \ldots, v_n) \geq_B g(x, v_1, \ldots, v_n)$ is true. Hence by transitivity $g(u, v_1, \ldots, v_n) >_B 0$ is true. Therefore, all the constraints in S' derived by Case II must also be true using the same substitutions for the variables as in S.

Case II Second Direction: Suppose that S' is true for some substitution of the variables in it. Then S is true with the same substitutions of the variables as in S' and the substitution of x by u. This is because the augmentation rule implies for each i that $f_i \geq_B u$, which is equivalent to (9.5) with x replaced by u. Also, with that substitution, each $g(x, v_1, \ldots, v_n) >_B 0$ constraint in S becomes equivalent to the corresponding constraint in S'. Hence S must also be true. ∎

Example 9.1.1   We can represent the information in Exercise 7.9 as the following conjunction of constraints in the specific Boolean algebra B_W of Example 2.1.3, where capitalized strings are words in $\mathcal{W}$ and lower case letters are variables:

$$\{Lilla\} \subseteq p$$
$$\{Bob, Peter\} \subseteq f$$
$$t \subseteq \{Bob, Jenny, Peter, Tom\}$$
$$o \subseteq p$$
$$t \subseteq f$$
$$p \subseteq d$$
$$v \subseteq g$$
$$v \subseteq p$$
$$f \cap g \neq \emptyset$$
$$d \cap p \neq \emptyset$$
$$t \cap (v \cup p) \neq \emptyset$$

These constraints can be rewritten as the conjunction of eight simple upper bound constraints and three monotone inequality constraints as follows:

$$p' \subseteq \{Lilla\}'$$
$$f' \subseteq \{Bob, Peter\}'$$
$$t \subseteq \{Bob, Jenny, Peter, Tom\}$$
$$o \cap p' \subseteq \emptyset$$
$$f' \cap t \subseteq \emptyset$$
$$d' \cap p \subseteq \emptyset$$
$$g' \cap v \subseteq \emptyset$$
$$p' \cap v \subseteq \emptyset$$
$$f \cap g \neq \emptyset$$
$$d \cap p \neq \emptyset$$
$$t \cap (v \cup p) \neq \emptyset$$

Let us eliminate the variable p. Note that p occurs unnegated in only one upper bound constraint, which is equivalent to $p \subseteq d$. Hence we get:

$$f' \subseteq \{Bob, Peter\}'$$
$$t \subseteq \{Bob, Jenny, Peter, Tom\}$$
$$f' \cap t \subseteq \emptyset$$
$$d' \subseteq \{Lilla\}'$$
$$d' \cap o \subseteq \emptyset$$
$$d' \cap v \subseteq \emptyset$$

$$g' \cap v \subseteq \emptyset$$
$$f \cap g \neq \emptyset$$
$$d \neq \emptyset$$
$$t \cap (v \cup d) \neq \emptyset$$

9.1.1   Satisfiability

We say that a conjunction of constraints S is true if there is an instantiation of the variables in the formula by constants in the allowed domain that makes the formula true.

Suppose that S is a conjunction of constraints with variables $x_1, \ldots, x_n$. Then it is satisfiable if and only if $S^* = \exists x_1 (\ldots (\exists x_n S) \ldots)$ is satisfiable. In other words, we can test the satisfiability of S by successively eliminating all variables from S and then testing whether the remaining variable-free formula is true. Usually this test is easy to do.

Theorem 9.1.12   In any constraint theory $\mathcal{C}$, it can be tested whether a conjunction of constraints is satisfiable if there is a closed form existential quantifier elimination algorithm in $\mathcal{C}$.   ∎

9.2   Evaluation of Relational Algebra Queries

In the following we write *points*(R) for the set of tuples that make R true. Hence $r = points(R)$ in this case. If there are several constraint relations in a database DB then *points*(DB) is the set of infinite relations *points*(R_i) such that $R_i \in DB$. If R contains k attributes and the domain of the attributes is D, then the *complement* of R is the set of all tuples in D^k that are not in r.

Before describing the relational algebra operators, note that we can find the complement of any constraint relation R by at first taking the formula that is the disjunction of all the constraint tuples of R and then taking its negation and putting the negated formula back into disjunctive normal form as discussed in Section 2.1.3.

Suppose now that we have a relational algebra query Q. We understand from Section 3 how the relational algebra operators work and hence how Q can take as input an infinite relational database and give as output an infinite relation. The problem is that this would take an infinite amount of time, hence we have to use a finite constraint database representation of the input and output as shown in Figure 9.2. However, the relational algebra operators that we have within the query do not work on constraint relations. Therefore we replace them with their counterparts that perform on the constraint representation what is logically expected of the original operators.

We define the following relational algebra operators for constraint databases corresponding to the operators in Section 3.1.1. We refer to the original definitions and highlight only the differences. We also assume that each distinct attribute corresponds to the same distinct variable in each constraint relation in the database.

Intersection: The constraint intersection of two relations A and B, denoted $A\hat{\cap}B$, returns the same relation scheme as the intersection operator and all satisfiable conjunctions of S_i and T_j such that S_i is a constraint tuple of A and T_j is a constraint tuple of B.

Union: The constraint union of two relations A and B, denoted $A\hat{\cup}B$, returns the set of constraints tuples that belong to either A or B or both.

Difference: The constraint difference of two relations A and B, denoted $A\hat{\setminus}B$ takes first the complement B' of B and then the intersection of A and B'.

Product: The constraint product of two relations A and B, denoted $A\hat{\times}B$, returns the same relation scheme as the product operator and all conjunctions of S_i and T_j such that S_i is a constraint tuple of A and T_j is a constraint tuple of B. Note that S_i and T_j have no common variables because the product requires that A and B have no common attributes. Hence the conjunctions of S_i and T_j are always satisfiable if S_j and T_j are satisfiable.

Project: The constraint project operator $\hat{\pi}_L A$ eliminates from each constraint tuple of A all the variables that correspond to attributes that are not in L. Then it reorders the attribute columns in the order given in L.

Select: The constraint select operator $\hat{\sigma}_F A$ first expresses F as a conjunction of disjunctions of constraints, i.e., of the form $F_1 \vee \ldots \vee F_k$ where each F_i is a conjunction of constraints. Second, it returns all satisfiable conjunctions of S_i and F_j such that S_i is a constraint tuple of A.

Rename: The constraint rename operation $\hat{\rho}$ renames the attributes and the name of the constraint relation as ρ did for the infinite relations.

Natural Join: The constraint natural join operator $A\hat{\bowtie}B$ returns the same relation scheme as the natural join operator and all satisfiable conjunctions of S_i and T_j such that S_i is a constraint tuple of A and T_j is a constraint tuple of B.

In the following let us define for any constraint theory $\mathcal{C}$ that is closed under negation the following functions:

1. The function *elim* from pairs of variables and conjunction of constraints in $\mathcal{C}$ to conjunction of constraints in $\mathcal{C}$ such that $elim\,(x, S) = \exists S$.

2. The function *sat* from conjunction of constraints in $\mathcal{C}$ to {*true, false*} such that *sat* (S) is *true* if S is satisfiable and *false* otherwise.

3. The function *compl* (R) that returns the complement of the constraint relation R.

Theorem 9.2.1   Let DB be any constraint database over a constraint theory and let Q be any relational algebra query. Let $\hat{Q}$ be the query obtained by replacing each relational algebra operator with a corresponding constraint database operator. Then:

$$Q(points(DB)) = points(\hat{Q}(DB))$$

Proof. The theorem can be proven by induction on the operators in Q. This is done as follows. Let R, R_1, R_2 be constraint relations. Then, do the following:

Rename: $points(\hat{\rho}_C(R)) \equiv \rho_C(points(R))$ follows from the fact that substituting variables by other variables does not change the set of models of a constraint formula.

Select: $points(\hat{\sigma}_C(R)) \equiv \sigma_C(points(R))$ is true.

Project: We show that $points(\hat{\pi}_{X'}(R)) \equiv \pi_{X'}(points(R))$. Suppose that

$$t = a_1, \ldots, a_{j-1}, a_{j+1}, \ldots, a_k$$

is a tuple in $\pi_{X'} points(R)$. Then there must be a tuple $a_1, \ldots, a_k$ in $points(R)$. Also, $a_1, \ldots, a_k$ must be a model of some constraint tuple t_i of R. Then by definition of variable elimination t is a model of $elim(x_j, t_i)$. By the definition of $\hat{\pi}$ the tuple t must belong to $points(\hat{\pi}_{X'} R)$.

For the reverse direction, suppose that t is a tuple in $points(\hat{\pi}_{X'} R)$. Then there must be a constraint tuple t' in R such that t is a model of $elim(x_j, t')$. Therefore, there is some a_j value such that $a_1, \ldots, a_k$ is a model of t'. Then $a_1, \ldots, a_k$ must be in $points(R)$. Hence t must be in $\pi_{X'} points(R)$.

Natural Join: We show that $points(R_1 \hat{\bowtie} R_2) \equiv points(R_1) \bowtie points(R_2)$. Suppose that $a_1, \ldots, a_{k1}$ is in $points(R_1)$ and $b_1, \ldots, b_{k2}$ is in $points(R_2)$, and $c_1, \ldots, c_k$ is the combination of $a_1, \ldots, a_{k1}$ and $b_1, \ldots, b_{k2}$ such that the same attributes are assigned the same values in $points(R_1) \bowtie points(R_2)$. Then $a_1, \ldots, a_{k1}$ is a model of some constraint tuple t_i in R_1 and $b_1, \ldots, b_{k2}$ is a model of some constraint tuple s_j in R_2. By the definition of $\hat{\bowtie}$ then (t_i, s_j) is a constraint tuple in $R_1 \hat{\bowtie} R_2$ and $c_1, \ldots, c_k$ is a model of $R_1 \hat{\bowtie} R_2$. Hence $c_1, \ldots, c_k$ must be in $points(R_1 \hat{\bowtie} R_2)$.

For the reverse direction, suppose that $c_1, \ldots, c_k$ is in $points(R_1 \hat{\bowtie} R_2)$. Then by the definition of $\hat{\bowtie}$ there must be a tuple of the form (t_i, s_j) in $R_1 \hat{\bowtie} R_2$ such that t_i is a constraint tuple in R_1 and s_j is a constraint tuple in R_2. That means that there must be projections of $c_1, \ldots, c_k$ onto the attributes of R_1 and R_2 that yield tuples $a_1, \ldots, a_{k1}$ and $b_1, \ldots, b_{k2}$, respectively, and that $a_1, \ldots, a_{k1}$ is a model of R_1 and $b_1, \ldots, b_{k2}$ is a model of R_2. Hence $a_1, \ldots, a_{k1}$ is in $points(R_1)$ and $b_1, \ldots, b_{k2}$ is in $points(R_2)$. Therefore $c_1, \ldots, c_k$ must be in $points(R_1) \bowtie points(R_2)$.

The intersection is proved similarly to natural join. Difference also follows from natural join and the definition of complement. Union is obvious, and set difference follows from union and intersection. This shows that the theorem is true. ∎

Example 9.2.1 Consider again the *Broadcast* relation in Chapter 2. The following relational algebra query finds which areas are reached by station 1 but not by station 3.

$$\pi_{X,Y}(\sigma_{\text{Radio}=1} Broadcast) - \pi_{X,Y}(\sigma_{\text{Radio}=3} Broadcast)$$

Here $\pi_{X,Y}(\sigma_{\text{Radio}=1} Broadcast)$ can be evaluated as:

$$(x - 8)^2 + (y - 9)^2 \le 25$$

Similarly, $\pi_{X,Y}(\sigma_{\text{Radio}=3} Broadcast)$ can be evaluated as:

$$(y - 1) \ge (x - 3)^2, \quad y \le 10$$

Set difference is implemented by taking first the complement of the second relation, which yields:

$$(y - 1) < (x - 3)^2 \text{ or } y > 10$$

and then finally joining the first relation with the preceding. The final result, in disjunctive normal form, will be:

$$((x - 8)^2 + (y - 9)^2 \le 25, \quad (y - 1) < (x - 3)^2) \text{ or}$$
$$((x - 8)^2 + (y - 9)^2 \le 25, \quad y > 10)$$

The output can be recognized to be a constraint relation with two constraint tuples.

9.3 Evaluation of SQL Queries

Evaluation of SQL queries without aggregate operators can be done by reduction to relational algebra, as we mentioned in Section 3.2. The evaluation of *Avg* and *Sum* operators is straightforward, because these are only applied to attributes that are constants and do not involve constraints.

The *Max* and *Min* aggregate operators can be applied to any linear constraint relation without any restriction. The evaluation of these operators is based on *linear programming*. Linear programming is the problem of finding the maximum or minimum of a linear function $f(x_1, \ldots, x_n)$ where the solution also must satisfy a conjunction of linear inequality constraints. The solution space of the conjunction of linear inequality constraints is called the *feasible region*.

To find the maximum value of a linear function on the attributes of a linear constraint relation R, we apply linear programming to each constraint tuple of R. Then we can take the maximum of all the linear programming solutions as the output of the aggregate query.

Example 9.3.1 Let us consider again the relation *Crops* of Chapter 1 and Example 5.4.1 where we expressed in Datalog with aggregation the query that finds the maximum profit for the farmer. In SQL the query can be expressed as follows:

SELECT Max(30 Corn + 25 Rye + 8 Sunflower + 15 Wheat)
FROM Crops

Because *Crops* contains only one constraint tuple, a single call to a linear programming subroutine can evaluate the query.

The evaluation of aggregate operators described in Chapter 5 is similar to the evaluation of the aggregate operators within SQL queries.

9.4 Evaluation of Datalog Queries

The constraint proof-based semantics of Datalog queries defines the set of constraint tuples that can be derived in the following way.

We call a *constraint instantiation* of a rule the substitution of each relation R_i in the body by a constraint tuple t_i that is in R_i. Note that the substitution renames the variables in t_i to those variables with which R_i occurs in the rule.

Let Q be a query, I an input constraint database, and $R_0(x_1, \ldots, x_k)$ a constraint relation scheme and let t be a constraint over the variables $x_1, \ldots, x_k$. We say that $t \in R_0$ has a constraint proof using Q and I, written as $\vdash^c_{Q,I} t \in R_0$, if and only if:

$R_0 \in \mathcal{I}$ and $t \in R_0$ or
$R_0 \in \mathcal{D}$ and for some rule of form (4.1) in Q there is a constraint instantiation

$$R(a_1, \ldots, a_k) :\!- t_1(x_{1,1}, \ldots, x_{1,k_1}), \ldots, t_n(x_{n,1}, \ldots, x_{n,k_n}).$$

where $\vdash^c_{Q,I} t_i \in R_i$ for each $1 \leq i \leq n$ and

$$t = \exists * t_1(x_{1,1}, \ldots, x_{1,k_1}), \ldots, t_n(x_{n,1}, \ldots, x_{n,k_n}).$$

where $*$ is the list of the variables in the body of the rule that do not occur in the head of the rule.

We call *constraint rule application* the constraint substitution of a rule and perform the implied existential quantifier elimination.

The *constraint proof-based* semantics of Datalog queries is the following. Each Datalog query Q is a function that on any input constraint database I returns for each relation name R the relation $\{t : \vdash^c_{Q,I} t \in R\}$.

When the query and the input constraint database are obvious, then we will write $\vdash^c$ without any subscript.

The following theorem shows that the proof-based semantics and the constraint proof-based semantics are equivalent.

Theorem 9.4.1 The following equality is true:

$$\{(a_1, \ldots, a_k) : \ \vdash_{Q,I} R(a_1, \ldots, a_k)\} = \{points(t) : \ \vdash^c_{Q,I} t \in R\} \qquad \blacksquare$$

The *bottom-up constraint evaluation* of Datalog queries starts from an input constraint database and query and repeatedly applies some rule of the query until no new constraint tuples can be derived and added to the constraint database. We consider a constraint tuple of a relation new if there is some instantiation that makes it true but does not make any other constraint tuple of that relation true.

It is also possible to extend the least fixpoint semantics similarly. Then it can be shown that the constraint least fixpoint and the constraint proof-based semantics are equivalent. Hence in the following, we keep using $lfp(Q(D))$ to describe the semantics of a Datalog query Q on input constraint database D.

There are a few general techniques to prove the termination of the bottom-up evaluation in various cases of constraints. The first technique we consider is the following.

Theorem 9.4.2 Let C be any constraint theory with a closed form existential quantifier elimination. Let Q be any Datalog with C query and D be any C constraint input database D. Then $lfp(Q(D))$ is finitely computable if C can express only a finite number of atomic constraints using only a finite number of variables.

Proof. Consider any defined relation $R(x_1, \ldots, x_n)$ in Q. The constraint bottom-up evaluation can add to R only constraint tuples that are conjunctions of atomic constraints over the variables $x_1, \ldots, x_n$, which is a finite set. Hence if there is only a finite number of possible atomic constraints, then there is also a finite number of possible constraint tuples that can be added to R. Because the bottom-up evaluation never adds to R the same tuple twice, it must stop adding new tuples to R after a finite number of rule applications. The same happens to every other defined relation in Q. Hence the bottom-up evaluation must terminate after a finite number of rule applications. $\qquad \blacksquare$

We give some examples where Theorem 9.4.2 can be applied.

Theorem 9.4.3 The least fixpoint of any Datalog query and input database with infinite domain equality and inequality constraints is closed-form evaluable.

Proof. Let D be the set of constants that occur in the Datalog program or the input database. Clearly D is a finite set. The constraint theory of infinite domain equality and inequality constraints and D set of constant symbols has a closed existential quantifier elimination (see Theorem 9.1.1) and can express only a finite number of atomic constraints using a finite set F of variables, i.e., the set $u\theta v$ where $u, v \in (D \cup F)$ and θ is either $=$ or $\neq$. Therefore, by Theorem 9.4.2 the least fixpoint is closed-form evaluable. $\qquad \blacksquare$

Theorem 9.4.4   The least fixpoint of any Datalog query and input database with rational order constraints is closed-form evaluable.

Proof. Let D be the set of constants that occur in the Datalog program or the input database. Clearly D is a finite set. The constraint theory of rational order constraints and D set of constant symbols has a closed existential quantifier elimination (see Theorem 9.1.2) and can express only a finite number of atomic constraints using a finite set F of variables, i.e., the set $u\theta v$ where $u, v \in (D \cup F)$ and θ is either $\geq$ or $>$. Therefore, by Theorem 9.4.2 the least fixpoint is closed-form evaluable.   ∎

Now we look at free Boolean algebras.

Theorem 9.4.5   The least fixpoint of any Datalog query and input database with free Boolean algebra constraints is closed-form evaluable if (1) there are only Boolean upper bound constraints, (2) there are only simple Boolean upper bound and monotone inequality constraints, or (3) the free algebra represents an atomless Boolean algebra.

Proof. Let $D = \{c_1, \ldots, c_m\}$ be the set of distinct constants that occur in the Datalog program or the input database. Clearly m is finite. The constraint theory of free Boolean algebras with m distinct constant symbols has a closed existential quantifier elimination in cases 1–3 (see Theorems 9.1.9, 9.1.11, and 9.1.10).

In case 1 with k variables, there are $3^k - 1$ different left-hand sides, because each variable appears unnegated, negated, or does not appear in the conjunction of the left-hand side. Also, only ground terms appear on the right-hand side. By Lemma 2.1.1 there can be only 2^{2^m} different right-hand sides. Constraints with the same left-hand sides can be combined into one upper bound constraint. Therefore, there could be only $(3^k - 1)2^{2^m}$ different atomic constraints.

In case 2 with k variables, because simple upper bound constraints are a subclass of upper bound constraints, the argument in case 1 also implies that there are $O((3^k - 1)2^{2^m})$ simple upper bound constraints. We can put each monotone inequality constraint with k variables into disjunctive normal form. By Lemma 2.1.1, there are $2^{2^{m+k}}$ different monotone inequality constraints in disjunctive normal form.

In case 3 we can argue similarly to case 2 that there are a finite number of different Boolean equality and inequality constraints formable from k variables and the constants in D.

In each case, because there is a finite number of atomic constraints, by Theorem 9.4.2 the least fixpoint is closed-form evaluable.   ∎

Example 9.4.1   We can ask a number of questions about the musical group described in Exercise 9 of Chapter 7. For example, who could play the piano? We can find that out using the following query:

$$piano\,(p) \quad :\!\!-\quad plays\,(d, f, g, o, p, v, t).$$

Similarly, we can find out whether any person plays both the drum and the flute, by the following query:

$$drum\_and\_flute\,(d, f) \quad :\!-\quad plays\,(d, f, g, o, p, v, t).$$

We can evaluate these Datalog queries by successive existential quantifier elimination as described in Example 9.1.1. For example, the output of the second query is the constraint tuple $d \cap f \neq \emptyset$, which means that there is someone who can play both the drum and the flute.

The second technique to prove termination is based on geometry. We say that a point *dominates* another point if it has the same dimension and all of its coordinate values are greater than or equal to the corresponding coordinate values in the other point.

Lemma 9.4.1   In any fixed dimension, any sequence of distinct points with only natural number coordinates must be finite, if no point dominates any earlier point in the sequence.

Proof. We prove the theorem by induction on the dimension k of the space in which the points lie. For $k = 0$, the whole space is only a single point, hence the theorem holds. Now we assume that the theorem holds for k dimensions and show that it is true for $k + 1$ dimensions.

Let S be any arbitrary sequence of points in which no point dominates any earlier point. Let $x_1, \ldots, x_{k+1}$ be the coordinate axis of the $k + 1$ dimensional space, and let $(a_1, \ldots, a_{k+1})$ be the first point in S. By the requirement of nondominating and distinctness, for any later point $(b_1, \ldots, b_{k+1})$ for some $i, 0 < i \leq k + 1$ it must be true that $b_i < a_i$. That means that any point in the sequence after $(a_1, \ldots, a_{k+1})$ must be within one or more of the k-dimensional regions $x_1 = 0$, $x_1 = 1, \ldots, x_1 = a_1, \ldots, x_{k+1} = 0, x_{k+1} = 1, \ldots,$ or $x_{k+1} = a_{k+1}$.

As we add points to each of these regions from S, no point can dominate any earlier one within these regions. Therefore, by the induction hypothesis, only a finite number of points from S can be placed into each of these k-dimensional regions. Because the number of these regions is finite, S must also be finite.   ∎

Theorem 9.4.6   Let $\mathcal{C}$ be any constraint theory subset of linear inequality constraints. Let Q be any Datalog with $\mathcal{C}$ query and D be any $\mathcal{C}$ constraint input database D. Then $lfp(Q(D))$ is finitely computable over both integers and rational numbers as the domain of the variables if there exists an $l_{\min} \leq 0$ and a p such that $\mathcal{C}$ has a closed existential quantifier elimination that creates only conjunctions of atomic constraints such that:

1. there is a finite number N of different left-hand sides of the atomic constraints, and

2. in each atomic constraint the bound is an integer or rational number with denominator p and is greater than or equal to $l_{\min}$.

Proof. Let us fix any ordering of the N possible left-hand sides of the atomic constraints. Using this fixed ordering, we can represent any conjunction S of C atomic constraints as an N-dimensional point in which the ith coordinate value will be $p(b - l_{\min}) + 1$ if S contains one or more atomic constraints with the ith left-hand side and b is the largest bound in them, and 0 otherwise.

Let $R(x_1, \ldots, x_n)$ be any defined relation in Q. Because quantifier elimination is closed in C, the constraint bottom-up evaluation derives only new constraint tuples for R that are conjunctions of atomic constraints satisfying conditions 1 and 2. The sequence of derived constraint tuples can be represented as described earlier using a point sequence:

$$p_1, p_2, \ldots$$

It is easy to see that if point p_i dominates point p_j, then p_i and p_j represent conjunctions S_i and S_j of atomic constraints such that the set of solutions of S_i is included in the set of solutions of S_j. This shows that the constraint bottom-up evaluation adds only points that do not dominate any earlier point in the sequence. Note that each coordinate value of each point must be a natural number in the preceding representation. Therefore by Lemma 9.4.1 only a finite number of constraint tuples will be added to relation R. This shows that for each relation we can add only a finite number of constraint tuples. Hence the constraint bottom-up evaluation must terminate. ∎

Next we see a few applications of Theorem 9.4.6.

Theorem 9.4.7   The least fixpoint of any Datalog query and input database with gap-order, lower bound, and upper bound constraints is closed-form evaluable when the domain of the variables is integers or rational numbers.

Proof. We can always find an $l < 0$ and a $p > 0$ for each query Q and input database D such that in each atomic constraint the bound is $\geq l$ and each constant is an integer or a rational number with denominator p. By Theorem 9.1.3 the existential quantifier elimination is closed for conjunctions of such atomic constraints.

Further, if a relation has n variables $x_1, \ldots, x_n$ in it, then it can easily be seen that each atomic constraint can have as its left-hand side only one of the following: $x_i - x_j$, x_i, or $-x_i$ where $1 \leq i, j \leq n$, and $i \neq j$. Hence there are only $n(n + 1)$ different left-hand sides. Therefore, by Theorem 9.4.6 the least fixpoint is closed-form evaluable. ∎

Theorem 9.4.8   The least fixpoint of any Datalog query and input database with half-addition, lower bound, and upper bound constraints is closed-form evaluable when the domain of the variables is integers or rational numbers.

Proof. We can always find an $l < 0$ and a $p > 0$ for each query Q and input database D such that in each atomic constraint the bound is $\geq l$ and each constant is an integer or rational number with denominator p. By Theorem 9.1.4 existential quantifier elimination is closed in this theory.

If a relation has n variables $x_1, \ldots, x_n$ in it, then it can easily be seen that each half-addition, lower bound, and upper bound constraint with at least one variable can be written to have as its left-hand side only one of the following: x_i and $-x_i$ and $x_i - x_j$ where $i \neq j$, $x_i + x_j$, or $-x_i - x_j$ where $i < j$ and $1 \leq i, j \leq n$. Hence there are only $n(n+1) + n(n-1) = 2n^2$ different left-hand sides. Therefore, by Theorem 9.4.6 the least fixpoint is closed-form evaluable. ■

Theorem 9.4.9 The least fixpoint of any Datalog query and input database with gap-order, lower bound, upper bound, and positive linear constraints is closed-form evaluable when the domain of the variables is integers or rational numbers.

Proof. Put each positive linear constraint in the query and the input database into normal form. After that we can always find l, m, p, and s as required in the conditions of Theorem 9.1.5. By the same theorem the existential quantifier elimination is closed for conjunctions of such atomic constraints.

If a relation has n variables $x_1, \ldots, x_n$ in it, then it can easily be seen that each gap-order, lower bound, and upper bound atomic constraint can have as its left-hand side only one of the following: $x_i - x_j$, x_i, or $-x_i$ where $1 \leq i, j \leq m$, and $i \neq j$.

Further, in each positive normal linear constraint each coefficient is a positive integer and the sum of the coefficients is at most s. Therefore each coefficient is an integer between 1 and s. Because the maximum arity is m of any positive normal linear constraint, the number of possible left-hand sides is at most $s^m \binom{n}{m}$. Therefore, by Theorem 9.4.6 the least fixpoint is closed-form evaluable. ■

The following is similar to the preceding, but uses negative linear constraints and the quantifier elimination in Theorem 9.1.6.

Theorem 9.4.10 The least fixpoint of any Datalog query and input database with gap-order, lower bound, upper bound, and negative linear constraints is closed-form evaluable when the domain of the variables is integers or rational numbers. ■

There is another type of application of Theorem 9.4.6. The main idea behind this is that in a linear constraint the value of the bound may be so small that we do not care too much about it. This leads to the idea of placing a limit l on the allowed smallest bound. To avoid smaller bounds than l, we may do two different modifications to a constraint tuple:

Modification 1: We change in the constraint tuple the value of any bound b to be $\max(b, l)$.

Modification 2: We delete from each constraint tuple any constraint with a bound that is less than l.

We can apply either of these modifications to each tuple in an input constraint database. During the constraint bottom-up evaluation we can also apply either of the modifications to the result of each rule application. In this way, we obtain modified bottom-up evaluations.

Given a query Q, input database D, and a fixed constant l, let $Q(D)_l$ and $Q(D)^l$ denote the output of the first and second modified evaluation algorithms, respectively. We can show the following.

Theorem 9.4.11 For any Datalog with integer or rational addition constraint program Q, input database D, and constant $l < 0$, the following is true:

$$Q(D)_l \subseteq lpf(Q(D)) \subseteq Q(D)^l$$

Further, $Q(D)_l$ and $Q(D)^l$ can be evaluated in finite time.

Proof. This is like the case in Theorem 9.4.8, except that half-addition is replaced with addition constraints. Therefore, the Datalog bottom-up evaluation can be done similarly, except that after each rule application some bounds may become less than l and have to be changed by one of the modifications.

In the case of the first modification, the modified tuple implies the original one. Therefore, after any number of rule applications the output relations obtained by the modified algorithm also imply the output relations obtained by the original algorithm. This shows that $Q(D)_l \subseteq lpf(Q(D))$.

In the case of the second modification, the original tuple implies the modified one. Therefore, after any number of rule applications the output relations obtained by the original algorithm also imply the output relations obtained by the modified algorithm. This shows that $lpf(Q(D)) \subseteq Q(D)^l$.

Clearly, there is a finite number of different left-hand sides of atomic addition constraints. That satisfies condition 1 of Theorem 9.4.6. Condition 2 we get free by choosing $l = l_{min}$. Therefore, by that theorem both $Q(D)_l$ and $Q(D)^l$ can be evaluated in finite time. ∎

We can also get better and better approximations using smaller and smaller values as bounds. In particular, we have the following theorem.

Theorem 9.4.12 For any Datalog with addition constraints program Q, input database D, and constants l_1 and l_2 such that $l_1 \leq l_2 < 0$, the following hold:

$$Q(D)_{l_2} \subseteq Q(D)_{l_1} \quad \text{and} \quad Q(D)^{l_1} \subseteq Q(D)^{l_2} \qquad ∎$$

Theorem 9.4.13 For any Datalog with integer or rational difference, lower bound, upper bound, and positive linear constraints program Q, input database D, and constant $l < 0$, the following is true:

$$Q(D)_l \subseteq lpf(Q(D)) \subseteq Q(D)^l$$

Further, $Q(D)_l$ and $Q(D)^l$ can be evaluated in finite time.

Proof. We can argue similarly to Theorem 9.4.11 for the containment. We can argue similarly to Theorem 9.4.9 for the finite number of left-hand sides. Again we can choose $l = l_{min}$ and apply Theorem 9.4.6 to show termination. ∎

Example 9.4.2 Consider the Datalog program in Example 4.1.7. This program contains only difference constraints. Therefore by Theorem 9.4.13 the lower and upper approximations of its least fixpoint model can be found in finite time. Before discussing the approximation, let us note that in this case the least fixpoint of the Datalog program can be expressed as the relation

$$\{(x, y, z) \ : \ \exists k \ \ x \geq z, \ z - x \geq -200k, \ z - y \geq 300k\}$$

This relation is not expressible as a finite set of gap-order constraint facts. However, we can express for each fixed $l < -200$ the relation

$$\{(x, y, z) \ : \ \exists k \ \ x \geq z, \ z - x \geq max(l, -200k), \ z - y \geq 300k\}$$

as a finite set of gap-order constraint facts. This would be a lower bound of the semantics of the *Balance* relation. We can also express the relation

$$\{(x, y, z) \ : \exists k \ \left\{ \begin{array}{ll} x \geq z, z - x \geq -200k, z - y \geq 300k & \text{if } -200k \geq l \\ x \geq z, \ z - y \geq 300k & \text{otherwise} \end{array} \right\}\}$$

as a finite set of difference constraint tuples. This would be an upper bound of the least fixpoint of the *Balance* relation.

The approximation could be used to decide whether some particular tuple of constants is in the least fixpoint. For example, is it possible that the account balances are at any time $x = 1500$, $y = 200$, and $z = 1000$? When we use an approximate evaluation with $l = -1000$, we see that it is not in the upper bound of the semantics of the *Balance* relation. Hence $(1500, 200, 1000)$ is not in the least fixpoint of the *Balance* relation.

9.4.1 Relations with Different Types of Constraints

From a practical point of view, we can allow the variables in a constraint relation to range over different domains. Then the constraint tuple contains conjunctions of two or more types of atomic constraints. For example, some variables may be Boolean and other variables may be integers. In this case, the constraints over the Boolean variables can be separated from the constraints over the integer variables. When we have to eliminate a Boolean variable we do variable elimination using only the Boolean constraints and preserve intact all the constraints on the integer variables. Similarly, if we have to eliminate an integer variable, we use the variable elimination over the integer constraints and do not change the Boolean constraints within the constraint tuple.

9.4.2   Parametric Evaluation

For Boolean algebras there is a representation theorem, known as *Stone's theorem*: "Every Boolean algebra is isomorphic to Boolean algebra of sets (where $\wedge$, $\vee$, $'$ are interpreted as $\cap$, $\cup$, and set difference from 1, respectively) and every finite Boolean algebra is isomorphic to the power set of a finite set." Thus, there is a unique (up to isomorphism) finite Boolean algebra for every cardinality 2^m.

By Stone's representation theorem, if we know the interpretation ahead of time, then we can substitute the constants and functions of the Boolean algebra and obtain a set algebra, which we know how to evaluate. If we do not know the interpretation ahead of time, then we can evaluate the query using the free Boolean algebra. What we obtain is a *parametric evaluation* of the query.

Theorem 9.4.14   The least fixpoint of any Datalog query Q and input database D with free Boolean algebra constraints is closed-form evaluable under any specific interpretation $I = (B, \sigma)$ if (1) there are only Boolean equality constraints, (2) there are only simple Boolean upper bound and monotone inequality constraints, or (3) B is an atomless Boolean algebra. The evaluation can be done on the free Boolean algebra and then the result interpreted, or the input database and program can be interpreted and the evaluation can be done on the specific Boolean algebra. That is,

$$I(Q(D)) = Q(I(D)) \qquad\blacksquare$$

Parametric tuples should not be confused with constraint tuples. A constraint tuple describes the set of all tuples that one gets by substituting values for its variables. A parametric tuple describes a single tuple, given a substitution for its parameters. Parametric constraint tuples do both.

Example 9.4.3   Consider again the parity query in Example 4.3.1. Under the parametric evaluation using the free Boolean algebra B_n, we would get:

$$Paritybit(x) :\!\!- x =_{B_n} c_1 \oplus c_2 \oplus \ldots \oplus c_n$$

Now suppose that we have the interpretation B_0 as in Example 2.1.1 and each c_i is interpreted as *false* for i odd and *true* for i even. Under this interpretation *Paritybit* will be *false* if n is odd and *true* if n is even.

Alternatively, by making the interpretation of the parametric tuples in relation *Parity* and then evaluating the query in B_0 instead of B_n, we would get the same result.

Example 9.4.4   Let us now consider the parametric evaluation of Example 4.3.2. Replacing the CS_Minor subgoal with its only constraint tuple yields:

$$Can\_Apply\_CS\_MS\,(y) \quad :\!\!- \quad x \leq_B c' \wedge (d \vee s), \ \ x' \wedge y \leq_B c.$$

Here we have to eliminate the variable y from a conjunction of Boolean upper bound constraints. Using the procedure described in the proof of Theorem 9.1.9 we get the following:

$$Can\_Apply\_CS\_MS\,(y) \quad :\!\!- \quad y \leq_B c \vee (c' \wedge (d \vee s)).$$

Now let us assume the interpretation B for the Boolean algebra operators as in Example 2.1.8, and for the constants σ_4 as follows:

$$\sigma_4(a) = \{1, 2, 5, 6\}$$
$$\sigma_4(c) = \{5, 6, 7, 8\}$$
$$\sigma_4(d) = \{2, 4, 6, 8\}$$
$$\sigma_4(m) = \{1, 2, 3, 4\}$$
$$\sigma_4(s) = \{3, 6\}$$

Hence the last constraint tuple becomes $y \subseteq \{2, 3, 4, 5, 6, 7, 8\}$ after using substitution for the constants.

Alternatively, we can consider the evaluation of the Datalog query by first substituting. Then we obtain the following.

$Math\_Minor(x)$:— $x \subseteq \{5, 6, 7, 8\} \cap \{1, 2, 5, 6\}.$

$CS\_Minor(x)$:— $x \subseteq \{1, 2, 3, 4\} \cap (\{2, 4, 6, 8\} \cup \{3, 6\}).$

$Can\_Apply\_CS\_MS(y)$:— $CS\_Minor(x), x' \cap y \subseteq \{5, 6, 7, 8\}.$

It can be seen that when we evaluate this, we get the same result.

Bibliographic Notes

Quantifier elimination algorithms have a long history. One simple quantifier elimination method for conjunctions of Boolean equality constraints can be said to originate with George Boole. It was used in [159], but it is rather inefficient. Theorem 9.1.7 is another early quantifier elimination method for rational linear equality constraints and is due to Fourier [99]. Theorem 9.1.8 on real polynomial constraints is by Tarski and is described in [303]. Both of the last two algorithms are computationally inefficient, but better algorithms were developed by several other authors for both linear constraints [199, 198, 200] and for polynomial constraints, including Basu [19], Ben-Or et al. [26], Caviness and Johnson [53], Collins [69], Renegar [254] and Van Den Dries [312]. Quantifier elimination with linear constraints over the integers was considered by Williams [327] and over the reals by Ferrante and Rackoff [94].

Theorems 9.1.1 and 9.1.2 on variable elimination, as well as Theorems 9.4.3, 9.4.4, and 9.4.5 on closed-form least fixpoint evaluations, are from Kanellakis et al. [158, 159]. An efficient quantifier elimination algorithm for rational order constraint formulas was also given by Ferrante and Geiser [93]. All of these closed-form evaluation results relied on the observation that only a finite number of atomic constraints are expressible in these cases. Theorem 9.4.2 is a generalization of that observation.

Some additional finite cases were discovered later. These include Boolean upper bound and monotone Boolean inequality constraints in free Boolean algebras as well as equality and inequality constraints in atomless Boolean algebras. Theorems 9.1.9, 9.1.11, and 9.4.5 are from Revesz [265]. The quantifier elimination method for atomless Boolean algebras in Theorem 9.1.10 is by Marriott and Odersky [204]. Further discussion on Boolean constraint solving can be found in Buttner and Simonis [47] and in Martin and Nipkow [206]. Upper bound constraints in Boolean algebras include the case of set containment constraints between set variables in the specific Boolean algebra B_Z. A Datalog least fixpoint evaluation for this specific case was described in Revesz [258].

Lemma 9.4.1 is variously known as Dickson's or Higman's lemma and is used in several different types of well-structured transition systems, which are reviewed by Finkel and Schnoebelen [95]. It has been rediscovered several times in the literature, including by the author, and its present form and proof is from Revesz [255, 257]. Several fixpoint evaluation termination results rely on that lemma, and Theorem 9.4.6 is a new summary of that fact. Kuijpers et al. [190] discusses termination of spatial Datalog queries.

In particular, gap-order constraints were considered and Theorems 9.1.3 and 9.4.7 were proven in Revesz [255, 257]. Half-addition, positive, and negative linear constraints were considered and Theorems 9.1.4, 9.1.5, and 9.1.6 on variable elimination and Theorems 9.4.8, 9.4.9, and 9.4.10 on least fixpoint evaluation were proven in Revesz [266]. The modified least fixpoint evaluation algorithms and Theorems 9.4.11, 9.4.12, and 9.4.13 are from Revesz [268].

Quantifier elimination for difference constraints over the rational numbers is studied in Koubarakis [179]. Efficient variable elimination algorithms for difference constraints, addition constraints, and their disjunctive extensions can be found in [182, 183, 184]. Variable elimination for addition constraints and for two-variable-per-inequality linear constraints is studied in Hochbaum and Naor [144], Goldin and Kanellakis [112], Jaffar et al. [152], and Harvey and Stuckey [140].

Parametric evaluation of Datalog queries was considered in [159]. Example 9.4.3 is from that paper, and Example 9.4.4 is from [265]. Stone's representation theorem and other general background on Boolean algebras is described in Burris and Sankappanavar [46] and Halmos [138].

The general relational algebra evaluation method in Theorem 9.2.1 is from [267]. Specific relational algebra evaluation methods will be discussed in Chapter 12, and more bibliography references can be found at the end of that chapter.

Evaluation of SQL queries with *Max* and *Min* aggregate operators based on linear programming were considered in Brodsky et al. [44] and Revesz and Li [274]. The classic book on linear programming is by Dantzig [74]; the method described there is known as the simplex method. In the worst case the simplex algorithm requires an exponential number of steps in the size of the problem. Efficient polynomial time algorithms have been found for this problem by Khachiyan [171] and Karmarkar [163]. Chvatal [64] and Schrijver [284] are more recent books on linear programming that include the newer methods.

Megiddo [210] considers the computational complexity of linear programming when the dimension is fixed. Yannakakis [334] is a recent review of linear programming and its applications.

Exercises

1. Assume that x, y, z, and w are variables. Eliminate variable x from the following conjunctions of rational half-addition, lower bound, and upper bound constraints:

    $$x - z \geq 3$$
    $$y - z \geq 8$$
    $$w - y \geq 2$$
    $$w - x \geq 4$$
    $$-w \geq -40$$
    $$z \geq 20$$

2. Assume that x, y, z, and w are variables. Eliminate variable x from the following conjunctions of rational linear constraints:

    $$x + 3y - z \geq 5$$
    $$-2x + 4y - 8z \geq -8$$
    $$-x + 3z \geq 4$$
    $$3x - 27y \geq 3$$

3. Assume that x, y, z, and w are variables and a, b, c, d, and e are constant symbols of a free Boolean algebra. Eliminate variable x from the following conjunctions of constraints:

    $$x \wedge y \leq (a \vee b) \wedge c'$$
    $$x' \wedge y' \wedge z \leq (a \wedge d') \vee (a \wedge e)$$
    $$x \wedge w \leq (d \vee e)$$
    $$x' \wedge w' \leq (a \vee c)$$
    $$(x \wedge y) \vee z \neq 0$$

4. Which of the conjunction of constraints in the previous exercises are satisfiable? Prove your answer.

5. Are conjunctions of integer order constraints closed under existential quantifier elimination? Why or why not?

6. Are conjunctions of integer linear inequality constraints closed under existential quantifier elimination? Why or why not?

10

Computational Complexity

In this chapter we consider the computational complexity of evaluating constraint queries. In Section 10.1 we start with a brief review of the most important complexity classes, models of computation, and complexity measures. Section 10.2 discusses the computational complexity of relational algebra, Section 10.3 discusses the complexity of Datalog queries, and finally Section 10.4 discusses the complexity of stratified Datalog queries.

10.1 Complexity Classes and Measures

In this chapter readers are assumed to be familiar with the following complexity classes:

- LOGSPACE—deterministic logarithmic space with one processor

- NC—deterministic logarithmic time with a polynomial number of processors

- P—deterministic polynomial time with one processor

- PSPACE—deterministic polynomial space with one processor

- EXP—deterministic exponential time with one processor

- iEXP—deterministic i levels of exponential time with one processor

These complexity classes are increasingly powerful. Later ones include all earlier ones. We also assume familiarity with the concept of hardness and completeness of complexity classes and Turing machines, which is the computation model for all complexity classes, except that in the class NC we can use the PRAM computational model.

The size of the query evaluation problem is often divided into two parts: the program part and the data part. When we are interested in the complexity of query evaluation we would sometimes like to know how much the complexity depends on the size of each part. Hence we may talk of three different measures of computational complexity.

- **Data Complexity:** This measures the computational complexity of a fixed program and a variable size database.

- **Expression Complexity:** This measures the computational complexity when the size of the program may change and the database is fixed.

- **Combined Complexity:** This measures the computational complexity when both the size of the program and the database may change.

Data complexity makes sense when we think about the library of programs that is provided to users. Because the set of programs in the library is fixed, the users may be interested in knowing the computational complexity of those programs on their variable size databases.

Another motivation for data complexity may be that the size of the database often dominates the size of the program. This certainly seems true for relational database systems in practice. However, it may be unwarranted to jump to the conclusion that it will also be true for constraint databases. In fact, because constraint tuples can describe an infinite number of constant tuples, we may expect that they could sometimes provide a very condensed description of the user's data. Therefore, the size of the constraint databases may be much smaller than the relational databases. Hence in the following we will consider both complexity measures. Also, whenever we use logarithms we assume that the base is two unless otherwise indicated.

10.2   Complexity of Relational Algebra

As we mentioned in Chapter 3, relational algebra can be easily rewritten to relational calculus. The rewriting is a simple mapping that replaces some symbols of relational algebra with other symbols in relational calculus. We also mentioned that constraint relations can be viewed as a disjunction of constraint tuples, that is, as a disjunctive normal form formulas of some type of atomic constraints. If we replace in the relational calculus expressions the relational symbols with the corresponding disjunctive normal form formula we get what is called a *first-order formula of constraints*.

Quantifier elimination from a first-order formula of constraints is similar to existential quantifier eliminations from conjunctions of constraints as described in Chapter 9, but it is more complex, because we also have to deal with disjunctions and negations in the formula. We do not give details of these more complex quantifier eliminations because they have been studied extensively by many researchers, and good descriptions can be found in many other books. We note, however, the following connection between quantifier eliminations from first-order formulas and relational algebra query evaluations.

Theorem 10.2.1   Let C be any type of constraint. If we can do closed-form quantifier elimination from C constraint formulas of size n in $f(n)$ time, then the output of each relational algebra query on C constraint relations can be evaluated in $O(f(n))$ time.

∎

This translation from relational algebra query evaluation to quantifier elimination from formulas does not yield a nicely structured algebraic evaluation like that described in Section 9.2.1. However, Theorem 10.2.1 is useful to prove several computational complexity results, by taking advantage of what is known about the complexity of various quantifier elimination from formulas. In particular, some of the relational algebra with constraints combined complexity results that can be shown using Theorem 10.2.1 are summarized in Figure 10.1. In Figure 10.1 and most of this section we are interested only in complexity class classifications.

10.2.1 Normal Form Relations

The problem of relational algebra query evaluation is greatly simplified when we know that there can be only a finite number of different atomic constraints. In these cases it is also possible to describe the maximum size that any constraint relation can contain. Therefore, in these cases the complexity of the query evaluation can be analyzed in a simpler way than by using Theorem 10.2.1.

Domain	Constraint	Data complexity	Combined complexity
Q, Z	Lower bound, upper bound, gap-order	LOGSPACE-comp	PSPACE-comp
Q, Z	Lower bound, upper bound, half-addition	LOGSPACE-comp	PSPACE-comp
Q, Z	Difference	LOGSPACE-comp	PSPACE-comp
Q, Z	Addition	in NC	PSPACE-comp
Q, Z	Linear	in NC	EXP-comp
R	Polynomial	in NC	EXP-comp

FIGURE 10.1. Relational algebra computational complexity (I).

Query evaluation is more efficient when the constraint relations are in *normal form*. The main purpose of normal forms is to reduce the size of the representation of constraint tuples and to eliminate redundancies of representation.

Let $A = \{a_1, \ldots, a_l\}$ be the set of constant symbols that appear in the input database or the relational algebra program. Note that for each instance of query evaluation (input database and program) A is only a small finite part of a larger domain of possible constant symbols. We consider in this section only constraints for which the output relation can also be represented by using only constants in A.

The following lemma can be used to simplify the query evaluation in the case of Boolean constraints.

Lemma 10.2.1 Query evaluation in any free Boolean algebra with l constants can be translated to a query evaluation in a Boolean algebra with $m = 2^l$ constants where the conjunction of any pair of constant symbols is 0.

Proof. Let $D = \{c_1, \ldots, c_m\}$ for $m \leq 2^l$ be the distinct ground minterms of the Boolean algebra defined by $A = \{a_1, \ldots, a_l\}$. Then we have that $c_i \wedge c_j = 0$.

We can eliminate the constants in A by replacing each with some equivalent disjunction of the minterms. Therefore, the query evaluation in B_A can be translated to a query evaluation in B_D, which is a Boolean algebra where conjunction of any two constant symbols is the zero element. After the query evaluation, we can translate back from B_D to B_A by writing each c_i in terms of the constants in A. ∎

Before defining normal forms, we need some more definitions in the case of Boolean constraints. Recall that for any set of constant symbols D as earlier and set of variable symbols $\{x_1, \ldots, x_k\}$ we can define a free Boolean algebra B_{k+m}. We already defined minterms of B_{k+m}. We will refine that concept in the following definitions:

- We call *ground minterm* a minterm of the subalgebra B_m, i.e., conjunctions of unnegated or negated constants.

- We call *variable minterm* a minterm of the subalgebra B_k, i.e., conjunctions of unnegated or negated variables.

- We call *monotone minterm* any conjunction of one or more unnegated variables and a ground minterm. That is, in a monotone minterm each variable is either unnegated or absent and each constant appears either negated or unnegated.

Example 10.2.1 If we have a query in B_Z such that the constants that appear in the query are $D = \{\{2\}, \{5\}, \{9\}\}$, then there will be four nonzero ground minterms in the transformed algebra, namely, $\{2\}, \{5\}, \{9\}$, and $Z - \{2, 5, 9\}$.

Hence in the rest of this section, we will assume that $D = \{c_1, \ldots, c_m\}$ is the set of constants that appear in the query and that for each pair $c_i \wedge c_j = 0$.

- We call *minterm equality constraints* those equality constraints in which the left-hand side is a minterm. We call *(monotone) minterm inequality constraints* those inequality constraints in which the left-hand side is a (monotone) minterm.

- We call *minterm upper bound constraints* those upper bound constraints in which the left-hand side is a variable minterm and the right-hand side is a ground minterm.

- We call *minterm order constraints* monotone minterm inequality constraints and those precedence constraints in which the left-hand side is an unnegated variable and the right-hand side is a monotone Boolean minterm.

Remark 10.2.1   Each order constraint is equivalent to a conjunction of minterm order constraints.

Now we define for various types of constraints *normal form constraint tuples* with k variables as follows:

Equality: Each constraint tuple contains at most k equality constraints between variables. For each equivalence class with variables $x_1, \ldots, x_n$ and optionally some constant c we have a conjunction of constraints $x_1 = x_2, \ldots, x_{n-1} = x_n, x_n = c$. The constant must appear as the last element in the conjunction that represents the equivalence class.

Equality and Inequality: Each constraint tuple contains a conjunction of equality constraints as described earlier. In addition, for each pair of equality classes, including single variables, the tuple also contains an inequality constraint between their last elements, unless those are both constants. Finally, if the last element x of an equivalence class is a variable, then there is also an inequality constraint $x \neq c_i$ for each $1 \leq i \leq m$.

Rational Order: We may assume that $c_i < c_j$ whenever $i < j$. Each constraint tuple contains for each variable x one of the following: $x < c_1, c_m < x, c_i < x, x < c_{i+1}$, or $x \geq c_i, x \leq c_i$ for some $1 \leq i \leq m$. In addition, the tuple contains for some permutation $x_1, \ldots, x_k$ of the variables either $x_i < x_{i+1}$ or $x_i \leq x_{i+1}, x_{i+1} \leq x_i$ for each $1 \leq i < m$.

Boolean Equality: Each constraint tuple contains only constraint of the form $m_i \wedge c_j = 0$, where m_i is a variable minterm and c_j is a constant.

Atomless Boolean Equality and Inequality: Each constraint tuple contains for each variable minterm m_i and constant c_j either $m_i \wedge c_j = 0$ or $m_i \wedge c_j \neq 0$.

Boolean Order: Each constraint tuple contains for each variable and one element on one side at most one order constraint with the monotone function in monotone disjunctive normal form. In addition, the tuple contains minterm monotone inequality constraints of the form $m_i c_j \neq 0$, where m_i is a monotone variable minterm.

Boolean Binary Order: Each constraint tuple contains at most k^2 binary order constraints between pairs of variables and $2k$ binary order constraints between a variable on one side and disjunctions of constants on the other side.

We say that a $\mathcal{C}$ constraint relation is in normal form if each constraint tuple in it is in normal form, and there are no duplicate tuples. We say that a $\mathcal{C}$ constraint database is in normal form if each constraint relation in it is in normal form.

Remark 10.2.2   Some details are skipped here about orderings of the constraints and specific forms of the constraints. These details are important to efficiently check for duplicate tuples, because otherwise the same constraint could be in different forms and the atomic constraints may appear in any permutations if we do not fix some standard forms and orderings. We give one example. In B_{k+m} we can fix an order of the variables and the constant symbols. Then we keep in each minterm the variables and constants in increasing order, and we keep an ordering of the minterms similar to that in Lemma 2.1.1. We also keep the constraint tuples in sorted order. Having these fixed orderings enables us to check for duplicates in linear time in the size of the constraint relations.

Remark 10.2.3   In this section we take the size of the representation of each constant and variable to be a constant.

The following theorem shows that in the normal forms, the maximum number of atomic constraints in each tuple and the maximum number of constraint tuples in each relation depends only on k and m.

Theorem 10.2.2   Let $\mathcal{C}$ be any type of constraint listed earlier. Let m be the number of different constants in use. Then each k-arity normal form $\mathcal{C}$ constraint tuple contains at most as many atomic constraints and has size, and each k-arity normal form $\mathcal{C}$ constraint relation contains at most as many tuples as shown in Figure 10.2.

Proof.   For each type of constraint we analyze the maximum number of atomic constraints in a normal form tuple, the maximum number of tuples in a normal form relation, and the maximum size of a normal form relation.

Equality

Number of Atomic Constraints: Each equivalence class with n elements is represented using $n - 1$ equality constraints. Hence we need at most k equality constraints in each normal form tuple.

Domain	Constraint	Number of tuples in relation
$\mathcal{Q}, \mathcal{Z}$	Equality	$(m+k)^k$
$\mathcal{Q}, \mathcal{Z}$	Equality, inequality	$(m+k)^k$
$\mathcal{Q}$	Order	$k!\,(4m)^k$
$\mathcal{B}$	Equality	$2^{2^{k+\log m}}$
$\mathcal{B}^{aless}$	Equality, inequality	$2^{2^{k+\log m}}$
$\mathcal{B}$	Order	$2^{2^{k+\log k+\log m}}$
$\mathcal{B}$	Binary order	2^{k^2+2km}

FIGURE 10.2. Normal form sizes: O(number of tuples).

Number of Constraint Tuples: We can assign to the first variable any of the m constants or some new unspecified constant. We can assign to the second variable any of the m constants or the previously assigned unspecified constant or some new unspecified constant. We can continue in this way untill the last variable. Each assignment clearly describes a unique constraint tuple. Therefore, there are $O((m+1)(m+2)\ldots(m+k)) = O((m+k)!/m!) \leq O((m+k)^k)$ different normal form constraint tuples.

Size: By Remark 10.2.3, the size of each normal form relation is a constant factor of the number of tuples.

Equality and Inequality

Number of Atomic Constraints: We have $O(k)$ equality and $O(k^2+km)$ inequality constraints in each normal form tuple.

Number of Constraint Tuples: We have the same number of tuples as in the case of only equality constraints because each constraint tuple describes a partition into equivalence classes as in the case of only equality constraints. We only add inequality constraints to each partition to make sure that elements of different equivalence classes are different for each instantiation of the constraint tuple.

Size: By Remark 10.2.3, the size of each normal form relation is a constant factor of the number of tuples.

Order

Number of Atomic Constraints: We have at most $2k$ constraints between variables. We also have at most $2k$ constraints between variables and constants.

Number of Constraint Tuples: We have $k!$ possible permutations of k variables. Each permutation can be extended to a total ordering by adding between adjacent elements either $>$ or two $\leq$ to denote equality. Hence there are $k!2^k$ total orderings of the variables. Each variable must belong to one of the $m+1$ intervals between constants or to one of the m constants. Hence for each variable there are $2m+1$ choices. Therefore, there are $O(k!\, 2^k (2m+1)^k) = O(k!\, (4m)^k)$ choices.

Size: By Remark 10.2.3, the size of each normal form relation is a constant factor of the number of tuples.

Boolean Equality

Number of Atomic Constraints: There are 2^k different left variable minterms and m different constants, therefore $2^k m = 2^{k+\log m}$ different atomic constraints.

Number of Constraint Tuples: Each atomic constraint may or may not be present in a constraint tuple. Hence there are at most $2^{2^{k+\log m}}$ different constraint tuples.

Size: The size of each minterm equality constraint is k, therefore, the size of each constraint tuple is $O(k2^{k+\log m}) \leq O(2^{k+\log k+\log m})$.

Atomless Boolean Equality and Inequality

Number of Atomic Constraints: There are $2^k m$ different left-hand sides in the minterm equality and inequality constraints. Therefore, there are that many atomic constraints in each constraint tuple.

Number of Constraint Tuples: There are $2^{2^{k+\log m}}$ possible constraint tuples.

Size: The size of each minterm equality and inequality constraint is $O(k)$. Therefore the total size of each constraint tuple is at most $O(k2^{2^{k+\log m}})$.

Boolean Order

Number of Atomic Constraints: There are at most $k+1$ monotone upper bound constraints because there are k variables and the one element. Also, there are at most $2^{k+\log m}$ monotone minterm inequality constraints in each tuple because there are that many different monotone minterms.

Number of Constraint Tuples: There are at most $2^{k-1}m$ different monotone minterms with $k-1$ variables. Therefore, for each of the variables there are $2^{2^{k-1}m} = O(2^{2^{k+\log m-1}})$ different monotone disjunctive normal form upper bounds. Hence there can only be $O((2^{2^{k+\log m-1}})^k) = O(2^{2^{k+\log k+\log m-1}})$ combinations. In addition, there are $2^{2^{k+\log m}}$ different monotone disjunctive normal form upper bounds for the one element and the monotone inequality constraints. Hence the number of different constraint tuples is at most

$$O(2^{2^{k+\log k+\log m-1}}(2^{2^{k+\log m}})^2) \le O(2^{2^{k+\log k+\log m}})$$

Size: The size of each order constraint is $O(2^k m)$. The size of each monotone-minterm inequality constraint is $O(k)$. Therefore the size of each constraint tuple is at most $O(2^k m(k+1) + 2^k mk) \le O(2^{k+\log k+\log m})$.

Boolean Binary Order

Number of Atomic Constraints: There are k^2 different binary order constraints between pairs of variables. There are $2k2^m$ different binary order constraints between variables and constants. In each constraint tuple by the merge rule, each variable needs at most two binary order constraints with constants, one lower bound and one upper bound.

Number of Constraint Tuples: There are 2^{k^2} combinations of binary order constraints between variables. Also, there are 2^m possible right-hand sides in the binary order constraints between variables and constants. Hence there are at most $(2^{k^2})(2^m)^2 k \le 2^{k^2+2km}$ different constraint tuples.

Size: The size of each var-var set containment constraint is a constant, and the size of each var-constant set containment constraint is $O(m)$. Therefore the size of each constraint tuple is $O(k^2 + 2km) = O(k^2 + km)$.   ∎

We call a normal form constraint tuple C a *cell* if either all the models or none of the models of C satisfy each relational algebra query.

Lemma 10.2.2   The normal form constraint tuples for infinite domain equations and inequations, rational order, and atomless Boolean equality and inequality constraints are cells.

∎

It is easy to take the complement of the difference of relations that are composed of cells.

Next we look at algebraic evaluations assuming that the input constraint relations are in normal form. We will show for each case of constraints that the relational algebra operators can be evaluated efficiently such that the normal forms are preserved.

Lemma 10.2.3 For normal form relations, the project, join, and difference operators can be evaluated in the times shown in Figure 10.3.

Proof. We show the theorem for each case as follows.

Equality

Project: Because this is a subcase of equality and inequality where only equality constraints appear, we may use Theorem 9.1.1 to eliminate variable x. We show that this preserves normal form as follows.

If x appears in the equality constraint tuple, then it must belong to some equivalence class with at least two members. If x appears at the beginning or end of the conjunction of equality constraints that represent the equivalence class x, then just drop the equality constraint in which x appears. Otherwise, if x appears somewhere in the middle of a conjunction of the form $\dots, y = x, x = z, \dots$ Then replace the constraints $y = x$ and $x = z$ with $y = z$. Clearly, this preserves the normal form.

Join: Let us consider the join of two tuples. For each pair of equivalence classes, check that they have any element in common, i.e., that they need to be merged. If we have two equivalence classes that need to be merged of the form $u_1 = u_2, \dots, u_{n-1} = u_n$ and $v_1 = v_2, \dots, v_{m-1} = v_m$, where u_n and v_m are the same

Domain	Constraint	Project (Elim x)	Join	Difference
Q, Z	Equality	$(m+k)^k$	$(m+k)^k$	
Q, Z	Equality, inequality	$(m+k)^k$	$(m+k)^{2k}$	$(m+k)^k$
Q	Order	$k!\,(4m)^k$	$(k!)^2\,(4m)^k$	$k!\,(4m)^k$
B	Equality	$2^{2^{k+\log m}}$	$2^{2^{k+\log m}}$	
B^{aless}	Equality, inequality	$2^{2^{k+\log m}}$	$2^{2^{k+\log m}}$	$2^{2^{k+\log m}}$
B	Order	$2^{2^{k+\log k+\log m+1}}$	$2^{2k+2\log m+\log k}$	
B	Binary order	$2^{k^2+2mk}\,km$	$2^{k^2+2mk}\,km$	

FIGURE 10.3. Relational algebra operator complexity $O(\ )$.

constants, then replace them with $u_1 = u_2, \ldots, u_{n-1} = v_1, v_1 = v_2, \ldots, v_{m-1} = v_m$. If only u_n is a constant or there are no constants, then replace them with $v_1 = v_2, \ldots, v_{m-1} = v_m, v_m = u_1, u_1 = u_2, \ldots, u_{n-1} = u_n$. If only v_m is a constant replace them with $u_1 = u_2, \ldots, u_{n-1} = u_n, u_n = v_1, v_1 = v_2, \ldots, v_{m-1} = v_m$. Delete tuple if it is unsatisfiable. Also delete duplicate tuples.

Equality and Inequality

Project:

Use Theorem 9.1.1 to eliminate equality and inequality constraints. Clearly this preserves normal form.

Join: For each pair of tuples, do the join similarly to the earlier equality case. Note that it may occur that some pair of equivalence classes that do not have a common element do not have an inequality constraint between them. To make the constraint tuple a cell, we can do two things: either add a new inequality constraint between the last elements of these equivalence classes or merge the two equivalence classes. These options create different cells that are all added to the output relation. The number of options is clearly fewer than the total number of possible tuples. Hence we get the result shown in Figure 10.3. Finally, we delete duplicate tuples.

Difference: The output will be those cells that are in the first but not the second argument. This is correct because of the disjointness of cells and Lemma 10.2.2. If we store the cells in each relation in some sorted order, then the difference can be done in linear time in the size of the input relations.

Rational Order

Project: Use Theorem 9.1.2 to eliminate equality and inequality constraints. Eliminate all but the highest lower bound and all but the smallest upper bound constraint for each variables. Clearly this preserves normal form.

Join: For each pair of tuples, if the conjunction of their constraints is satisfiable, then we create several cells by extending the order of the variables in the two arguments into a total order. We add all of the cells to the output relation. The number of options is clearly fewer than $k!$. Hence we get the result shown in Figure 10.3. Finally, we delete duplicate tuples.

Difference: This is similar to the case of infinite domain equality and inequality constraints.

Boolean Equality

Project: We may use Theorem 9.1.9 to eliminate variable x. Let m_x be the minterm m with variable x deleted from it.

Let $x m_{1_x} c_1 = 0$ and $x' m_{2_x} c_2 = 0$ be equality constraints. Then Theorem 9.1.9 will create the equality constraint $m_{1_x} m_{2_x} c_1 c_2 = 0$. Note that the left-hand side is zero if $c_1 \neq c_2$ or $m_{1_x} \neq m_{2_x}$, hence the constraint can be deleted. Otherwise, we create the constraint $m_{1_x} c_1 = 0$, which is equivalent to $m_{2_x} c_2 = 0$. Therefore, the created constraints are simply the original ones with x or x' deleted from them. Clearly this preserves normal form and can be done in linear time.

Join: If the conjunction of constraints is satisfiable, then we create several normal form tuples by extending all possible combinations in each argument the minterms with the variables that occur only in the other argument. We add all of the normal form tuples to the output relation.

Atomless Boolean Equality and Inequality

Project: We can use Theorem 9.1.10. However, we can note a simplification in this case because of the normal form. The elimination of a variable x from a satisfiable normal form atomless Boolean equality and inequality constraint tuple, i.e., cell, can be done by simply deleting x and x' in each minterm within the Boolean equality and inequality constraints. Note that each cell is satisfiable except the one that contains only inequality constraints. That cell can be deleted from any relation. This preserves normal form and can be done in linear time.

Join: This is similar to the case of Boolean equality constraints.

Difference: This is similar to the case of infinite domain equality and inequality constraint.

Boolean Order

Project: We can use Theorem 9.1.11 to eliminate variable x. In this case, u will be the order of x, which we already have in disjunctive normal form, i.e., of the form

$$v_{1,1} c_1 \vee \ldots \vee v_{1,n_1} c_1 \vee \ldots \vee v_{m,1} c_m \vee \ldots \vee v_{m,n_m} c_m$$

where each $v_{i,j}$ is a variable monotone minterm and each c_i is a ground minterm, for $1 \leq i \leq m$ and each $j \leq n_i \leq 2^k$.

In the monotone minterm inequalities, each monotone minterm has the form $v c_i$ where v is a variable monotone minterm and c_i is a ground minterm.

After the substitution of x by u and rewriting using distributivity the left-hand side of the monotone minterm of the preceding form, we get a formula of the form

$$v_{i,1} v c_i \vee \ldots \vee v_{i,n_1} v c_i \neq 0 \qquad (10.1)$$

Note that all terms of u that did not have c_i in them dropped out because the conjunction of two constants is zero. Formula (10.1) has at most 2^k disjuncts. We simplify the formula by eliminating in each $v_{i,j} v$ the duplicate variables and then deleting duplicate disjuncts.

We can do the preceding substitution and simplification for each monotone minterm inequality constraint of the form (10.1). Note that each of the results is equivalent to a disjunction of at most 2^k inequality constraints. Because there are at most $2^k m$ monotone inequality constraints, we have the conjunction of at most that many disjunctions. We can rewrite this conjunctive normal form formula into a disjunctive normal form formula.

The process of rewriting can be done by first taking the conjunction of the first two disjuncts and then eliminating duplicates. Then we take the conjunction of the result with the third disjunct. Then we again eliminate duplicates, and so on until the last disjunct. The elimination of duplicates guarantees that in each disjunct of the temporary relation obtained after each conjunction, we have only $2^k m$ different monotone inequality constraints. Hence the size of the temporary relation is at most $2^{2^{k+\log m}}$ tuples.

We can do the preceding for each constraint tuple. Because originally there are at most $2^{2^{k+\log k+\log m}}$ different tuples, we will get a temporary relation that has at most $2^{2^{k+\log k+\log m+1}}$ tuples before we eliminate duplicate tuples in the output relation.

Note that the conjunction of the order constraints and each disjunct of the formula is a normal form constraint tuple. We add all of these to the database.

Join: We merge the order constraints with the same variable on the right-hand side.

For each variable, there is at most one order constraint in each argument of the join. Because in each of these there are at most $2^k m$ disjuncts on the left-hand side. Merge takes the conjunction of the left-hand sides. When we put that conjunction back into monotone disjunctive normal form, we obtain at most $(2^k m)^2 = 2^{2k+2\log m}$ disjuncts. Then we eliminate duplicates. Doing this for each of the k variables requires at most $O(k2^{2k+2\log m}) = O(2^{2k+2\log m+\log k})$ time.

We also eliminate duplicate monotone inequality constraints, which can be done within the same time.

Boolean Binary Order

Project: Because each Boolean binary order constraint is also an upper bound constraint, we can use Theorem 9.1.9 to eliminate variable x. Then we merge those binary order constraints that have the same variable in them on the same side. We show that this preserves normal form.

The application of Theorem 9.1.9 can be shown to create a binary order constraint $y \leq z$ for each pair of binary order constraints $y \leq x$ and $x \leq z$. Before normalization, x had only one upper bound u and one lower bound v. We take the conjunction (or disjunction) of u (or v) and the upper bound (or the lower bound) of each y for which we have the constraint $y \leq x$ (or $x \leq y$).

Because the constant sides of binary order constraints are disjunctions of minterms, the conjunction of constants will be a disjunction of those minterms that are in each of the constants, and the disjunction of constants will be a disjunction of those minterms that are in at least one of the constants. Therefore, this preserves closed form. For each constraint tuple, the projection of of x requires merging two sets of at most m minterms, each at most $2k$ times. Hence this takes $O(km)$ time for each constraint tuple.

Join: We again merge binary order constraints with the same variable in them in the same side as in the preceding project. Then we eliminate duplicate constraints.

∎

It is now obvious that any relational algebra query can be evaluated using normal form relations. However, to improve the space efficiency of the query evaluation, it is better to test one at a time for each normal form tuple C whether it satisfies the query (or more precisely, whether all the models of C satisfy the query). We do that by going recursively down the structure of the relational algebra expression. If the top level operator is:

- *Project:* Recall that the project means the elimination of some variables. We find all possible extensions of C with the eliminated variables and test whether any of those satisfies the argument.

- *Join:* We find the projections of C onto the variables of the first and second arguments. Then we test whether the projections satisfy the corresponding arguments.

- *Difference:* This is applicable for cells only. We test whether the cell satisfies the first and not the second argument.

The cases for the other operators are similar to these three.

What we do in each case is to implement the reverse of each of the three operators. Note that in the case of project, there are at most as many extensions as there are number of normal form tuples. In the case of join, the two projections are unique. In the case of difference we do not change the cell. This shows that the inverse operations take the same time as the original operators.

Example 10.2.2   Suppose that $A = \{2, 5, 9\}$ and we have the normal form tuple C with the following equality constraints $y = z = 2, u = v = 9$. Suppose that the top-level operator is a project that eliminates the variable x.

While extending C with x we have to make a decision as to which equivalence class to add x and if the equivalence class does not include a constant whether to make it equal to one of the constants in A. Therefore there are the following cases:

$x = y = z = 2,\; u = v = 9$ add to first equivalence class

$y = z = 2,\; x = u = v = 9$ add to second equivalence class

$y = z = 2,\; u = v = 9,\; x$ make it a new equivalence class

$y = z = 2,\; u = v = 9,\; x = 5$ make it a new equivalence class with 5.

Note that there are no more cases because there are only three constants in A, and if x is neither unspecified nor 5 then it must be either 2, in which case x belongs to the first equivalence class, or 9, in which case x belongs to the second equivalence class.

Note that the four normal form tuples are the only normal form tuples whose projection onto u, v, y, z is C.

We can now show the following theorem.

Theorem 10.2.3 Let C be any of the constraints listed in Figure 10.2. Then any relational algebra query on C constraint relations can be evaluated in the combined complexity shown in Figure 10.4.

Proof. *Upper bounds:* When we evaluate the relational algebra query using the reverse operators as described earlier, we need to repeatedly read the relational algebra query and the input database. Also, we have to use space to store our current positions in the query and the input database. We use space to store the normal form tuples in use and their order number, so that we can always get the next normal form tuple. As we noted earlier, the reverse operators can be done in at most as much time as the number of possible tuples in a normal form relation,

Domain	Constraint	Difference okay?	Data complexity	Combined complexity
Q, Z	Equality	No	in LOGSPACE	PSPACE-comp
Q, Z	Equality, inequality	Yes	in LOGSPACE	PSPACE-comp
Q	Order	Yes	in LOGSPACE	PSPACE-comp
B	Equality	No	in PSPACE	2EXP-comp
B^{aless}	Equality, inequality	Yes	in PSPACE	2EXP-comp
B	Order	No	in PSPACE	2EXP-comp
B	Binary order	No	in PSPACE	EXP-comp

FIGURE 10.4. Relational algebra computational complexity (II).

because there are at most that many possible extensions of each normal form tuple.

Therefore, when there are a polynomial (exponential) number of normal form tuples, we need to use some logarithmic (polynomial) size counter to do the query evaluation. Finally, for data complexity we can take k to be fixed, hence the first four cases can contain at most some polynomial and the last three cases at most some exponential number of normal form tuples.

Lower bounds: The lower bounds in the non-Boolean cases follow from the P-hardness combined complexity of relational algebra queries without constraints. For the lower bound proofs note that each fixed Datalog program restricted to a number n of iterations can be expressed by a relational algebra query of $O(n)$ size. Hence if there is a fixed Datalog program that has with n iterations some C-hard data complexity then there is also a (positive) relational algebra query that has C-hard combined complexity where C is any complexity class used in this chapter. We will analyze the computational complexity of Datalog queries in Section 10.3, hence we skip further details here.   ∎

In the space-efficient evaluation described earlier, we did not have to assume that the input database is normalized. However, the following is convenient to know in case of bottom-up evaluation.

Lemma 10.2.4   Let C be any of the constraints for which we defined normal forms. Then any C constraint relation of size n can be put into normal form in $O(nT)$ where T is the number of tuples shown in Figure 10.2.   ∎

10.3   Complexity of Datalog

In Section 10.3.1 we consider the problem of defining counters in Datalog with constraints. By *counters* we mean binary relations where the second attribute value is always one more than the first. In Section 10.3.2 we show that if a relation can be defined to count from 1 to t using a Datalog query with C constraints, then we can simulate t time-bounded Turing machines. This implies for Datalog queries with C constraints a number of computational complexity lower bounds. The computational complexity of various constraint query languages is examined in Section 10.3.3.

10.3.1   Counting

In this section we describe how we can define a counting or successor function in several cases of constraint query languages.

Lemma 10.3.1   There is a Datalog program with gap-order constraints, that given as inputs two relations containing the numbers s and 2^s and a relation that enables counting from 0 to s, defines a relation that enables counting from 0 to 2^s.

Proof. Let us assume that the input relations are $Next\,(0, 1), \ldots, Next\,(s - 1, s)$, $No\_Digits\,(s)$, and $Two\_to\_s\,(2^s)$. Using a Datalog query we define an output relation $Succ\,(0, 1), \ldots, Succ\,(2^s - 1, 2^s)$.

It helps to think of each number being written in binary notation. Because the number 2^s has s binary digits, what we really need is, given a counter on the digits and the value 2^s, to define a counter from 0 to 2^s.

We start by representing the value of each digit using a constraint interval, where the bound is the actual value. That is, for each $1 \leq i \leq s$, we want to represent the value of the ith digit from the right as: $Digit\,(i, x_1, x_2) :\!\!-\; x_2 - x_1 \geq 2^{(i-1)}$. The following rules define the desired constraint tuples:

$$Digit\,(j, x_1, x_2) \quad :\!\!-\quad Next\,(i, j),\; Digit\,(i, x_1, x_3),\; Digit\,(i, x_3, x_2).$$
$$Digit\,(1, x_1, x_2) \quad :\!\!-\quad x_2 - x_1 \geq 1.$$

Note that we can represent each number i by a pair of constraints: $i \leq x$ (which is equivalent to $x \geq i$) and $x \leq i$ (which is equivalent to $-x \geq -i$). Because each number can be expressed as the sum of a subset of the values of the n digits, if we start out from the constraint $1 \leq x$ and $x \leq 2^s$ and choose to either increase the first or decrease the second bound by the value of the ith digit for each $1 \leq i \leq s$, then we will get a single integer between 1 and 2^s as output.

This gives an idea about how to define any number we need. We can use a separate x_1 and x_2 to represent x to make it easy to tighten either the lower or upper bound on x while preserving the other bound.

We can define any integer n between 1 and 2^s if for each binary digit value we add it to the lower bound if the corresponding binary digit is 1 in $n - 1$ or subtract it from the upper bound as if the corresponding binary digit is 0 in $n - 1$.

To express the successor function, we define pairs of integers. Let x_1 and x_2 represent the first and y_1 and y_2 represent the second integer. The following rules make sure that when we add a digit to the xs we also add the same digit to the ys the right way:

$$Succ\,(x, y) \qquad\qquad\qquad :\!\!-\quad Succ2\,(x, x, y, y, s),\, No\_Digits\,(s).$$

$$Succ2\,(x_3, x_2, y_3, y_2, j) \quad :\!\!-\quad Succ2\,(x_1, x_2, y_1, y_2, i),\, Next\,(i, j),$$
$$Digit\,(j, x_1, x_3),\; Digit\,(j, y_1, y_3).$$

$$Succ2\,(x_1, x_3, y_1, y_3, j) \quad :\!\!-\quad Succ2\,(x_1, x_2, y_1, y_2, i),\, Next\,(i, j),$$
$$Digit\,(j, x_3, x_2),\; Digit\,(j, y_3, y_2).$$

$$Succ2\,(x_1, x_3, y_3, y_2, j) \quad :\!\!-\quad Succ3\,(x_1, x_2, y_1, y_2, i),\, Next\,(i, j),$$
$$Digit\,(j, x_3, x_2),\; Digit\,(j, y_1, y_3).$$

$$Succ3\,(x_3, x_2, y_1, y_3, j) \quad :\!\!-\quad Succ3\,(x_1, x_2, y_1, y_2, i),\, Next\,(i, j),$$
$$Digit\,(j, x_1, x_3),\; Digit\,(j, y_3, y_2).$$

$$Succ3\,(x_1, x_2, y_1, y_2, 0) \quad :\!- \quad 1 \leq x_1,\ x_2 \leq n,\ 1 \leq y_1,\ y_2 \leq n,$$
$$Two\_to\_s\,(n).$$

In this program, in each recursive step, x_1 will be bounded by higher and higher constants from below and x_2 will be bounded by lower and lower constants from above. In the second rule the possible values of x_1 and x_2 will overlap on exactly one integer. A similar note applies to y_1 and y_2. ∎

Example 10.3.1 Let $s = 3$. Then we can prove that $Succ\,(5, 6)$ is true. It helps to think that the numbers 4 and 5 are written in binary notation as 100 and 101. The sequence of derived constraint tuples leading to the conclusion is the following:

$Succ3\,(x_1, x_2, y_1, y_2, 0)\!:\!-1 \leq x_1,\ x_2 \leq 8,\ 1 \leq y_1,\ y_2 \leq 8$ by the last rule

$Succ2\,(x_1, x_2, y_1, y_2, 1)\!:\!-1 \leq x_1,\ x_2 \leq 7,\ 2 \leq y_1,\ y_2 \leq 8$ by the fifth rule

$Succ2\,(x_1, x_2, y_1, y_2, 2)\!:\!-1 \leq x_1,\ x_2 \leq 5,\ 2 \leq y_1,\ y_2 \leq 6$ by the fourth rule

$Succ2\,(x_1, x_2, y_1, y_2, 3)\!:\!-5 \leq x_1,\ x_2 \leq 5,\ 6 \leq y_1,\ y_2 \leq 6$ by the third rule

$Succ\,(x, y)$ $\qquad\qquad :\!-5 \leq x,\ x \leq 5,\ 6 \leq y,\ y \leq 6$ by the second rule

Lemma 10.3.2 There is a stratified Datalog program with gap-order constraints and a single negation of a one-arity relation that, given as inputs a relation containing the number s and a relation that enables counting from 0 to s, defines a relation containing the number 2^s.

Proof. Let us assume that $No\_Digits\,(s)$ and $Next\,(0, 1), \ldots, Next\,(s - 1, s)$ are the input relations. We define the relation $Two\_to\_s\,(2^s)$.

First we write a rule for exponentiation as follows:

$$Exp(j, x_1, x_2) \quad :\!- \quad Next\,(i, j),\ Exp(i, x_1, x_3),\ Exp(i, x_3, x_2).$$
$$Exp(1, x_1, x_2) \quad :\!- \quad x_2 - x_1 > 1.$$

This will define the constraint tuples $Exp(i, x_1, x_2) :\!- x_2 - x_1 \geq 2^i$ for each $1 \leq i \leq s$. Therefore, $Exp(s, 0, x) :\!- x \geq 2^s$ is one of the constraint tuples defined. We can find the value 2^s as follows. First we write the Datalog program Q_1:

$$Grt\_Two\_to\_s\,(x) \quad :\!- \quad x - y \geq 0,\ Geq\_Two\_to\_s\,(y).$$
$$Geq\_Two\_to\_s\,(x) \quad :\!- \quad No\_Digits\,(s),\ Exp(s, 0, x).$$

Then we finds its complement using negation query Q_2:

$$Not\_Grt\_Two\_to\_s(x) \quad :\!- \quad not\ Grt\_Two\_to\_s(x).$$

Note that we negated only a single attribute relation. Finally, we use the following Q_3:

$$Two\_to\_s\,(x) \quad :\!- \quad Geq\_Two\_to\_s\,(x),\ Not\_Grt\_Two\_to\_s\,(x).$$

Clearly, the stratified Datalog query $Q_3(Q_2(Q_1()))$ will find the number 2^s as required. ∎

Lemma 10.3.3 There is a stratified Datalog program with gap-order constraints and i negations of one-arity relations that given as inputs a relation containing the number s and a relation that enables counting from 0 to s defines a relation that enables counting from 0 to $2^{\cdot^{\cdot^{s}}}$ with i levels of exponentiations.

Proof. We can build a stratified Datalog program in which the strata of Lemma 10.3.2 and the strata of Lemma 10.3.1 alternate i times. ∎

Lemma 10.3.4 There is a Datalog program with B_Z Boolean algebra equality constraints that, given a database input of size $s \log s$, can define a function that enables counting from 0 to $2^s - 1$.

Proof. We can encode any number n as the set N that contains the place numbers of the digits that are one in the binary notation of n where we count the digits from right to left. For example, the number 9 can be represented as the set $N = \{1, 4\}$.

We define as an input relation $Next\,(\{1\}, \{2\}), \ldots, Next\,(\{s-1\}, \{s\})$ and the relations $First\,(\{1\})$ and $Last\,(\{s\})$, where s is the number of binary digits we need to count to $2^s - 1$. This database input requires only size $O(s \log s)$ because we have s number of constraint tuples each with one integer and the size of each integer is at most $\log s$.

We can now express the successor relation $Succ\,(N, M)$, which is true if and only if N and M represent the numbers n, m respectively and $m = n + 1$ for any $0 \leq n, m < 2^s - 1$:

$$Succ\,(N, M) \quad :\!- \quad Succ2\,(N, M, S),\ Last\,(S).$$

$$Succ2\,(N, M, I) \quad :\!- \quad Succ2\,(N, M, J),\ Next\,(J, I),$$
$$Zero\,(N, I),\ Zero\,(M, I).$$

$$Succ2\,(N, M, I) \quad :\!- \quad Succ2\,(N, M, J),\ Next\,(J, I),$$
$$One\,(N, I),\ One\,(M, I).$$

$$Succ2\,(N, M, I) \quad :\!- \quad Zero\,(N, I),\ One\,(M, I),\ First\,(I).$$

$$Succ2\,(N, M, I) \quad :\!- \quad Succ3\,(N, M, J),\ Next\,(J, I),$$
$$Zero\,(N, I),\ One\,(M, I).$$

$$Succ3\,(N,M,I) \quad :\!- \quad Succ3\,(N,M,J),Next\,(J,I),$$
$$One\,(N,I),Zero\,(M,I).$$

$$Succ3\,(N,M,I) \quad :\!- \quad One\,(N,I),\,Zero\,(M,I),\,First\,(I).$$

$$Zero\,(N,I) \quad\quad :\!- \quad N \wedge I =_{B_Z} 0.$$

$$One\,(N,I) \quad\quad\; :\!- \quad N' \wedge I =_{B_Z} 0.$$

Note that the constraint $N \wedge I =_{B_Z} 0$ is equivalent to $N \subseteq_{B_Z} I'$ and the constraint $N' \wedge I =_{B_Z} 0$ is equivalent to $I \subseteq_{B_Z} N$. Therefore, in the preceding, $Zero\,(N,I)$ is true if and only if the Ith digit of N is zero. Similarly, $One\,(N,I)$ is true if and only if the Ith digit of N is one.   ■

Lemma 10.3.5   There is a Datalog program with B_Z Boolean algebra variable-variable and variable-constant set containment constraints that, given a database input of size $s^2 \log s$, can define a function that enables counting from 0 to $2^s - 1$.

Proof. The proof is similar to Lemma 10.3.4, however, we replace the definitions of *zero* and *one*. Let I^0 be the complement of I with respect to the set $\{0,\ldots,s\}$. We replace *zero* with an input relation that contains s constraint tuples for each $I = \{0\}$ to $I = \{s\}$, as follows:

$$Zero\,(I,N) \quad :\!- \quad N \subseteq I^0.$$

We also replace *one* with an input relation that contains only one constraint tuple, as follows:

$$One\,(I,N) \quad :\!- \quad I \subseteq N.$$

This database input requires only size $O(s^2 \log s)$ because we have only s number of constraint tuples in which we have at most s integer constants and the size of each integer constant is at most $\log n$.   ■

Lemma 10.3.6   There is a Datalog program with free B_s Boolean algebra simple upper bound constraints that, given a database input of size $s^2 \log s$, can define a function that enables counting from 0 to $2^{2^s} - 1$.

Proof. Let $g_1,\ldots,g_s$ be the constant symbols of the free Boolean algebra B_s. We first define the input database relations $Next\,(g_1,g_2)$, ..., $Next\,(g_{m-1},g_m)$, $First\,(g_1)$, and $Last\,(g_m)$. Note that the $Next$ relation can be defined using s simple Boolean upper bound constraint tuples, one for each $1 \leq j \leq s$, as follows:

$$Next\,(J,I) \quad :\!- \quad J \leq g_j,\; J' \leq g'_j,\; I \leq g_{j+i},\; I' \leq g'_{j+1}.$$

The first and last relations can be defined similarly using only simple Boolean upper bound constraints.

We can form 2^s minterms from the constant symbols of B_s. These can be ordered according to the binary value of the superscripts of $g_1, \ldots, g_m$ read in this order. (Here a one (or zero) superscript means that the constant symbol (or its complement) is in the conjunction defining the minterm.)

Then we define in Datalog the relation $M\_Succ\,(X, Y)$ that is true if and only if X and Y are minterms generated by $g_1, \ldots, g_m$ and the minterm number of X is one less than the minterm number of Y. The structure of this program is the same as that for $Succ$ in Lemma 10.3.4, except that we can define $Zero$ and One using Boolean equality constraints, as follows:

$$Zero\,(N, I) \quad :- \quad N \wedge I =_{B_s} 0.$$
$$One\,(N, I) \quad :- \quad N \wedge I' =_{B_s} 0.$$

Note that if N is a minterm of B_s then it is equivalent to the conjunction of constant symbols or their negations. Because I is a constant symbol, it occurs in N exactly if $N \wedge I' =_{B_s} 0$ and does not occur but its negation does occur in N if $N \wedge I =_{B_s} 0$.

Similarly to Lemma 10.3.5, we can replace the definitions of $zero$ and one with s simple Boolean upper bound constraint tuples. Now let I^0 be the complement of I with respect to the set $\{g_1, \ldots, g_s\}$. We replace $zero$ with an input relation that contains s constraint tuples one for each $I = \{g_1\}$ to $I = \{g_s\}$, as follows:

$$Zero\,(N, I) \quad :- \quad N \le I^0.$$

We replace one by a single constraint tuple as follows:

$$One\,(N, I) \quad :- \quad N \wedge I' \le_{B_s} 0.$$

We can form 2^{2^s} elements out of the minterms of B_s. These elements can be ordered according to the binary value of the superscripts of the minterms read in the order of the minterms. (Here a one (or zero) superscript means that the minterm is (or is not) in the disjunctive normal form of the element.) We can define in Datalog the relation $E\_Succ\,(N, M)$ that is true if and only if N and M are elements of the free Boolean algebra B_s and the number of M is one less than the number of N. The structure of this program is the same as that for $succ$ in Lemma 10.3.4, except that again the Boolean equality constraints need to be replaced by simple Boolean upper bound constraints in the corresponding relations E_Zero and E_One.

We first define a complement relation $comp\,(N, M)$ that is true if and only if N and M are elements of B_s such that each minterm is in N exactly if it is not in M, as follows:

$$Comp\,(N, M) \quad :- \quad Comp2\,(N, M, S),\ Last\,(S).$$

$$Comp2\,(N, M, I) \quad :- \quad Comp2\,(N, M, J),\ Next\,(J, I),$$
$$One\,(N, I),\ Zero\,(M, I).$$

$$Comp2\,(N, M, I) \quad :\!\!- \quad Comp2\,(N, M, J),\; Next\,(J, I),$$
$$Zero\,(N, I),\; One\,(M, I).$$

$$Comp2\,(N, M, I) \quad :\!\!- \quad One\,(N, I),\; Zero\,(M, I),\; First\,(I).$$

$$Comp2\,(N, M, I) \quad :\!\!- \quad Zero\,(N, I),\; One\,(M, I),\; First\,(I).$$

Using the complement function, we can define E_Zero and E_One using only simple Boolean upper bound constraints, as follows:

$$E\_Zero\,(N, I) \quad :\!\!- \quad Comp\,(N, M),\, M' \wedge I \leq_{B_s} 0.$$

$$E\_One\,(N, I) \quad :\!\!- \quad N' \wedge I \leq_{B_s} 0,\, .$$

Note that if N is an element of B_s then it can be written as a disjunction of minterms. Because I is a minterm, it is in N exactly if $N' \wedge I =_{B_s} 0$, which is true if and only if $N' \wedge I \leq_{B_s} 0$, and it is not in N if $N \wedge I =_{B_s} 0$, which is true if and only if $M' \wedge I \leq_{B_s} 0$ where M is the complement of N. ■

Remark 10.3.1 Let t_i denote the ith minterm of B_s. We can encode each integer number from 0 to $2^{2^s} - 1$ as some element of B_s. Each number n is represented by the element that contains the minterm t_i if and only if in the binary encoding of n the ith digit from the right is 1. For example, the number 9 is represented in the free Boolean algebra B_s by the element $\{t_4, t_1\}$. Note that the ordering of the elements of B_s given earlier and the ordering of the integers from 0 to $2^{2^s} - 1$ described here are the same.

10.3.2 Turing Machines

Theorem 10.3.1 Let C be any type of constraint. If in Datalog with C constraints we can define the relation $Succ$ that enables counting from 0 to n and the relations $First$ and $Last$ that contain a representation of 0 and n, respectively, then we can write a Datalog query with C constraints that can simulate an n time-bounded Turing machine.

Proof. In this proof let #i denote the representation of integer i using the $Succ$ relation. In particular let #0 and #n be the representations of the numbers 0 and n. We have in $Succ$ the tuples (#i, #$i + 1$) for $0 \leq n - 1$.

Note that the successor function can also be used to define the greater function between pairs of integers from 0 to n as follows:

$$Greater\,(i, j) \quad :\!\!- \quad Succ\,(i, k),\; Greater\,(k, j).$$
$$Greater\,(i, j) \quad :\!\!- \quad Succ\,(i, j).$$

Let $\mathcal{T} = \langle K, \sigma, \delta, s_0, h \rangle$ be the deterministic n time-bounded Turing machine, where K is the set of states of the machine, σ is the alphabet, δ is the transition function, s_0 is the initial state, and h is the halt state. We record the value of n into the $Tape\_Size$ relation:

Tape_Size (#*n*).

First let relation T describe the initial content of the tape, that is, let $T(\#i, c_i)$ for each $1 \leq i \leq n$ describe the content of the ith tape cell.

Second we use relations *Left*, *Right*, and *Write* to describe the transition function δ of T. We create for each possible machine input state s_1, output state s_2, and tape symbols c and w, a fact *Left* (s_1, c, s_2), *Right* (s_1, c, s_2), or *Write* (s_1, c, s_2, w) if according to δ when the machine is in state s_1 and pointing to c, then the machine must go to state s_2 and move one tape cell to the left or to the right or stay and write w on the tape, respectively.

Third we use a relation C to describe the configuration of the machine. The relation $C(t, i, s)$ describes that at time step t the machine is pointing to tape position i and is in state s. We can assume at time zero that the Turing machine is pointing to the first tape cell. Therefore we create a fact:

$$C(\#0, \#1, s_0)$$

Fourth we express the sequence of transitions of the machine by a relation $R(t, j, c)$ that is true if and only if at time t the jth tape cell contains the tape symbol c. To initialize R we write the rule:

$$R(\#0, j, c) :- T(j, c)$$

We express the requirements for a valid deterministic computation of the machine as follows:

$$C(t_2, o, s_2) \quad :- \quad Succ\,(t, t_2),\ C(t, i, s_1),\ R(t, i, c),\ Left\,(s_1, c, s_2),$$
$$Succ\,(o, i).$$

$$C(t_2, o, s_2) \quad :- \quad Succ\,(t, t_2),\ C(t, i, s_1),\ R(t, i, c),\ Right\,(s_1, c, s_2),$$
$$Succ\,(i, o).$$

$$C(t_2, i, s_2) \quad :- \quad Succ\,(t, t_2),\ C(t, i, s_1),\ R(t, i, c),\ Write\,(s_1, c, s_2, w).$$

$$R(t_2, i, c) \quad :- \quad Succ\,(t, t_2),\ C(t, i, s_1),\ R(t, i, c),\ Left\,(s_1, c, s_2).$$
$$R(t_2, i, c) \quad :- \quad Succ\,(t, t_2),\ C(t, i, s_1),\ R(t, i, c),\ Right\,(s_1, c, s_2).$$
$$R(t_2, i, w) \quad :- \quad Succ\,(t, t_2),\ C(t, i, s_1),\ R(t, i, c),\ Write\,(s_1, c, s_2, w).$$
$$R(t_2, p, c) \quad :- \quad Succ\,(t, t_2),\ C(t, i, s_1),\ R(t, p, c),\ i < p.$$
$$R(t_2, p, c) \quad :- \quad Succ\,(t, t_2),\ C(t, i, s_1),\ R(t, p, c),\ i > p.$$

$$Yes\,() \quad :- \quad C(t, i, h),\ Time\_Bound\,(t_2),\ t < t_2.$$

The last rule expresses that by time n the machine is in state h. ∎

10.3.3 Complexity Results

The evaluation of Datalog queries in general was discussed in Section 9.4. It follows from the discussion there that the constraint consequence operator can be implemented by repeatedly taking in each Datalog rule the join of the subgoal relations of the rule body and then projecting out the variables from the join relation that occur on the left-hand side and adding the result to the relation defined by the rule. We do this until there is no new tuple added to any defined relation.

Fortunately, for the constraints discussed in Section 10.2.1, we know the maximum number of normal form tuples that may be added to each defined relation. Let us define the following list of parameters:

- m—the number of constants that occur in either the input database or the Datalog program

- k—the maximum arity of any relation

- M—the maximum number of normal form constraint tuples in k-arity relations with m constants in use

- s—the maximum size of a constraint tuple

- d—the number of defined relations

- i—the number of input relations

- t_1—the time to evaluate each d relational algebra query on an input database with i normal form relations of size at most Ms

- t_2—the time to eliminate duplicates from a database with d normal form relations of size at most Ms

Using these parameters it is now possible to show the following.

Lemma 10.3.7 Let C be any type of constraint discussed in Section 10.2.1. Let Q be a Datalog program and I a normal form input constraint database with C constraints. Let the other parameters be as earlier. Then the least fixed point of the Datalog program Q on input I can be evaluated in $O(dM(t_1 + t_2))$ time.   ∎

Now let us look at the data and combined complexities of Datalog queries.

Theorem 10.3.2 Datalog queries with C constraints have data complexity and combined complexities as shown in Figure 10.5.

Proof. In each case the upper bounds follow from Lemma 10.3.7 and Theorem 10.2.3. For the first three cases the lower bound follows from the fact that we can define an input relation that can count from 0 to some number m. Using that relation we can define in Datalog a relation of arity k to count from 0 to $m^{k/2} - 1$, where the numbers are represented as $k/2$ digit base m numbers. Therefore, by Theorem 10.3.1 we can simulate any $m^{k/2} - 1$ time-bounded Turing machine.

Domain	Constraint	Data complexity	Combined complexity
Q, Z	Equality	P-comp	EXP-comp
Q, Z	Equality, inequality	P-comp	EXP-comp
Q	Order	P-comp	EXP-comp
Q, Z	Lower and upper bound, gap-order	EXP-hard	EXP-hard
B	Binary order	EXP-comp	EXP-comp
B	Equality	2EXP-comp	2EXP-comp
B^{aless}	Equality, inequality	2EXP-comp	2EXP-comp
B	Order	2EXP-comp	2EXP-comp

FIGURE 10.5. Datalog computational complexity.

For gap-order, upper bound, and lower bound constraints the complexity lower bound follows from Lemma 10.3.1 and Theorem 10.3.1. Hence the three cases all include the same computational lower bound.

For B_Z Boolean constraints the lower bound follows from Lemmas 10.3.4 and 10.3.5.

For B_{k+m} Boolean constraints the lower bounds follow from Lemma 10.3.6. Note that the query described there used only simple Boolean upper bound constraints, which are included in each of the three B_{k+m} constraint cases. ∎

10.4 Complexity of Stratified Datalog

In this section we analyze the computational complexity of stratified Datalog queries with C constraints. We either look at cases where C constraints are closed under negation or restrict the negation to unary in certain cases when C constraints are closed under unary negation.

Theorem 10.4.1 Stratified Datalog queries with C constraints have data and combined complexities as shown in Figure 10.6.

Proof. For the first three cases, for each strata we first find the complement of the negated relations and then repeat the evaluation of a Datalog program as in Theorem 10.3.2. For i unary negations and gap-order, upper bound, and lower bound constraints or theories that include these, the lower bound follows from Lemma 10.3.3. ∎

Domain	Constraint	Data complexity	Combined complexity
$\mathcal{Q}, \mathcal{Z}$	Equality, inequality	P-comp	EXP-comp
$\mathcal{Q}$	Order	P-comp	EXP-comp
$\mathcal{B}^{aless}$	Equality, inequality	2EXP-comp	2EXP-comp
$\mathcal{Q}, \mathcal{Z}$	Lower bound, upper bound, gap-order	$(i+1)$EXP-hard with i unary neg.	$(i+1)$EXP-hard with i unary neg.

FIGURE 10.6. Stratified Datalog computational complexity.

Bibliographic Notes

We gave an extensive bibliographic reference at the end of Chapter 9 for Datalog with constraints. Here we concentrate on the computational complexity references.

Papadimitriou [230] is a book on computational complexity in general. The definition of data complexity is from Vardi [318] and Immerman [150]. The data complexity of Datalog with inequality and rational order constraints as well as the data complexity of relational algebra with real polynomial constraints was studied by Kanellakis et al. [158, 159]. For Datalog with gap-order the data complexity is studied in [255, 256, 257] and the combined complexity in those, in Cerans [54], and in Cox and McAloon [72]. Stolboushkin and Taitslin [295] show that no query language can express precisely those Datalog with gap-order constraints that are safe.

The expressive power of first-order queries with linear and polynomial constraints is considered in Afrati et al. [5, 6], Benedikt et al. [28, 29, 30, 31], Grumbach and Su [125, 126, 127, 128], Ibarra and Su [147], Kuper [192], Otto and Van den Bussche [225], and Paredaens et al. [233].

Gyssens et al. [133] studied constraint-based geometric query languages that are complete. Dumortier et al. [84, 85] consider the problem of deciding whether a constraint relation with real polynomial constraints can be simplified and expressed with only linear constraints. Jeavons et al. [155] studied the tractability of constraint queries in general. Koubarakis [182] studied the complexity of query evaluation in indefinite temporal constraint databases; and van der Meyden [313, 314] studied indefinite order databases. Kozen [185] and Kanellakis and Revesz [161] study the complexity of Boolean algebras.

Baudinet et al. [20] study constraint-generating dependencies and Zhang and Ozsoyoglu [338] study implication constraints. Kolaitis and Vardi [174] study the complexity of conjunctive query containment. Lemma 10.3.6 and the Boolean case of Theorem 10.3.2 are from Revesz [265]. Lemma 10.3.4 is from Revesz [258, 267]. Lemmas 10.3.1, 10.3.2, and 10.3.3 and the set order and gap-order constraint cases of Theorems 10.3.2 and 10.4.1 are from Revesz [259, 267].

Exercise

1. Find any NP-complete problem not seen before in the text and express it in:

   (a) Datalog with Boolean binary constraints.

   (b) Datalog with Boolean equality constraints.

   (c) Stratified Datalog with lower bound, upper bound, and gap-order constraints.

2. A pet shop has a finite number of dalmatian dogs, with each dog having a finite number of spots. Each day one dalmatian dog is sold or exchanged for a finite number of dogs that each have fewer spots. Prove that one day the shop will run out of dogs. (**Hint:** Use Lemma 9.4.1.)

11

Certification

In Chapter 8 we saw one approach to guarantee the termination of queries. It placed various syntactic restrictions on the constraint query language used such that every query expressible in the restricted constraint query language was safe.

Certification is another approach to safety. The idea is to certify that a query is safe before adding it to a query library. Certification is not based on simple syntax checking but on more complicated tests. Certification either runs a special algorithm that verifies that a query is safe or uses some ad hoc arguments.

In both cases certification is better done by expert programmers. In the latter case an expert is needed because the ad hoc arguments require some knowledge about the evaluation of queries that cannot be expected from naive database users. In the former case, if certification fails an expert may rewrite the query to make it safe, something that again cannot be expected from naive database users.

Certification is important because it can sometimes yield guarantees when the first approach fails. There are many certification techniques. We describe and illustrate some of them in this chapter.

11.1 Constant Propagation

Constant propagation occurs when in a rule body some of the attributes of some relations are known to contain only constants. That information is passed to the other relations within the same rule. This may lead to a simplification of the constraints in the rules and restriction may become applicable to prove safety.

Example 11.1.1   In Example 4.1.4 about the *Travel* query we can assume that the third argument of *Go2* is a constant. Then at each rule application we have only a (half)-addition constraint. Hence the *Travel* query is safe, by Figure 8.2.

11.2 Variable Independence

Variable independence occurs when knowing the value of a variable does not improve our knowledge of the value of another variable. For example, consider gap-order constraint tuples over the variables $x_1, \ldots, x_k$. If there is no gap-order constraint between any two of the variables then they are independent. There could be other constraints between variables and constants, for example, we could have $x_1 - 10 \geq 30$, but even if knowing the exact value of x_1 does not help us know more about x_2.

We say that the variables are independent in a relation if they are independent in each tuple of the relation. Negation is closed-form safe for gap-order relations in which the variables are independent. This is stronger than being simply evaluation safe. Therefore, if we have a stratified Datalog query with some alternation of Datalog queries and negations such that the variables are independent in the relations negated, then the stratified program is also closed-form evaluation safe. Based on this observation we can define very complex queries that are closed-form evaluation safe. Following is just a simple example.

Example 11.2.1 We computed relation $Travel(x, y, t)$ in Example 4.1.3. It is easy to see that the three variables are independent in this relation. Hence let us define the following query:

$$Not\_Fastest(x, y, t_2) \quad :- \quad Travel(x, y, t_1), Travel(x, y, t_2), t_1 < t_2.$$
$$Fastest(x, y, t) \quad :- \quad Travel(x, y, t), \ not\, Not\_Fastest(x, y, t).$$

Here the first rule computes for each pair of cities the set of time instances that are not fastest. The variables are independent in relation $Not\_Fastest$. Hence $Not\_Fastest$ can be negated in the second rule to get a new gap-order constraint relation, which is then joined with the $Travel$ relation. Therefore relation $Fastest$ can be evaluated in gap-order closed form. Hence this is a closed-form evaluation safe query.

11.3 Monotonicity

Monotonicity occurs when a value is monotone increasing. Monotonicity conditions can be often used to prove termination.

Example 11.3.1 In the subset sum query of Example 4.1.10 the first argument of Sum is 0 in the very first tuple that can be derived. With all applications of the second and third rules, the value of the first attribute increases by one. Therefore, there are at most 2^n different tuples that can be derived when there are n items numbered 1 to n in the $Item$ relation. This proves that $Q_{subsetsum}$ is a safe query.

11.4   Acyclicity

Acyclicity means that the database input can be considered a directed acyclic graph. If the query is traversing the edges in a direction, then the query must terminate.

Example 11.4.1   The query in Example 4.1.6 about water flowing in a river contains only linear constraints in the second and third rules of the query. However, we can expect that the river is acyclic. Therefore, the first, second, and third rules need to be applied only as many times as source, dam, and merge tuples we have. Therefore, the query will have to terminate.

11.5   Tightening Bounds

Tightening bounds is another technique of proving termination. This occurs when we have a constraint that is almost like a negative linear constraint except that its bound is a variable that increases on each rule application while the other variables are bounded from below.

Example 11.5.1   A possible solution for Exercise 7.3.4 would be a constraint automaton that can be translated to the following Datalog program:

$$Money \, (500, 3000, -100, 0, 3300).$$
$$Money \, (x', y', z', i', b') \qquad\qquad :\!- \quad Money \, (x, y, z, i, b),$$
$$-x' - y' - z' \geq -b,$$
$$x' \geq 0, \ y' \geq 0, \ z' \geq -1000,$$
$$i' = i + 1, \ b' = b - 100.$$

Here the constraint $-x' - y' - z' \geq -b$ is a tightening negative linear constraint, where the bound $-b$ increases by one hundred on each rule application, and all the other variables are bounded from below. Therefore this second rule can be applied only a finite number of times to derive anything; thus it is a safe query. Note that this is a recursive query with linear constraints that cannot be shown to be safe by restriction.

11.6   Tightening Coefficients

Tightening coefficients is similar to the previous technique. This occurs when the domain is the nonnegative integers and we have a constraint that is like a negative linear constraint except that the bound and one or more coefficients are variables and on each rule application the coefficients are all growing with a faster rate than the bound.

Example 11.6.1   The annual purchase automaton in Figure 6.1.5 with only the left arc results in a Datalog program with polynomial constraints. However, the polynomial constraint $ax' + by' + cz' \leq d$ is like a linear constraint where a, b, and c are coefficients and d is the bound that takes on different values for each rule application. Namely a, b, and c grow by 5, 10, and 5 percent, respectively, while d grows by only 2 percent. Hence this rule can be applied only a finite number of times.

Note that the Datalog rule corresponding to the other arc of the automaton can also be applied only a finite number of times successively. That is because there the value of i decreases by one on each rule application but must stay above 0. Because the second rule cancels the effect of the other and restores the values of the variables, it can be seen that the Datalog query can derive only a finite number of different tuples, no matter what are the initial values of the variables.

11.7   Vector Addition System

Sometimes a Datalog program with addition constraints can be recognized to define a vector addition system. In a vector addition system there is a vector of variables to which we only add constant vectors to go to different states. Vector addition systems also correspond to constraint automata whose transitions contain only comparison constraints and only add or subtract from each state variable a constant.

Vector addition systems are recognition safe. A special case of vector addition systems is when they are *lossy*. In a lossy system if $(a_1, \ldots, a_n)$ is the state of the automaton at a time instance, then at any later time and state $(b_1, \ldots, b_n)$ it must be the case that for some $1 \leq i \leq n$ $b_i < a_i$. Lossy vector addition systems are evaluable in closed form.

Example 11.7.1   The Datalog query in Example 6.1.1 about the tourist is a vector addition system. Hence it is recognition safe. In fact, because some part of the tourist's money is used to pay commissions, it is not possible for the tourist to have more or equal amount of dollars, euros, and yens at a later state than at an earlier state due to the commission charges. Hence this is also a lossy vector addition system and is evaluable in closed form.

11.7.1   Recognition Safety

Suppose that the initial values for a vector addition system with n variables are $a = (a_1, \ldots, a_n)$. Is the configuration $b = (b_1, \ldots, b_n)$ possible? Let $v_1, \ldots, v_m$ be the transition vectors, and let $M = (v_1, \ldots, v_m)$ be the $n \times m$ matrix of transitions.

For configuration b to be possible we have to have a vector $x \in \mathcal{N}^n$ such that:

$$a + Mx = b$$

But this is not enough, because there must exist a sequence of vectors $x_0, \ldots, x_k$ where x_0 is the zero vector, $x_k = x$, and each x_{i+1} is obtained from

x_i by adding 1 to one of its elements, such that the following is true for each $0 \leq i \leq k$:

$$a + M x_i \geq 0$$

In Example 6.1.1 the transition matrix is:

$$\begin{pmatrix} -100 & -100 & 99 & 0 & 99 & 0 \\ 198 & 0 & -200 & -200 & 0 & 198 \\ 0 & 29700 & 0 & 29700 & -30000 & -30000 \end{pmatrix}$$

Suppose that $a = (0, 600, 0)$ and $b = (98, 0, 59400)$. Then a solution for the equality is $x = (0, 1, 2, 1, 0, 0)$, which means that we need to exchange dollars into yens once, euros into dollars twice, and euros into yens once. There are 4! possible vector sequences from the zero vector to x. Out of these, the sequence $(0, 0, 1, 0, 0, 0)$, $(0, 0, 2, 0, 0, 0)$, $(0, 0, 2, 1, 0, 0)$, $(0, 1, 2, 1, 0, 0)$ is one that satisfies the inequality. This sequence corresponds to exchanging euros to dollars twice, then exchanging euros to yens, and then exchanging dollars to yens. There are other possible solutions, but this solution shows that the configuration is reachable.

This technique works well if there are only a few solutions of the equality. This may happen if the equality solved in the rationals is a hyperplane that intersects the all-positive quadrant in only a few integer solutions (this is true for Example 6.1.1) or when the rank of the matrix is m (i.e, it contains m linearly independent rows). For a vector addition system if there is only one way to reach from a to b and that requires n transitions, then we can find this solution in $O(n!)$ time. There are more general but also more complex techniques for solving the reachability problem in vector addition systems where the equality yields many solutions in nonnegative integers.

Now we will look at how we can certify that a vector addition system is evaluation safe by checking for the lossy property. We use the following theorem.

Theorem 11.7.1   A vector addition system with n variables is lossy if and only if there exist positive constants $c = (c_1, \ldots, c_n)$ such that for each transition v_i we have $\sum_j c_j v_{i,j} < 0$.

Proof. (*If*) If there exist such positive constants c, then on each transition from some configuration a to another configuration b the dot product of the cs and the configuration value decreases. Hence $ca > cb$. Now if each $b_i \geq a_i$, then $ca \leq cb$, which is a contradiction. Hence, there must be some i such that $b_i < a_i$. Therefore, the system must be lossy.

(*Only if*) If the vector addition system is not lossy then it is possible to go from a configuration a to a configuration b such that $b_i \geq a_i$ for each $1 \leq i \leq n$. Then for any set of positive constants c we have $ca \leq cb$. Hence at least for some transition v_i that was made when going from a to b, it must be the case that $\sum_j c_j v_{i,j} > 0$. Hence if the system is not lossy, then there cannot be positive constants as required. ■

Corollary 11.7.1   It can be tested whether a vector addition system is lossy.

Proof. By Theorem 11.7.1 it is enough to write a formula $\exists c\ \forall i\,(cv_i < 0)$. This formula is a linear Diophantine formula, which can be solved in general. ∎

For the vector addition system in Example 6.1.1 a set of positive constants that satisfies the condition of Theorem 11.7.1 is $c = (300, 150, 1)$. This shows that it is a lossy vector addition system.

For lossy vector addition systems one can find all possible configurations by either breadth-first or depth-first search. Each branch of the search tree will be finite length because for some set of positive constants c, the dot product of c and the value of the state variables monotone decreases in discrete steps (because the values are integers) and only down to zero (because the value of each state variable must be always a nonnegative integer).

11.8   Positive Stochastic Matrix Multiplication

Sometimes it is possible to recognize that a Datalog program with linear constraints defines repeated multiplication of a vector by a *positive stochastic matrix*. A positive stochastic matrix is a square matrix that has only positive entries and in each column the sum of its elements is 1. It can be shown that during repeated positive stochastic matrix multiplication the values of the variables are monotone converging to some steady state with values $(s_1, \ldots, s_n)$. This steady state can be computed even though an infinite number of matrix multiplications may be needed to reach it.

Suppose we wish to test whether there is ever a derived tuple such that each of its values is ϵ close to the corresponding value in some tuple $(a_1, \ldots, a_n)$. We can do this test by first testing whether $(a_1, \ldots, a_n)$ is ϵ close to $(s_1, \ldots, s_n)$. If it is, then the answer is yes. Otherwise, we just repeatedly perform the matrix multiplication and check that the current state is ϵ close to $(a_1, \ldots, a_n)$. We keep doing this until the last derived tuple is so close to the steady state that there is no chance for any derived tuple between the last derived tuple and the steady state to be ϵ close to $(a_1, \ldots, a_n)$. Hence Datalog programs that correspond to repeated positive stochastic matrix multiplication are ϵ-recognition safe.

Example 11.8.1   The query about the water cycle in Example 6.1.7 is safe for years $3n$ for each integer n. Suppose that we want to test whether vector w is a configuration that can occur after some $3n$ number of years. In Example 6.1.7 the matrix A is:

$$
\begin{pmatrix}
\frac{1}{2} & \frac{1}{3} & \frac{1}{6} & \frac{1}{60} \\
\frac{1}{2} & 0 & 0 & 0 \\
0 & \frac{1}{3} & \frac{2}{3} & 0 \\
0 & \frac{1}{3} & \frac{1}{6} & \frac{59}{60}
\end{pmatrix}
$$

Note that A is not positive stochastic because it has some zero entries, but $B = A^3$ is positive stochastic. To answer the question it is enough to consider whether for any n the vector $B^n u$ where u is the initial value of the state variables is ϵ-close to w.

11.8.1 ϵ-Recognition Safety

In this section we assume some familiarity with basic concepts in linear algebra. Positive stochastic matrix multiplication is also called *Markov chains*; we will use this term for simplicity. For Markov chains the most important theorem is the following.

Theorem 11.8.1 Let A be any positive stochastic matrix. Then there exists a unique distribution v such that $Av = v$. Further, let u be any vector different from v, and let $\sum u_i = c$. Then

$$\lim_{k \to \infty} A^k u = cv$$

Proof. One can show that any positive stochastic matrix has 1 as an eigenvalue and for any other eigenvalue λ it may have it must be true that its absolute value is less than 1.

Suppose that A has n distinct eigenvalues $\lambda_1 = 1, \lambda_2, \ldots, \lambda_n$, where $|\lambda_i| < 1$ for $i \geq 2$. (The proof is similar but has to be modified slightly if the eigenvalues are not distinct.) It has corresponding eigenvectors $v_1, \ldots, v_n$ where v_1 is a distribution and the vs are linearly independent. This implies that the matrix $V = (v_1, \ldots, v_n)$ is invertible. Let V^{-1} be the inverse of V and let Λ be the matrix where the eigenvalues appear on the main diagonal.

Then $A = V\Lambda V^{-1}$. Hence $A^k = V\Lambda^k V^{-1}$ for any k. Note that $\lim_{k \to \infty} \Lambda^k = D$, where D is the matrix that has all 0 entries except in its upper-left corner, which is 1. Therefore, $\lim_{k \to \infty} A^k = VDV^{-1} = V(DD)V^{-1} = (VD)(DV^{-1}) = (v_1, 0, \ldots, 0)(w_1, 0, \ldots, 0)^{-1}$, where w_1 is the first row of the matrix V^{-1}.

Hence we have $\lim_{k \to \infty} A^k u = v_1 c$ where c is the dot product of w_1 and u. Because multiplication of a positive stochastic matrix by any vector yields a vector in which the sum of the entries is the same, and v_1 is a distribution, $\sum u_i = c$. ∎

We can use Theorem 11.8.1 to evaluate ϵ-recognition safe queries.

Theorem 11.8.2 For any vectors w and u and matrix M we can find whether there exists a k such that $M^k \sim_\epsilon w$.

Proof. By Theorem 11.8.1 the value $A^k u$ converges to cv, where v and c are as defined there. We test first whether $w \sim_\epsilon cv$. If yes, then clearly w can be reached with ϵ-closeness. Otherwise, we calculate repeatedly $A^k u$ for $k = 1, 2, \ldots$ until either $(A^k u) \sim_\epsilon w$ or $(A^k u) \sim_\epsilon cv$. In the former case w can be still reached

Domain	Constraint	Property Verified
$\mathcal{N}$	Addition	Vector addition system[r]
$\mathcal{N}$	Addition	Lossy vector addition system
$\mathcal{Q}$	Linear	Positive stochastic matrix multiplication[ε]
$\mathcal{Z}$	Linear	Tightening (pseudo-negative)
$\mathcal{N}$	Polynomial	Constricting (pseudo-linear)

FIGURE 11.1. Certifications that Guarantee Safety.

with ϵ-closeness, while in the latter case w cannot be reached with ϵ-closeness because for all larger k the vector $A^k u$ will just get closer and closer to cv, which we already know is not close to w.   ∎

For example, consider Example 6.1.7 with A as given earlier, $B = A^3$, $u = (8, 16, 2, 8)$, $w = (2, 1.5, 1, 29.5)$, and $\epsilon = 0.5$. Because B is positive stochastic, by Theorem 11.8.1 there is a unique distribution v such that $Bv = v$. Solving this system of linear equations $Bv = v$ together with the distribution requirement $\sum v_i = 1$ we obtain the unique solution $v = (1/34)(2, 1, 1, 30)$. Here $c = 34$. Therefore by Theorem 11.8.1 the value of $B^k u$ converges to $cv = (2, 1, 1, 30)$. Because $w \sim_\epsilon cv$ is true, we know that the configuration w is ϵ-reachable.

Figure 11.1 summarizes some conditions that can be verified to guarantee the safety of a constraint automaton. Superscripts r, ϵ mean recognition and ϵ-recognition safe, respectively.

Bibliographic Notes

Vector addition systems were introduced in an equivalent but different notation by Petri; hence they are sometimes called Petri nets [237, 250]. The recognition problem in vector addition systems was shown to be decidable by Kosaraju [177] and Mayr [208]. A recognition algorithm that requires double exponential space in the size of the automaton was developed recently by Bouziane [40].

Constraint automata with a single self-transition with positive stochastic matrix multiplication, are also called Markov chains, because they were studied by Markov, who showed that there is a steady-state vector to which the nth power of the matrix converges. More about steady states of matrix multiplication can be found in [221, 282, 296].

Certification using lossy constraint automata, tightening, and constricting transitions is new. Certification algorithms using constraint simplification by constant passing for stratified Datalog queries with gap-order and set-order constraints are described in Revesz [267].

Exercises

1. Prove that the following queries are safe:

   (a) Example 4.1.1 about the taxes due.
   (b) Example 4.1.8 about the broadcast areas of radio stations.
   (c) Example 6.1.2 about the elevator system.
   (d) Example 6.1.4 about the subway train control system.
   (e) Example 6.1.6 about the cafeteria.

2. Is the query you wrote for the following exercises safe? Why or why not?

   (a) Exercise 6.4 about the thermostat.
   (b) Exercise 6.8 about employment.
   (c) Exercise 6.9 about the wealth of people.

3. Prove that the following queries in Chapter 5 are safe:

   (a) The Q_{profit} query.
   (b) The Q_{edge} query.
   (c) The $Q_{\text{not\_cover}}$ query.
   (d) The Q_{fastest} query.
   (e) The Q_{Alice} query.

4. Prove that lossy vector addition systems are evaluable in closed form. (**Hint:** Use Lemma 9.4.1 and König's Lemma, which says that any infinite tree must have an infinite path.)

Implementation Methods

Chapter 9 discussed the evaluation of constraint query languages in general based on several assumptions, for example, that existential quantifier elimination and satisfiability can be implemented as functions. From a practical point of view there are many lower-level details that need to be considered for implementation of a constraint database system. In this chapter, we discuss two implementation approaches.

The first approach is a graph-based approach described in Section 12.1. This approach takes a step toward implementation by giving a graph data structure to the constraint data represented. Then it develops the algebraic operators in terms of this new data structure.

The second approach, described in Section 12.2, is a matrix-based approach that is even more concrete. In this, the graph data structure is replaced by matrices that lead to simple computer implementations. Throughout this chapter we will consider integer difference constraints as our main example. Similar graph-based or matrix-based implementation structures could be described for other types of constraints. We give just a brief outline for Boolean constraints in Section 12.3.1.

12.1 Evaluation with Gap-Graphs

In this section we assume that all atomic constraints in the input relations are difference constraints. Note that each lower bound constraint of the form $x \geq a$ and each upper bound constraint of the form $-x \geq b$ can be represented by the difference constraints $x - 0 \geq a$ and $0 - x \geq b$, respectively. Similarly, we can express equality constraint $x = y$ by the conjunction of $x - y \geq 0$ and $y - x \geq 0$.

Unlike gap-order constraints, which always have a nonnegative bound, difference constraints are closed under negation. More precisely, $not\,(x - y \geq b)$

is equivalent to $x - y < b$, which can be rewritten as the difference constraint $y - x > -b$. If the domain of the variables is the integers, then the latter can be further rewritten as $y - x \geq -b + 1$. Therefore, we will assume in the following that we have only integer difference constraints of the form $x - y \geq c$, where x and y are variables or 0 and c is some integer. We call this the normal form of integer difference constraints.

Conjunctions of integer difference constraints over the variables $x_1, \ldots, x_n$ can be represented as a *gap-graph* $G(V, E)$, where V is the set of vertices and E is the set of edges. V contains a vertex representing the constant 0 and one vertex for each variable. For each integer difference constraint of the form $x - y \geq c$, E contains a directed edge from y to x with label c. This edge is denoted as $y \xrightarrow{c} x$. We define the following operators.

Graph: This operator takes as input a set of constraint tuples and returns their gap-graph representations.

Example 12.1.1 Consider the following conjunction of difference constraints:

$$0 - x_1 \geq 5$$
$$0 - x_2 \geq 2$$
$$x_1 - x_3 \geq -2$$
$$x_1 - x_5 \geq -9$$
$$x_2 - x_1 \geq -6$$
$$x_3 - x_2 \geq 3$$
$$x_3 - x_4 \geq -3$$
$$x_4 - x_3 \geq -5$$
$$x_5 - x_4 \geq 3$$
$$x_5 - x_6 \geq 3$$
$$x_6 - 0 \geq 1$$

This can be represented by gap-graph G_1, shown in Figure 12.1. Similarly, the conjunction

$$0 - x_2 \geq 1$$
$$x_1 - x_5 \geq -10$$
$$x_2 - x_1 \geq -3$$
$$x_3 - x_2 \geq 6$$
$$x_4 - x_3 \geq -4$$
$$x_5 - x_4 \geq 3$$
$$x_5 - 0 \geq 2$$

can be represented by G_2, shown in Figure 12.2.

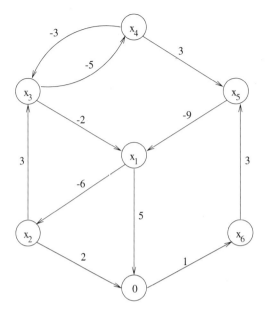

FIGURE 12.1. Gap-graph G_1.

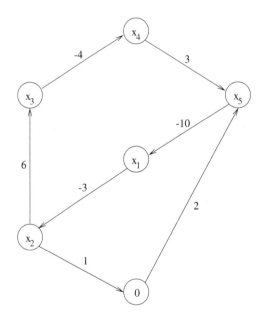

FIGURE 12.2. Gap-graph G_2.

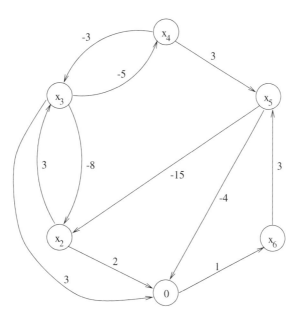

FIGURE 12.3. Shortcut of x_1 from G_1.

Note that between any pair of vertices, at most two edges are enough because we need to keep in each direction only the highest labeled edges, as the others represent only weaker constraints. Therefore, each gap-graph with $k + 1$ vertices can be represented with at most $O(k^2)$ size.

Shortcut: This operator takes as input a variable x and a gap-graph $G(V, E)$ and returns a gap-graph $G'(V \setminus \{x\}, E')$, where E' is all the edges in E that are not incident on x and the edges

$$u \xrightarrow{a+b} v \text{ if } u \xrightarrow{a} x \text{ and } x \xrightarrow{b} v \in E$$

This operator implements existential quantifier elimination on gap-graphs.

Example 12.1.2   The shortcut of vertex x_1 from G_1 is shown in Figure 12.3. Because $x_5 \xrightarrow{-9} x_1$ and $x_1 \xrightarrow{5} 0$ are edges in Figure 12.1 we have the new edge $x_5 \xrightarrow{-4} 0$ in the shortcut graph because $-9 + 5 = -4$.

Merge: This operator takes as input two gap-graphs $G_1(V_1, E_1)$ and $G_2(V_2, E_2)$ and gives as output the gap-graph $G(V, E)$ where $V = V_1 \cup V_2$ and $E = E_1 \cup E_2$. This operator implements taking the conjunction of two constraint tuples.

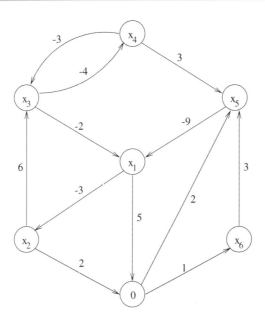

FIGURE 12.4. Merge of G_1 and G_2.

Example 12.1.3 The merge of G_1 and G_2 is shown in Figure 12.4. Because $x_5 \xrightarrow{-9} x_1$ is an edge in Figure 12.1 and $x_5 \xrightarrow{-10} x_1$ is an edge in Figure 12.2 we have the first edge in the new gap-graph because $-9 > -10$.

Sat: This operator takes as input a gap-graph and returns it if the constraint tuple represented by the gap-graph is satisfiable. Otherwise the sat returns nothing.

We call a chain of directed edges a *path*. If the path starts and ends at the same vertex, then we call it a *cycle*. We call the *length* of a path the sum of the gap values in the labels of its directed edges. For example, in G_2 the path $x_1 \xrightarrow{-3} x_2 \xrightarrow{6} x_3 \xrightarrow{-4} x_4$ has length 1.

Lemma 12.1.1 Let T be a difference constraint tuple. Then T is satisfiable if and only if in *graph* (T) there is no cycle with length greater than 0. ∎

For example, suppose that in a gap-graph there is a directed edge from vertex x to vertex y with label 3, and there is another edge from y to x with label -2. Then there is a cycle in the gap-graph where the sum of the labels is 1. Hence the gap-graph is not satisfiable by Lemma 12.1.1.

Instead of using Lemma 12.1.1 we could reason as follows. The first edge represents the constraint $x + 3 \leq y$, while the second edge represents the constraint $y - 2 \leq x$, which is equivalent to $y \leq x + 2$. Hence the two constraints together would imply that $x + 3 \leq x + 2$, which is impossible.

The transitive closure G^* of a gap-graph G is the gap-graph with the same vertices as G and with a single directed edge $v_i - v_j \geq b$ between each pair of vertices v_i and v_j between which there is at least one directed path and the length of the longest directed path is b. Lemma 12.1.1 implies the following theorem.

Theorem 12.1.1   Let T be a difference constraint tuple. Then $G = graph(T)$ is satisfiable if and only if in G^* there is no vertex v with $v \xrightarrow{b} v$ and $b > 0$. ∎

Corollary 12.1.1   Let T be a difference constraint tuple with k variables and size $O(n)$. Then it can be decided in $O(n + k^3)$ time whether T is satisfiable.

Proof. We can build a gap-graph to represent T in $O(n)$ time such that there is at most one edge from each vertex to another vertex. Therefore, the size of the gap-graph will be $O(k^2)$. Then we can find the transitive closure of this gap-graph in $O(k^3)$ time. Finally, we can check that there is no edge from any vertex to itself with a bound greater than zero. ∎

Dnf: This operator takes as input a formula with difference constraints and puts it into disjunctive normal form.

Compl: This operator takes as input a formula with difference constraints, finds its complement, and puts it into disjunctive normal form.

Lemma 12.1.2   For any fixed k and variable n, the complement of any integer difference constraint relation R of arity k and size n can be found in $O(n^{k^2})$ time.

Proof. Without loss of generality let $R(x_1, \ldots, x_k)$ be the schema of R. The complement of R will be a relation with a set of integer difference constraint tuples. Each atomic constraint in these constraint tuples will have a left-hand side of the form $x_i - x_j$ where $1 \leq i, j \leq k$. Therefore, there are k^2 different left-hand sides. In each constraint tuple there need be at most one atomic constraint with each left-hand side. (This corresponds to having at most one edge from any vertex to another vertex in a gap-graph representation.)

Let B be the set of bound values that occur in R. Let also $\overline{B} = \{-b + 1 : b \in B\}$. Clearly both B and $\overline{B}$ have size $O(n)$. It can be seen from De Morgan's laws that each constraint tuple in the complement of R can be represented as a conjunction of atomic constraints in which the bound is in $\overline{B}$.

We can build only at most $O(n^{k^2})$ different constraint tuples using atomic constraints with at most $O(k^2)$ distinct left-hand sides and $O(n)$ right-hand sides. (This corresponds to assigning to each directed edge in a gap-graph a value from $\overline{B}$.)

Each of these disjuncts can be tested to be in the relation in $O(n)$ time. We know that a constraint tuple t is in the complement of R if t and t_i is unsatisfiable for any constraint tuple t_i in R. Therefore, we can build and test each of the possible constraint tuples. Corollary 12.1.1 implies that satisfiability can be done in $O(k^3)$ time. Therefore, the complement can be found in at most $O(n^{k^2})$ time.

■

Remark 12.1.1   For small k, there are special algorithms that can be used to take the complement of R. For example, when $k = 1$ then each constraint tuple of R represents an interval. Hence in this case the problem reduces to finding the complement of n intervals. The complement in this case can be represented by at most $n + 1$ intervals or constraint tuples, which can be found in $O(n \log n)$ time.

Based on these operators, we define the constraint relational algebra operators as follows:

$$A \hat{\cap} B = \{merge\,(G_1, G_2) : G_1 \in graph\,(A) \text{ and } G_2 \in graph\,(B)\}$$

$$A \hat{\cup} B = \{G : G \in graph\,(A) \text{ or } G \in graph\,(B)\}$$

$$A \hat{\backslash} B = A \hat{\cap} compl\,(B)$$

$$A \hat{\times} B = \{G(V_1 \cup V_2, E_1 \cup E_2) : G_1(V_1, E_1) \in graph\,(A) \text{ and}$$
$$G_2(V_2, E_2) \in graph\,(B)\}$$

$$A \hat{\bowtie} B = \{merge\,(G_1, G_2) : G_1 \in graph\,(A) \text{ and } G_2 \in graph\,(B)\}$$

$$\hat{\pi}_L A = \{shortcut\,(x_i, G) : G \in graph\,(A)\}$$

$$\hat{\sigma}_F A = \{merge\,(G, graph\,(F)) : G \in graph\,(A) \text{ and } F_i \in dnf\,(F)\}$$

As a final step in each operation, we apply the sat operator to keep only the satisfiable gap-graphs in the output relation. The preceding list of relational algebra operators left out the rename operator, which just relabels the vertices of the gap-graph. Using the defined constraint relational algebra operators, it is possible to evaluate any relational algebra query.

12.2   Evaluation with Matrices

12.2.1   From Graphs to Matrices

We represent each gap-graph by a matrix M in which each entry $M[i, j] = b$ if there is an edge $x_i \xrightarrow{b} x_j$ and it is $-\infty$ otherwise. If there are several edges from x_i to x_j, then we take the maximum of the bounds.

Example 12.2.1   The following matrix represents G_1 in Figure 12.1:

	0	x_1	x_2	x_3	x_4	x_5	x_6
0	$-\infty$	$-\infty$	$-\infty$	$-\infty$	$-\infty$	$-\infty$	1
x_1	5	$-\infty$	-6	$-\infty$	$-\infty$	$-\infty$	$-\infty$
x_2	2	$-\infty$	$-\infty$	3	$-\infty$	$-\infty$	$-\infty$
x_3	$-\infty$	-2	$-\infty$	$-\infty$	-5	$-\infty$	$-\infty$
x_4	$-\infty$	$-\infty$	$-\infty$	-3	$-\infty$	3	$-\infty$
x_5	$-\infty$	-9	$-\infty$	$-\infty$	$-\infty$	$-\infty$	$-\infty$
x_6	$-\infty$	$-\infty$	$-\infty$	$-\infty$	$-\infty$	3	$-\infty$

Similarly, the following is the representation of G_2 in Figure 12.2:

	0	x_1	x_2	x_3	x_4	x_5
0	$-\infty$	$-\infty$	$-\infty$	$-\infty$	$-\infty$	2
x_1	$-\infty$	$-\infty$	-3	$-\infty$	$-\infty$	$-\infty$
x_2	1	$-\infty$	$-\infty$	6	$-\infty$	$-\infty$
x_3	$-\infty$	$-\infty$	$-\infty$	$-\infty$	-4	$-\infty$
x_4	$-\infty$	$-\infty$	$-\infty$	$-\infty$	$-\infty$	3
x_5	$-\infty$	-10	$-\infty$	$-\infty$	$-\infty$	$-\infty$

The satisfiability testing algorithm can be now given as follows:

Sat(M,n)
input: Matrix M representing a gap-graph over $n+1$ vertices.
output: True or False depending on whether M is satisfiable.

```
m := 0
```
repeat
```
      m := m + 1
```
      for i := 0 to n **do**
        for j := 0 to n **do**
          for k := 0 to n **do**
            $M[i, j] := max(M[i, j], M[i, k] + M[k, j])$
          end-for
        end-for
      end-for
until $m = \log(n + 1)$

```
Flag := True
```

for i := 0 to n **do**
   if $M[i, i] > 0$ **then**
      Flag := False
end-for

return(Flag)

The repeat-until loop finds the transitive closure of M. For the body of the innermost for loop, note that $(-\infty) + (-\infty) = -\infty$ and $-\infty + b = -\infty$ for any integer b. The last for loop checks the condition in Theorem 12.1.1.

Example 12.2.2   The satisfiability algorithm for input G_1 will compute the transitive closure G_1^*, which is the following:

	0	x_1	x_2	x_3	x_4	x_5	x_6
0	0	-5	-11	-8	-13	4	1
x_1	5	0	-6	-3	-8	9	6
x_2	6	1	-5	3	-2	10	7
x_3	3	-2	-8	-5	-5	7	4
x_4	0	-5	-11	-3	-8	4	1
x_5	-4	-9	-15	-12	-17	0	-3
x_6	-1	-6	-12	-9	-14	3	0

Because in the main diagonal of this matrix there is no entry greater than 0, the gap-graph G_1 is satisfiable.

12.2.2   Shortcut and Project

Now we give an implementation of the shortcut function. We assume that there are already two functions available that can delete the kth row or column of a matrix.

Shortcut(k,M,n)
input: A matrix $M[0..n][0..n]$ and an integer k between 1 and n.
output: The submatrix M' with the kth vertex shortcut.

```
for i := 0 to n do
    for j := 0 to n do
        M[i, j] := max(M[i, j], M[i, k] + M[k, j])
    end-for
end-for

M := delete_row(k,M)
M := delete_column(k,M)
```

return (M,n-1)

Example 12.2.3   Let us apply the shortcut algorithm for the input matrix for G_1. We obtain the following matrix, which represents the gap-graph shown in Figure 12.3:

	0	x_2	x_3	x_4	x_5	x_6
0	$-\infty$	$-\infty$	$-\infty$	$-\infty$	$-\infty$	1
x_2	2	$-\infty$	3	$-\infty$	$-\infty$	$-\infty$
x_3	3	-8	$-\infty$	-5	$-\infty$	$-\infty$
x_4	$-\infty$	$-\infty$	-3	$-\infty$	3	$-\infty$
x_5	-4	-15	$-\infty$	$-\infty$	$-\infty$	$-\infty$
x_6	$-\infty$	$-\infty$	$-\infty$	$-\infty$	3	$-\infty$

Based on the *shortcut* operation, we can now define projection. We assume that we have a function *insert* that inserts a matrix into the linked list, which represents a relation:

Project(X,R,n)
input: R is a linked list of matrices $[0..n]$ times $[0..n]$.
        A set X of indices of vertices to be projected out.
output: The project of R onto X.

$V := \{0, \ldots, n\}$
$S := V \setminus X$

```
T := empty-list
```

for each matrix M in R **do**
    for each x in S **do**
        M := *shortcut*(x,M)
    end-for
    T := insert(M,T)
end-for

return(T,n-1)

12.2.3   Merge and Join

Suppose we have two matrices T and M such that T includes all the variables of M. We would like to add M to T, that is, change T such that it will contain the merge of T and M.

The main problem is that the order of the variables in T and M may be different. For example, in T the columns may be in the order $0, x, y, t, z, t_2$ while in M they may be in the order $0, x, z, t_2$.

Although it is possible to implement an operator that reorders the columns and rows of M, it would be a time-consuming operation and would require extra storage space for an entire matrix. Instead we can just define an order vector $e[0, \ldots, 6]$ such that $e[0] = 0$, and for $i > 0$ each $e[i]$ equals the order in M of the ith variable in T or blank if it does not occur in M. In this case, the vector would be the second row of the following matrix:

0	x	y	t	z	t_2
0	1			2	3

Similar orderings can be found between any pair of T and M where the variables of T contain those of M. We assume that the order vector is known before calling merge. We pass the order vector e along with the matrices T and M and n the number of variables in T as parameters into the merge operator, which now can be implemented as follows:

Merge(T, M, e, n)
input: Matrices, order vector, and number of variables.
output: T will be updated to be the merge of T and M.

for i := 0 to n **do**
    for j := 0 to n **do**
        if $e[i] \neq blank$ and $e[j] \neq blank$ **then**
            $T[i, j] := max(T[i, j], M[e[i], e[j]])$
    end-for
end-for

return (T, n)

Example 12.2.4   Let's consider the matrix representations of G_1 and G_2 shown in Example 12.2.1. Here the variables of G_1 include those of G_2. Therefore, we have the order vector $e = [0, 1, 2, 3, 4, 5, blank]$. The result of the merge operation will be the following matrix:

	0	x_1	x_2	x_3	x_4	x_5	x_6
0	$-\infty$	$-\infty$	$-\infty$	$-\infty$	$-\infty$	2	1
x_1	5	$-\infty$	-3	$-\infty$	$-\infty$	$-\infty$	$-\infty$
x_2	2	$-\infty$	$-\infty$	6	$-\infty$	$-\infty$	$-\infty$
x_3	$-\infty$	-2	$-\infty$	$-\infty$	-4	$-\infty$	$-\infty$
x_4	$-\infty$	$-\infty$	$-\infty$	-3	$-\infty$	3	$-\infty$
x_5	$-\infty$	-9	$-\infty$	$-\infty$	$-\infty$	$-\infty$	$-\infty$
x_6	$-\infty$	$-\infty$	$-\infty$	$-\infty$	$-\infty$	3	$-\infty$

Now suppose that we would like to merge two matrices M_1 and M_2 in which neither contains all the variables of the other. We can do this by first taking the union of all the variables in the two matrices and creating a template matrix T that contains some ordering of all the variables. By a template matrix we mean a matrix in which all entries are $-\infty$. Next we find the order vectors of both M_1 and M_2 and then successively merge into T first M_1 and then M_2.

Similarly to the merge, we can implement the join of two relations represented by a linked list of matrices. Again we assume that the scheme of the first relation includes all the attributes in the scheme of the second relation. We also assume that the number of matrices in the linked lists can be found by the *size* function:

Join(T, R, e, n)
input: T and R, linked lists of matrices, e and n as in merge.
output: The join of T and M.

```
L := empty-list

for i := 1 to size(T) do
    for j := 1 to size(R) do
        Temp := T[i]
        Temp := merge(Temp, R[j], e, n)
        if sat(Temp) then
            L := insert(Temp, L)
    end-for
end-for

return(L)
```

12.2.4   Datalog Evaluation

It is easy to see that we can write each Datalog rule into a form where each subgoal contains only distinct variables. This is because we can always add some equality constraints to the end of the rule body and consider them as additional subgoals in the rule. We also assume that the same defined relation always contains the same list of variables in every rule. We say that Datalog programs in this form are in *rectified form*. From now on we assume that Datalog programs are in rectified form.

With each Datalog rule with n distinct variables and m subgoals we associate a matrix $M[0..m][0..n]$. The header of this matrix lists the constant 0 and the variables that occur in the rule in some fixed order, for example, the order of their occurrence as we read the rule from left to right. Then each ith row of the matrix corresponds to the ith subgoal in the rule and contains the order vector of the ith subgoal. More precisely, for each $1 \leq j \leq n$ the $M[i, j]$ entry is the rank of the jth variable within the ith relation. If a variable does not occur in the relation, then we will leave it blank. The $M[i, 0]$ entry will always be 0 for any i. For example, let us consider the following rule of Example 4.1.3:

   Travel $(x, y, t) :-$ *Travel* (x, z, t_2), *Go* (z, t_2, y, t).

To this rule we assign the list: x, y, t, z, t_2 as the list of occurrence of the variables from left to right. For this rule, the order vectors of the two subgoals are shown as the second and third rows of the following matrix:

0	x	y	t	z	t_2
0	1			2	3
0		3	4	1	2

Eval-Datalog(Q,D,l_{min})
input: Query Q, an input database D, and minimum bound l_{min}.
output: Approximation of the least fixpoint model of $Q(D)$.

Rectify each rule of Q.

repeat
    MoreAdded := False
    for each rule r_k with n_k variables and m_k subgoals **do**

        Create a template matrix $Temp[0..n_k][0..n_k]$.
        Create a relation T containing only the $Temp$ matrix.

        for $i := 1$ to m_k **do**
            R := subgoal(k,i)
            e := order(k,i)
            T := join(T,R,e,n)
        end-for

        Suppose output relation R_0 has j number of variables
        X := $\{0, \ldots, j\}$
        P := project(X,T,n)

        for each matrix M_1 in P **do**
            In M_1 change each entry less than l_{min} to $-\infty$
            Need-to-Add := True
            for each matrix M_2 in R_0 **do**
                if dominates(M_1, M_2) **then**
                    Need-to-Add := False
            if Need-to-Add = True **then**
                $R_0 := insert(M_1, R_0)$
                MoreAdded := True
            end-if
        end-for
    end-for
until MoreAdded = False

The equality matrix really is an implicit representation of the renaming required of the variables in the subgoals. We will use this in the evaluation of Datalog queries.

To evaluate a Datalog rule, we have to do for each rule a join of the subgoals in the rule body and then a projection of the variables in the head of the rule. We have to do this repeatedly until there are no more matrices that can be added to the database. We only need to add to the database those matrices that do not dominate any earlier matrix. We assume that *dominates* (M_1, M_2) is a function that returns true if M_1 dominates M_2. We also assume that each *bound* must have a value greater than or equal to l_{min} as explained in Chapter 9. The *Eval-Datalog* program evaluates a Datalog query.

The program assumes that we already defined the order matrices for each rule, and the function *subgoal* (k, i) returns the ith subgoal of the kth rule and the function *order* (k, i) returns its order vector.

Note that in the project it is enough to know the number of variables in the rule head because the rules are rectified and because of our assumption that variables in each rule are ordered according to their occurrence in the rule as it is read from left to right. An evaluation of a lower bound of the least fixpoint of a Datalog query can be done by changing in M_1 any bound that is less than l_{min} to l_{min} instead of to $-\infty$. This requires only changing one line in the preceding program.

Compl-Matrix(M,n)
input: A matrix $M[0..n][0..n]$.
output: The complement of M as a list of matrices and n.

```
L := emptyset
```

for i := 1 to n **do**
    for i := 1 to n **do**
        if $M[i, j] \neq -\infty$ **then**
            `Create a template matrix` $Temp[0..n][0..n]$
            `Temp[j,i] := -M[i,j]+1`
        end-if
        `L := insert(Temp,L)`
    end-for
end-for

return `(T,n)`

12.2.5 Complement and Difference

At first we give an algorithm *Compl_Matrix* that takes the complement of a matrix M. Note that the complement of M is a linked list of matrices, where in each matrix we have one of the entries that is not $-\infty$ in M negated. Negation of an entry $[i, j]$ with value b is equivalent to a value of $-b+1$ in the entry $[j, i]$. Hence we can implement the complement by at first defining an a function *Compl-Matrix* as shown in the preceding environment.

Using this function and another called *remove_duplicate*, which removes duplicate copies from a linked list of matrices, we describe the complement of a relation as follows:

Compl(R,n)
input: R is an array of $[0..n] \times [0..n]$ matrices.
output: The complement of R.

for i = 1 to m **do**
　　$e[i] := i$
end-for

$T := compl\_matrix(R[1])$

for i := 2 to size(R) **do**
　　$T := join(T, compl\_matrix(R[i]), e, n)$
　　$T := remove\_duplicates(T)$
end-for
return (T)

The difference of relations R and P, written $R - P$ is equivalent to the join of R and the complement of P. Hence the difference operator can also be defined for integer difference constraint relations.

Remark 12.2.1　Using the difference operator it is possible to improve the Datalog evaluation slightly by replacing the dominance test (last two for loops of algorithm *Eval-Datalog*) with a test whether *Difference* (M_1, R_0) is nonempty. Nonemptiness of a relation can be tested by checking the satisfiability of each matrix in the relation. The relation is empty if each of the matrices in it is unsatisfiable.

12.3　Boolean Constraints

Suppose that $R(x_1, \ldots, x_k)$ is a relation where the domain of the variables is some Boolean algebra and each constraint tuple of R contains only Boolean algebra upper bound constraints.

We saw in Theorem 9.4.5 that there can be only $3^k - 1$ possible left-hand sides in all the upper bound constraints with variables $x_1, \ldots, x_k$. We can fix an ordering of these left-hand sides.

In a constraint tuple there is no need to have two different upper bound constraints with the same left-hand sides, because using the merge rule for precedence constraints we can show that

$$x \leq a \text{ and } x \leq b \quad \text{iff} \quad x \leq (a \wedge b) \qquad (12.1)$$

Hence each constraint tuple can be represented by an array $A[0..3^k - 1]$ of Boolean constants, where the ith entry corresponds to the right-hand side of the ith upper bound constraint.

Example 12.3.1   The conjunction of upper bound constraints:

$$x \wedge y \wedge z \leq_B (a \vee b)$$
$$x \wedge y' \leq_B (a \wedge c) \vee d$$
$$x' \wedge y' \wedge z' \leq_B (b' \wedge e)$$

can be represented by the array:

	Upper Bound
xyz	$(a \vee b)$
$\vdots$	1
xy'	$(a \wedge c) \vee d$
$\vdots$	1
$x'y'z'$	$(b' \wedge e)$

which has all its entries 1 except for the three entries that show the right-hand sides of the Boolean upper bound constraints.

In this case, the merge of two constraint tuples represented by arrays A_1 and A_2 can be done by applying rule (12.1) for each corresponding pair of entries in A_1 and A_2 and then simplifying and putting the right-hand sides back to disjunctive normal form.

Existential quantifier elimination of a variable x can be done following Theorem 9.1.9 by taking each pair of left-hand sides such that one contains x and the other contains x' and then finding their implication and merging that with the corresponding entry in the array.

12.3.1   Evaluation with Set-Graphs

Consider again the Boolean algebra B_Z defined in Chapter 2. When this Boolean algebra is in use, the left-hand sides are simpler because we can have only 2^D possible sets or their complements on the right-hand side where D is the set of integer constants that occurs in the input database or the query.

In B_Z the zero element is $\emptyset$ and the one element is $\mathcal{Z}$. Recall from Chapter 2 that these can be used within constraints as well as with any set constant $\{c_1, \ldots, c_n\}$ where all of c_i are integer constants or complements of set constants.

We also defined in B_Z the constraint $\subseteq$ as equivalent to the precedence constraint. Hence, let us use $\subseteq$ for the precedence constraint in this section. The following constraints are possible to express using only $\subseteq$ and set constants:

$$\{c\} \subseteq x \tag{12.2}$$

which means that c is in x, and

$$x \subseteq \{c\}' \tag{12.3}$$

which means that c is not in x.

If B_Z is the domain and we use only $\subseteq$ constraints, including constraints of the form (12.2) and (12.3), then we can express constraint tuples in an even simpler structure called *set-graphs*. Set-graphs provide a visual representation of conjunctions of set containment constraints. For example, the conjunction of the constraints:

$$\{3, 6, 9\} \subseteq X_1$$
$$\{1, 2, 3, 4\} \subseteq Y$$
$$Y \subseteq X_1$$
$$Y \subseteq X_2$$
$$X_3 \subseteq Y$$
$$X_3 \subseteq X_2$$
$$X_1 \subseteq \{1, 2, 3, 4, 5, 6, 7, 8, 9\}$$
$$X_2 \subseteq \{1, 2, 3, 4, 5, 6, 7, 8, 9\}$$

can be represented by the set-graph shown on the left in Figure 12.5. In the set-graph, each directed edge from a vertex labeled X to another vertex labeled Y represents the constraint $X \subseteq Y$.

Set-graphs with n variables can also be represented by a matrix of size $n \times n$ and an array of size $n \times 3$. In the first matrix the i, jth entry will be a 1 if the ith variable is a subset of the jth variable or 0 otherwise. For example, the set-graph on the left of Figure 12.5 can be represented by the matrix:

	x_1	x_2	x_3	y
x_1	0	0	0	0
x_2	0	0	0	0
x_3	0	1	0	1
y	1	1	0	0

In the second matrix there will be a row for each variable and two columns. The first column will list the lower bound and the second the upper bound for each set variable. In the example the second matrix would be:

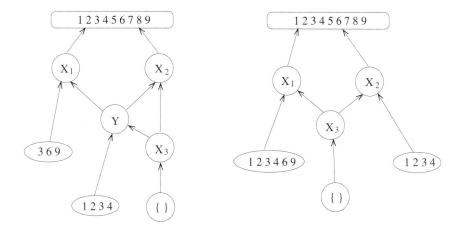

FIGURE 12.5. Example of variable elimination from a set-graph.

	L	U
x_1	{3,6,9}	{1,2,3,4,5,6,7,8,9}
x_2	{}	{1,2,3,4,5,6,7,8,9}
x_3	{}	{}'
y	{1,2,3,4}	{}'

In this matrix the upper bound of x_3 is $\{\}' = \mathbf{Z}$, i.e., the entire set of integers.

We define the transitive closure G^* of a set-graph G with vertices $v_1, \ldots, v_n$ as the set-graph that has an edge from v_i to v_j whenever there is a directed path from v_i to v_j in G. The satisfiability of set-graphs can be tested based on the following lemma.

Lemma 12.3.1   Let G be a set-graph with vertices $v_1, \ldots, v_n$. G is satisfiable if and only if in G^* for each pair of vertices v_i and v_j if there is a directed edge from v_i to v_j, then $L_i \subseteq U_j$ is true.   ∎

The variable elimination operation can be defined similarly to the one for gap-graphs. If we want to eliminate variable Y, then we have to add for each pair of vertices V_i and V_j with $V_i \subseteq Y$ and $Y \subseteq V_j$ the edge $V_i \subseteq V_j$. Further we have to make the lower bound of V_j the union of the lower bounds of V_i and V_j, and we have to make the upper bound of V_i the intersection of the upper bounds of V_i and V_j.

For example, if we want to eliminate variable Y from the set-graph on the left of Figure 12.5, then we get the set-graph on the right side of the figure.

The merge operation can be defined between set-graphs as well. The merge returns a set-graph that contains all the edges of the two input set-graphs plus the lower and upper bounds are also merged as in the variable elimination algorithm. For example, the merge operation on the inputs that is the right side of

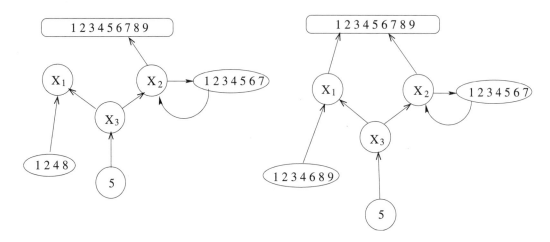

FIGURE 12.6. Example of merge of set-graphs.

Figure 12.5 and the left side of Figure 12.6 will return the set-graph on the right side of Figure 12.6.

The relational algebra operators rename, select, and join can be defined similarly to the definitions for relations with gap-graphs. Finally, the evaluation of Datalog queries with B_Z precedence constraints can be defined similarly to Section 12.2.

12.4 Optimization of Relational Algebra

Because relational algebra is a procedural language, each relational algebra query can be evaluated simply by following the sequence of operations in the relational algebra expression. However, this simple evaluation method is not always the best possible.

Relational algebra query optimization algorithms rely on the fact that a relational algebra expression can be rewritten into other logically equivalent relational algebra expressions by using several rewriting rules. The rewritten relational algebra expression can often be evaluated much more simply than the original one, although they always yield the same output relation.

The following are some rewriting rules that can be used by query optimization algorithms:

1. *Commutative laws for join and products:*

$$R_1 \bowtie R_2 \equiv R_2 \bowtie R_1$$
$$R_1 \times R_2 \equiv R_2 \times R_1$$

2. *Associative law for joins and products:*

$$(R_1 \bowtie R_2) \bowtie R_3 \equiv R_1 \bowtie (R_2 \bowtie R_3)$$
$$(R_1 \times R_2) \times R_3 \equiv R_1 \times (R_2 \times R_3)$$

3. *Cascade of projections:*

$$\pi_{A_1,\dots,A_k}(\pi_{B_1,\dots,B_l}(R)) \equiv \pi_{A_1,\dots,A_k}(R)$$

if $\{A_1, \dots, A_k\} \subseteq \{B_1, \dots, B_l\}$

4. *Cascade of selections:*

$$\sigma_{F_1}(\sigma_{F_2}(R)) \equiv \sigma_{F_1 \wedge F_2}(R) \equiv \sigma_{F_2}(\sigma_{F_1}(R))$$

5. *Commuting selections and projections:*
   If the set of attributes in condition F is the subset of $\{A_1, \dots, A_k\}$:

$$\pi_{A_1,\dots,A_k}(\sigma_F(R)) \equiv \sigma_F(\pi_{A_1,\dots,A_k}(R))$$

   If the set of attributes in F is $\{A_{i_1}, \dots, A_{i_m}\} \cup \{B_1, \dots, B_l\}$:

$$\pi_{A_1,\dots,A_k}(\sigma_F(R)) \equiv \pi_{A_1,\dots,A_k}(\sigma_F(\pi_{A_1,\dots,A_k,B_1,\dots,B_l}(R)))$$

6. *Commuting selection with join:*
   If all the attributes of F are the attributes of R_1:

$$\sigma_F(R_1 \bowtie R_2) \equiv \sigma_F(R_1) \bowtie R_2$$

   If $F = F_1 \wedge F_2$, the attributes of F_1 are only in R_1, and the attributes in F_2 are only in R_2, then:

$$\sigma_F(R_1 \bowtie R_2) \equiv \sigma_{F_1}(R_1) \bowtie \sigma_{F_2}(R_2)$$

   If $F = F_1 \wedge F_2$ and the attributes of F_1 are only in R_1, but the attributes in F_2 are in both R_1 and R_2:

$$\sigma_F(R_1 \bowtie R_2) \equiv \sigma_{F_2}(\sigma_{F_1}(R_1) \bowtie R_2)$$

7. *Commuting a projection with a join:*
   $\{A_1, \dots, A_k\} = \{B_1, \dots, B_l\} \cup \{C_1, \dots, C_m\}$, where B_is are attributes of R_1, and C_is are attributes of R_2:

$$\pi_{A_1,\dots,A_k}(R_1 \bowtie R_2) \equiv \pi_{B_1,\dots,B_l}(R_1) \bowtie \pi_{C_1,\dots,C_m}(R_2)$$

The following description of the optimization algorithm is clearer if we visualize each relational algebra expression as a tree in which each internal node is a relational algebra operator and its children are the operands. Then the general principles behind the query optimization algorithm can be stated as follows:

1. Perform selections as early as possible.

2. Perform projections as early as possible.

3. Combine sequences of selection operations.

These principles lead to a basic optimization algorithm that at first uses for each selection the identities 4—6 to move the selections down. Second, it uses the identities 3 or 7 to move the projections down, and if possible to delete some projections. Finally, it uses the identity 4 to combine cascades of selections into one selection.

Example 12.4.1   Consider the following relational algebra formula:

$$\pi_{x,y} \left(\sigma_{x \cap y \neq \emptyset} \left(\sigma_{y \cap \{4\} = \emptyset} \left(\sigma_{x \cap \{6,8\} = \emptyset} \left(\sigma_{x \cap \{2,4\} = \emptyset} \right. \right. \right. \right.$$
$$\left. \left. \left. \left. (A(x, z) \bowtie B(v, y) \bowtie C(x) \bowtie D(v, y)) \right) \right) \right) \right)$$

This formula can be visualized as the tree shown in Figure 12.7. We now briefly illustrate each of these steps of the optimization.

Perform Selections as Early as Possible: To apply this step, we find which relations and selections have common variables. Suppose that in a (sub)formula a set of selections $(S_1, S_2, \ldots, S_k)$ follows the join of a set of relations $(R_1, R_2, \ldots, R_l)$. Let V_i be the set of relations that have common variables with S_i, that is:

$$V_i = \{R_n \mid (variables\ in\ R_n) \cap (variables\ in\ S_i) \neq \emptyset\}$$

A selection (S_i) can be executed if the join of all the relations mentioned in V_i is already calculated. This gives an obvious limit for how far we can move down the selection S_i.

Whenever there are several selections to choose to move down, then we check whether there is any i such that $\forall j : V_i \subseteq V_j$. In this case S_i will be moved down before all the other selections. If there is no such i, then the algorithm chooses some index i with a minimal cardinality V_i. After a selection is moved down, the V_is are updated and the preceding is repeated.

In Figure 12.7 there are four selections to choose from to move down first. For the four selections $\sigma_{y \cap \{4\} = \emptyset}, \sigma_{x \cap \{6,8\} = \emptyset}, \sigma_{x \cap \{2,4\} = \emptyset}$, and $\sigma_{x \cap y \neq \emptyset}$, we calculate the values $V_1 = \{A, B, C, D\}$, $V_2 = \{B, D\}$, $V_3 = \{A, C\}$, and $V_4 = \{A, C\}$, respectively.

Because no V_i is the subset of all the other V_js, the algorithm chooses the minimal cardinality V_i with the smallest index, that is, V_2. When S_2 is moved down over the join of the relations B and D, the subformula $\sigma_{y \cap \{4\} = \emptyset}(B(v, y) \bowtie D(v, y))$ will be treated as a single relation S_2.

The process is repeated and the values $V_1 = \{A, C, S_2\}$, $V_3 = \{A, C\}$, and $V_4 = \{A, C\}$ are found. Because $V_3 \subseteq V_1$ and $V_3 \subseteq V_4$, we now choose S_3 to move down. From now on the subformula $\sigma_{x \cap \{6,8\} = \emptyset}(C(x) \bowtie A(x, z))$ will be

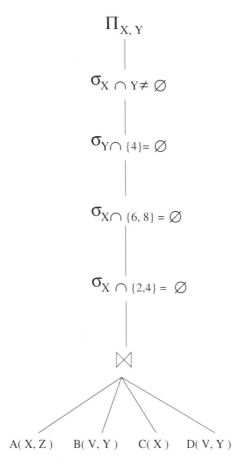

$\Pi_{X, Y}$

$\sigma_{X \cap Y \neq \varnothing}$

$\sigma_{Y \cap \{4\} = \varnothing}$

$\sigma_{X \cap \{6, 8\} = \varnothing}$

$\sigma_{X \cap \{2,4\} = \varnothing}$

⋈

A(X, Z)   B(V, Y)   C(X)   D(V, Y)

FIGURE 12.7. The formula before the optimization.

treated as the single relation S_3. Then the process is repeated again and the values $V_1 = \{S_2, S_3\}$ and $V_4 = \{S_3\}$ are found. Because $V_4 \subseteq V_1$, we choose S_4 to move down. Now, let S_4 be the formula

$$\sigma_{x \cap \{2,4\} = \varnothing}(\sigma_{x \cap \{6,8\} = \varnothing}(C(x) \bowtie A(x, z)))$$

The process is repeated again and V_1 cannot be pushed down further. Hence we obtain the formula shown in Figure 12.8.

Perform Projections as Early as Possible: The optimization algorithm also moves down the projection operations. The set of variables used in each branch of the formula tree is calculated and the variables that are not needed higher up are eliminated. Moving down projections in Figure 12.8 results in the formula shown in Figure 12.9.

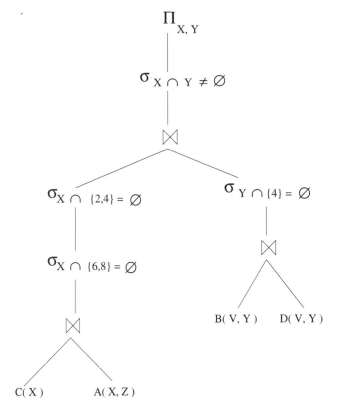

FIGURE 12.8. The formula after the first step of the optimization.

Combine Sequences of Selection Operations: The optimization algorithm combines cascades of selections into one selection. The optimization algorithm checks every edge in the tree, and if both vertices of an edge are selection operations, then combines them. In this example one pair of selections between the joins on the top and the left can be combined.

Bibliographic Notes

Although the quantifier elimination algorithms in Section 9.1 are only subcases of Fourier's method extended to the integers [327], the interesting point here is that these subcases are closed. Gap-graphs are considered as a representation in Revesz [256, 257]. Temporal constraint networks that are similar to gap-graphs are considered in the area of artificial intelligence by Dechter et al. [77]. Stone's representation theorem is described in Burris and Sankappanavar [46] and Halmos [138].

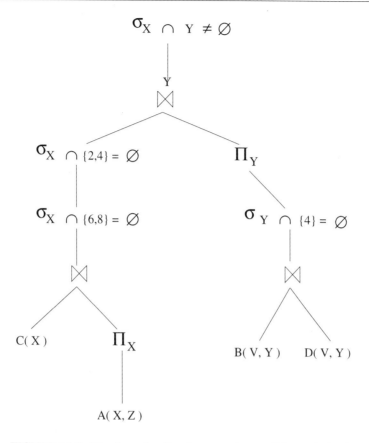

FIGURE 12.9. The formula after the second step of the optimization.

The Datalog evaluation in Section 12.2.4 is based on the naive evaluation described in Ullman [310]. The use of an equality matrix in the Datalog evaluation method is new. More details about the evaluation of Datalog queries within the DISCO system will be described in Section 19.2.

Michaylov [212], Ramakrishnan and Srivastava [244, 292], and Stuckey and Sudarshan [298] consider the optimization of constraint logic programs pushing constraint selections and efficient subsumption testing.

The discussion about the relational algebra identities follows Ullman [310]. Example 12.4.1 about relational algebra optimization is from Salamon [277]. Another algebraic optimization technique based on an efficient parallel algorithm for hypergraph partitioning is described in Ouyang [226].

Exercises

1. Consider the following conjunction of half-addition constraints:

$$x - z \geq 3$$
$$y - z \geq 8$$
$$w - y \geq 2$$
$$w - x \geq 4$$
$$-w \geq -40$$
$$z \geq 20$$

(a) Draw the conjunction as a gap-graph.

(b) Draw the transitive closure of the gap-graph.

(c) Represent the transitive closure of the gap-graph as a matrix.

(d) Is the gap-graph satisfiable? Why or why not?

2. A constraint database relation $R(x, y, z)$ consists of two constraint tuples t_1 and t_2, where t_1 is:

$$y - x \geq 5$$
$$z - y \geq 4$$

and t_2 is:

$$y - x \geq 6$$
$$z - y \geq 3$$

(a) Find the complement of R.

(b) Suppose that another relation $Q(x, y, z)$ consists of only one constraint tuple as follows:

$$y - x \geq 5$$
$$z - y \geq 3$$
$$z - x \geq 9$$

Find the difference $Q - R$. (Simplify the relation $Q - R$ by deleting unsatisfiable constraint tuples.)

(c) Is the relation $Q - R$ nonempty?

(d) Suppose relation $S(x, y, z)$ consists of only the constraint tuple t_1. Is the relation $Q - S$ nonempty?

3. (a) Represent the following conjunction of half-addition constraints as a gap-graph:

$$u - x \geq 9$$
$$y - x \geq 4$$
$$z - y \geq 2$$

$$z - u \geq 3$$
$$z - x \geq 5$$

(b) Find an assignment to the variables that satisfies the gap-graph.

(c) Find the gap-graph obtained by shortcutting vertex u from the gap-graph.

(d) Represent the following conjunction of half-addition constraints as a gap-graph:

$$y - x \geq 6$$
$$z - y \geq 3$$

(e) Find the merge of the gap-graphs in parts (c) and (d).

4. Consider the following conjunction of $\subseteq$ constraints in B_Z:

$$S \subseteq E$$
$$S \subseteq T$$
$$E \subseteq \{2, 4, 6, 8, 12\}$$
$$T \subseteq \{3, 6, 9, 12\}$$
$$\{2, 4, 8\} \subseteq E$$
$$\{6, 12\} \subseteq S$$
$$\{3, 9\} \subseteq T$$

(a) Draw the conjunction as a set-graph.

(b) Represent the set-graph by two matrices.

(c) Draw the transitive closure of the set-graph.

(d) Represent the transitive closure set-graph by two matrices. (**Hint:** This needs merging of set-constant lower bounds and set-constant upper bounds.)

(e) Is the set-graph satisfiable? Why or why not?

5. Implement the algebraic operators of project, join, union, and intersection for *integer half-addition* constraint databases.

You can assume that we are given the values of u and l. The input relations will be a number of files. Each file represents a relation. Each file will have in it a, the arity of the relation, followed by a list of matrices of size $1 + a$ by $1 + a$ each. Each matrix represents a gap-graph of the input relation. (The header and the first column of the matrices are not present, and you can use any large negative integer instead of $-\infty$.)

The program should prompt users with a menu that lists the available relational algebra operators, the print operator, and quit. If one of the relational algebra operators is entered, the system should prompt for the names of the files that contain the input relations (one or two) and will contain the output relation. In addition, the selection and the join operations should be followed by a prompt asking for the conditions.

For the selection operation the condition may look like this:

$$\$i = c$$

which means that the ith attribute variable should be replaced by the constant c.

For the join operation the condition may look like this:

$$i = j, \ldots, k = l$$

which means that the ith attribute of the first relation equals the jth attribute of the second relation ... and the kth attribute of the first relation equals the lth attribute of the second relation.

The print operator should be followed by a prompt for the name of the file to be displayed. (The relation may be displayed as a set of matrices or as a set of graphs.)

After each operation, except quit, display the menu again.

6. Implement similarly to Exercise 5 the algebraic operators of complement and difference for *integer half-addition* constraint databases.

7. Implement similarly to Exercise 5 the algebraic operators of project, join, union, and intersection for *rational linear* constraint databases.

8. Implement similarly to Exercise 5 the algebraic operators of complement and difference for *rational linear* constraint databases.

9. Implement similarly to Exercise 5 the algebraic operators of project, join, union, and intersection for B_Z constraint databases with only $\subseteq$ constraints.

13

Spatiotemporal Databases

Each spatiotemporal object has a spatial extent and a temporal extent. By *spatial extent* we mean the set of points in space that belong to an object. By *temporal extent* we mean the set of time instances when an object exists. Each spatiotemporal data model attempts to represent both the spatial and temporal extents of the objects. In this chapter we introduce three different sets of spatiotemporal data models.

Section 13.1 describes two *extreme point* data models. By extreme points we mean either the endpoints of intervals or the corner vertices of polygonal or polyhedral shaped objects. The two extreme point data models discussed are the *rectangle* data model and *Worboys'* data model.

Section 13.2 describes *parametric extreme point* data models, which extend the extreme point data models by specifying the extreme points as linear, polynomial, or periodic functions of time. The two main extreme point parametric data models introduced are the *parametric rectangles* and the *parametric 2-spaghetti* data models.

Section 13.3 describes *geometric transformation* data models. These data models generalize geometric transformations by using a time parameter. There are several types of geometric transformations that are considered, including affine, linear, scaling, and translation transformations, which are reviewed and defined in their traditional and parametric forms.

Section 13.4 describes query languages for spatiotemporal databases. The query languages are based on relational algebra, SQL, and Datalog with some minor restrictions and the addition of some new spatiotemporal operators. The spatiotemporal operators introduced in Section 13.4 are the *buffer*, the *compose*, the *block*, and the *collide* operators. These operators are useful for many types of spatiotemporal queries.

13.1   Extreme Point Data Models

There are several spatiotemporal data models that can be classified as *extreme point* data models. We define two of the most important extreme point data models next.

The Rectangles Data Model: As the name indicates, this data model assumes that the spatial extent of each object is either a rectangle or the union of a set of rectangles. It assumes that the sides of the rectangles are parallel to the x- or y-axes. In this data model the temporal extent of an object is a time interval or the union of a set of time intervals.

The rectangles data model represents the spatial extent of a d-dimensional rectangle as the cross product of d intervals, one for each dimension. The temporal extent of each object is represented as a set of time intervals. Each spatial and temporal interval is represented by its endpoints. The endpoints of the intervals are also called the *extreme points* of the intervals. We allow the special constants $-\infty$ or $+\infty$ as endpoints of temporal intervals.

Further, each tuple of the rectangle model represents just the combination of one rectangle and one time interval. Therefore, several tuples need to be used to describe objects whose spatial or temporal extents are composed of a set of intervals. An ID number unique to each object connects the different tuples representing the same object.

Example 13.1.1   Suppose an archaeologist excavating a settlement finds three houses built at different periods, as shown in Figure 13.1. The figure shows for each house its area and the time interval when it existed.

The first house was built in year 100 and lasted until year 200. The second house was built in year 150 and lasted untill year 350. The third house was built in year 250 and lasted untill year 400. Note that by the time the third house was built the first house was demolished; hence the areas of the two houses did not overlap in any year.

Here the spatial extent of the first two houses are single rectangles, while the spatial extent of the third house is the union of two rectangles. The spatial extent of the third house can be described in several ways, depending on how we partition the house area into rectangular areas. One way to partition is to add in our imagination the line segment from $(2, 8)$ to $(4, 8)$ to the representation of the third house. We could choose other divisions of the area of the third house into rectangles, even a division in which the areas of the rectangles overlap. Any division leads to a good representation as long as the union of the points in the rectangles equals the points in the area of the third house.

Relation *House* (Id, X, Y, T) is a rectangles data model representation of the archaeological site, where Id refers to the house ID number, the X and Y to the intervals in the x and y dimensions, respectively, and T to the time interval.

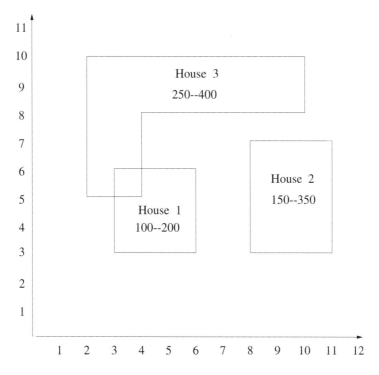

FIGURE 13.1. Archaeological site.

In the *House* relation the first house is represented by its ID, which is 1, the cross product of the interval [3, 6] in the *x* and *y* dimensions, and the temporal interval [100, 200]. The second house is represented similarly to the first. The third house is more complicated by the use of two tuples, one for each rectangular piece of the area of the third house. The time dimension, of course, is the same interval [250, 400] in each tuple representing the third house.

House

Id	X	Y	T
1	[3, 6]	[3, 6]	[100, 200]
2	[8, 11]	[3, 7]	[150, 350]
3	[2, 4]	[5, 10]	[250, 400]
3	[2, 10]	[8, 10]	[250, 400]

In the rectangles model, as in other models, the *Id* number is optional and usually used only if we are representing several objects. If we are only interested in representing one object then we do not use the *Id* fields. In the absence of an *Id* it is implicitly assumed that all the tuples represent just one object.

Although there are many problems where the objects are rectangular, the rectangles data model is clearly limited when the objects have a more complex shape or the sides of the rectangles are not parallel to either the *x*- or *y*-axis. The next data model we introduce can deal with more complex shapes. It is a slightly simplified version of a popular data model used within several geographic information systems to describe spatiotemporal information. It is named after the author who introduced it.

Worboys' Data Model: In this data model the spatial extent of each spatial object can be decomposed into a set of triangles (some are special triangles like points or lines) where each triangle is represented by its three corner vertices. The three corner points can be described using the special attributes *Ax*, *Ay*, *Bx*, *By*, *Cx*, and *Cy* in a relation, where the pairs (Ax, Ay), (Bx, By), and (Cx, Cy) represent the (x, y) coordinate values of the first, second, and third corner vertices, respectively.

In addition, the temporal extent is represented by two special attributes called *From* and *To*. The *From* and *To* values represent the endpoints of a time interval that belongs to the temporal extent of an object.

Example 13.1.2 Figure 13.2 shows a map of a rectangular-shaped park with a road, a fountain, a pond, and a tulip garden. The map shows the location of the objects in the park and indicates the time intervals of their existence. For example, the tulip garden ceased to exist in 1990, the year before the pond was created.

The park can be represented in Worboys' data model as follows. First, the fountain, which is a single point $(10, 4)$ is treated as the special rectangle with three corner vertices, each of which is $(10, 4)$. The road, which is composed of two separate line segments is treated as the union of two special cases of rectangles. For example, the first line segment between points $(5, 10)$ and $(6, 9)$ is represented as the triangle with one corner vertex $(5, 10)$ and the other two corner vertices being $(6, 9)$. The tulip is represented as one, the park as two, and the pond as the union of three triangles.

13.2 Parametric Extreme Point Data Models

In the rectangles data model all the spatial and temporal extents are independent of each other. In Worboys' data model the spatial extents are related to each other, but the spatial and temporal extents are still independent of each other. Therefore, the extreme point spatiotemporal data models only represent objects that appear and disappear suddenly. Hence they cannot represent continuously moving objects. Next we consider some data models that use a time parameter *t* and can represent continuously moving objects.

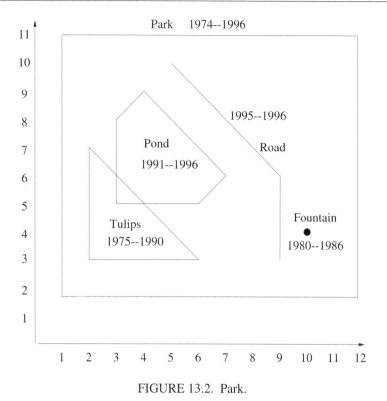

FIGURE 13.2. Park.

Park

Id	Ax	Ay	Bx	By	Cx	Cy	From	To
Fountain	10	4	10	4	10	4	1980	1986
Road	5	10	9	6	9	6	1995	1996
Road	9	6	9	3	9	3	1995	1996
Tulip	2	3	2	7	6	3	1975	1990
Park	1	2	1	11	12	11	1974	1996
Park	12	11	12	2	1	2	1974	1996
Pond	3	5	3	8	4	9	1991	1996
Pond	4	9	7	6	3	8	1991	1996
Pond	3	5	7	6	3	8	1991	1996

The Parametric Rectangles Data Model: In this data model, a d-dimensional *parametric rectangle* is a moving and growing or shrinking rectangle represented as the cross product of d intervals, whose endpoints are functions of time, and a temporal interval, whose endpoints are constants.

Example 13.2.1   Suppose that a plankton-rich area of the ocean is located at time $t = 0$ in a rectangular area with left lower corner $(5, 5)$ and upper right corner $(10, 15)$ and it is moving with an ocean stream. Between $t = 0$ and $t = 20$, the right edge of the plankton-rich area is moving east with two and the left edge with one unit speed. At the same time, the top edge is moving north with three and the bottom edge with one unit speed. Relation *Plankton* represents the plankton-rich area using one parametric rectangle.

Plankton

X	Y	T
$[5 + t,\ 10 + 2t]$	$[5 + t,\ 15 + 3t]$	$[0,\ 20]$

The *Plankton* relation uses only linear functions of time. However, the parametric rectangles model also allows polynomial functions or even quotients of two polynomials as functions of time. The following is an example with quadratic parametric rectangles.

Example 13.2.2   Suppose a plane drops a bomb with one unit width, one unit length, and two units height at time $t = 0$ from a height of 100 meters to hit a target as shown in Figure 13.3. If we assume that the gravity constant is 9.8 meters per second and time is measured in seconds, then the movement of the bomb while it falls can be represented by the parametric rectangle relation *Bomb*, as shown here:

Bomb

X	Y	Z	T
$[t,\ t + 1]$	$[t,\ t + 1]$	$[100 - 9.8t^2,\ 102 - 9.8t^2]$	$[0, 3.19]$

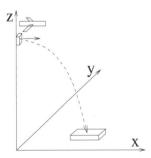

FIGURE 13.3. The trajectory of a bomb.

Each of the previous two examples used only a single parametric rectangle. To represent moving objects that change their direction or speed due to additional forces not present initially, we may need to use several parametric rectangles.

Example 13.2.3   Suppose a sailboat, which at time $t = 0$ occupies the space $9 \leq x \leq 19$, $10 \leq y \leq 20$, first moves east with a speed of 5 ft/sec until $t = 10$. Then it goes northeast until $t = 20$, with a speed of 10 ft/sec in both the x- and y-axes. Finally, it goes north with a speed of 8 ft/sec until $t = 25$. We can represent the sailboat in this data model as follows:

Sailboat

X	Y	T
$[5t + 9,\ 5t + 19]$	$[10,\ 20]$	$[0,\ 10]$
$[10t - 41,\ 10t - 31]$	$[10t - 90,\ 10t - 80]$	$[10,\ 20]$
$[159,\ 169]$	$[8t - 50,\ 8t - 40]$	$[20,\ 25]$

We can find the first parametric tuple that represents the movement between $t = 0$ and $t = 10$ as in the previous examples. Note that at $t = 10$, the boat is located in the rectangle with sides $[59, 69]$ and $[10, 20]$. Hence moving east 10 ft/sec means to change the x dimension as $[59 + 10(t - 10),\ 69 + 10(t - 10)] = [10t - 41,\ 10t - 31]$. Similarly, to move north 10 ft/sec means to change the y dimension as $[10 + 10(t - 10),\ 20 + 10(t - 10)] = [10t - 90,\ 10t - 80]$.

Finally, at $t = 20$ the boat is located in the rectangle with sides $[159, 169]$ and $[110, 120]$. To go directly north 8 ft/sec does not change the x dimension, but the y dimension changes as $[110 + 8(t - 20),\ 120 + 8(t - 20)] = [8t - 50,\ 8t - 40]$.

The next data model is a parametric generalization of Worboys' data model. For historical reasons it is called the parametric 2-spaghetti data model.

The Parametric 2-Spaghetti Data Model: The parametric 2-spaghetti data model generalizes Worboys' data model by allowing the vertex coordinates to be functions of time.

Net

Ax	Ay	Bx	By	Cx	Cy	From	To
3	$3 - t$	$4 + 0.5t$	$4 - 0.5t$	$5 + t$	3	0	10

Example 13.2.4   Suppose three fishing boats each hold one corner of a fishing net. Suppose at time $t = 0$ the three boats are at locations $(3, 3)$, $(4, 4)$, and $(5, 3)$, respectively. The first boat goes south with a speed of one mile per hour, the second goes southeast with a speed of half mile per hour in both the south and the east directions, and

the third goes east with a speed of one mile per hour for ten hours. The shape of the fishing net can be represented in this data model as follows.

13.2.1   Periodic Parametric Data Models

Periodic movements can be classified as either cyclic or acyclic. By a *cyclic periodic movement*, we mean that an object repeats its movement from the same position and with the same velocity every period. For example, a pendulum clock shows cyclic periodic movement.

An *acyclic periodic movement* is the composition of cyclic periodic movement and nonperiodic movement. For example, the movement of a light particle is a wave that is composed of an up-down movement and a linear movement.

In the previous section we considered only linear or polynomial functions of time. To represent periodic movements we need to consider more complicated functions. We use trigonometric functions like sines or cosines to represent periodic movement. However, trigonometric functions have not yet been implemented in any constraint database system. Therefore, we prefer to use periodic functions of time that use the modulus operator. The modulus operator is quite powerful, and as we will see in Example 13.2.5, it can be used to approximate trigonometric functions. The modulus operator is defined as follows:

$$x \bmod p = x - p \times \left\lfloor \frac{x}{p} \right\rfloor$$

where x is a real variable or constant and p is a positive rational constant. For example, $f(t) = (5t + 7) \bmod 8$ is a periodic function of time with $f(0) = 0$ and $f(0.2) = 1$. To use periodic functions we make some extensions to the parametric extreme point data models. First let us introduce some definition.

Let the temporal extent of the first period of a periodic object be the interval [*from*, *to*]. If the period is p and the periodic movement repeats until time *end*, then we write this as [*from*, *to*]$_{p,end}$, which we call a *periodic interval*. Note that [*from*, *to*]$_{p,end}$ is equal to the following:

$$\left\{ [\textit{from} + ip,\ \min(\textit{to} + ip, \textit{end})] : 0 \leq i \leq \frac{\textit{end} - \textit{from}}{p} \right\}$$

where i is an integer variable. For example, $[80, 82]_{10,111}$ is equivalent to the union of the intervals $[80, 82]$, $[90, 92]$, $[100, 102]$, and $[110, 111]$. We also allow $\textit{end} = +\infty$ for periodic movement that repeats without a time limit.

The Periodic Parametric Rectangles Data Model: We extend the parametric rectangles data model by allowing periodic functions of time in the spatial attributes and periodic intervals in the temporal attribute.

Example 13.2.5   Suppose a person A is swimming in a wavy sea. Figure 13.4 shows the position of A at four different time instances.

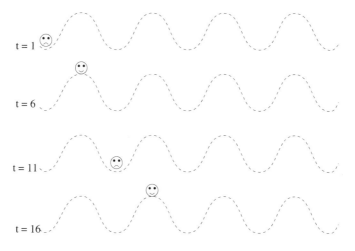

FIGURE 13.4. Periodic movements.

We represent the head of the person A as one foot in the swimming direction, along the x-axis, and one foot in height, along the z-axis. We also assume that A swims along the x-axis with a speed of one foot per second. Then we may approximate A's movement using a trigonometric function with a period of length 10 as shown in relation *Swimmer1*:

Swimmer1

X	Z	T
$[t,\ t+1]$	$\left[4.5\sin\left(\frac{\pi}{5}(t-1)-\frac{\pi}{2}\right),\ 4.5\sin\left(\frac{\pi}{5}(t-1)-\frac{\pi}{2}\right)+1\right]$	$[0,+\infty]$

Alternatively, we may approximate A's movement using modulus functions. First we approximate the wave as shown in part (1) of Figure 13.5. We still assume that A swims along the x-axis with a speed of 1 ft/sec. However, in every period A moves only horizontally at the bottom of the wave for two seconds, and at the top of the wave for another two seconds as shown in parts (2) and (4) of Figure 13.5. Between these, A moves either up with a speed of 3 ft/sec in the z direction or down with the same speed for three seconds as shown in parts (3) and (5) of Figure 13.5. Hence the movement of A can be decomposed into four simple periodic functions.

Each piece can be represented as a periodic parametric rectangle as shown in relation *Swimmer*. In each row, the x coordinate is defined as $[t, t+1]$ because the swimmer moves continuously with uniform speed in the x-axis and has width one. In the first and third periodic parametric rectangles, representing when the swimmer is at the bottom or top of the wave, respectively, there is no change in the height, hence the z-coordinate values will be defined by the intervals $[0, 1]$ and $[9, 10]$.

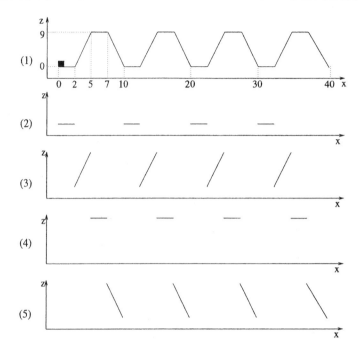

FIGURE 13.5. Approximate representation of the swimmer.

The second periodic parametric rectangle represents the upward movements displayed as part (3) in Figure 13.5. Note that $3t - 6$ is zero when $t = 2$ and nine when $t = 5$; hence it is the function that correctly describes the first upward movement. Because it is repeated every ten seconds, the periodic parametric rectangle contains the function $(3t - 6)$ mod 10.

Swimmer

X	Z	T
$[t, t+1]$	$[0, 1]$	$[0, 2]_{10,\infty}$
$[t, t+1]$	$[(3t - 6) \bmod 10, ((3t - 6) \bmod 10) + 1]$	$[2, 5]_{10,\infty}$
$[t, t+1]$	$[9, 10]$	$[5, 7]_{10,\infty}$
$[t, t+1]$	$[(-3t + 30) \bmod 10, ((-3t + 30) \bmod 10) + 1]$	$[7, 10]_{10,\infty}$

Similarly, the fourth periodic parametric rectangle represents the downward movements displayed as part (5) in Figure 13.5. Note that $-3t + 30$ is nine when $t = 7$ and zero when $t = 10$; hence it is the function that correctly describes the first downward movement. Because it is repeated every ten seconds, the periodic parametric rectangle contains the function $(-3t + 30)$ mod 10.

Next we see that the parametric 2-spaghetti data model can also be generalized with periodic functions.

The Periodic Parametric 2-Spaghetti Data Model: This extends the parametric 2-spaghetti data model by allowing periodic parametric functions instead of only polynomial functions of time. Instead of using periodic intervals for time, we add two special columns for each relation. The first is *P*, which represents the period value, and the second is *End*, which represents the ending time of the periodic movement. Hence a periodic parametric 2-spaghetti tuple with *From, To, P, End* values *from, to, p, end* is applicable only at times in the periodic interval $[from, to]_{p, end}$.

Example 13.2.6   Figure 13.6 shows a rectangular area on a seashore. Suppose that a shoreline is changing continuously with the tide as shown by the set of parallel lines tagged by some of the time instances when the water level reaches them. The time instances shown are for the first period, which starts at 12:00 midnight, then expands linearly untill 5:45 a.m. and retreats in the opposite direction for the next 5 hours and 45 minutes, that is, untill 11:30 a.m. The tide repeats its movement every 11 hours and 30 minutes.

For example, the shoreline will be at the same level at 2:00 a.m. (during expansion) and at 9:30 a.m. (during recession). Similarly, it will be at the same level

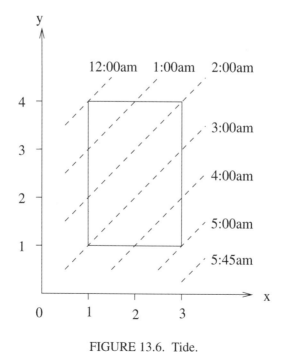

FIGURE 13.6. Tide.

at 3:00 a.m. and 8:30 a.m. and at 5:00 and 6:30 a.m. The tide can be represented in the parameric 2-spaghetti data model by noting that the shape of the area flooded by the tide will be a triangle, a quadrangle, or a pentagon in different time intervals. Hence each of these can be represented as areas are broken into triangles with each triangle having the proper time interval. In the following representation, time t is measured in hours from the first 12:00 midnight. Hence 5.75 represents 5:45 a.m., and 33 represents 9:00 a.m. the second day.

Tide

Ax	Ay	Bx	By	Cx	Cy	From	To	P	End
1	4	1	$4-t'$	$t'+1$	4	0	2	11.5	∞
1	4	1	2	3	4	2	9.5	11.5	∞
1	2	3	4	3	$6-t'$	2	3	11.5	∞
1	2	1	$4-t'$	3	$6-t'$	2	3	11.5	∞
1	2	3	4	3	3	3	8.5	11.5	∞
1	2	1	1	3	3	3	8.5	11.5	∞
1	1	3	3	3	$6-t'$	3	5	11.5	∞
1	1	$t'-2$	1	3	$6-t'$	3	5	11.5	∞
1	1	3	4	3	1	5	6.5	11.5	∞
1	1	3	4	1	4	5	6.5	11.5	∞
1	1	3	3	3	t'-5.5	6.5	8.5	11.5	∞
1	1	9.5-t'	1	3	t'-5.5	6.5	8.5	11.5	∞
1	1	3	4	3	t'-5.5	8.5	9.5	11.5	∞
1	2	1	t'-7.5	3	t'-5.5	8.5	9.5	11.5	∞
1	4	1	t'-7.5	12.5-t'	4	9.5	11.5	11.5	∞

where $t' = (t \bmod 11.5)$

13.3 Geometric Transformation Data Models

Before introducing the next data model, recall that a *geometric transformation* is a bijection of d-dimensional space into itself. Let A be a nonsingular $d \times d$ matrix and B be a d-vector of constants in $\mathcal{R}$. The following are some common geometric transformations that move the point $\overline{x} = (x_1, \ldots, x_d)$ to the point $\overline{x'} = (x'_1, \ldots, x'_d)$ according to *transformation functions* of the following form:

Affine Motion: $\overline{x'} = A\overline{x} + B$
Linear Motion: $\overline{x'} = A\overline{x}$
Scaling: $\overline{x'} = A\overline{x}$ where A is diagonal
Translation: $\overline{x'} = \overline{x} + B$
Identity: $\overline{x'} = \overline{x}$

The restriction that A be nonsingular is required to assure that for every $\overline{x'}$ there exists a unique $\overline{x}$ that satisfies the system of linear equations. However, in special cases we allow A to be singular.

We can generalize affine, linear, scaling, and translation geometric transformations into parametric affine, parametric linear, parametric scaling, and parametric translations, respectively, by allowing within the matrix A and vector B functions of t wherever nonzero constants are allowed. Note that for each instance of t, the parametric geometric transformations give a corresponding geometric transformation.

The Geometric Transformation Data Model: This data model defines each spatiotemporal object as some spatial object together with a continuous transformation that produces an image of the spatial object for every time instant. More precisely, a *geometric transformation object* G of dimension d is a triple (V, I, f) where:

- $V \subseteq \mathcal{R}^d$ is a *representative spatial object*,

- $I \subseteq \mathcal{R}$ is a *time domain*, and

- f is a parametric geometric transformation function from $\mathbf{R}^{d+1}$ to $\mathcal{R}^d$.

Example 13.3.1   Suppose a group of whales is moving in the ocean. At time $t = 0$ they are located in the rectangular area with lower-left corner $(20, 20)$ and upper-right corner $(30, 30)$. The whales are moving until $t = 20$ directly west with a speed of one unit, and they do not go north or south. The whales can be represented by the geometric transformation *Whales* (V, I, f) where V is the set of points $[20, 30] \times [20, 30]$, $I = [0, 20]$, and f is:

$$f(\overline{x}, t) = \overline{x} + \begin{bmatrix} -t \\ 0 \end{bmatrix}$$

To express the *Whales* relation we needed only a transformation function that was a parametric translation. The following examples use parametric scalings.

Example 13.3.2   Suppose a water lily is growing on the surface of the water. At $t = 1$ its leaf is a unit circle. As the water lily grows, the radius of its leaf is expanding linearly with time until $t = 5$. The leaf of the water lily can be represented by the geometric transformation object *Lily* $= (x^2 + y^2 \leq 1, [1, 5], f)$ where f is the following parametric scaling from (x, y) points to (x', y') points:

$$\begin{bmatrix} t & 0 \\ 0 & t \end{bmatrix}$$

Suppose the water lily has some plant virus infection in area V. The virus is growing at an exponential rate in each direction at the same time the lily grows. The virus can be represented by $Virus = (V, [1, 5], g)$ where V is a subset of the unit circle at time 1 and g is:

$$\begin{bmatrix} e^t & 0 \\ 0 & e^t \end{bmatrix}$$

Example 13.3.3   Suppose a ball B centered at the origin and having a radius of 0.1 meter is thrown at time $t = 0$ into the air with an initial velocity of 40 meters/sec on the x- and 30 meters/sec on the z-axis along the y-axis. We may represent the ball as the geometric transformation object $B = (x^2 + y^2 + z^2 \leq 0.1, [0, 6], f)$ where f is the parametric scaling

$$f(x, y, t) = \begin{bmatrix} x \\ y \\ z \end{bmatrix} + \begin{bmatrix} 40t \\ 0 \\ 30t - 0.5gt^2 \end{bmatrix}$$

and g is the gravitational force.

13.4 Queries

In Section 13.4.1 we describe the *logical level* of spatiotemporal databases. In Sections 13.4.2 and 13.4.3 we describe queries based on the logical meaning of spatiotemporal databases. The last section also introduces several spatiotemporal operators.

13.4.1 The Logical Level of Spatiotemporal Relations

The spatiotemporal data models can be placed at the constraint level within the abstraction hierarchy described in Chapter 1. Each spatiotemporal database means at the logical level some infinite relational database.

For a rectangles relation $R(Id, X_1, \ldots, X_d, T)$, the corresponding infinite relational database $r(id, x_1, \ldots, x + d, t)$ contains all the tuples $(x_1, \ldots, x_d, t) \in \mathcal{R}^{d+1}$ such that $(x_1, \ldots, x_d)$ is a d-dimensional point within the rectangle with identification id at time t. The same is true for parametric rectangles.

A Worboys relation $W(Id, Ax, Ay, Bx, By, Cx, Cy, From, To)$ similarly corresponds to an infinite relational database $w(id, x, y, t)$ that contains all the tuples $(x, y, t) \in \mathcal{R}^3$ such that (x, y) is a point in the triangle with identification id at time t. The same is true for parametric 2-spaghetti relations.

Finally, the meaning of a geometric transformation object (V, I, f) is the following subset of $\mathcal{R}^{d+1}$:

$$\{(f(\overline{x}, t), t) : \overline{x} \in V, t \in I\}$$

In practice spatiotemporal relations may contain other attributes that are regular relational database attributes that always have a constant value.

As we learned in Chapter 1, the logical level should be used for querying databases. We used that rule in describing the query languages for constraint databases. We use it again in describing the query languages for spatiotemporal databases.

Whenever data abstraction is used, one both gains and loses a few things. What is gained by using the logical level is the simplicity of query languages. What is lost is the ability to ask some details of the data representation because of lost access to the special spatial and temporal attributes. For example, we may not write the query:

$$\pi_{Ax}(\sigma_{Id='road'} \; Park)$$

which would be evaluated to be $\{5, 9\}$. However, the same road could have been represented by different pairs of tuples from the ones shown in the *Park* relation. For example, the second tuple of the park relation could be $(9, 6, 5, 10, 5, 10, 1995, 1996)$, in which case the query output would be $\{9\}$. As this example shows, giving access to the special attributes leads to queries whose output depends not on the represented data but on the data representation. The represented data is the logical meaning of the database, while the data representation is something lower that should be hidden by data abstraction.

Of course, the logical level may be queried by relational algebra, SQL, and Datalog. However, as described in Section 13.4.2 in the case of parametric rectangles we place some restrictions on these three languages to guarantee that the query output can be represented by parametric rectangles.

In addition, for spatiotemporal relations it makes sense to introduce some extra operators, which may be used embedded within the query languages of relational algebra, SQL, or Datalog. Following is one example operator. In Section 13.4.3 we define several other operators.

Buffer: The buffer operator takes as input a spatiotemporal relation A and returns a spatiotemporal relation B that includes A and all spatiotemporal points $(\bar{x}, t)$ such that there is a point $(\bar{x}', t) \in A$ with a distance between $\bar{x}$ and $\bar{x}'$ less than some constant d. In other words, $Buffer(A, d)$ returns A and its surrounding points that are within d distance. Note that there are several variations of the buffer operator because there are several ways of measuring distance.

In the next few sections we give example queries, first in English and then we translate them into relational algebra, SQL, or Datalog queries. These examples are provided only to illustrate translation from English into spatiotemporal queries. We postpone discussion of query evaluation until Chapter 14.

13.4.2   Querying Parametric Extreme Point Databases

For querying (periodic) parametric rectangle databases the only restriction is that in any atomic constraint of either a selection condition of a relational algebra or a SQL query or in the body of a Datalog rule we allow only the constraints of the type $x = c$, $x \leq c$, or $x \geq c$ where x is a spatiotemporal variable and c is a constant. For example, if x and y are special spatial attributes, then $x \leq y$ is not allowed as a selection condition. This is needed to guarantee that the output relation is representable by parametric rectangles. We make no such restrictions for querying parametric 2-spaghetti relations.

Example 13.4.1   Let us consider again Example 13.2.5, but with two swimmers. Suppose a swimmer can see another swimmer if both of them are at least partly 9 feet high on the waves (so that at least the top of their heads are above the crest of the waves). Let *SwimmerA* and *SwimmerB* be two periodic parametric rectangle relations representing the swimming movements of A and B, respectively.

Query: When can A and B see each other?
This can be expressed as:

$$(\pi_t \, \sigma_{z \geq 9} \, SwimmerA) \, \cap \, (\pi_t \, \sigma_{z \geq 9} \, SwimmerB)$$

Suppose now that a ship moves in the area. Then a natural query is:

Query: Can the swimmers be rescued by the ship?
Let relation *Ship* represent the movement of the ship and suppose that there is a limited visibility of d feet. Then the movement of the ship together with its visibility region can be found using the buffer operation. Hence, the query can be expressed as follows:

$$Buffer(Ship, d) \, \cap \, (SwimmerA \, \cup \, SwimmerB)$$

Example 13.4.2   Suppose the relation *Clouds*$(X, Y, T, humidity)$ is a parametric rectangle relation with the regular attribute *humidity*, which indicates the humidity of the cloud. Let *Region*$(X, Y, T, temperature)$ be a spatiotemporal relation with an additional attribute *temperature* that gives the temperature of each region in degrees Fahrenheit. Suppose that it snows when a cloud with greater that 80 percent humidity moves into a region where the temperature is less than 32 degrees.

Query: Where and when will it snow?

```
SELECT   x, y, t
FROM     Clouds
WHERE    Humidity ≥ 80
         INTERSECT
SELECT   x, y, t
```

FROM   Region
WHERE   Temperature ≤ 32

The next example uses a Datalog query. When writing Datalog queries we make the assumption that for each d-dimensional spatiotemporal relation, there is a corresponding relation in which the first argument denotes Id, if it exists, the next d arguments denote attribute variables for the d spatial dimensions, and the next argument denotes an attribute variable for the time dimension. These may be followed by optional regular attributes in a specified order. We need this extra ordering assumption because in Datalog queries we do not have a rename operator. Hence we need the specified ordering of attributes and the ability to put different variable names in their places.

Example 13.4.3 Suppose $Window\,(id, x, y, t)$ is a rectangles relation that contains all windows that are open on a computer screen, where id is the number of the window, x and y are the locations that belong to the window, and t are the times when it is active, that is, the cursor is in the window. Assume that more recently active windows cover less recently active windows.

Query: Which windows are completely hidden by other windows?
We can express this by the following Datalog query:

$Seen\,(i)$:— $Window\,(i, x, y, t),$ *not* $Window\,(i_2, x, y, t_2),\ t_2 > t.$

$Hidden\,(i)$:— $Window\,(i, x, y, t),$ *not* $Seen\,(i).$

Example 13.4.4 Let us return to Example 13.1.1, but imagine that we have many more houses excavated at the archaeological site. Suppose a ghost haunts house number 1. The ghost remains in the area of a house even after it is demolished. However, if a new house is built whose area at least partially overlaps the old house that the ghost is haunting, then the ghost may move to the new house. This process may continue each time a house is demolished and a new house is built on top of it.

Query: Which houses and at what time may the ghost haunt?
We can express this by the following Datalog query.

$Haunt\,(1, t)$:— $House\,(1, x, y, t_1),\ t \geq t_1.$
$Haunt\,(n, t)$:— $Haunt\,(m, t_1),\ House\,(m, x, y, t_2),$
                              $House\,(n, x, y, t),\ t \geq t_1.$

The next few examples use parametric 2-spaghetti relations.

Example 13.4.5 Consider again the fishing net described in Example 13.2.4. Suppose that relation *Dolphin* describes a dolphin swimming in the area.

Query: Will the dolphin be caught in the fishing net?

Dolphin ∩ *Net*

Suppose that it is illegal to have dolphins in the fishing net north of the line $y = x + 10$. Note that this includes catching the dolphin south of the line and dragging it north.

Query: Will the dolphin be caught illegally?

$\sigma_{y \geq x + 10}(Dolphin \cap Net)$

The next example uses periodic parametric 2-spaghetti relations.

Example 13.4.6   Suppose that in Example 13.2.6 the rectangular area is a parking lot with slightly uneven level that the tide is flooding. Let *Car* be the location of cars parked on the parking lot, with the *Id* attribute describing the license plate number of the cars.

Query: Which cars will be flooded between 33 and 36 hours?

$\Pi_{Id} (Car \cap \sigma_{(33 \leq t \text{ and } t \leq 36)} Tide)$

The following is another query, which we express in Datalog with aggregation.

Query: What is the total area that will be flooded at 36 hours?

$Tide36(x, y)$:— $Tide (x, y, 36).$
$Tide36\_Area (area\langle x, y\rangle)$:— $Tide36(x, y).$

13.4.3 Querying Geometric Transformation Databases

In this section we introduce several new spatiotemporal operators that are convenient to use in many applications.

Compose: $Compose(G_1, G_2)$ is a function where the inputs $G_1 = (V_1, I_1, f_1)$ and $G_2 = (V_2, I_2, f_2)$ are two geometric transformation relations with $V_1 \subseteq V_2$ and $I_1 \subseteq I_2$ and f_1 and f_2 are geometric transformations with the same dimension. The output of compose is the geometric transformation $(V_1, I_1, f_1 f_2)$ where $f_1 f_2$ is the functional composition of f_1 and f_2, i.e., it takes each point $\overline{x}$ to $f_1(f_2(\overline{x}))$.

Example 13.4.7   Suppose we have the relations *Lily* and *Virus* as in Example 13.3.2.

Query: Which areas of the water lily will be infected at time 3?

$A \leftarrow Compose (Virus, Lily)$

This query yields the geometric transformation relation $A = (V, [1, 5], gf)$. Note that the areas infected at time $t = 3$ must still be within the area of the leaf at that time. Hence we can express the query as:

$$(\pi_{x,y} (\sigma_{t=3} A)) \cap (\pi_{x,y} (\sigma_{t=3} Lily))$$

Block: Another operator that we allow is the *block* operator. This operator considers the set of points in the spatial reference object to be independent. Hence if some of the points are blocked by the presence of another object, then the rest of the points just continue moving along the trajectory determined by the transformation function. Let $G_1(V, [from, to], f)$ and G_2 be two geometric transformation relations. Then the meaning of *Block* (G_1, G_2) is defined as follows.

$$\{(\overline{x}, t) : \exists \overline{x_0} \in V, f(\overline{x_0}) = \overline{x}, t \leq to, (\{\overline{x_0}\}, [from, t], f) \cap G_2 = \emptyset\}$$

This means the combination of a d-dimensional spatial point $\overline{x}$ and a temporal instance t is in the output of the block operator, if there is a point $\overline{x_0}$ in V from which the point $\overline{x}$ derives at time t, t is less than to, and as the point $\overline{x_0}$ moves to $\overline{x}$, it is not intersected by any point in G_2.

Example 13.4.8   Let L be a light source illuminating from behind a screen in a shadow theater. Let B be the ball as in Example 13.3.3.

Query: What will be the shadow of the ball on the screen?
    We can find what remains from the light by the following:

Block (L, B)

This gives what remains of the light when it is blocked by the ball. Suppose the screen is parallel to the plane $y = 10$. Then we need the projection of the light onto that plane to find the illuminated areas:

$\pi_{y=10}$ *Block* (L, B)

This is the illuminated area. To find the shadow area we subtract the screen area from the illuminated area. Let S be the screen area. Then the final query is:

$S - (\pi_{y=10}$ *Block* $(L, B))$

Collide: This operator assumes an extra attribute for spatiotemporal objects, namely, *mass*. For simplicity we describe this operator in two dimensions. Suppose there are two objects that do not change their shape and that are traveling at uniform speeds defined by the transition functions:

$$\begin{bmatrix} v_{1,x} & 0 \\ 0 & v_{1,y} \end{bmatrix} \text{ and } \begin{bmatrix} v_{2,x} & 0 \\ 0 & v_{2,y} \end{bmatrix}$$

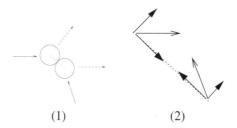

(1)   (2)

FIGURE 13.7. (1) Dotted line joining centers (LC) at t_c; (2) collision along LC.

Suppose both objects are valid in a time interval that includes time t_c when they collide with an angle of θ as shown in Figure 13.7. Depending on the degree of elasticity of the collision, we may calculate the transition functions of the two objects after the collision as

$$\left[\begin{array}{cc} v'_{1,x} & 0 \\ 0 & v'_{1,y} \end{array} \right] \quad \text{and} \quad \left[\begin{array}{cc} v'_{2,x} & 0 \\ 0 & v'_{2,y} \end{array} \right]$$

For example, if the x-axis is along the line connecting the centers of the objects and the collision is completely elastic, then the velocities in the y dimension do not change, i.e., $v'_{1,y} = v_{1,y}$ and $v'_{2,y} = v'_{2,y}$ and the other parameters may be calculated from the equations for the conservation of energy and momentum.

Example 13.4.9   The nine planets of the solar system revolve around the sun in periodic orbits. They are represented by relations *Mercury, Venus, ..., Pluto*. The motion of an asteroid is represented by the relation *Asteroid*.

Query: What will happen if the asteroid collides with any of the planets?

    Collide (Asteroid, (Mercury $\cup$ *Venus* $\cup \dots \cup$ *Pluto))*

The output describes the movement of the asteroids and the planets before and after a collision.

Bibliographic Notes

Several temporal and spatial data models precede and in fact form the basis of the spatiotemporal data models presented in this chapter. Tansel et al. [302] review temporal data models, including the TQuel data model, which is an extreme point data model that uses the endpoints of time intervals for the representation of time. Snodgrass [291] reviews the TSQL temporal database language, and Frank et al. [101] review the Chorochronos research project on temporal and spatiotemporal databases. Temporal data models that can represent periodicity constraints with the modulus operator over the integers are described in [34, 306], with linear repeating points in [21, 157] and an extension of Datalog with the successor function in [58]. These data models do not represent spatial dimensions or continuous movements of objects. Temporal databases with indefinite information are considered in Koubarakis [180] and Koubarakis and Skiadopoulos [184]. Efficient temporal constraint solving is considered in Dean and Boddy [76], Dechter et al. [77], and Vilain and Kautz [320].

The surveys by Bittner and Frank [37] and Kemper and Wallrath [169] and the book by Laurini and Thompson [201] review the area of spatial databases, including the 2-spaghetti data model often used in geographic information systems [4, 80, 294] such as the ARC/INFO system [219, 220, 240]. The 2-spaghetti data model is an extreme point data model that uses the corner vertices of polygons for the representation of polygonal-shaped areas. It can be extended to the 3-spaghetti data model for the representation of three-dimensional objects. The 3-spaghetti data model represents three-dimensional objects as a set of faces, and each face is a polygon and can be further extended as described in Paoluzzi et al. [229]. Egenhofer [86], Svensson and Zhexue [300], and Waugh and Healey" [324] extend relational databases and SQL with spatial operators.

Helm et al. [142] describe a spatial data model based on Boolean constraints and range queries. Topological data models are considered in Egenhofer and Franzosa [87, 88], Egenhofer and Mark [89], Grigni et al. [119], Kuijpers [188], Kuijpers and Smits [191], Kuijpers and Van den Bussche [189], Papadimitriou et al. [231], Paredaens et al. [235, 234, 232], and Segoufin and Vianu [285]. Geerts et al. [107] considers the efficient maintenance of topological properties. Fournier and Montuno [100] present algorithms for triangulating polygons. Ooi [224] discusses query processing in geographic information systems. Scholl and Voisard [283] present an object-oriented approach to building geographic information systems.

Worboys' data model, which is simplified in the presentation in this chapter, is described in [332, 333]. Worboys [332] also describes a query language that contains more special spatiotemporal operators. Grumbach et al. [123] propose another spatiotemporal data model based on constraints in which, like in [332], only discrete change can be modeled. Frank and Wallace [103] use constraint databases for modeling orad design.

There are other temporal geographic information system data models, for example, the Raster Snapshot Model [18], the Temporal Map Set Model [23], the Event-Based Spatiotemporal Model [239], the Space-Time Composite Model [197], and Yuan's data model that represent spatiotemporal information as a sequence of raster or vector snapshots. These also cannot represent continuous change.

Sistla et al. [289] and Wolfson et al. [329] present a model for moving objects along with a query language. This model represents the position of each object as a continuous function of time $f(t)$ and updates the database when the parameters of the motion, like speed or direction, change. However, the model captures just the *current* part of motions that are composed of several parts described by different functions. It does not describe complete trajectories and the spatial extents of moving objects. Some other object-relational models for spatiotemporal data are also available in Oracle8i [287] and PostgreSQL [218].

Data models based on moving points and regions are described by Erwig et al. [92] and Forlizzi et al. [98] but in these data models the moving objects do not change their shapes over time and periodic movements are not considered. These spatiotemporal models are used within the Chorochronos project [104].

The parametric 2-spaghetti data model with linear constraints is from Chomicki and Revesz [61, 62]. Example 13.1.2 is modified from [61, 62]. The extension of the parametric 2-spaghetti data model to polynomial and periodic constraints is new to this chapter. Chomicki et al. [60] describes an application of the parametric 2-spaghetti data model in the animation of linear constraint databases (see Chapter 16).

The parametric rectangle model is from Cai et al. [50]. This data model also considered polynomial and periodic constraints. Examples 13.2.3 and 13.2.2 and most of the queries in Section 13.4.2 are modified from [50]. An extension to non-cyclic periodic constraints and the computational complexity of query evaluation is considered in [271, 272]. The block and collide operators are presented in a simpler form in [50].

The geometric transformation model is by Chomicki and Revesz [63]. Hae-sevoets and Kuijpers [134] study the closure properties of geometric object transformation relations. We postpone review of other issues in spatiotemporal databases until later chapters on interoperability (Chapter 14) and indexing (Chapter 17).

Exercises

1. Represent using a rectangles relation the location at $t = 0$ of the plankton-rich area of Example 13.2.1. (**Hint:** Use the time interval $[0, 0]$.)

2. Represent using a Worboys relation the town map shown in Figure 1.4, assuming that the town exists between times $t = 0$ and $t = 300$.

3. Represent using a Worboys relation the state of Florida as shown in Figure 2.2, using the fact that Florida became the 27th state of the United States in 1845.

4. (a) Suppose that at time $t = 0$ a person stands at a rectangular location with lower-left corner $(20, 20)$ and upper-right corner $(21, 21)$ measured in meters and starts walking toward the east with a speed of 1 meter per second until $t = 100$. For simplicity assume the x and y dimensions of this person are one meter each. Represent the person as (i) a parametric rectangle and (ii) a geometric transformation relation.

   (b) Suppose a ship is located at time $t = 0$ in a rectangular area with lower-left corner $(20, 20)$ and upper-right corner $(130, 30)$ and is moving east with a speed of 5 meters per second until time $t = 100$ seconds. Represent the ship as (i) a parametric rectangle and (ii) a geometric transformation relation.

(c) Suppose an iceberg at time $t = 0$ is in a rectangular location with lower-left corner $(690, 80)$ and upper-right corner $(700, 100)$ and is floating southwest with a speed of 2 meters per second in the west and 1 meter per second south. Represent the iceberg as (i) a parametric rectangle and (ii) a geometric transformation relation.

5. Continuing the previous example, write queries to find out the following:

   (a) Will the iceberg hit the ship?

   (b) Suppose the person stands on the ship. What is the combined movement of the person and the ship?

   (c) Suppose there is a visibility of 50 meters. Will the person on the ship see the iceberg?

6. Suppose an eagle nest sits at location $(0, 0)$. At time $t = 0$ an eagle leaves the nest and flies northeast with a speed of 15 ft/sec north and 10 ft/sec east for 10 seconds. Another eagle leaves the same nest at time $t = 0$ and flies west with a speed of 8 ft/sec for 5 seconds and then flies south with the same speed for 5 more seconds. Represent by a parametric 2-spaghetti relation the triangular area of the nest and the two birds between times $t = 0$ and $t = 10$.

7. In this example you have to supply some of the specific data values. Represent using periodic parametric rectangle relations the following:

   (a) Any shuttle bus running periodically around a route. First draw the route of the bus as a polygon, then specify the speed on each piece of the route, and finally give the periodic parametric rectangle relation that represents the movement of the shuttle bus. Assume that the shuttle bus has a width and length of one unit distance.

   (b) The bus stops along the route of the shuttle bus.

   (c) A passenger walking toward some bus stop during some part of the day.

8. Suppose that relations *Shuttle* (id, x, y, t) and *Bus_Stop* (x, y) represent a number of shuttle buses and bus stops. Write a Datalog query that finds the ID number of the shuttle buses one can transfer to from shuttle bus number 1 either directly or indirectly.

9. Consider a bicycle wheel with an air-pump valve. Represent the motion of the air-pump valve assuming that the wheel moves with a constant speed on a flat road (a) using trigonometric functions and (b) using modulus functions. (**Hint:** Use a linear approximation for one complete rotation of the wheel, then extend the representation with a period.)

10. Suppose that *Castle* (x, y, t) represents the ground area of a castle. The owner would like to build a water canal around the castle such that its

area contains exactly the points (x, y) such that either x or y is at most 10 meters from some point (x', y') of the castle using the *Manhattan distance* measure, i.e., such that $|x - x'| \leq 10$ or $|y - y'| \leq 10$. Write a query that finds the location of the water canal around the castle.

11. Represent the *Plankton* relation of Example 13.2.1 using the geometric transformation data model.

12. Represent the *Whales* relation of Example 13.3.1 using the parametric rectangles data model.

13. Assuming we have geometric transformation relations that represent the plankton-rich area and the whales of Examples 13.2.1 and 13.3.1, write a query to find the plankton-rich area at time $t = 10$ assuming that the whales are eating the plankton as they swim.

14. Using the given spatiotemporal input relations, express the following queries in (i) SQL and (ii) Datalog:

   (a) Relations *Snow*, which describes the snow cover on the top of a mountain, and *Rock*, which describes a rocky area on its side.

      Query: What part of the rock will be free from snow at time 10?

   (b) Relation *Lake*, which describes the changing shape of a lake.

      Query: What is the total area of the lake at time 20?

   (c) Relation *Mall*, which describes the shops in a mall, and *Customer*, which describes customers that visit the mall.

      Query: Which pairs of customers are one or more floors at least partially directly above or below each other at any time?

      Query: Which pairs of customers visit the same shop at the same time?

14

Interoperability

Database interoperability is the problem of making the data and queries of one database system usable to the users of another database system. Obviously, interoperability involves many issues, such as networking, and security. However, interoperability between databases that are written in different data models poses an especially challenging task. We focus here on the issues arising from data model incompatibility. Section 14.1 describes the problem of *data interoperability*, which occurs when the data of one database system needs to be made available for users of another database system. For each of the spatiotemporal data models in Chapter 13 we give an equivalent constraint data model with some type of constraints. We also describe data interoperability between parametric extreme point and geometric transformation databases. Section 14.2 describes the problem of *query interoperability*, in which case the queries of one database system need to be made available for users of another system. This section describes three ways of accomplishing query interoperability, namely, the approaches via *query translation*, *data translation*, and the use of a *common basis*. Section 14.3 looks at other issues of database interoperability that are not limited to spatiotemporal databases.

14.1 Data Interoperability

Data interoperability between two database systems Δ_1 and Δ_2 requires that the data models used in them have the same *data expressiveness*. That means that each database written in the data model used in Δ_1 can be translated into an equivalent database in the data model of Δ_2. This section describes several pairs of spatiotemporal data models that have the same data expressiveness and between which translation is possible in either direction. Section 14.1.1 describes equivalences between cases of constraint and extreme point data models, Section 14.1.2 between constraint and parametric extreme point data models, Section 14.1.3 between parametric and geometric transformation data models, and Section 14.1.4 between constraint and geometric transformation data models.

14.1.1   Constraint and Extreme Point Data Models

In this section we show that each database in the rectangles data model and Worboys' data model is equivalent to a constraint database with some suitable types of constraints. We start with rectangles databases.

Theorem 14.1.1   Any rectangle relation R is equivalent to a constraint relation C with only inequality constraints between constants and variables.

Proof. $R \rightarrow C$: Let $T = ([a_1, b_1], \ldots, [a_d, b_d], [from, to])$ be any tuple in a rectangle relation. This can be represented by the constraint tuple $a_1 \leq x_1$, $x_1 \leq b_1, \ldots, a_d \leq x_d, x_d \leq b_d, from \leq t, t \leq to$. If $from = -\infty$ or $to = +\infty$, then the constraints with the last two constraints are omitted.

$C \rightarrow R$:   Let T be any constraint tuple. Find the highest lower bound a_i and lowest upper bound b_i for each x_i. Also find the highest lower bound $from$ and lowest upper bound to for t. The rectangle relation will be $([a_1, b_1], \ldots, [a_d, b_d], [from, to])$. ■

Example 14.1.1   Using Theorem 14.1.1 the *House* relation in Example 13.1.1 can be translated to relation *House2* shown here:

House2

ID	X	Y	T	
1	x	y	t	$3 \leq x$, $x \leq 6$, $3 \leq y$, $y \leq 6$, $100 \leq t$, $t \leq 200$
2	x	y	t	$8 \leq x$, $x \leq 11$, $3 \leq y$, $y \leq 7$, $150 \leq t$, $t \leq 300$
3	x	y	t	$2 \leq x$, $x \leq 4$, $5 \leq y$, $y \leq 10$, $250 \leq t$, $t \leq 400$
3	x	y	t	$2 \leq x$, $x \leq 10$, $8 \leq y$, $y \leq 10$, $250 \leq t$, $t \leq 400$

Theorem 14.1.2   Any Worboys relation W is equivalent to a constraint relation C with two spatial variables with linear constraints and one temporal variable with inequality constraints.

Proof. $W \rightarrow C$: Let $T = (a_x, a_y, b_x, b_y, c_x, c_y, from, to)$ be any tuple in a Worboys relation where $a_x, a_y, b_x, b_y, c_x, c_y$ are rational constants and $from, to$ are rational constants or $-\infty$ or $+\infty$. We translate T into a linear constraint tuple with variables (x, y, t). The tuple will be the conjunction of the linear inequalities in (x, y) that define the area of the triangle with corner vertices (a_x, a_y), (b_x, b_y), and (c_x, c_y) and the constraints $t \geq from$ if $from \neq -\infty$ and $t \leq to$ except if $to \neq +\infty$. We obtain the equivalent linear constraint relation by repeating for each tuple in the Worboys relation the preceding translation.

$C \rightarrow W$: Let T be any conjunction of a set of linear inequality constraints over the variables x and y. By replacing each $\leq, \geq$ with an $=$ we get a corresponding set of linear equations L. Let S be the set of intersection points of each pair of lines in L. Let $H \subseteq S$ be the set of points in S that satisfy all of the constraints in T. The convex hull of the points in H is an ordered list of points $P_1, \ldots, P_n$ that are the corner vertices of the convex polygon that encloses precisely the points that are the solutions of T. We find the convex hull and then divide it into the set of triangles (P_1, P_{1+i}, P_{2+i}) for $1 \leq i \leq n - 2$. Finally, we represent each of these triangles by a single Worboys tuple. ∎

Example 14.1.2 We represented the park in a Worboys relation in Example 13.1.2. Using the algorithm described in Theorem 14.1.2 that relation can be translated to the linear constraint relation *Park2* shown here:

Park2

ID	X	Y	T	
fountain	x	y	t	$x = 10, y = 4, 1980 \leq t, t \leq 1986$
road	x	y	t	$5 \leq x, x \leq 9, y = -x + 15, 1995 \leq t, t \leq 1996$
road	x	y	t	$x = 9, 3 \leq y, y \leq 6, 1995 \leq t, t \leq 1996$
tulip	x	y	t	$2 \leq x, x \leq 6, y \leq 9 - x, 3 \leq y, y \leq 7,$ $1975 \leq t, t \leq 1990$
park	x	y	t	$1 \leq x, x \leq 12, 2 \leq y, y \leq 11, 1974 \leq t, t \leq 1996$
pond	x	y	t	$x \geq 3, y \geq 5, y \geq x - 1, y \leq x + 5, y \leq -x + 13,$ $1991 \leq t, t \leq 1996$

Example 14.1.3 Suppose that T is the following set of linear inequality constraints:

$$y \geq 0$$
$$y \leq x + 1$$
$$y \leq 2x$$
$$y \leq -2x + 4$$

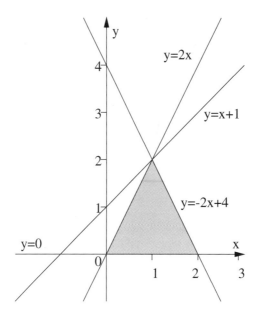

FIGURE 14.1. A set of lines.

By changing it into a set of equations we get L:

$$y = 0$$
$$y = x + 1$$
$$y = 2x$$
$$y = -2x + 4$$

Figure 14.1 shows the set of lines. Here the first line intersects the second line at $(-1, 0)$, the third line at $(0, 0)$, and the fourth line at $(2, 0)$. The other three lines intersect each other only at point $(1, 2)$. Hence S is these four points. Because $(-1, 0)$ does not satisfy the third linear inequality, i.e., $y \leq 2x$, it is eliminated. The other three points satisfy all four inequalities; hence they will be H. The convex hull is therefore the triangle with corner vertices $(0, 0)$, $(2, 0)$, and $(1, 2)$. This can be represented by the Worboys tuple $(0, 0, 2, 0, 1, 2, -\infty, +\infty)$.

14.1.2 Constraint and Parametric Extreme Point Data Models

Next we look at the translation from parametric relations into constraint relations.

Theorem 14.1.3 Any parametric rectangle relation R with m-degree polynomial parametric functions of t is equivalent to a constraint relation C with inequality constraints in which the spatial variables are bounded from above or below by m-degree polynomial functions of t and t is bounded from above and below by constants.

Proof. $R \rightarrow C$: Let $T = ([X_1^{[}, X_1^{]}], \ldots, [X_d^{[}, X_d^{]}], [\textit{from}, \textit{to}])$ be any tuple in a R where each $X_i^{[}$ and $X_i^{]}$ are m-degree polynomial functions of t and $\textit{from}, \textit{to}$ are real constants or $-\infty$ or $+\infty$. We translate T into the constraint tuple with variables $(x_1, \ldots, x_d, t)$ and the constraints:

$$X_1^{[} \leq x_1, \ x_1 \leq X_1^{]}, \ldots, X_d^{[} \leq x_d, \ x_d \leq X_d^{]}, \ \textit{from} \ \leq t, \ t \leq \textit{to}$$

except for the special cases when either $\textit{from} = -\infty$ or $\textit{to} = +\infty$, when we omit from the preceding the constraint involving $\textit{from}$ or $\textit{to}$, respectively.

$C \rightarrow R$:   The translation is similar to Theorem 14.1.1 except we have functions of t instead of constants. Therefore, the highest lower bound and the lowest higher bound will be different functions of t in different time intervals. The endpoints of the time intervals will be the time instances when two functions will be equivalent, or their difference is zero. Therefore, this translation requires finding the roots of polynomials. That can be done precisely for $m \leq 5$ and for higher degree to any desired precision using numerical analysis techniques. ∎

Example 14.1.4 The parametric rectangle relation of Example 13.2.2 can be translated to the following constraint relation:

Bomb2

X	Y	T	
x	y	t	$t \leq x, \ x \leq t + 1, \ t \leq y, \ y \leq t + 1,$
			$100 - 9.8t^2 \leq z, \ z \leq 102 - 9.8t^2, \ 0 \leq t, \ t \leq 3.19$

Theorem 14.1.4 Any parametric 2-spaghetti relation W with quotient of polynomial functions of t is equivalent to a constraint relation C with polynomial constraints over the variables x, y, t such that for each instance of t all the constraints are linear.

Proof. $W \rightarrow C$: Let $T = (a_x, a_y, b_x, b_y, c_x, c_y, \textit{from}, \textit{to})$ be any tuple in W. We translate T into a constraint tuple with variables (x, y, t) as in Theorem 14.1.2, except that all the constraints will be parametric functions of t. For example, the parametric line between (a_x, a_y) and (b_x, b_y) can be represented for instances of t when $b_x - a_x = 0$ as $x = a_x$ and otherwise as:

$$y = (x - a_x) \frac{b_y - a_y}{b_x - a_x} + a_y$$

or by first subtracting a_y and then multiplying by $b_x - a_x$ as:

$$(y - a_y)(b_x - a_x) = (x - a_x)(b_y - a_y) \tag{14.1}$$

The other sides of the parametric triangle can be represented similarly. We can represent the points within T by turning the $=$ signs into $\leq$ or $\geq$ signs as appropriate. Note that each inequality contains only polynomial constraints and for each instance of t only linear constraints. The translation of *from* and *to* to constraints are like in Theorem 14.1.2, and they only introduce inequality constraints.

$C \rightarrow W$: Do the following:

1. For each pair of parametric lines find a parametric intersection point and find out when it is valid, i.e., satisfies all the constraints.
2. Find which set of parametric points are valid in which time interval. Order the time intervals $I_1, \ldots, I_k$.
3. For each time interval the valid parametric points define a parametric convex polygon, i.e., for each instance of t in the interval define a convex polygon. Triangulate that parametric polygon and represent each triangle as a parametric 2-spaghetti tuple.   ∎

Example 14.1.5   We translate the *Net* relation of Example 13.2.4 to a constraint relation. After substituting into Equation (14.1) we obtain:

$$(y - (3 - t))((4 + 0.5t) - 3) = (x - 3)((4 - 0.5t) - (3 - t))$$

This simplifies to:

$$y = x - t$$

Similarly, substituting into Equation (14.1) with B replaced by C we get:

$$(y - (3 - t))((5 + t) - 3) = (x - 3)(3 - (3 - t))$$

Simplifying we get:

$$y(t + 2) = xt - t^2 - 2t + 6$$

Substituting into Equation (14.1) with A replaced by B we get:

$$(y - 3)((4 + 0.5t) - (5 + t)) = (x - (5 + t))((4 - 0.5t) - 3)$$

Simplifying we get:

$$y(t + 2) = x(t - 2) - t^2 + 16$$

Finally we find whether the equality symbols should be replaced by $\leq$ or $\geq$ symbols by checking which of these the third point satisfies. The translation will yield the following constraint relation:

Net2

X	Y	T	
x	y	t	$y \leq x - t$
			$y(t + 2) \geq xt - t^2 - 2t + 6,$
			$y(t + 2) \geq x(t - 2) - t^2 + 16$

Example 14.1.6 Consider the conjunction of constraints C:

$$y \geq 0$$
$$y \leq (2t + 1)x$$
$$y \leq (t + 1)(1 - x)$$

From these we create the system of equations:

$$y = 0$$
$$y = (2t + 1)x$$
$$y = (t + 1)(1 - x)$$

Now we can calculate that the intersection of the first two lines is $(0, 0)$ except for $t = -0.5$ when the two lines overlap, the intersection of the first and third lines is $(1, 0)$ except for $t = -1$ when these lines overlap, and the intersection of the last two lines is $((t + 1)/(3t + 2), ((t + 1)(2t + 1))/(3t + 2))$. These three points define the corner vertices of a triangle. The substitution of $(0, 0)$ makes the three inequalities true simultaneously only when $t \geq -1$. The substitution of $(1, 0)$ makes the three inequalities true simultaneously only when $t \geq -0.5$. The substitution of $((t + 1)/(3t + 2), ((t + 1)(2t + 1))/(3t + 2))$ makes the three inequalities true simultaneously only when t is in the interval $[-1, -2/3)$ or $[-1/2, +\infty]$. Hence the parametric 2-spaghetti relation that contains the single tuple:

$$\left(0, 0, 1, 0, \frac{t + 1}{3t + 2}, \frac{(t + 1)(2t + 1)}{3t + 2}, -0.5, +\infty\right)$$

is equivalent to C.

Example 14.1.7 Consider the moving region P represented by the following conjunction of linear constraints:

$$l_1 : \quad y \geq x$$
$$l_2 : \quad y \leq 26 - x$$
$$l_3 : \quad y \leq x + 10$$
$$l_4 : \quad y \geq 16 - x$$
$$l_5 : \quad x \geq 5 + t$$
$$t \geq 0$$
$$t \leq 4$$

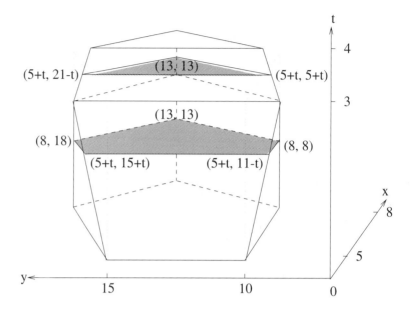

FIGURE 14.2. A polygon with one side moving.

This moving object is a polygon with one side moving linearly with t, that is, the side represented by the linear constraint $x \geq 5 + t$. At times 0, 2, 3, and 4 this moving region looks as shown in Figure 14.2. At time 0 the region is a pentagon. Between 0 and 3 the front side of the pentagon moves backward until at time 3 it becomes a triangle. Between 3 and 4 the moving object remains a triangle as the front side of the triangle moves backward. Note that the object only exists between times 0 and 4.

We translate P using the algorithm described in Theorem 14.1.4.

Step 1:   First we calculate the parametric intersection points and when they are valid. Each row of the following table shows a pair of parametric lines, their intersection and when it is valid. We only list those intersections that are valid at some time:

$$
\begin{array}{lll}
l_1, l_2 & (13, 13) & [0, 4] \\
l_1, l_4 & (8, 8) & [0, 3] \\
l_1, l_5 & (5 + t, 5 + t) & [3, 4] \\
l_2, l_3 & (8, 18) & [0, 3] \\
l_2, l_5 & (5 + t, 21 - t) & [3, 4] \\
l_3, l_5 & (5 + t, 15 + t) & [0, 3] \\
l_4, l_5 & (5 + t, 11 - t) & [0, 3]
\end{array}
$$

Step 2:   We see that during $[0, 3]$ the following points are valid:

$$(8, 18), (13, 13), (8, 8), (5 + t, 11 - t), (5 + t, 15 + t)$$

During the interval $[3, 4]$ the following points are valid:

$$(5 + t, 21 - t), (13, 13), (5 + t, 5 + t)$$

Step 3:   By triangulating these parametric pentagons for $[0, 3]$ and using directly the parametric triangle for $[3, 4]$ we get the following parametric 2-spaghetti representation of P:

Ax	Ay	Bx	By	Cx	Cy	From	To
8	18	13	13	8	8	0	3
8	18	8	8	$5 + t$	$11 - t$	0	3
8	18	$5 + t$	$11 - t$	$5 + t$	$15 + t$	0	3
$5 + t$	$21 - t$	13	13	$5 + t$	$5 + t$	3	4

Now we look at the translation of periodic parametric relations. The following can be proven similarly to the previous theorem.

Theorem 14.1.5   Any periodic parametric 2-spaghetti relation with periodic parametric functions of t is equivalent to a constraint database relation with periodic constraints over the variables x, y, t such that for each instance of t all the constraints are linear.

∎

Example 14.1.8   The *Tide* relation of Example 13.2.6 is a periodic parametric 2-spaghetti relation. We can simplify the translation by noting that the edge of the tide water is always described by the constraint $y = x - (t \bmod 11.5) + 3$ during the expansion and by $y = x + (t \bmod 11.5) - 8.5$ during the recession phase.

Tide2

X	Y	T	
x	y	t	$1 \le x$, $x \le 3$, $1 \le y$, $y \le 4$, $0 \le t'$, $t' \le 5.75$, $y \ge x - t' + 3$.
x	y	t	$1 \le x$, $x \le 3$, $1 \le y$, $y \le 4$, $5.75 \le t'$, $t' \le 11.5$, $y \ge x + t' - 8.5$.

where $t' = (t \bmod 11.5)$.

14.1.3 Parametric and Geometric Transformation Models

In this section we investigate the relationship between the parametric and geometric transformation models. First we show an equivalence between parametric rectangles and a restricted type of geometric transformation objects. We start with some definitions. A parametric rectangle $R = (\Pi_{i=1}^{d}[X_i^[, X_i^]], [from, to])$ is in *normal form* if $X_i^[(t) \leq X_i^](t)$ for each $1 \leq i \leq d$ and $t \in [from, to]$.

Example 14.1.9 Consider the two-dimensional parametric rectangle $R = ([2t - 10, t], [t + 12, 3t], [6, 10])$. Note that $2t - 10 \leq t$ for any $t \leq 10$ and $t + 12 \leq 3t$ for any $t \geq 6$. Hence $2t - 10 \leq t$ and $t + 12 \leq 3t$ are both true for each $t \in [6, 10]$. Therefore, R is a normal form parametric rectangle.

It is always possible to represent a parametric rectangle as a set of normal form parametric rectangles.

Example 14.1.10 Consider the one-dimensional parametric rectangle $R = ([0, t^2 - 3t + 2], [0, 3])$. Note that $0 \leq t^2 - 3t + 2$ only if $t \leq 1$ or $t \geq 2$. Hence R can be expressed as the union of the normal form parametric rectangles $R_1 = ([0, t^2 - 3t + 2], [0, 1])$ and $R_2 = ([0, t^2 - 3t + 2], [2, 3])$.

A geometric transformation object $G = (\Pi_{i=1}^{d}[a_i, b_i], [from, to], f)$ where f is definable as the system of equations $x_i' = g_i x_i + h_i$ where g_i and h_i are functions of t for $1 \leq i \leq d$ is in *normal form* if $g_i(t) \geq 0$ for all $t \in [from, to]$ or $g_i(t) \leq 0$ for all $t \in [from, to]$ and $a_i < b_i$ for all $1 \leq i \leq d$.

It is always possible to represent a geometric transformation object as a set of normal form geometric transformation objects.

Example 14.1.11 Consider the one-dimensional geometric transformation object $G = ([10, 20], [0, 3], (t^2 - 4t + 3)x)$. This is not in normal form because $t^2 - 4t + 3 \geq 0$ for $t \in [0, 1]$ and $t^2 - 4t + 3 \leq 0$ for $t \in [1, 3]$. We can represent G as the union of two normal form geometric transformation objects $G_1 = ([10, 20], [0, 1], (t^2 - 4t + 3)x)$ and $G_2 = ([10, 20], [1, 3], (t^2 - 4t + 3)x)$.

Theorem 14.1.6 Let $[a_i, b_i]$ for $1 \leq i \leq d$ be any set of d intervals with $a_i < b_i$. Let

$$R = (\Pi_{i=1}^{d}[X_i^[, X_i^]], [from, to])$$

be any normal form parametric rectangle. Let

$$G = (\Pi_{i=1}^{d}[a_i, b_i], [from, to], f)$$

be any normal form geometric transformation object where f is definable as the system of equations $x_i' = g_i x_i + h_i$ where g_i and h_i are functions of t for $1 \leq i \leq d$. Then R and G are equivalent if:

$$\begin{cases} g_i = \dfrac{X_i^] - X_i^[}{b_i - a_i} \quad \text{and} \quad h_i = -\dfrac{X_i^] - X_i^[}{b_i - a_i}a_i + X_i^[\end{cases}$$

or alternatively if:

$$\begin{cases} X_i^{[} = g_i\, a_i + h_i \text{ and } X_i^{]} = g_i\, b_i + h_i & \text{if } g_i(t) \ge 0 \ \forall t \in [\textit{from, to}] \\ X_i^{[} = g_i\, b_i + h_i \text{ and } X_i^{]} = g_i\, a_i + h_i & \text{if } g_i(t) \le 0 \ \forall t \in [\textit{from, to}] \end{cases}$$

Proof. $R \to G$: We can choose f such that it maps each point $(x_1, \dots, x_d)$ in $\Pi_{i=1}^{d}[a_i, b_i]$ to another point $(x_1', \dots, x_d')$ at time $t \in [\textit{from, to}]$ such that if $X_i^{[} \ne X_i^{]}$ then x_i' is always located at a fixed ratio of the distance between the endpoints of the ith interval, or else $x_i' = X_i^{[}$. Therefore,

$$\frac{x_i' - X_i^{[}}{X_i^{]} - X_i^{[}} = \frac{x_i - a_i}{b_i - a_i}$$

We can rewrite this as:

$$x_i' = \frac{X_i^{]} - X_i^{[}}{b_i - a_i}(x_i - a_i) + X_i^{[}$$

Further simplifying we get:

$$x_i' = \frac{X_i^{]} - X_i^{[}}{b_i - a_i}x_i - \frac{X_i^{]} - X_i^{[}}{b_i - a_i}a_i + X_i^{[}$$

Hence we can take

$$g_i = \frac{X_i^{]} - X_i^{[}}{b_i - a_i} \text{ and } h_i = -\frac{X_i^{]} - X_i^{[}}{b_i - a_i}a_i + X_i^{[}$$

Note that when $X_i^{[} = X_i^{]}$, the preceding gives $x_i' = X_i^{[}$ and $g_i = 0$ and $h_i = X_i^{[}$.

$G \to R$: For each i and $t \in [\textit{from, to}]$ the interval $[a_i, b_i]$ is mapped by f to a set of points in $[X_i^{[}, X_i^{]}]$. ∎

Next we look at some applications of Theorem 14.1.6.

Example 14.1.12 Consider the parametric rectangle $R = ([2t - 10, t], [t + 12, 3t], [6, 10])$, which we know by Example 14.1.9 to be normal. Suppose that $a_1 = 6, b_1 = 8, a_2 = 20,$ and $b_2 = 24$. We can calculate for the first dimension that:

$$g_1 = \frac{t - (2t - 10)}{8 - 6} = -0.5t + 5$$

$$h_1 = -6\frac{t - (2t - 10)}{8 - 6} + (2t - 10) = 5t - 40$$

Similarly, for the second dimension, we have:

$$g_2 = \frac{3t - (t + 12)}{24 - 20} = 0.5t - 3$$

$$h_2 = -20\frac{3t - (t + 12)}{24 - 20} + (t + 12) = -9t + 72$$

By Theorem 14.1.6, R is equivalent to the geometric transformation object $G = (V, [6, 10], f)$ where V is the set of points in the rectangle $[6, 8] \times [20, 24]$ and f is:

$$f(\overline{x}, t) = \begin{bmatrix} -0.5t + 5 & 0 \\ 0 & 0.5t - 3 \end{bmatrix} \overline{x} + \begin{bmatrix} 5t - 40 \\ -9t + 72 \end{bmatrix}$$

Example 14.1.13   Consider the parametric rectangle $R = ([5t, 5t], [0, 2t - t^2], [0, 2])$. Suppose that $a_1 = 0$, $b_1 = 1$, $a_2 = 0$, and $b_2 = 1$. By Theorem 14.1.6 we have for the first dimension:

$$g_1 = \frac{5t - 5t}{1 - 0} = 0$$

$$h_1 = -0\frac{5t - 5t}{1 - 0} + (5t) = 5t$$

For the second dimension, we have:

$$g_2 = \frac{(2t - t^2) - (0)}{1 - 0} = 2t - t^2$$

$$h_2 = -0\frac{(2t - t^2) - (0)}{1 - 0} + 0 = 0$$

By Theorem 14.1.6, R is equivalent to the geometric transformation object $G = (V, [0, 2], f)$ where V is the set of points in the rectangle $[0, 1] \times [0, 1]$ and f is:

$$f(\overline{x}, t) = \begin{bmatrix} 0 & 0 \\ 0 & 2t - t^2 \end{bmatrix} \overline{x} + \begin{bmatrix} 5t \\ 0 \end{bmatrix}$$

The preceding example shows that nonsingularity cannot be guaranteed if the parametric rectangle has a dimension in which the lower bound and upper bound functions are equivalent. In this case, like for the first dimension in the preceding example, all the points in the interval will be mapped to one point. The following is an example of translation from a geometric transformation to a parametric rectangle object.

Example 14.1.14   Consider the geometric transformation objects G_1 and G_2 of Example 14.1.11. By Theorem 14.1.6 the parametric rectangle $R_1 = ([t^2 - 4t + 3)10, (t^2 - 4t + 3)20], [0, 1])$ is equivalent to G_1 and $R_2 = ([t^2 - 4t + 3)20, (t^2 - 4t + 3)10], [1, 3])$ is equivalent to G_2.

Now we look at parametric 2-spaghetti relations.

Theorem 14.1.7   Any parametric 2-spaghetti relation W with m-degree polynomial functions of t is equivalent to a two-dimensional parametric affine transformation object relation G with m-degree polynomial functions of t and a polygonal reference object.

Proof. $W \rightarrow G$: We represent separately each parametric 2-spaghetti tuple as a geometric transformation object. Let S be any parametric 2-spaghetti tuple with the attributes Ax, Ay, Bx, By, Cx, Cy, which are functions of time, and *from* and *to*, which are constants. We choose any $t_0 \in [from, to]$ such that the parametric 2-spaghetti tuple is a nonempty triangle T at time t_0. If there is no such t_0, then the parametric 2-spaghetti tuple only represents the empty relation and need not be translated. We translate the parametric 2-spaghetti tuple into the geometric transformation tuple $(T, [from, to], f)$ where f is a parametric affine transformation of the form:

$$f(x, y, t) = \begin{bmatrix} a & b \\ c & d \end{bmatrix} \begin{bmatrix} x \\ y \end{bmatrix} + \begin{bmatrix} e \\ f \end{bmatrix}$$

where a, b, c, d, e, f are functions of t. Because an affine transformation in the plane is uniquely defined by the transformation of three points, we can find the parametric affine transformation by substituting the values of the corner vertices of T for (x, y) and then solving the system of equations using Gaussian elimination. During Gaussian elimination we only multiply by constants or add together the right-hand sides, which are the only ones to contain functions of t. Therefore, if initially the right-hand sides are at most m-degree polynomials of t, then in the solution we also get at most m-degree polynomials of t.

$G \rightarrow W$: Let $G = (S, I, f)$ be a parametric affine transformation object relation with m-degree polynomial functions of t. If S is not a triangle, i.e., it is a general n-degree polygon, then we break S into a set of triangles $T_1, \ldots, T_{n-2}$ and create new geometric transformation objects $G_i = (T_i, I, f)$ for $1 \leq i \leq (n-2)$. Similarly, if I is not describable as a single interval of time, then we break I into a set of intervals $I_1, \ldots, I_m$. We also further break each G_i into m smaller pieces $G_{i,j}$ by replacing I with I_j for $1 \leq j \leq m$. We now created $(n-2)m$ geometric transformations. By the definition of geometric transformations, the union of the $G_{i,j}$s has the same meaning as G has. Therefore, it is enough to show that each $G_{i,j}$ can be transformed into an equivalent parametric 2-spaghetti relation. Hence without loss of generality for the rest of the proof we assume that S is a triangle and I is a single time interval of the form $[from, to]$ where *from, to* are real constants. Let $(a_x, a_y), (b_x, b_y)$, and (c_x, c_y) be the vertices of S at time $t = 0$. Let $(Ax, Ay) = f(a_x, a_y, t), (Bx, By) = f(b_x, b_y, t)$, and $(Cx, Cy) = f(c_x, c_y, t)$. Then the vertices $(Ax, Ay), (Bx, By)$, and (Cx, Cy) describe a triangle for each instance of t. Therefore, it can be represented as the parametric 2-spaghetti relation

$$T = (Ax, Ay, Bx, By, Cx, Cy, from, to)$$

Finally, note that if f contains only m-degree polynomial functions, then T will also contain only m-degree polynomial functions. ∎

Example 14.1.15   Let us translate the *Net* parametric 2-spaghetti relation of Example 13.2.4 into a geometric transformation object. This relation has only one tuple. The spatial extent of the fishing net at time $t = 0$ is a triangle T with corner vertices $(3, 3)$, $(4, 4)$, and $(5, 3)$. We choose T as the spatial reference object. We now substitute as described in Theorem 14.1.7 to obtain a parametric affine transformation function f. The vertex $(3, 3)$ is always mapped to $(3, 3 - t)$, hence the transformation must satisfy:

$$\begin{bmatrix} a & b \\ c & d \end{bmatrix} \begin{bmatrix} 3 \\ 3 \end{bmatrix} + \begin{bmatrix} e \\ f \end{bmatrix} = \begin{bmatrix} 3 \\ 3 - t \end{bmatrix}$$

Similarly, vertex $(4, 4)$ is always mapped to $(4 + 0.5t, \ 4 - 0.5t)$; hence the transformation must also satisfy:

$$\begin{bmatrix} a & b \\ c & d \end{bmatrix} \begin{bmatrix} 4 \\ 4 \end{bmatrix} + \begin{bmatrix} e \\ f \end{bmatrix} = \begin{bmatrix} 4 + 0.5t \\ 4 - 0.5t \end{bmatrix}$$

Finally, $(5, 3)$ is mapped to $(5 + t, 3)$, hence:

$$\begin{bmatrix} a & b \\ c & d \end{bmatrix} \begin{bmatrix} 5 \\ 3 \end{bmatrix} + \begin{bmatrix} e \\ f \end{bmatrix} = \begin{bmatrix} 5 + t \\ 3 \end{bmatrix}$$

The preceding yields the following system of equations:

$$3a + 3b + e = 3$$
$$3c + 3d + f = 3 - t$$
$$4a + 4b + e = 4 + 0.5t$$
$$4c + 4d + f = 4 - 0.5t$$
$$5a + 3b + e = 5 + t$$
$$5c + 3d + f = 3$$

By solving this system, we can find that the affine parametric transformation f is:

$$\begin{bmatrix} 1 + 0.5t & 0 \\ 0.5t & 1 \end{bmatrix} \begin{bmatrix} x \\ y \end{bmatrix} + \begin{bmatrix} -1.5t \\ -2.5t \end{bmatrix}$$

Therefore, $(T, [0, 10], f)$ is a geometric transformation object that is equivalent to the *Net* relation. Note that in this example both the *Net* and the parametric affine transformation contain only linear functions of t. As a check, let us now translate back G to a parametric 2-spaghetti relation. Because T is a triangle and the time domain is a single interval, we do not need to break up G. By substituting the coordinate values of the first vertex for x and y we get that:

$$\begin{bmatrix} 1 + 0.5t & 0 \\ 0.5t & 1 \end{bmatrix} \begin{bmatrix} 3 \\ 3 \end{bmatrix} + \begin{bmatrix} -1.5t \\ -2.5t \end{bmatrix} = \begin{bmatrix} 3 \\ 3 - t \end{bmatrix}$$

For the second vertex we find:

$$\begin{bmatrix} 1 + 0.5t & 0 \\ 0.5t & 1 \end{bmatrix} \begin{bmatrix} 4 \\ 4 \end{bmatrix} + \begin{bmatrix} -1.5t \\ -2.5t \end{bmatrix} = \begin{bmatrix} 4 + 0.5t \\ 4 - 0.5t \end{bmatrix}$$

Finally, for the third vertex we obtain:

$$\begin{bmatrix} 1 + 0.5t & 0 \\ 0.5t & 1 \end{bmatrix} \begin{bmatrix} 5 \\ 3 \end{bmatrix} + \begin{bmatrix} -1.5t \\ -2.5t \end{bmatrix} = \begin{bmatrix} 5 + t \\ 3 \end{bmatrix}$$

Therefore, we can say that G is equivalent to the parametric 2-spaghetti tuple $(3, 3 - t, 4 + 0.5t, 4 - 0.5t, 5 + t, 3, 0, 10)$, which is exactly the original definition of the *Net* relation.

Note that the restriction in Theorem 14.1.7 that the reference object is a polygon is important. For example, a geometric transformation object may be a circle that is growing with a circle reference object. It is easy to see that this geometric transformation object cannot be represented as a parametric 2-spaghetti, because at any instance of time it is a circle, while any instance of the parametric 2-spaghetti relation is a 2-spaghetti relation, which is a union of triangles.

Figure 14.3 gives a summary of the equivalences among spatiotemporal data models. All the parts of the table follow from the theorems given earlier except the equivalence between rectangles relations and identity transformations with rectangular reference objects, and the equivalence between Worboys relations and identity transformations with polygonal reference objects. These two follow directly from the definition of these models and the fact that each polygon reference object can be broken into triangles and represented separately as a tuple in a Worboys relation.

Constraint	(Parametric) Extreme Point	(Parametric) Geometric Transformation
Inequality	Rectangles	Identity transformation Rectangle reference object
x, y linear t inequality	Worboys	Identity transformation Polygon reference object
Each x_i bounded by functions of t	Parametric Rectangles	Parametric scaling + translation Rectangle reference object
x, y linear for each t	Parametric 2-spaghetti	Parametric affine motion Polygon reference object

FIGURE 14.3. Equivalences among spatiotemporal data models.

14.1.4   Constraint and Geometric Transformation Models

If the reference spatial object is not a polygon or set of polygons, but, for example, a circle, then we cannot use Theorem 14.1.7 to achieve a two-step transformation from a geometric relation to a constraint relation. However, we can still say the following.

Theorem 14.1.8   Any d-dimensional parametric affine transformation object relation with m-degree polynomial functions of t can be represented as a $(d + 1)$-dimensional constraint relation with polynomial constraints.

Proof. Let $G = (S, I, f)$ be any parametric affine transformation object as stated. At first create a $(2d + 1)$-dimensional constraint relation $C = (x_1, \ldots, x_d, t, x'_1, \ldots, x'_d)$ with the d equality constraints that describe the system of equations implied by:

$$f(x_1, \ldots, x_d, t) = (x'_1, \ldots, x'_d)$$

as its conjunction of constraints. Then find $\pi_{x'_1, \ldots, x'_d, t} C$. Because projection is doable from conjunctions of real polynomial constraints in closed form, the result is a constraint relation with real polynomial constraints that represents the meaning of G.   ∎

Example 14.1.16   Let $G = (x^2 + y^2 = 1, [1, 5], f)$ where f is the following parametric scaling from (x, y) points to (x', y') points:

$$\begin{bmatrix} t & 0 \\ 0 & t \end{bmatrix} \begin{bmatrix} x \\ y \end{bmatrix} = \begin{bmatrix} x' \\ y' \end{bmatrix}$$

This defines a unit circle centered at the origin with radius 1 at time $t = 1$. The circle is expanding linearly with time until $t = 5$. At each time its radius will be equal to t. Here f is also expressible as the following system of equations:

$$tx = x'$$
$$ty = y'$$

Hence the geometric transformation object is equivalent to the following conjunction of constraints:

$$tx = x', \ ty = y', \ x^2 + y^2 = 1, \ 1 \leq t, \ t \leq 5$$

We can rewrite this as:

$$x = \frac{x'}{t}, \ y = \frac{y'}{t}, \ x = \sqrt{1 - y^2}, \ 1 \leq t, \ t \leq 5$$

Eliminating x yields:

$$\frac{x'}{t} = \sqrt{1 - y^2}, \ y = \frac{y'}{t}, \ 1 \leq t, \ t \leq 5$$

This we rewrite as:

$$y^2 = 1 - \left(\frac{x'}{t}\right)^2, \quad y = \frac{y'}{t}, \ 1 \le t, \ t \le 5$$

Eliminating y yields:

$$\left(\frac{x'}{t}\right)^2 + \left(\frac{y'}{t}\right)^2 = 1, \quad 1 \le t, \ t \le 5$$

It is easy to see that the last conjunction of constraints defines a circle with radius t as expected.

14.2 Query Interoperability

Query interoperability between two database systems Δ_1 and Δ_2 requires that the queries of Δ_2 be usable by the users of Δ_1. Typically, a user wants to find the result of running Q_2 on D_1 where D_1 is a local Δ_1 database and Q_2 is a distant site Δ_2 query. Here we assume that the user is unaware of the issue of different data models and knows only what Q_2 is supposed to do normally if run on Δ_2 databases. There are three different approaches to query interoperability. Section 14.2.1 describes the approach of query translation, Section 14.2.2 data translation, and Section 14.2.3 the use of a common basis to solve the query interoperability problem. Several of the query interoperability examples will solve the problem of intersection in spatiotemporal data models via the use of constraint databases. Section 14.2.4, which discusses the difficulties of defining intersection of linear parametric rectangles directly without the use of query interoperability.

14.2.1 Query Interoperability via Query Translation

One approach to solving the problem mentioned earlier is to translate query Q_2 to a logically equivalent Δ_1 query Q_1 before the execution. This process requires *query translation* and is illustrated in Figure 14.4.

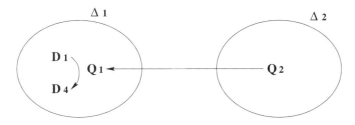

FIGURE 14.4. Query interoperability via query translation.

By insisting that the query languages use the logical level of data in any spatiotemporal and constraint data model, the queries written for different databases are very similar. Hence query translation is not a major problem in the case of queries that use only relational algebra, SQL, or Datalog and the database systems allow all these languages. However, we may still need query translation when one database system allows only one of these query languages and the other allows another. For example, we may still need to translate from Datalog to SQL. In addition, we learned about some special spatiotemporal operators that may not be available in all database systems.

Example 14.2.1   Suppose Δ_1 is a constraint database system that contains the *Castle* relation of Exercise 13.10 and uses only Datalog. Suppose also that Δ_2 is a rectangles database system that allows the buffer operator. To find the water canal around the castle we can write the query *Buffer(Castle, 10)*. However, this works only in Δ_2. Hence we have to translate this query to Datalog, which we can do as follows:

$$Buffer(x, y) \quad :— \quad Castle\,(x_2, y_2),\ 0 \leq x - x_2 \leq 10,\ 0 \leq y - y_2 \leq 10.$$

$$Buffer(x, y) \quad :— \quad Castle\,(x_2, y_2),\ 0 \leq x - x_2 \leq 10,\ 0 \leq y_2 - y \leq 10.$$

$$Buffer(x, y) \quad :— \quad Castle\,(x_2, y_2),\ 0 \leq x_2 - x \leq 10,\ 0 \leq y - y_2 \leq 10.$$

$$Buffer(x, y) \quad :— \quad Castle\,(x_2, y_2),\ 0 \leq x_2 - x \leq 10,\ 0 \leq y_2 - y \leq 10.$$

The *Buffer* relation will contain all the locations that belong to either the castle or the water. To find only the areas of the water canal we can subtract from *Buffer* the *Castle* relation using Datalog with negation.

Note that we may expect the *Buffer* operator in Δ_2 to be closed, i.e., to give a rectangles relation if the input is a rectangles relation. Analogously, the *Buffer* operator always gives an inequality constraint database output if the input is an inequality constraint database. If we wrote a *Buffer* operator in Datalog that uses the Euclidean distance measure, then the output could be a polynomial constraint relation, which cannot be translated into a rectangles relation.

14.2.2   Query Interoperability via Data Translation

Another approach to solving the query interoperability problem is to translate D_1 (or at least its part relevant to Q_2) into a logically equivalent Δ_2 database D_2, then execute Q_2 on D_2 to obtain a new Δ_2 database D_3, and finally translate it to a Δ_1 database D_4. This approach is shown in Figure 14.5. Clearly, D_4 is logically equivalent to the database we obtained using the previous approach with query translation. However, in this alternative process we used only *data translation*. In other words we reduced the problem to data interoperability.

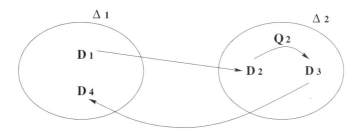

FIGURE 14.5. Query interoperability via data translation.

Example 14.2.2   Consider again Example 14.2.1 and suppose that the definition of the *Castle* relation contains only inequality constraints. Then by Theorem 14.1.1 the *Castle* relation can be translated into a rectangles relation D_2. Then the query *Buffer*$(D_2, 10)$
can be executed in Δ_2, resulting in a rectangles database D_3. Finally, D_3 can be
translated back to an inequality constraint relation that is equivalent to D_4 of Example 14.2.1.

In theory all the query languages of relational algebra, SQL, and Datalog can
be made available in any spatiotemporal database system because of the closure
of the data models mentioned in Figure 14.3, as shown by the following theorem.

Theorem 14.2.1   All the spatiotemporal models appearing in Figure 14.3 are closed under intersection, complement, union, join, projection, and selection with inequality constraints that contain spatiotemporal variables and constants.

Proof. All the operators are easily seen to be closed in the four cases of constraint
data models shown in Figure 14.3. Because the other data models are equivalent
to one of the four constraint data models, they are also closed.   ■

In practice, some spatiotemporal database systems do not even implement the
full relational algebra. In these cases, query interoperability via data translation
to a constraint database can be used to enhance the query capabilities of other
spatiotemporal databases. We illustrate that in the following examples.

Example 14.2.3   Suppose Δ_1 is a parametric 2-spaghetti database system that does not allow the
intersection operator. Suppose also that Δ_2 is a constraint database system that
allows intersection. Let D_1 contain the parametric 2-spaghetti relations

$$R_1 = (0, 0, 1, 0, 0, t + 1, -\infty, +\infty)$$

and

$$R_2 = (0, 0, 1, 0, 1, 2t + 1, -\infty, +\infty)$$

We can use query interoperability to find the intersection of R_1 and R_2. First,
we translate R_1 to the constraint relation:

$$C_1 = \{y \geq 0, \ x \geq 0, \ y \leq (t + 1)(1 - x)\}$$

and R_2 to the constraint relation

$$C_2 = \{y \geq 0, \ x \leq 1, \ y \leq (2t + 1)x\}$$

Then the intersection of C_1 and C_2 is:

$$C = \{y \geq 0, \ y \leq (t + 1)(1 - x), \ y \leq (2t + 1)x, \ x \geq 0, \ x \leq 1\}$$

Because the first three constraints imply the last two, the preceding simplifies to:

$$C = \{y \geq 0, \ y \leq (t + 1)(1 - x), \ y \leq (2t + 1)x\}$$

Finally, as in Example 14.1.6, we translate C back to the parametric 2-spaghetti relation

$$R = (0, 0, 1, 0, \frac{t + 1}{3t + 2}, \frac{(t + 1)(2t + 1)}{3t + 2}, -0.5, +\infty)$$

This example shows that parametric 2-spaghetti relations with linear functions of time are not closed under intersection, because R_1 and R_2 both contain only linear functions, but their intersection R contains a rational of polynomial functions of t.

Example 14.2.4 Suppose Δ_1 is a geometric transformation database system that does not allow the intersection operator. Suppose also that Δ_2 is a constraint database system that allows intersection. Let D_1 contain $G_1 = ([0, 1] \times [0, 1], \ (1, +\infty), \ f_1)$ where f is the identity transformation and $G_2 = ([0, 1] \times [0, 1], \ (1, +\infty), \ f_2)$ where f_2 is:

$$f_2(x, y, t) = \begin{bmatrix} 1 & t \\ -1 & 1 \end{bmatrix} \begin{bmatrix} x \\ y \end{bmatrix}$$

We can use query interoperability to find the intersection of G_1 and G_2. First, we translate G_1 to:

$$C_1 = \{0 \leq x, \ x \leq 1, \ 0 \leq y, \ y \leq 1, \ t \geq 1\}$$

Note that G_2 maps the unit square at each time $t \geq 0$ into a parallelogram with corner vertices $(0, 0)$, $(1, -1)$, $(t + 1, 0)$, and $(t, 1)$ as shown in Figure 14.6.

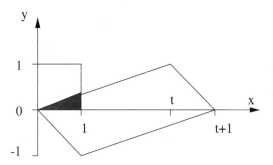

FIGURE 14.6. Unit square mapped to a parallelogram.

Hence we can translate G_2 to:

$$C_2 = \left\{ y \geq -x, \ y \leq -x + t + 1, \ y \leq \frac{x}{t}, \ y \geq \frac{x-1}{t} - 1 \right\}$$

Therefore, after simplifying the intersection of C_1 and C_2 is:

$$C = \left\{ y \leq \frac{x}{t}, \ x \geq 0, \ y \geq 0, \ t \geq 1 \right\}$$

Finally, we translate C to the geometric transformation $G(T, [1, +\infty], f)$ where T is the triangle with corner vertices $(0, 0)$, $(1, 0)$, and $(1, 1)$, and f is:

$$f(x, y, t) = \begin{bmatrix} 1 & 0 \\ 0 & 1/t \end{bmatrix} \begin{bmatrix} x \\ y \end{bmatrix}$$

This example shows that parametric affine transformation objects with rectangle spatial reference objects are not closed under intersection even if the rectangles have sides parallel to the x- and y-axes.

14.2.3   Query Interoperability via a Common Basis

We would need to write a total of $2n(n-1)$ data and query translation algorithms to interoperate directly between each pair of n data models. Instead, we simplify the interoperability problem by finding a *common basis* database system into which the data and queries of every other data model are translated. The common basis approach requires only $4n$ data and query translations. Let us see how the query interoperability problem, as discussed earlier, can be solved using a common basis. Let Δ_0 be the common basis. Then in this approach, D_1 is translated into a logically equivalent database D_0 in Δ_0 and query Q_2 is translated into a logically equivalent Δ_0 query Q_0. Then Q_0 is executed and the resulting relation D_5 is translated into a Δ_1 relation D_4. This approach is shown in Figure 14.7.

Example 14.2.5   Suppose Δ_0 is a parametric 2-spaghetti and Δ_1 is a geometric transformations database system and that they do not allow the intersection operator. Suppose also that Δ_2 is a constraint database system that allows intersection. Let D_1 contain

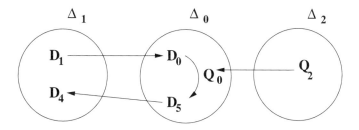

FIGURE 14.7. Query interoperability via a common basis.

$G_1 = (T_1, (-\infty, +\infty), f_1)$ where T_1 is a triangle with vertices $(0, 0)$, $(0, 1)$, and $(1, 0)$, and f_1 is:

$$f_1(x, y, t) = \begin{bmatrix} 1 & 0 \\ 0 & 1+t \end{bmatrix} \begin{bmatrix} x \\ y \end{bmatrix}$$

and $G_2 = (T_2, (-\infty, +\infty), f_2)$ where T_2 is a triangle with vertices $(0, 0)$, $(0, 1)$, and $(1, 1)$, and f_2 is:

$$f_2(x, y, t) = \begin{bmatrix} 1 & 0 \\ 0 & 2+t \end{bmatrix} \begin{bmatrix} x \\ y \end{bmatrix}$$

We can use query interoperability via a common basis to find the intersection of G_1 and G_2. First, we translate G_1 and G_2 to the parametric 2-spaghetti relations R_1 and R_2, respectively. These happen to be the same as those of Example 14.2.3. We also translate the intersection operator from Δ_2 to Δ_0. Then we evaluate in Δ_0 the intersection of R_1 and R_2 to be the parametric 2-spaghetti relation R of Example 14.2.3. Finally, we translate R to the geometric transformation $G(T_1, [-0.5, +\infty], f)$ where T_1 is as in Example 14.2.3 and f is:

$$f(x, y, t) = \begin{bmatrix} 1 & \dfrac{-t}{3t + 2} \\ 0 & \dfrac{2(t + 1)(2t + 1)}{3t + 2} \end{bmatrix} \begin{bmatrix} x \\ y \end{bmatrix}$$

This example shows that parametric scaling transformation objects with triangle spatial reference objects are not closed under intersection, because G is a parametric affine transformation that is not a parametric scaling transformation.

The common basis also facilitates the addition of new data models. For example, suppose one would like to use a new data model Δ_n that is not already available in some database system. One needs only to define data and query translations between the common basis Δ_0 and Δ_n. Then any Q_n query on D_n database in Δ_n can be executed by translating the query and the database to the common basis, executing the query in the common basis and translating the result back into Δ_n. Hence the common basis could also save writing separate query processors for data models that are used only infrequently. Constraint databases are a good common basis for many types of databases for the following reasons:

1. *Precise data translation:* We can translate each of the spatiotemporal data models of Chapter 13 into a syntactically restricted type of constraint database. We can also easily compare the expressive power of several different data models by translating them to restricted types of constraint databases.

2. *Easy query translation:* Many spatiotemporal query languages contain numerous special operators and other special language features. In general, it is difficult to translate directly from a query language with a set of special

operators to another query language with a different set of special operators. It is usually easier to translate between constraint queries and specialized languages. Many query processors also work better and more robustly
if the query language contains only a few or no special operators.

3. *Safety and complexity:* By knowing the allowed syntax of the constraints in
the common basis, we can gain valuable information about the safety and
computational complexity of queries following the results of Chapters 8
and 10.

14.2.4 Intersection of Linear Parametric Rectangles

Query interoperability via data translation to a constraint database is not the only
way to evaluate the intersection of parametric extreme point relations or geometric transformation relations. It is possible but cumbersome to define directly the
intersection of relations in those spatiotemporal data models. To hint at some of
the difficulties, let us consider the simple question of just finding out whether two
linear parametric rectangles intersect. For added simplicity, the following lemma
is stated only for one spatial dimension.

Lemma 14.2.1   The parametric rectangles

$$R_1 = ([a_1t + b_1, \ c_1t + d_1], \ I_1)$$

and

$$R_2 = ([a_2t + b_2, \ c_2t + d_2], \ I_2)$$

where $a_1, b_1, c_1, d_1, a_2, b_2, c_2, d_2$ are constants and I_1 and I_2 are time intervals
intersect if and only if

$$I_1 \cap I_2 \cap I_3 \cap I_4 \cap I_5 \cap I_6$$

is nonempty, where:

I_3 is the time interval when $a_1t + b_1 \leq c_1t + d_1$ is true;

I_4 is the time interval when $a_2t + b_2 \leq c_2t + d_2$ is true;

I_5 is the time interval when $a_1t + b_1 \leq c_2t + d_2$ is true;   and

I_6 is the time interval when $a_2t + b_2 \leq c_1t + d_1$ is true.

Proof. It is obvious that R_1 and R_2 can intersect only at times t, which are within
both I_1 and I_2. Also, R_1 must have a lower bound than is less than its upper bound,
which occurs exactly when I_3 is true. Similarly, R_2 must have a lower bound than
is less than its upper bound, which occurs exactly when I_4 is true. In addition, at
any time t when R_1 and R_2 intersect the lower bound of R_1 must be less than the
upper bound of R_2 and the lower bound of R_2 must be before the upper bound of
R_1, which are true in the intervals I_5 and I_6, respectively.   ■

We can use Lemma 14.2.1 to prove the following theorem for d dimensions.

Theorem 14.2.2   Whether two d-dimensional linear parametric rectangles intersect can be checked in $O(d)$ time.

Proof. For each ith dimension we can easily calculate the values of all the intervals in Lemma 14.2.1 and express those intervals in terms of constraints on the permissible values of t. For example, we have the following cases of intervals for I_3:

$$
I_3 = \begin{cases}
\emptyset & \text{if } a_1 = c_1 \quad \text{and} \quad b_1 > d_1 \\
t & \text{if } a_1 = c_1 \quad \text{and} \quad b_1 \leq d_1 \\
t \leq (d_1 - b_1)/(a_1 - c_1) & \text{if } a_1 > c_1 \\
t \geq (d_1 - b_1)/(a_1 - c_1) & \text{if } a_1 < c_1
\end{cases}
$$

We can similarly express the other intervals as constraints on t. The conjunctions of these constraints is either satisfiable or not and can be easily checked. Furthermore, we can take the conjunction of all the constraints in all the dimensions. The two linear parametric rectangles intersect if and only if the resulting constraint is satisfiable. Note that picking for each ith dimension for each of the intervals $I_1, \ldots, I_6$ one of the four cases takes a constant time. Therefore, for the d dimensions together it takes $O(d)$ time to build the large constraint that needs to be checked for satisfiability. Checking satisfiability also takes $O(d)$ time because as we scan the constraint from left to right we can keep track of the highest lower bound c_1 constraint and lowest upper bound c_2 constraint on t and whether any $\emptyset$ was seen. If $\emptyset$ occurs anywhere or $c_1 > c_2$ then the constraint is not satisfiable; otherwise it is satisfiable. ∎

Theorem 14.2.2 can be extended to yield a theorem that actually states the precise intersection for any two d-dimensional linear parametric rectangles.

14.3   Other Types of Interoperability

There are many possible sources of mismatches between different databases that are not due to the use of different data models. For example, the schemas of the relations may not match even in the case of two relational databases. For example, in one database Δ_1 the attribute name "cars" is used while in the other database Δ_2 the attribute name "vehicles" is used. Then before executing a query Q_2 that was written originally for Δ_2 on some Δ_1 database instance, we have to change Q_2 by replacing "vehicles" with "cars" before execution, along with other changes that may be necessary.

There is also a potential for mismatch when some data are missing or inconsistent. For example, suppose that in Δ_2 we can assume that each employee works in only one company. Suppose further that some query Q_2 is written for that database to find the total salary of each employee. Therefore Q_2 could be easily expressed using only select, project, and join operations. However, if each employee in Δ_1 may work in several companies, then Q_2 has to be modified, for example, by inserting into it the maximum aggregate function where appropriate, before running it in Δ_1. Another type of mismatch occurs when the same attribute, for example, weight, is measured in different units, for example, in pounds in one database relation and kilograms in another database relation.

These issues are sometimes called *application-dependent* interoperability issues. In this chapter we limited our attention to the differences in the data models and were concerned only with *application-independent* interoperability, because that is the part where constraint databases could be most useful. Obviously, for practical applications the two types of interoperability should be considered together.

Bibliographic Notes

Interoperability is traditionally motivated by several possible sources of mismatches between different relational databases [172]. Interoperability between a GIS database and application programs was studied in Scheck and Wolf [281]. Interoperability in the sense of combining spatial and attribute data managers for the implementation of GIS systems was studied in Kolovson et al. [176]. A functional specification facilitating interoperability of GIS systems were studied by Frank and Kuhn [102]. Application-dependent interoperability issues of resolving semantic and representational mismatches and conflict detection and resolution have found a very elegant formulation using the language of first-order logic by Qian and Lunt [242].

Data interoperability of a number of temporal databases via a common basis, that is, a unifying temporal database, was studied in Jensen et al. [156]. More recent work on the interoperability of temporal databases, e.g., Wang et al. [322, 36] also consider interoperability among different temporal data models.

Chomicki and Revesz [61, 62] initiated a study of the interoperability of constraint and spatiotemporal databases, emphasizing the interoperability problem that derives from differences in data models. Theorem 14.1.2 is from that paper, and it gave a translation from linear constraint databases to parametric 2-spaghetti databases with linear functions of time, which is a subcase of Theorem 14.1.4. Chomicki et al. [60] provide a use of the one-way translation, and the paper contains Exercise 3. The other data interoperability results are new.

Theorem 14.2.1 is a culmination of previous work on the closure of spatiotemporal data models under relational algebra. The previous approaches did not have the benefit of the data translation results and were based on direct arguments on the structure of various spatiotemporal data models. Such direct arguments are more complicated but desirable for potentially more efficient implementations of the operators. Examples of direct arguments include Theorem 14.2.2, which checks whether two linear parametric rectangles intersect, and a definition of the intersection of two parametric scaling + translation objects with rectangle reference objects in [63].

The nonclosure of parametric 2-spaghetti relations with linear functions of time, which is illustrated in Example 14.2.3, was noticed by Chomicki and Revesz [61, 62]. The closure of parametric rectangles even with periodic and polynomial constraints is from Cai et al. [50]. A generalization of the periodic functions in [50] and the computational complexity of query evaluation is considered in [271, 272]. The closure of parametric scaling and translation transformations with rectangle spatial reference objects is from Chomicki and Revesz [63]. An earlier version of Example 14.2.5 also appeared in Chomicki and Revesz [63] but was solved incorrectly.

As mentioned earlier, Example 14.2.5 illustrates that parametric scaling transformations with polygonal spatial reference objects are not closed under intersection. This result was also proven by Haesevoets and Kuijpers [134] as well as some other results on the closure properties of geometric transformation objects.

The result that parametric affine transformations with rectangle spatial reference objects (with sides parallel to the x- and y-axes) are not closed under intersection is new. This follows from Example 14.2.4 and the fact that the intersection is a parametric triangle and parametric affine transformations cannot map any rectangle to parametric triangles.

Exercises

1. Translate the following instance of the *Window* relation of Example 13.4.3 into an inequality constraint relation:

Window

Id	X	Y	T
1	[60, 90]	[10, 60]	[0, 3]
1	[60, 90]	[10, 60]	[17, 20]
2	[0, 100]	[0, 80]	[3, 8]
3	[50, 80]	[40, 50]	[8, 12]
4	[20, 60]	[30, 70]	[12, 17]

2. Translate the parametric 2-spaghetti relation of Exercise 13.6 into a constraint relation.

3. Translate the following constraint relation *Desert*, which describes a changing desert area, into a parametric 2-spaghetti relation:

$$Desert\,(x, y, t) :- x \geq 0$$
$$y \geq 0$$

$$x - t \leq 10$$
$$x + y \leq 20$$
$$t \geq 0$$
$$t \leq 10$$

$$Desert\,(x, y, t) :\!-\; x \geq 0$$
$$y \geq 0$$
$$x + y + t \leq 30$$
$$t \geq 10$$
$$t \leq 20$$

4. Translate the following constraint relation into a parametric 2-spaghetti relation:

$$x \geq 5, \quad x \leq 10, \quad y \leq xt^2, \quad y \geq -xt^3, \quad t \geq -20, \quad t \leq 20$$

5. For each of the following parametric rectangles (i) test whether it is normal, and if it is not normal, then rewrite it into a set of normal parametric rectangles and (ii) translate them into geometric transformation relations, assuming the spatial reference object is $[0, 1] \times [0, 1]$:

   (a) $R_1 = ([0,\ t+1],\ [2t,\ t],\ [-1,\ 0])$

   (b) $R_2 = ([2t+5,\ 3t],\ [8t^3,\ 8t^3],\ [0,\ 10])$

   (c) $R_3 = ([2t,\ 50-3t],\ [t^2,\ 4t-77],\ [-20,\ 20])$

6. Find the intersection of the following pair of parametric rectangles. (**Hint:** Translate them to constraint relations, take their intersection, and translate the intersection relation back into a parametric rectangles relation.)

   (a) $R_1 = ([5,\ 15],\ [3t,\ 3t+8],\ [0,\ 24])$ and
   $R_2 = ([3,\ 7],\ [2t+8,\ 2t+24],\ [0,\ 30])$

   (b) $R_3 = ([3+t,\ 8+t],\ [2-t,\ 6-t],\ [0,\ 10])$ and
   $R_4 = ([2t,\ 12+3t],\ [t,\ 10-2t],\ [0,\ 20])$

7. Suppose you use a rectangles database system Δ_1 that allows only SQL queries. Suppose you have the instance of relation *Window* given in Exercise 1 and would like to execute the Datalog query of Example 13.4.3 that finds the windows that are completely hidden on a computer screen. However, Datalog queries are available only in some constraint database system Δ_2:

   (a) Use query interoperability via query translation to solve the problem. (**Hint:** Translate the Datalog query to a SQL query.)

   (b) Use query interoperability via data translation to solve the problem.

   (c) Compare these two approaches for query interoperability.

15

Approximation by Constraints

Many natural data, such as the surface of a landscape or the continuously changing temperature at a location, are hard to record in any database as we illustrate here. Generally it is possible to record surface elevation values or the temperature only at some finite set of points in space and time. However, that does not capture the entire continuously changing surface or temperature curve. Hence there is a need for *interpolation*, i.e., some approximation of the value at a given place and time from the values at other places and times. The interpolation function is usually expressed by constraints, hence the approximate representation of the data can be represented by constraint databases.

Another advantage of approximate representation is *data compression*. In general, the constraint representation requires fewer tuples and less computer memory than the original representation, that is, uninterpolated data. As a result, queries can often be evaluated much faster on the constraint approximation.

Section 15.1 describes *triangulated irregular networks*, or TINs, which are used in several geographic information systems to approximate the surface of a landscape. Each TIN can be represented by a constraint relation.

Section 15.2 describes *piecewise linear approximations* of time series data, such as the temperature data recorded at a finite number of time instances. Each piecewise linear approximation can also be easily represented by a linear constraint relation. As we show in this section the constraint relation is more compact than the original one. Constraint relations can be queried with the output of the query having a high *precision* and *recall*. Constraint relations representing time series can also be easily updated.

Section 15.3 describes *parametric triangulated irregular networks*, or PTINs. Each PTIN is a combination of a TIN and a separate piecewise linear approximation for a number of locations. PTINs can be used to represent data that vary over time at each (x, y) location. PTINs can also be represented by linear constraint databases.

Finally, Section 15.4 describes an approximation of a raster movie by parametric rectangles. Parametric rectangles approximation can then be translated to a constraint approximation as was shown in Chapter 13.

15.1   Triangulated Irregular Networks

Figure 15.1 shows a natural landscape surface with a mountain range. Such a landscape is hard to represent in a database system because it would require an infinite number of tuples. One way to approximate this representation is to first take a *sample* of points on the surface. For example, for the mountain range surface we may select the points shown in Figure 15.2. The solid black points are on the visible and the gray points are on the hidden part of the surface of the mountains.

The selection of the sample points can be arbitrary. For example, it can be a random set of points or some regular pattern of points. Often the points are

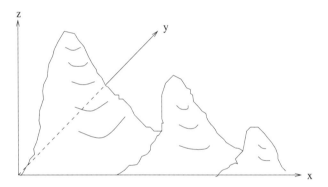

FIGURE 15.1. The mountain range.

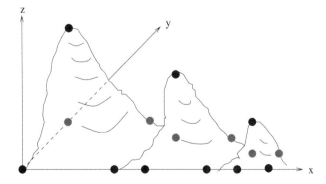

FIGURE 15.2. Sample points from the surface of a mountain range.

special points of the landscape, for example, mountain tops or the deepest points in valleys. The exact (x, y, z) coordinates of the sample points of Figure 15.2 are given in relation *Sample_Points*.

Using the sample points, we can reconstruct an approximation of the surface called a *triangulated irregular network* (TIN). To find a TIN, we project the sample points to the (x, y) plane, as shown in Figure 15.3.

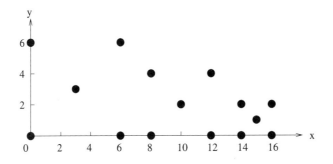

FIGURE 15.3. The spatial points.

Sample_Points

ID	X	Y	Z
1	0	0	0
2	0	6	0
3	3	3	9
4	6	0	0
5	6	6	0
6	8	0	0
7	8	4	0
8	10	2	6
9	12	0	0
10	12	4	0
11	14	0	0
12	14	2	0
13	15	1	3
14	16	0	0
15	16	2	0

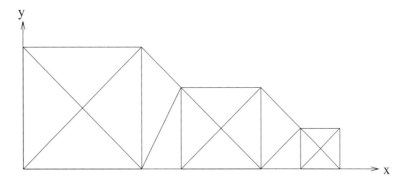

FIGURE 15.4. The triangulation.

Next we find a *triangulation* of the sample points, that is, we add a set of edges to the sample points until the whole set of sample points is within a polygon and each inside region is a triangle. There are many different possible triangulations of the given set of sample points. One triangulation is shown in Figure 15.4.

While the resulting triangulation is a two-dimensional structure, the triangulated irregular network is a three-dimensional structure. It is found by raising, in the two-dimensional triangulation, each sample point to its proper elevation, that is, its z-coordinate value, as shown in Figure 15.5.

The mountain range is now approximated by a TIN that contains three adjacent pyramids. The sample points were used to interpolate the elevation data of the whole space, by taking, for each triangle, the surface above the triangle that is a flat plane going through the corner vertices. For example, the east side surface of the large pyramid, shown shaded in Figure 15.5, is a part of the TIN that corresponds to the triangle with corner vertices $(3, 3)$, $(6, 0)$, and $(6, 6)$.

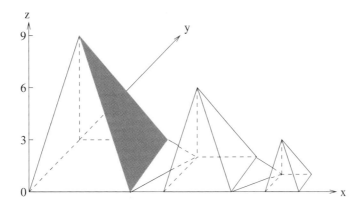

FIGURE 15.5. The triangulated irregular network corresponding to the mountain range.

Pyramid

X	Y	Z	
x	y	z	$y \geq 0$, $y \leq x$, $x + y \leq 6$, $z = 3y$
x	y	z	$x \geq 0$, $y \geq x$, $x + y \leq 6$, $z = 3x$
x	y	z	$y \leq 6$, $y \geq x$, $x + y \geq 6$, $z = -3y + 18$
x	y	z	$x \leq 6$, $y \leq x$, $x + y \geq 6$, $z = -3x + 18$

The TIN surface can be naturally represented in a constraint database. For example, the largest pyramid can be represented as shown in relation *Pyramid*. There, in the last tuple the east side surface of the large pyramid is represented by the conjunction of the three inequality constraints $x \leq 6$, $y \leq x$, and $x + y \geq 6$, which define the triangle mentioned in the (x, y) plane and the equality constraint $z = -3x + 18$, which represents the elevation of each point of the triangle.

15.2   Piecewise Linear Approximation of Time Series

A time series is a sequence of data points $(t_1, y_1), \cdots, (t_n, y_n)$ where t_i are monotone increasing real number time instances and y_i are real number measured values at those times for $1 \leq i \leq n$. Databases are often used to record data in the form of a time series.

For example, consider four weather stations at different locations. A database may record the daily high temperature for the first weather station on Mondays and Fridays, for the second on Tuesdays and Thursdays, for the third on Saturdays, and for the fourth on Sundays. These measurements yield a separate time series for each of the four weather stations, and assuming that day 1 is a Monday, the first month of these four time series may be represented as shown in relation *Temperature*.

Suppose we want to find the location where the daily high temperature was the highest on the second Wednesday, i.e., day 10. Because none of the four weather stations measures the temperature on Wednesdays, we cannot know the answer precisely, but we may use approximation to estimate the temperature on any particular day.

One approximation that we can use is called *piecewise linear approximation* or *piecewise linear interpolation*. For a time series S and any given error tolerance value Ψ we find a piecewise linear function f, i.e., a function composed of line segments such that the following holds:

$$|f(t_i) - y_i| \leq \Psi \text{ for each } (t_i, y_i) \in S \tag{15.1}$$

The relation *Temperature* can be approximated with piecewise linear functions, and the approximation can be represented in a constraint database. For ex-

Temperature

SN	t	Temp
1	1	68
1	5	71
1	8	76
1	12	73
1	15	71
1	19	68
1	22	70
1	26	74
1	29	73
2	2	71
2	4	69
2	9	68
2	11	66
2	16	70
2	18	68
2	23	71
2	25	75
2	30	77
3	6	75
3	13	78
3	20	72
3	27	68
4	7	72
4	14	75
4	21	72
4	28	74

ample, relation *Temperature2* gives one constraint database approximation when $\Psi = 5$.

Piecewise linear approximations have several advantages. They can be used for data compression because the number of pieces in an approximation is usually much fewer than the number of points in the time series. For example, relation *Temperature* has 9 tuples, while relation *Temperature2* has only 2 tuples corresponding to the first weather station. Second, querying can be done faster using the compressed data as will be shown in Examples 15.2.2 and 15.2.3. Third, the approximation gives an interpolation that allows us to find the temperature at *any* time instance. For example, we can get the daily high temperature for each station

Temperature2

SN	t	Temp	
1	t	y	$y = 0.5(t-1) + 68,\ t \geq 1,\ t \leq 15$
1	t	y	$y = -0.5(t-15) + 75,\ t \geq 15,\ t \leq 29$
2	t	y	$\ldots$
$\vdots$	$\vdots$	$\vdots$	$\vdots$

on the second Wednesday, i.e., day 10, with the following SQL query, which uses the constraint representation:

> **select**   *Temp*
> **from**   *Temperature2*
> **where** $t = 10$

We will describe a piecewise linear approximation algorithm that runs in linear time in the number of time series data points. First we give some definitions.

Definition 15.2.1   Given two points (t_b, y_b) and (t_e, y_e) where $(b < e)$, and the maximum approximation error threshold is Ψ, we denote by:

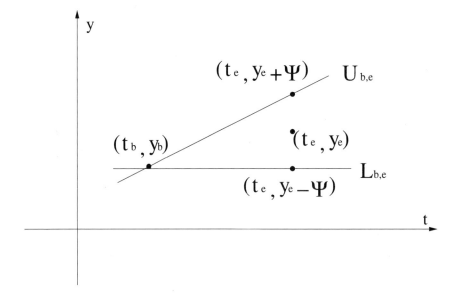

FIGURE 15.6. Lines $Y_{b,e}$, $U_{b,e}$, and $L_{b,e}$.

$L_{b,e}(t)$ the *lower line* passing through (t_b, y_b) and $(t_e, y_e - \Psi)$ and

$U_{b,e}(t)$ the *upper line* passing through (t_b, y_b) and $(t_e, y_e + \Psi)$.

The lower and upper lines are shown in Figure 15.6. Note that any line that passes through (t_b, y_b) and has a slope between that of the lower and the upper lines is a line that at t_e must have a value between $y_e - \Psi$ and $y_e + \Psi$.

In the following algorithm, we assume that if A and B are points, then the function $slope(A, B)$ returns the slope of the line segment between those two points.

The idea behind the algorithm is that it tries to extend each piece until it cannot because the upper line becomes lower than the lower line. This idea will become clearer following Example 15.2.1 and the proof of correctness in Theorem 15.2.1.

Piecewise Linear Approximation(S,Ψ)

input: A time series S and a maximum error threshold Ψ.
output: A piecewise linear approximation function.
local vars: Begin is start, S_L min and S_U max slope of a
                piece.

$Begin := (t_1, y_1)$
$S_L := -\infty$
$S_U := +\infty$

for $i = 1$ to $(n-1)$ **do**
  $S'_L := \max(S_L, \; slope(Begin, (t_{i+1}, y_{i+1} - \Psi))$
  $S'_U := \min(S_U, \; slope(Begin, (t_{i+1}, y_{i+1} + \Psi))$
  if $S'_L \leq S'_U$ **then**
      $S_L := S'_L$
      $S_U := S'_U$
  else
      Add line $f(t) = \frac{S_L + S_U}{2}(t - Begin.t) + Begin.y$
      $Begin := (t_i, f(t_i))$
      $S_L := slope(Begin, (t_{i+1}, y_{i+1} - \Psi))$
      $S_U := slope(Begin, (t_{i+1}, y_{i+1} + \Psi))$
  end-if
end-for

Add line $f(t) = \frac{S_L + S_U}{2}(t - Begin.t) + Begin.y$

Example 15.2.1   Let us find a piecewise linear approximation with $\Psi = 5$ for the time series that corresponds to the first weather station in relation *Temperature*, that is, for:

$$(1, 68), (5, 71), (8, 76), (12, 73), (15, 71), (19, 68), (22, 70), (26, 74), (29, 73)$$

The algorithm works as follows. The initialization sets $Begin := (1, 68)$, $S_L :=$ $-\infty$ and $S_U := +\infty$. Next we see what happens in the *for loop* for successive values of i.

$i = 1$:

$$S_L' := \max \left(-\infty, \frac{(71 - 5) - 68}{5 - 1} \right) = -0.5$$

$$S_U' := \min \left(+\infty, \frac{(71 + 5) - 68}{5 - 1} \right) = 2$$

The *if* condition is true, hence $S_L := S_L'$ and $S_U := S_U'$.

$i = 2$:

$$S_L' := \max \left(-0.5, \frac{(76 - 5) - 68}{8 - 1} \right) = \max(-0.5, 3/7) = 3/7$$

$$S_U' := \min \left(2, \frac{(76 + 5) - 68}{8 - 1} \right) = \min(2, 13/7) = 13/7$$

The *if* condition is true, hence $S_L := S_L'$ and $S_U := S_U'$.

$i = 3$:

$$S_L' := \max \left(3/7, \frac{(73 - 5) - 68}{12 - 1} \right) = \max(3/7, 0) = 3/7$$

$$S_U' := \min \left(13/7, \frac{(73 + 5) - 68}{12 - 1} \right) = \min(13/7, 10/11) = 10/11$$

The *if* condition is true, hence $S_L := S_L'$ and $S_U := S_U'$.

$i = 4$:

$$S_L' := \max \left(3/7, \frac{(71 - 5) - 68}{15 - 1} \right) = \max(3/7, -1/7) = 3/7$$

$$S_U' := \min \left(10/11, \frac{(71 + 5) - 68}{15 - 1} \right) = \min(10/11, 4/7) = 4/7$$

The *if* condition is true, hence $S_L := S_L'$ and $S_U := S_U'$.

$i = 5$:

$$S_L' := \max \left(3/7, \frac{(68 - 5) - 68}{19 - 1} \right) = \max(3/7, -5/18) = 3/7$$

$$S'_U := \min\left(4/7, \frac{(68+5)-68}{19-1}\right) = \min(4/7, 5/18) = 5/18$$

Because $3/7 > 5/18$, the *if* condition is false and the following line will be added as the first piece:

$$f(t) = 0.5(t-1) + 68$$

We also set *Begin* := $(15, 75)$ and

$$S_L := \frac{(68-5)-75}{19-15} = -3$$

$$S_U := \frac{(68+5)-75}{19-15} = -0.5$$

$i = 6$:

$$S'_L := \max\left(-3, \frac{(70-5)-75}{22-15}\right) = \max(-3, -10/7) = -10/7$$

$$S'_U := \min\left(-0.5, \frac{(70+5)-75}{22-15}\right) = \min(-0.5, 0) = -0.5$$

The *if* condition is true, hence $S_L := S'_L$ and $S_U := S'_U$.

$i = 7$:

$$S'_L := \max\left(-10/7, \frac{(74-5)-75}{26-15}\right) = \max(-10/7, -6/11) = -6/11$$

$$S'_U := \min\left(-0.5, \frac{(74+5)-75}{26-15}\right) = \min(-0.5, 4/11) = -0.5$$

The *if* condition is true, hence $S_L := S'_L$ and $S_U := S'_U$.

$i = 8$:

$$S'_L := \max\left(-6/11, \frac{(73-5)-75}{29-15}\right) = \max(-6/11, -7/14) = -0.5$$

$$S'_U := \min\left(-0.5, \frac{(73+5)-75}{29-15}\right) = \min(-0.5, 3/14) = -0.5$$

The *if* condition is true, hence $S_L := S'_L$ and $S_U := S'_U$.

Now we exit the *for loop* and in the last line we create the piece:

$$f(t) = -0.5(t - 15) + 75$$

Therefore, the algorithm returns the sequence of linear pieces $0.5(t - 1) + 68$ for $1 \leq t \leq 15$ and $-0.5(t - 15) + 75$ for $15 \leq t \leq 29$. This is exactly the same piecewise linear function that is represented as the first two constraint tuples in relation *Temperature2*.

Next we show the correctness of the piecewise linear approximation algorithm.

Theorem 15.2.1   The piecewise linear approximation algorithm is correct for any time series S and error tolerance value Ψ and runs in $O(n)$ time where n is the number of points in S.

Proof. To prove correctness, it is enough to show the following:

Claim: If the algorithm creates a piece $f(t)$ between (t_b, y_b) and (t_e, c), then that piece satisfies Formula (15.1) for each (t_i, y_i) where $b \leq i \leq e$.

The piece has a slope that is greater than or equal to the slope of all the lower lines $L_{b,i}$ and less than or equal to the slope of all the upper lines $U_{b,i}$, because the values of S_L and S_U are updated by taking the maximum of the lower lines and the minimum of the upper lines from $b \leq i \leq e$.

Let S_L^e and U_L^e be the values of the S_L and S_U variables at time t_e. It is obvious that any line that has a slope s such that $S_L^e \leq s \leq S_U^e$ satisfies Formula (15.1) for each $b \leq i \leq e$. Because the slope of the piece $f(t)$ is $(S_L^e + U_L^e)/2$, it is between S_L^e and S_U^e.

For computational complexity, it is easy to see that the for loop is entered $n - 1$ times, and within it each step takes a constant time. Therefore, the worst-case computational complexity of this algorithm is $O(n)$.   ∎

It is interesting to analyze the expected number of points spanned by a single piece of the piecewise linear approximation. In the following analysis we assume that the time series $(t_1, y_1), \ldots, (t_n, y_n)$ satisfies the following property, for some constant M and for each $1 < i \leq n$:

$$\begin{cases} y_1 = 0 \\ Prob(y_i - y_{i-1} = M) = 0.5 \\ Prob(y_i - y_{i-1} = -M) = 0.5 \end{cases} \tag{15.2}$$

For example, consider the time series that starts with $(0, 0)$ and records (t, y) pairs where t is the time a coin is flipped and y is the number of heads minus the number of tails seen since the beginning. This time series satisfies Property (15.2) with $M = 1$ if heads and tails have the same probability.

As another example, the daily temperature could be described by a time series that satisfies Property (15.2), if we use a thermometer in which the adjacent scales are M Fahrenheit degrees apart instead of the usual single Fahrenheit degrees, where M is the largest daily change, and if we record only on those days when there is a change in temperature according to the rougher thermometer.

Let $E(\Psi, M)$ be the expected number of original points spanned by a single piece of the piecewise linear approximation, including the two endpoints, when the approximation uses the tolerance Ψ and the time series satisfies Property (15.2). We can prove the following.

Theorem 15.2.2   If a time series satisfies Property (15.2), then

$$E(\Psi, M) \geq \left(\left\lfloor \frac{\Psi}{2M} \right\rfloor + 1 \right)^2 \qquad\qquad \blacksquare$$

For example, for the coin flipping time series, when $\Psi = 6$ each piece of the piecewise linear approximation function is expected to span at least 16 original time series points.

Experiments also show that the piecewise linear approximation algorithm provides good data compression. One experiment used two time series for weather station number 252820 in Nebraska. The first time series in relation *High_Temperature*(t, y) recorded the daily high temperature with a seven-day moving window, i.e., for each day t the y recorded the average temperature measured at days $t-3, t-2, t-1, t, t+1, t+2$, and $t+3$. Similarly, the second time series in relation *Low_Temperature*(t, y) recorded the daily low temperature with a seven-day moving window. Both time series recorded the moving averages for each day between January 1, 1987, and December 31, 1996. Because this period contained three leap years, the total number of data points was 3653 in each time series. Let us now consider some queries.

Example 15.2.2   Find all pair of days such that for each the high temperature in one day is greater than or equal to that in the other. This can be expressed in SQL as follows:

> **select** $R1.t$, $R2.t$
> **from**   *High_Temperature* **as** $R1$,   *High_Temperature* **as** $R2$
> **where** $R1.y > R2.y$

The output of this query is a relation with 6,645,646 tuples.

Example 15.2.3   Find all pair of days such that for each pair the first day has a high temperature greater than the high temperature of the second day and the first day has a low temperature greater than the low temperature of the second day. This can be expressed in SQL as follows:

> **select** $R1.t$, $R2.t$
> **from**   *High_Temperature* **as** $R1$, *High_Temperature* **as** $R2$
>   *Low_Temperature* **as** $R3$,   *Low_Temperature* **as** $R4$
> **where** $R1.t = R3.t$ **and** $R2.t = R4.t$ **and**
> $R1.y > R2.y$ **and** $R3.y > R4.y$

The output of this query is a relation with 6,091,441 tuples.

Neither of the preceding SQL queries is easy to evaluate because the output relations are so large. This is another reason to use approximation. Let $High\_temperature2(t, y)$ and $Low\_Temperature2(t, y)$ be the output constraint relations of the piecewise linear approximation. The following table shows the number of pieces in the piecewise linear approximations that are obtained using various Ψ error tolerance values.

Ψ	High_Temperature2	Low_Temperature2
—	3653	3653
1.0	1426	1084
2.0	790	594
4.0	428	335
8.0	197	140

These relations can be used in the preceding queries. Because the input is approximate, the output relation will also be approximate. We measure how good the approximation is by the values of *precision* and *recall*. Note that the original SQL output relations are pairs of integers, with each integer between 1 and 3653.

Let N be the number of (t_1, t_2) integer pairs with $1 \leq t_1, t_2 \leq 3653$ that satisfy the output constraint relation. In our context, *precision* is the percent of those N pairs that are also in the original SQL query output.

Similarly, let M be the number of (t_1, t_2) pairs that are the output of a SQL query. *Recall* is the percent of those M that satisfy the output constraint relation.

Usually, it is easy to achieve high precision at the expense of low recall or vice versa. A good system will have both high precision and high recall. Using the constraint approximation *High_Temperature2* instead of *High_Temperature*, the output of the first SQL query is shown in the following table.

Ψ	Constraint Approx.	Precision	Recall
—	6,645,646	100.00%	100.00%
1.0	2,006,001	99.39%	99.49%
2.0	1,208,010	98.54%	98.67%
4.0	235,639	96.83%	96.97%
8.0	51,681	93.39%	93.53%

Using *High_Temperature2* instead of *High_Temperature* and using *Low_Temperature2* instead of *Low_Temperature*, the output of the second SQL query is shown in the following table.

Ψ	Constraint Approx.	Precision	Recall
—	6,091,441	100.00%	100.00%
1.0	1,836,631	99.30%	99.44%
2.0	639,797	98.40%	98.66%
4.0	215,649	96.45%	96.67%
8.0	46,449	92.72%	92.68%

In both cases the output constraint relation is much smaller than the output relation of the original SQL queries, while the precision and recall are both high. Because of the smaller number of tuples, the constraint query can be evaluated much faster. Hence there is a trade-off between speed of evaluation and precision and recall of the output. Hence when time is critical and absolute precision is not necessary, the constraint query evaluation can be advantageous.

15.2.1 Updating Piecewise Linear Approximations

Updates modify the database as the user requests either the insertion or deletion of tuples in a relation. For example, a user may request the insertion or deletion of tuple (i, t, y) into the *Temperature* relation, where i is a weather station number, t is the time measured in days, and y is the temperature at that time and location. While modifying the *Temperature* relation is a trivial task, the corresponding modification of *Temperature2* merits some consideration.

In general, assume that f_0 is a piecewise linear approximation of a time series S. If the user requests a deletion of a time series data point (t, y) from S, then the request can be ignored because f_0 still satisfies the error tolerance for the remaining points.

However, the insertion of points is more complex, because it requires updating the piecewise linear function. Consider Figure 15.7. There the original piecewise linear function is shown as a solid black line in (1). In (2) the point P_1 is to be inserted, but the piecewise linear function is not changed because P_1 is in the error tolerance Ψ. In (3) the point P_2 is to be inserted, and the piecewise linear function is updated by splitting the middle piece into two pieces. In (4) the point P_3 is to be inserted, and the piecewise linear function is updated by splitting the third piece into two pieces.

Based on these ideas, the insertion algorithm for a single data point (t_α, y_α) is shown next. We assume that f_0 is the original piecewise linear function into

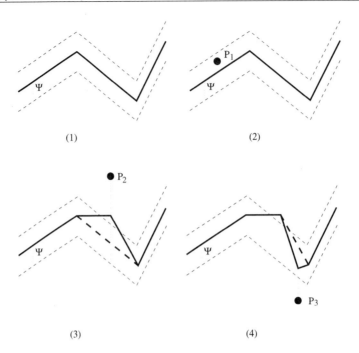

FIGURE 15.7. Inserting points into a piecewise linear function.

which we repeatedly insert data points. At any time, f is the current piecewise linear function after a number of insertions.

Insert($f_0, f, \Psi, t_\alpha, y_\alpha$)

input: The piecewise linear function f_0 before insertions.
       The piecewise linear function f after some insertions.
       Ψ the maximum error threshold in the f_0 approximation.
       (t_α, y_α) the next point to be inserted.
output: An updated f with (t_α, y_α) inserted.

if there is a piece AB of f such that
    $A = (t_i, y_i)$ and $B = (t_{i+1}, y_{i+1})$ and $t_i < t_\alpha < t_{i+1}$ **then**
    if $f_o(t_\alpha) - \Psi > y_\alpha$ **then**
        $C := (t_\alpha, \quad 0.5 \ (f_o(t_\alpha) + \Psi + y_\alpha))$
        delete AB and insert AC and CB into f
    end-if
    if $f_o(t_\alpha) + \Psi < y_\alpha$ **then**
        $C := (t_\alpha, \quad 0.5 \ (f_o(t_\alpha) - \Psi + y_\alpha))$
        delete AB and insert AC and CB into f
    end-if

```
else
      let (t_b, y_b) be leftmost and (t_e, y_e) be rightmost point in f
      if t_α < t_b then
            insert piece between (t_α, y_α) and (t_b, y_b) into f
      else
            insert piece between (t_e, y_e) and (t_α, y_α) into f
      end-if
end-if
```

We can show the following theorem.

Theorem 15.2.3 Suppose that a time series S is approximated by a piecewise linear function f_o with n "pieces" and Ψ error tolerance. Then any set I of m insertions such that each insertion point is at most some constant $\delta \geq \Psi$ distance from f_o can be done by the insertion algorithm such that the updated piecewise linear function f has at most $n + m$ "pieces" and the following holds:

$$|f(t_i) - y_i| \leq \frac{\Psi + \delta}{2} \text{ for each } (t_i, y_i) \in S \cup I \qquad (15.3)$$

Proof. There are four cases to insert one point (t_α, y_α), namely:

(1): $t_i < t_\alpha < t_{i+1}$ and $f_o(t_\alpha) - \Psi > y_\alpha$

(2): $t_i < t_\alpha < t_{i+1}$ and $f_o(t_\alpha) + \Psi < y_\alpha$

(3): $t_\alpha < t_b$

(4): $t_\alpha > t_e$

First we prove that the updated piecewise linear function f has at most $n + m$ pieces after m insertions. In each of the four cases, the algorithm adds one point to f. In other cases, the algorithm does not add any point to f. Therefore, for a sequence of m insertions, at most m points are added to f. Hence, f has at most $n + m$ points.

Next, we prove by induction that condition (15.3) holds. When $I = \emptyset$ the condition is obviously true. Let us assume that after a sequence of insertions the condition is true and we are inserting some new point (t_α, y_α). We prove that the condition also holds after the insertion.

Case (1): We have to prove that the condition is still true for the points of f that are between A and B. First let us consider the points on the piece AC.

Consider the original piecewise linear function f_0 between A and B shown by the bold line in Figure 15.8. Let D and E be points on the line $f_o(t) - \Psi$, and F and G be points on the line $f_o(t) + \Psi$ as shown in the figure. The coordinates of these four points can be calculated to be $D(t_i, f_o(t_i) - \Psi)$, $E(t_\alpha, f_o(t_\alpha) - \Psi)$, $F(t_i, f_o(t_i) + \Psi)$, and $G(t_\alpha, f_o(t_\alpha) + \Psi)$. For the point (t_α, y_α) to be inserted we

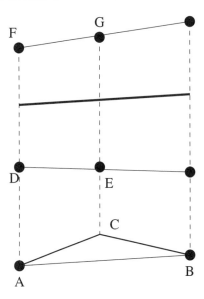

FIGURE 15.8. Insertion of a point.

calculate the following:

$$|f(t_\alpha) - y_\alpha| = 0.5 \, ((f_o(t_\alpha) + \Psi) + y_\alpha) - y_\alpha \text{ by } y\text{-coordinate of } C$$
$$= 0,5 \, ((f_o(t_\alpha) + \Psi) - y_\alpha)$$
$$= 0.5 \, (\Psi + (f_o(t_\alpha) - y_\alpha))$$
$$\leq \frac{\Psi + \delta}{2}$$

The last inequality follows from the condition that each point inserted is at most δ distance from f_0. Hence (t_α, y_α) satisfies the condition.

Note that there cannot be any other I point H before (t_α, y_α) that is between A and C and has more than Ψ distance from f_o. If we had, then we would have to use either AH or HB instead of AB when we are inserting (t_α, y_α).

Now we can assume that all S and I points before (t_α, y_α) and between A and C are at most Ψ distance from f_o. Therefore, these all fall into the trapezoid region $DEGF$, showing that any point within $DEGF$ satisfies the condition.

First we show the condition for the corner vertices. For D and F the condition is true by the induction hypothesis, that is, they are both at most $(\Psi + \delta)/2$ distance from A. Note that y_α is at most δ and both E and G are at most Ψ distance from f_o. Because the y-coordinate of C is at the midpoint of y_α and the y-coordinate of G, both G and E are at most $(\Psi + \delta)/2$ distance from C.

Let A' be the point exactly $(\Psi + \delta)/2$ below F, and let C' be the point exactly $(\Psi + \delta)/2$ below G. Suppose $M = (t, y)$ is any point within $DEGF$. Let M_1 be the point directly above M and intersecting the line segment FG and M_2 be the point

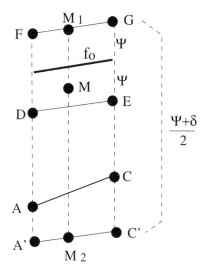

FIGURE 15.9. Proof condition for point M.

directly below M and intersecting the line segment $A'C'$ as shown in Figure 15.9. Clearly, the distance between M and AC is less than the distance between M_1 and M_2, which is exactly $(\Psi + \delta)/2$. Hence M must satisfy the condition. Therefore, all points within $DEGF$ satisfy the condition.

This took care for points between A and C. We can prove similarly that all points in S and in I before (t_α, y_α) and between C and B also satisfy the condition.

Case (2): This is similar to case (1).

Case (3): The condition is clearly true in this case, because the point (t_α, y_α) is contained in the new piece and there are no other points between it and (t_b, y_b).

Case (4): This is similar to case (3). ∎

For example, if $\delta = 3\Psi$, then the error tolerance for the updated piecewise linear approximation will be 2Ψ for all original and newly inserted data points.

15.3 Parametric Triangulated Irregular Networks

To represent approximately some spatiotemporal objects, for example, a changing landscape, we can combine the TIN representation for spatial data and the piecewise linear representation for time series data. The combined representation is called a *parametric triangulated irregular network* (PTIN).

A PTIN is created by fixing on the surface of the landscape a set of (x, y) locations. Unlike in a TIN, in a PTIN the z value of each (x, y) location changes over time, that is, it is associated with a time series, which we approximate by a piecewise linear function $z(t)$.

Let $A = (u_1, u_2)$, $B = (v_1, v_2)$, and $C = (w_1, w_2)$ be the (x, y) coordinates of the corner vertices of a PTIN triangle. Suppose that the elevation at these three locations changes with $u_3(t)$, $v_3(t)$, and $w_3(t)$, respectively. Then we can find the constraint representation of this PTIN triangle like in the TIN, but using t as an extra parameter. In particular, the surface of the PTIN triangle can be described by the equality

$$ax + by + cz + d = 0$$

where

$$a = u_2 v_3 - u_3 v_2$$
$$b = u_3 v_1 - u_1 v_3$$
$$c = u_1 v_2 - u_2 v_1$$
$$d = -(a w_1 + b w_2 + c w_3)$$

Example 15.3.1   Suppose that the mountain in Figure 15.1 is gradually eroding over a long period of time. In particular, suppose that the speed of erosion is one unit height per thousand years. This can be represented by the *Pyramid_Erode* constraint relation shown here:

Pyramid_Erode

X	Y	Z	T	
x	y	z	t	$y \geq 0$, $y \leq x$, $x + y \leq 6$, $3z = (9-t)y$, $t \geq 0$, $z \geq 0$
x	y	z	t	$x \geq 0$, $y \geq x$, $x + y \leq 6$, $3z = (9-t)x$, $t \geq 0$, $z \geq 0$
x	y	z	t	$y \leq 6$, $y \geq x$, $x + y \geq 6$, $3z = (9-t)(6-y)$, $t \geq 0$, $z \geq 0$
x	y	z	t	$x \leq 6$, $y \leq x$, $x + y \geq 6$, $3z = (9-t)(6-x)$, $t \geq 0$, $z \geq 0$

Suppose we know the (x, y) locations of the four weather stations in relation *Temperature*. Then we can use a PTIN to approximate the temperature at each location around the four weather stations at each time. The PTIN can be represented as a constraint relation *Temperature3*$(x, y, temp, t)$, where *temp* is the approximate temperature at location (x, y) at time t. This approximation can be used within spatiotemporal queries.

Example 15.3.2   The following SQL query finds the locations where the temperature rises above 75 degrees between days 180 and 230:

> **select**   *x, y*
> **from**   *Temperature3*
> **where**   *temp* > 75 **and** *t* ≥ 180 **and** *t* ≤ 230

15.4   Parametric Rectangles Approximation of Raster Movies

Imagine that a movie shows on a white screen some moving black objects. The video can be represented as a raster image every $t/20$ second. However, that representation requires a huge amount of computer memory if the movie lasts several hours. In this section we describe a space-efficient parametric rectangles approximation of raster movies. The parametric rectangles representation can also be translated into a constraint representation by the interoperability results of Chapter 13.

The idea behind the parametric rectangles representation is the following. We can expect in a typical movie that the objects move slowly and with uniform speed and change directions infrequently. In addition, they may be moving away from us, which makes their images gradually shrink, or toward us, which makes their images gradually grow on the screen.

As a simple example, suppose the black object is a rectangle. If it does not change direction between times t_1 and t_2, and it is $[x_1, x_2] \times [y_1, y_2]$ at time t_1 and $[x'_1, x'_2] \times [y'_1, y'_2]$ at time t_2, then there is a parametric rectangle:

$$([at + b, \ ct + d], \ [et + f, \ gt + h], \ [t_1, \ t_2])$$

where a, b, c, d, e, f, g, h are constants that describe the black object. For example, we have that:

$$x_1 = a \, t_1 + b$$
$$x'_1 = a \, t_2 + b$$

Subtracting the second from the first equation and then simplifying gives for a and b the following:

$$a = \frac{x_1 - x'_1}{t_1 - t_2} \quad \text{and} \quad b = x_1 - \frac{x_1 - x'_1}{t_1 - t_2} t_1$$

Therefore,

$$at + b = (x_1 - x'_1) \frac{t - t_1}{t_1 - t_2} + x_1$$

By doing similar simplifications for the other parametric endpoints, we see that the parametric rectangle can be written as:

$$([(x_1 - x_1')T + x_1, \ (x_2 - x_2')T + x_2],$$
$$[(y_1 - y_1')T + y_1, \ (y_2 - y_2')T + y_2], \ [t_1, \ t_2])$$

where

$$T = \frac{t - t_1}{t_1 - t_2}$$

If the shape of the black object is more complex than a rectangle, then we break it up into a set of rectangles at both time t_1 and time t_2, then we match the two sets of rectangles with each other. This can be done in a number of ways.

Let us assume that at time t_1 the object is within a rectangle that is ch_1 pixels in height and cw_1 pixels in width, and at time t_2 it is within another rectangle that is ch_2 pixels in height and cw_2 pixels in width.

Then we divide the first picture into $h_1 \times w_1$ size small rectangles and the second picture into $h_1 \times w_1$ size small rectangles. Note that this way we divide both big rectangles into the same c^2 number of smaller rectangles. For example, Figure 15.10 shows a glovelike image that fits into a square, which is subdivided into a set of small squares in part (a).

Next we mark each small rectangle as **on** if more than 50 percent of the pixels in it are black, otherwise we mark it as **off**. Part (b) of the figure shows as black squares those that are **on** and as white squares those that are **off**.

Next we merge in each row the adjacent black squares, yielding a set of rectangles in each row. This is shown as part (c) of the figure. We find these rectangles in each row in both pictures. Then for each row we pair the rectangles of the image at time t_1 with the rectangles of the image at time t_2. This can be done as follows. Let m and n be the number of rectangles in the two rows to be matched. There are three cases:

(1) If $m = n$ then we simply pair the ith rectangle of the first with the ith rectangle of the second row each for $1 \le i \le m$.

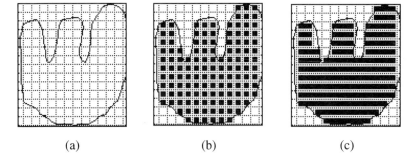

| (a) | (b) | (c) |

FIGURE 15.10. Dividing an image into rectangles.

(2) If $m < n$ then, then let $d = \lfloor m/n \rfloor$. We pair the first rectangle at t_1 with the first d rectangles at t_2, the second rectangle with the second d rectangles, and so on until we come to the mth rectangle at t_1, which we pair with all the remaining unpaired rectangles at t_2.

(3) If $m > n$, we can do the pairing similarly to the preceding.

Finally, for each pair we compute a parametric rectangle that takes the first rectangle into the second as we did earlier when we considered only one moving rectangle.

The preceding is an informal description of an algorithm that approximates by parametric rectangles a raster movie with only black objects on a white screen. There are many possible extensions. For example, in the presence of colors, the rectangles may be assumed to change color gradually. It is also not necessary to always make the assumption of linear motion. For example, in the y direction when an object is moving downward, it may be assumed that the motion is a quadratic polynomial motion due to the acceleration caused by gravity, similarly to the motion in relation *Bomb* of Chapter 13.

Bibliographic Notes

Triangulated irregular networks are used in several geographic information systems [4, 201, 333], including as an option by the ARC/INFO system [219]. Davis [75] is a book on approximation and interpolation.

The piecewise linear approximation problem for time series data has been studied by many researchers. The piecewise linear approximations can be divided into two main groups, namely (at least) time coordinate preserving approximations, in which the endpoints of the pieces have time coordinates that occur in the original time series data, or inventing approximations, in which the coordinate values can be any real numbers. The piecewise linear approximation algorithm in Section 15.2 is a preserving approximation. For example, in Example 15.2.1 the endpoints of the pieces are $(1, 68)$, $(15, 75)$, and $(29, 68)$ and 1, 15, and 29 all occur in the time series as time coordinates.

In 1991, Hakimi and Schmeichel [136] gave $O(n^2)$ preserving and an $O(n)$ inventing piecewise linear approximation algorithm that returns an approximation with a minimum number of possible pieces. Recently, Agarwal and Varadarajan [8] gave an improved preserving algorithm with complexity $O(n^{\frac{4}{3}+\epsilon})$, where ϵ is any arbitrarily small positive constant. The piecewise linear approximation and the update algorithms in Section 15.2 are improvements of algorithms by Chen et al. [56], and the weather data used in Section 15.2 was obtained from the Web site of the National Climatic Data Center at http://www.ncdc.noaa.gov.

In the preserving case, both [136] and [8] return fewer pieces but run slower than the $O(n)$ time piecewise linear algorithm presented in this section. It remains an open problem to find a preserving piecewise linear approximation algorithm that both returns the fewest number of pieces and runs in $O(n)$ time.

Parametric triangulated irregular networks are new. Grumbach et al. [124] also propose an alternative interpolation of spatiotemporal data. The parametric rectangles approximation of raster movies is adapted from Cai et al. [50].

Update operators can be classified as proper updates, revision, and arbitration operators. Revision methods are axiomatized in Alchourrón et al. [10], update methods in Katsuno and Mendelzon [165, 166, 167, 168], and arbitration in Revesz [261]. The complexity of propositional updates and revision is studied in Eiter and Gottlob [90], and the complexity of first-order updates is studied in Grahne et al. [117]. An extension of the update and the revision operators with weights is presented in Benczur et al. [27]. Three types of operators are extended for constraint databases in Revesz [260].

Exercises

1. Find the piecewise linear approximation of the following time series data using the given error tolerance values:

   (a) The following time series S when $\Psi = 1$:

   (1,2), (2,4), (3,2), (4,4), (5,5), (6,4), (7,5), (8,5), (9,6), (10,4), (11,4), (12,6), (13,6), (14,6), (15,7), (16,7), (17,9), (18,10), (19,11), (20,13)

   (b) The time series S when $\Psi = 2$.

   (c) The following time series when $\Psi = 3$:

   (0,0), (1,1), (2,3), (3,4), (4,2), (5,3), (6,5), (7,6), (8,8), (9,11), (10,12), (11,10), (12,9), (13,11), (14,13), (15,14), (16,17), (17,16), (18,18), (19,15), (20,13), (21,12), (22,11), (23,9), (24,10), (25,12), (26,11), (27,9), (28,8), (29,6), (30,5)

   (d) The following time series when $\Psi = 4$:

   (1,1), (3,3), (6,4), (7,7), (10,6), (13,9), (15,7), (18,4), (20,5), (22,4), (23,7), (25,9), (26,10), (28,9), (29,12)

2. Consider the time series:

   (1,1), (3,3), (10,6), (13,9), (15,7), (18,4), (22,4), (23,6), (28,9), (29,12)

   (a) Find a piecewise linear approximation when $\Psi = 2$.

   (b) Update the piecewise linear approximation by inserting into it the following points in order: (16, 5), (26, 5), (5, 12), and (8, 2).

3. Suppose that four weather stations in relation *Temperature* in Section 15.2 are located at $(0, 0)$, $(1, 0)$, $(0, 1)$, and $(1, 1)$, respectively.

   (a) Find a triangulation of the stations.

   (b) Find a piecewise linear approximation for the first month for each weather station. (**Hint:** Extend the first and last pieces in each approximation to day 1 and 31, respectively.)

(c) Find a parametric triangulated irregular network description of the temperature at each location.

(d) Represent the parametric triangulated irregular network as a constraint relation.

16

Data Visualization

In this chapter we consider visualization of constraint databases. The visualizations can be divided into static displays and *animations*, which are movielike displays of spatiotemporal objects that are represented implicitly by one of the spatiotemporal data models discussed in Chapter 13. Constraint databases are particularly well-suited for animation because they allow any granularity for the animation without requiring much data storage.

Section 16.1 describes *isometric color bands*, which are well-suited to visualize the triangulated irregular networks of Chapter 15. Isometric color bands are static displays, but a sequence of them can be used to animate parametric triangulated irregular networks.

Section 16.2 discusses value-by-area cartograms, which are different from regular maps in that in value-by-area cartograms the area of each cell corresponds to its value. For example, the area of a state is proportional to its population in a value-by-area cartogram. Value-by-area cartograms are static displays, but they can also be animated. For example, if the population values are not constants but functions of time, then value-by-area cartogram animation can be used to visualize the population changes over time. The functions of time that describe the value of a cell may be obtained in a number of ways. If we are given a time series, then we can use the piecewise linear approximations of Chapter 15.

Section 16.3 describes the animation of moving objects that are represented by either parametric extreme point databases or constraint databases that are equivalent to parametric 2-spaghetti databases.

16.1   Isometric Color Bands

Suppose a hill climber would like to know the landscape surface of the mountain range in Section 15.1 before planning a trip. A convenient way to indicate the elevation of a surface is by using colors. For example, we may color the surface areas that are below 2 black, the areas between 2 and 5 dark gray, and those areas that are above 5 units elevation gray. In this example, a unit may be a thousand feet. We summarize the elevation information in relation *Color_Configuration*:

Color_Configuration

Color	Z	
Black	z	$z \leq 2$
Dark gray	z	$z \geq 2, z \leq 5$
Gray	z	$z \geq 5$

We can give the hill climber a view of the landscape or some part of it, for example, the large pyramid, as shown in Figure 16.1.

The view given in Figure 16.1 is a natural side view of the large pyramid with color information added. However, it is not the most useful information for the hill climber, who would need to know, for example, the steepness on the other side of the mountain to plan for a trip. An alternative view of the mountain is called an *isometric color band map*. The isometric color band for the large pyramid is shown in Figure 16.2.

The isometric color band map is a two-dimensional map with color information added. It is the view of the mountain from the top as we would see it from an airplane. Even the color bands may sometimes be visible from the airplane, as for example, when there are pine trees below 2, grass lands between 2 and 5, and only snow above 5 units of height. Clearly, the isometric color band map provides elevation information for each point of the surface, as is needed by the hill climber. The map shows, for example, that the steepness of the large pyramid, ap-

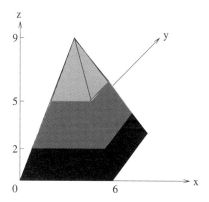

FIGURE 16.1. Side view of the pyramid.

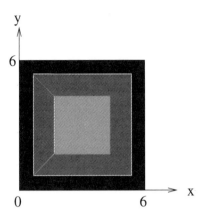

FIGURE 16.2. The view of the large pyramid from above.

proximating the largest mountain, is about the same from each of the four major directions.

16.1.1   An Isometric Color Band Map Display Algorithm

In this subsection we sketch an algorithm that finds and displays the isometric color band map for any given triangulated irregular network and color configuration. We assume that the TIN and color configuration are already represented using constraint databases similar to relations *Pyramid* and *Color_Configuration* described in Section 16.1. Then we define relation *Isometric_Map* as follows:

$$Isometric\_Map = \Pi_{X,Y,Color}(Pyramid \bowtie Color\_Configuration)$$

This is a simple relational algebra query as described in Chapter 3. We also know that it can be evaluated in closed form. In fact, the result will be the constraint relation shown next.

Now the preceding relation can easily be displayed. For each constraint tuple, we find the corner points of the convex polygon that is defined by the conjunction of linear inequality constraints over the x and y variables. Then we color the area of the isometric map corresponding to the polygon with the specified color. It is easy to verify that this would indeed result in the isometric color band map shown in Figure 16.2.

As a practical example, Figure 16.3 shows the isometric color band display for precipitation in the United States in the year 1997. The high precipitation areas are displayed by blue (darker gray) and the low precipitation areas by red (lighter gray). In this case the map contains more than eight thousand triangles.

Isometric Map

X	Y	Color	
x	y	Black	$y \leq x, \quad x + y \leq 6, \quad y \geq 0, \quad 3y \leq 2$
x	y	Dark gray	$y \leq x, \quad x + y \leq 6, \quad 3y \geq 2, \quad 3y \leq 5$
x	y	Gray	$y \leq x, \quad x + y \leq 6, \quad 3y \geq 5$
x	y	Black	$y \geq x, \quad x + y \leq 6, \quad x \geq 0, \quad 3x \leq 2$
x	y	Dark gray	$y \geq x, \quad x + y \leq 6, \quad 3x \geq 2, \quad 3x \leq 5$
x	y	Gray	$y \geq x, \quad x + y \leq 6, \quad 3x \geq 5$
x	y	Black	$y \geq x, \quad x + y \geq 6, \quad y \leq 6, \quad 3y \geq 16$
x	y	Dark gray	$y \geq x, \quad x + y \geq 6, \quad 3y \geq 13, \quad 3y \leq 16$
x	y	Gray	$y \geq x, \quad x + y \geq 6, \quad 3y \leq 13$
x	y	Black	$y \leq x, \quad x + y \geq 6, \quad x \leq 6, \quad 3x \geq 16$
x	y	Dark gray	$y \leq x, \quad x + y \geq 6, \quad 3x \geq 13, \quad 3x \leq 16$
x	y	Gray	$y \leq x, \quad x + y \geq 6, \quad 3x \leq 13$

FIGURE 16.3. Isometric color band map for U.S. precipitation in 1997.

16.1.2   Isometric Color Band Animation

Visualizing the eroding pyramid of Section 15.3 requires animation. The animation would display a sequence of snapshots of the pyramid at monotone increasing time instances. For each given t instance of time, we can generate a snapshot by substituting into the *Pyramid_Erode* relation the value of t, then eliminating the attribute T. The resulting relation is like the Pyramid relation discussed earlier and can be visualized using isometric color bands the same way.

Since the mountain is 9 units high initially, that is, at $t = 0$, it will be 8, 7, and 6 units high, respectively, at times $t = 1$, $t = 2$, and $t = 3$. Figure 16.4 shows the snapshots of the eroding mountain at four different times. If these pictures were

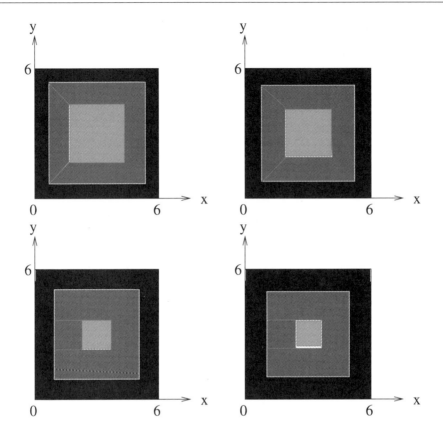

FIGURE 16.4. The mountain at $t = 0, 1, 2,$ and 3.

displayed one after the other on the computer screen at a reasonable speed, we would actually see the animation.

For each time instance t, let *Isometric_Map$_t$* be the relation that describes the snapshot of the isometric color animation of the *Pyramid_Erode* relation. *Isometric_Map$_t$* can be calculated using the following relational algebra expression:

$$\Pi_{X,Y,\text{Color}}(\sigma_{T=t} Pyramid\_Erode \bowtie Color\_Configuration)$$

16.2   Value-by-Area Cartogram

Now we consider maps that divide the plane into a set of disjoint regions, or *cells*. For example, the map of the continental United States consists of 48 cells, that is, one cell for each state. Maps give information only about the location of the individual cells, not other information like their populations.

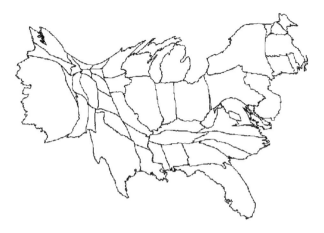

FIGURE 16.5. A value-by-area cartogram for the U.S. population in 1990.

Suppose someone would like to know the relative population of each state. We could use a *value-by-area cartogram*. A value-by-area cartogram is a map in which each cell is inflated or deflated so that its area is proportional to its associated "value." For example, Figure 16.5 is a value-by-area cartogram where the value of each cell is its population in 1990.

Value-by-area cartograms provide easy-to-understand visualizations. For example, one can learn from Figure 16.5 that California has a high population density because its area is greatly enlarged, while Nebraska has a small population density because its area is reduced.

16.2.1 Value-by-Area Cartogram Display Algorithm

We describe an algorithm that finds the value-by-area cartogram for any given map and set of cell values. We assume that the cells are polygons and the cell values are positive real numbers.

Let n be the number of cells and D_{AVG} be the *average cell density* of the map. For each $1 \leq i \leq n$, let C_i be the ith cell, V_i its value, AC_i its actual area, AD_i its *desired area*, Δ_i its *distortion*, and ER_i its *effective range*. The desired area is the area we best represent as the value of the cell. The distortion is the percent increase or decrease from the desired area to the actual area. The effective range ER_i is the area of the map that contains all the corner vertices that could change while inflating or deflating C_i. More formally, let us use the following definitions:

$$D_{AVG} = \frac{\sum_{i=1}^{n} V_i}{\sum_{i=1}^{n} AC_i}$$

$$AD_i = \frac{V_i}{D_{AVG}} \tag{16.1}$$

$$\Delta_i = \frac{|AD_i - AC_i|}{AD_i}$$

The *centroid* (x_c, y_c) of a polygon with corner vertices (x_1, y_1), (x_2, y_2), ..., (x_k, y_k) is defined as follows:

$$x_c = \frac{1}{k}\left(\sum_{i=1}^{k} x_i\right) \quad y_c = \frac{1}{k}\left(\sum_{i=1}^{k} y_i\right) \tag{16.2}$$

The effective range of a cell is a circle around its *centroid*. The radius of the effective range r_{eff} is:

$$r_{eff} = \frac{100|AD_i - AC_i|}{\sqrt{\pi}AC_i} \tag{16.3}$$

The algorithm, which is shown next, will iteratively inflate or deflate in sequence each cell whose distortion is greater than some error tolerance value ϵ. A cell is inflated if its actual area is smaller than its desired area, and it is deflated if its actual area is larger than its desired area. When we inflate a cell C_i, all its neighbors within the effective range ER_i are also influenced. Hence a change made for the ith cell may inadvertently negate a change made previously for an earlier cell. To minimize the effect of such inadvertent interactions, in each iteration, we order the cells according to their distortions. Hence we first change those cells that need a big change and then those cells that need only a small change.

Value-by-Area Cartogram Animation
Input: A map with n cells, a value for each cell,
         and an error tolerance value ϵ.
Output: A value-by-area cartogram in which each
         Δ_i is less than or equal to ϵ.
begin
  For each cell, compute its AD_i and AC_i.
  repeat
     Sort the cells by their distortions Δ_i.
     for $i = 1$ to n **do**
        Compute AC_i.
        Inflate/deflate C_i by changing corner vertices in ER_i.
     end-for
   until $\forall i \; \Delta_i \leq \epsilon$.
end

We still did not specify precisely how the corner vertices change within an effective range. There are many good alternative definitions, but the main idea is that the further a corner vertex is from the centroid of the inflated or deflated cell the less its location should be changed. Let (x_i, y_i) be the centroid of the cell C_i to be inflated or deflated. Then for each corner vertex (x, y) in the effective range of the cell, the new coordinates (x', y') will be:

$$
\begin{aligned}
x' &= x_i + (x - x_i)\sqrt{\tfrac{AD_i}{AC_i}} \\
y' &= y_i + (y - y_i)\sqrt{\tfrac{AD_i}{AC_i}}
\end{aligned}
\tag{16.4}
$$

These definitions are intuitive in the following sense. Suppose a cell has a circular shape approximated by a high-degree polygon. Suppose further that the desired area of the cell is $\pi r'^2$, but the actual area is πr^2. Then by making the preceding changes, we change r to r', which is exactly as desired.

A refinement of this would be to change according to Equation (16.4) only those corner vertices that are within the circle with radius $\sqrt{AC_i/\pi}$. If they are outside that circle, then we change them a little less, because they are in danger of intruding too much into the neighboring cells. For those corner vertices we choose the new coordinates as follows:

$$
\begin{aligned}
x' &= x_i + (x - x_i)\frac{AD_i - AC_i}{2\pi d^2} \\
y' &= y_i + (y - y_i)\frac{AD_i - AC_i}{2\pi d^2}
\end{aligned}
$$

For example, in Figure 16.6 the dotted lines represent the original cell division and C_5 is inflated. Here the effective range is shown by the dashed cycle. The corner vertices within the effective range are changed resulting in the new cell division shown in solid lines.

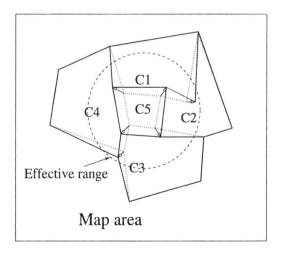

FIGURE 16.6. Effective range.

16.2.2   Value-by-Area Cartogram Animation

If the value of each cell is changing over time, we can represent each cell value as a function $V_i(t)$. For example, the cell value of a state with a population that is one million at $t = 0$ and growing each year by 2 percent can be represented by the function $1.02^t \times 1,000,000$.

Value-by-area cartogram animation can be used to visualize maps where cell values are functions of t. The animation displays a sequence of value-by-area cartogram "snapshots." Each snapshot is a value-by-area cartogram that corresponds to the cell values at a given time instance. There are three basic methods for value-by-area cartogram animation.

Parallel Method: For each time instance t to be displayed, this method takes the original map with the cell values at time t and gives an output map or snapshot. This is called the parallel method because the snapshots can be computed in parallel (see Figure 16.7).

Serial Method: In this method each cartogram snapshot is constructed from the previous cartogram snapshot (except for the first cartogram snapshot, which is constructed from the original map), as shown in Figure 16.8.

Hybrid Method: This method combines the previous two methods. It generates each $kn + 1$st snapshot from the original map and all the other snapshots from the previous snapshots (see Figure 16.9).

The serial method is faster than the parallel method on a single-processor computer because there is usually a smaller difference between two consecutive snap-

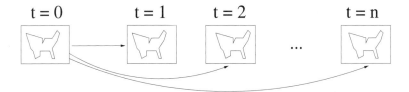

FIGURE 16.7. The parallel method for cartogram animation.

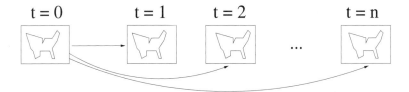

FIGURE 16.8. The serial method for cartogram animation.

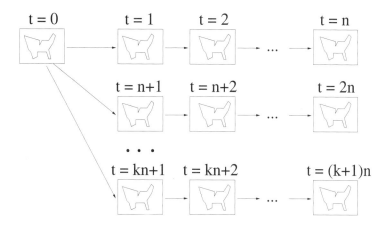

FIGURE 16.9. The hybrid method for cartogram animation.

shots than between the original map and a snapshot; hence calculating a snapshot from the previous snapshot requires generally fewer iterations of the value-by-area cartogram algorithm. However, in general, the cells are harder to recognize in the cartogram snapshots generated by the serial method, because in the serial method each snapshot will transmit to its successors some possible cell shape distortion, which may accumulate. The hybrid method is almost as fast as the serial method, but it avoids the accumulation of cell shape distortions.

16.2.3 Volume and Color Cartograms and Animations

A map may be displayed by a *volume cartogram*, which is a three-dimensional view in which each cell has a height that corresponds to its value. An example of this is shown in Figure 16.10, which shows for each continental U.S. state the daily mean temperature value in October 1990.

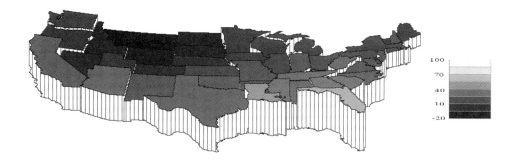

FIGURE 16.10. U.S. daily mean temperature in October 1990.

Besides using the height of the cells to represent the values, we may also use a *color cartogram* that colors the cells using some scale. For example, in Figure 16.10 lighter colors indicate greater cell values. This makes it clearer to see, for example, that the daily mean temperature in Texas is higher than in North Dakota.

When there is only one spatial variable to be displayed for each cell, then any of the three map visualizations we discussed could be used. Someone may prefer value-by-area cartograms because in them each cell is visible, while in volume cartograms some taller objects may obstruct the view of smaller objects in the background. Sometimes, a combination of the different visualizations could enhance each other as in Figure 16.10.

However, suppose we need to display a map with three different cell variables. In this case the three visualizations could be combined. For example, someone may wish to see the population, the per capita income, and the per capita energy consumption of the continental United States. This could be displayed by first computing a value-by-area cartogram using the population values then generating from that a volume cartogram using the gross income values, and finally coloring each state using the energy consumption values.

We may also animate volume and color cartograms similarly to the animation of value-by-area cartograms.

16.3   Animation of Moving Objects

Animation is the natural visualization of moving objects. As we saw in Chapter 13, moving objects may be described using several different data models. Each of these needs slightly different animation methods. We describe animation methods for periodic parametric databases in Section 16.3.1 and for linear constraint databases in Section 16.3.2.

16.3.1   Animation of Periodic Parametric Databases

Most computer systems provide in their graphics library as a primitive a display module for triangles and rectangles defined by their corner vertices. The animation algorithms we describe will assume that these primitives are available.

Periodic parametric 2-spaghetti and parametric rectangle databases can be easily animated. In order to display a relation at a time instant t_i, we first check each parametric rectangle tuple r whether it exists at time t_i, that is, whether $t_i \in T_r$, where T_r is the time interval of r.

If the tuple is a nonperiodic parametric rectangle (*period* $= +\infty$), it is easy to check whether $t_i \in T_r$.

If the tuple is a periodic parametric rectangle of form $T_r = [from, to]_{period, end}$, then we need to check the following:

$$from \ \leq \ t_i - \left\lfloor \frac{t_i - from}{period} \right\rfloor \cdot period \ \leq \ to \ \textbf{AND} \ t_i \ \leq \ end$$

If r exists at t_i, we substitute the variable t in the functions with t_i' and obtain the snapshot of r at t_i

Proceeding in this manner, we obtain a set of triangles or rectangles corresponding to the relation at time t_i. These can be displayed using the graphics primitives.

16.3.2 Animation of Constraint Databases

Constraint databases with two spatial and one temporal attributes, where for each instance of t the constraints are linear, the spatial variables can be animated by two different methods, called the *naive animation* and the *parametric animation* methods (see Figure 16.11).

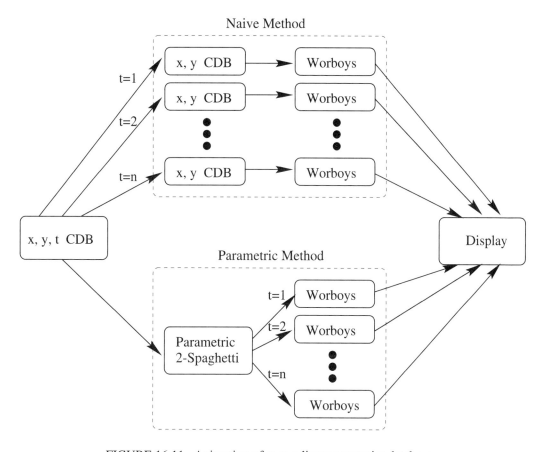

FIGURE 16.11. Animation of x, y, t linear constraint databases.

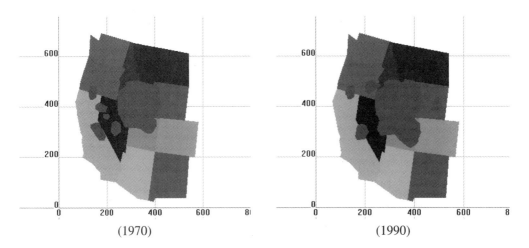

(1970)   (1990)

FIGURE 16.12. Two snapshots of a video on California gull ranges.

Naive Animation Method: This method works directly on constraint databases. It finds for each time instance t_i, by instantiating the variable t to t_i, a linear constraint relation that has only two spatial variables, namely, x and y. This linear constraint relation is translated into a Worboys relation where $from = to = t_i$. This translation uses Theorem 14.1.2. Finally, it displays as a set of triangles each Worboys relation.

Parametric Animation Method: This method has a *preprocessing* step and a *display* step. In the preprocessing step it constructs a parametric 2-spaghetti representation of the linear constraint relation using the algorithm outlined in Theorem 14.1.4. This construction needs to be done only once, before any user requests it. The construction also finds for each parametric triangle p a beginning time $t_{p.\text{from}}$ and an ending time $t_{p.\text{to}}$. Before $t_{p.\text{from}}$ or after $t_{p.\text{to}}$ the parametric triangle has no spatial extent and does not need to be displayed.

During the display step, which is done at the user's request, for each consecutive time instant t_i and for each parametric triangle it is checked first that t_i is between $t_{p.\text{from}}$ and $t_{p.\text{to}}$. Corresponding to the parametric triangles whose range includes t_i, the parametric method finds, by instantiating the variable t to t_i, a set of triangles defined by their corner vertices. Then it displays the set of triangles.

As an example, the habitat area of California gulls, a bird species usually found in the western United States, is a moving object described by a linear constraint database. It was first converted to a parametric 2-spaghetti representation before generating the two snapshots shown in Figure 16.12.

Example 16.3.1   A wilderness area is divided into grass land, pine forest, and oak forest. For various reasons these regions change over time. The left side of Figure 16.13 shows

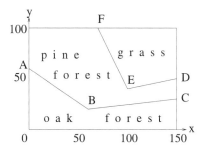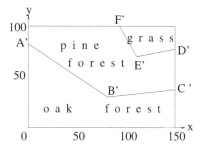

FIGURE 16.13. Wilderness area at $t = 0$ and $t = 10$.

the three regions at time $t = 0$ and the right side at $t = 10$ after a gradual expansion of the pine and oak forests to the northeast.

The changing of the grass land and trees can be represented by the linear constraint relation *Wilderness*. We assume that each of the four boundary lines moves linearly. For example, both boundary lines between the oak and pine forests move to the east with speed two units and north with one unit per year. Similarly, the boundary lines between the pine forest and grass land move to the east with speed one unit and north three units per year.

The oak forest area can be divided into two parts. The first part is a triangular area whose upper boundary is the line $2x + 3y - 7t \le 180$. The other area will be a quadrangle where this line is a lower bound and the line $x - 9y + 7t \ge -120$ is an upper bound. These lines can be obtained from the endpoints $(0, 60)$, $(60, 20)$, and $(150, 30)$ at $t = 0$ and the endpoints $(0, 250/3)$, $(80, 30)$, and $(150, 340/9)$. Considering the speed of the shifting lines, the entire relation can be represented as shown in relation *Wilderness*.

Wilderness

ID	X	Y	T	
G	x	y	t	$x \le 150$, $y \le 100$, $2x + y - 5t \ge 240$, $x - 5y + 14t \le -100$, $t \ge 0$, $t \le 10$
P	x	y	t	$x \ge 0$, $y \le 100$, $2x + y - 5t \le 240$, $2x + 3y - 7t \ge 180$, $x - 9y + 7t \le -120$, $t \ge 0$, $t \le 10$
P	x	y	t	$x \le 150$, $2x + y - 5t \ge 240$, $x - 5y + 14t \ge -100$, $x - 9y + 7t \le -120$, $t \ge 0$, $t \le 10$
O	x	y	t	$x \ge 0$, $y \ge 0$, $2x + 3y - 7t \le 180$, $t \ge 0$, $t \le 10$
O	x	y	t	$x \le 150$, $y \ge 0$, $2x + 3y - 7t \ge 180$, $x - 9y + 7t \ge -120$, $t \ge 0$, $t \le 10$

Finally, it can be translated to the parametric 2-spaghetti relation *Wilderness2* shown next (except for the *From* and *To* attributes, which are always 0 and 10, respectively):

Wilderness2

ID	Ax	Ay	Bx	By	Cx	Cy
G	$2.5t + 70$	100	$t + 100$	$3t + 40$	150	100
G	150	100	$t + 100$	$3t + 40$	150	$2.8t + 50$
P	0	100	0	$2.33t+60$	$2.5t + 70$	100
P	0	$2.33t+60$	$2t + 60$	$t + 20$	$2.5t + 70$	100
P	$2t + 60$	$t + 20$	$t + 100$	$3t + 40$	$2.5t + 70$	100
P	$2t + 60$	$t + 20$	$t + 100$	$3t + 40$	150	$.77t + 30$
P	$t + 100$	$3t + 40$	150	$.77t + 30$	150	$2.8t + 50$
O	0	$2.33t+60$	0	0	$2t + 60$	$t + 20$
O	0	0	$2t + 60$	$t + 20$	150	0
O	$2t + 60$	$t + 20$	150	0	150	$.77t + 30$

Bibliographic Notes

Isometric color bands are part of the display options in the MLPQ constraint database system and were discussed briefly in Revesz at al. [273] and in more detail in Chen [55]. The animation of parametric triangulated irregular networks is new.

Value-by-area cartogram algorithms using rubber-sheet-based algorithms were given by Dougenik [83] et al. and Gusein-Zade and Tikunov [131]. The value-by-area cartogram algorithm in Section 16.2 is by Ouyang and Revesz [227]. Ouyang and Revesz [227] is an extension of the previous algorithms by the introduction of an effective range and by sorting

Value-by-area cartogram animations were considered by House and Kocmoud [145], which gives an animation for the U.S. population change from 1900 to 1996, and White et al. (geog.qmw.ac.uk/gbhgis/gisruk98), which gives an animation for the infant mortality in the United Kingdom from 1856 to 1925. In these animations, each value-by-area cartogram is precomputed and stored, and there are fewer than 20 of them in the animation. They use precomputation because they are based on the slower cartogram display algorithms. The value-by-area cartogram animation in Section 16.2 is also by Ouyang and Revesz [227].

The animation of parametric rectangles was considered in Cai et al. [50]. The animation of linear constraint databases was considered in Chomicki et al. [60]. The constraint database animation in Section 16.3 is based on [60] but extends it from linear constraint databases to any x, y, t variable constraint database in which the constraints are linear for each instance of t. This extension is possible because of Theorem 14.1.4.

Exercises

1. Show each step of the evaluation of the relational algebra query that defines the *Isometric_Map* relation.

2. Give the corresponding constraint representations of the three snapshots of the *Pyramid_Erode* relation at $t = 1$, $t = 2$, and $t = 3$ in the isometric color animation.

3. Suppose a city is expanding by acquiring some suburban areas, while the suburbs are expanding by taking over some farmlands, as described in the following three relations, where x, y are spatial variables, t is time, and p is population. The population of the three areas also changes linearly with time.

$$city(x, y, t, p) :- x > 0, x < 50 + 20t$$
$$y > 0, y < 35 + 15t,$$
$$t > 0, t < 1,$$
$$p = 9000t + 7000.$$

$$suburb(x, y, t, p) :- x > 0, x < 50 + 20t,$$
$$y > 35 + 15t, y < 70,$$
$$t > 0, t < 1,$$
$$p = 2000t + 10000.$$

$$suburb(x, y, t, p) :- x > 50 + 20t, x < 100,$$
$$y > 0, y < 35 + 15t,$$
$$t > 0, t < 1,$$
$$p = 2000t + 9000.$$

$$farm\_land(x, y, t, p) :- x > 50 + 20t, x < 100,$$
$$y > 35 + 15t, y < 70,$$
$$t > 0, t < 1,$$
$$p = -3000t + 8000.$$

(a) Draw how the three relations would look at times $t = 0$ and $t = 1$.

(b) Translate the x, y, t projection of the relations into a parametric 2-spaghetti representation.

(c) What animation method would you use to show both the area and population changes?

17

Indexing

Applications such as air traffic control and weather forecasting require the monitoring of a large number of moving objects; hence they require large spatiotemporal databases. Efficient query processing for large spatiotemporal databases is an important challenge.

For example, when monitoring thousands of airplanes and clouds, even simple-looking queries like *"find all the airplanes that are currently traveling within some cloud"* become difficult to evaluate in a naive approach that tries to find for each pair of airplane and cloud whether they intersect. *Indexing* is a way to efficiently evaluate such queries.

In this chapter we assume that the moving objects are represented as linear parametric rectangles, and we describe an indexing method for *linear parametric rectangle* relations. For the rest of this chapter *parametric rectangle* will always mean linear parametric rectangle.

Section 17.1 describes *minimum bounding parametric rectangles*, which are parametric rectangles that enclose a set of other parametric rectangles. This section presents an algorithm to find a minimum bounding parametric rectangle.

Section 17.2 describes *parametric R-trees*, or PR-trees. This is a tree index structure in which each leaf node is a parametric rectangle and each internal node is a minimum bounding parametric rectangle for the leaves below it. This section describes algorithms for searching, insertion, and deletion of parametric rectangles from the PR-tree.

Section 17.3 describes an extension of the PR-trees from indexing moving objects that are linear parametric rectangles to indexing more general moving objects that are described by linear constraints.

17.1 Minimum Bounding Parametric Rectangles

The *minimum bounding parametric rectangle* (MBPR) of a set of parametric rectangles S is a parametric rectangle r such that:

1. r contains all the parametric rectangles in S.
2. The area of the project of r onto the (x_i, t) space is minimized for each $i = 1, \ldots, d$.

Let us consider how to compute the minimum bounding parametric rectangle. Suppose that S is a set of d-dimensional parametric rectangles. Let R be the MBPR of S. It is easy to see that the start time of R is the minimum of the start times of the parametric rectangles in S and the end time of R is the maximum of the end times of the parametric rectangles in S. Let t_{min} and t_{max} denote the start and end times of R, then

$$t_{min} = \min_{r \in S} \left(r.t^{\vdash} \right) \quad \text{and} \quad t_{max} = \max_{r \in S} \left(r.t^{\dashv} \right)$$

Hence the main task of computing R is to compute the functions for the lower and upper bounds of R in each x_i dimension. For each $i = 1, \ldots, d$, the projection of each parametric rectangle in S onto the (x_i, t) space corresponds to a trapezium with four extreme points, as shown in Figure 17.1 (left). The projection of S onto the (x_i, t) space corresponds to a set P of $4|S|$ extreme points in the (x_i, t) space. Let H_i be the convex hull of P. We show that the lower and upper bounds of R for the x_i are extensions of some edges of the convex hull H_i, which can be computed efficiently. For example, the thin solid line polygon in Figure 17.1 is the convex hull of four parametric rectangles in the (x_i, t) space, and the bold line trapezium in Figure 17.1 (right) is their MBPR projected on the (x_i, t) space.

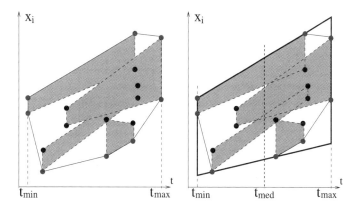

FIGURE 17.1. The convex hull and MBPR of parametric rectangles.

Lemma 17.1.1   For each x_i, let S_i be the projection of a set S of parametric rectangles onto the (x_i, t) space. Then the lower and upper bounds of the minimum bounding parametric rectangle R of S projected onto (x_i, t) overlaps some edge of the convex hull of S_i.

Proof. Let H_i be the convex hull of S_i. It is easy to see that the lower bound of R must touch at least one extreme point of the lower half of the convex hull. Otherwise, we can shift the lower bound upward until it touches one point. This shift only reduces the area of the trapezium, showing that R is not minimal as required in condition (2) for MBPRs.

Now let us prove that the lower bound of R overlaps one edge of H_i. Suppose the lower bound of R touches the convex hull H_i at the extreme point P_j as shown in Figure 17.2. Let P_{j-1} be the adjacent extreme point to the left of P_j and P_{j+1} be the adjacent extreme point to the right of P_j. Suppose also that the extension of $P_{j-1}P_j$ intersects with the left bound $t = t_{min}$ and the right bound $t = t_{max}$ at points A and B. The extension of $P_j P_{j+1}$ intersects with the left and right bounds at points C and D. Then the lower bound should fall in the range between AB and CD. Assume that the lower bound is the bold line EF, as shown in Figure 17.2. Let $t_{med} = (t_{min} + t_{max})/2$. If P_j is to the right of the line $t = t_{med}$ then the height of AP_jE is greater than that of BP_jF. We substitute EF by AB and get a parametric rectangle R' that includes all the parametric rectangles in S. The area of R' is

$$area(R') = area(R) + area(BP_jF) - area(AP_jE)$$

Because the triangle AP_jE is similar to BP_jF and the height of AP_jE is greater than that of BP_jF, the area of AP_jE is greater than that of BP_jF. Hence $area(R') < area(R)$. Then R is not an MBPR, because that contradicts minimality condition (2) for MBPR. Hence the lower bound must overlap AB. If P_j is to

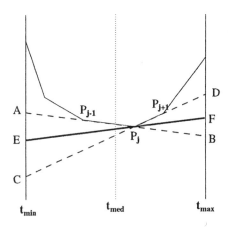

FIGURE 17.2. Lower hull and lower bound.

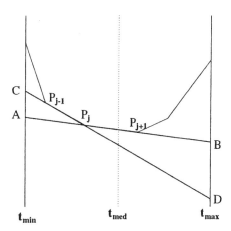

FIGURE 17.3. P_j is to the left of t_{med}; AB is a better bound than CD.

the left of the line $t = t_{med}$, we similarly prove that the choice of CD is better than that of EF. Hence, EF cannot be an optimal choice; it is either AB or CD, and in each case the minimum bounding parametric rectangle overlaps one edge of the convex hull.   ∎

Lemma 17.1.2   The lower and upper bounds of the minimum bounding parametric rectangle R of S projected onto (x_i, t) are the extensions of the edges of H_i that intersect the median line $t = t_{med}$, where $t_{med} = 0.5(t_{min} + t_{max})$.

Proof. By Lemma 17.1.1, if $P_{j-1}P_j$ is the edge of H that overlaps the lower bound of R, then P_j must be to the right of the median line $t = t_{med}$, otherwise, by substituting $P_j P_{j+1}$ for $P_{j-1}P_j$ we would get a bound parametric rectangle R' whose area is less than that of R, as shown in Figure 17.3. Similarly P_{j-1} must be to the left of the median line. Thus the lower bound of R overlaps the edge of the lower half of H_i that intersects with the median line $t = t_{med}$. Similarly, the upper bound of R overlaps the edge of the upper half of H_i that intersects with the median line.   ∎

For example, Figure 17.1 shows that in the x_i dimension the lower and upper bounds of the MBPR of a set of parametric rectangles are extensions of those edges of the convex hull that intersect the line $t = t_{med}$.

Theorem 17.1.1   The minimum bounding parametric rectangle R of a set S with n number of d-dimensional parametric rectangles can be computed in $O(d\, n \log n)$ time.

Proof. It is easy to see that t_{max} and t_{min} can be computed in $O(n)$ time. For each $i = 1, \ldots, d$, let S_i be the projection of S onto the (x_i, t) space; we can compute the corresponding extreme points of S_i in $O(n)$ time by substituting the start and end times of each parametric rectangle in S into the parametric functions. The convex hull of S_i can be computed in $O(n \log n)$ time. We can also find the edges of H_i that intersect with t_{med} in $O(n)$ time. By Lemmas 17.1.1 and 17.1.2, the functions of the lower and upper bounds of R in x_i are the functions of the edges of H_i that intersect with t_{med}. Therefore the bounds of R in x_i can be computed in $O(n) + O(n \log n) + O(n) = O(n \log n)$ time. Hence, for d dimensions, the complete R can be computed in $O(d\, n \log n)$ time.   ■

The algorithm that finds minimum bounding parametric rectangles is outlined next.

FindMBPR(S)

input: S, a set of parametric rectangles
$t_{min} = \min_{r \in S}(r.t^{[})$
$t_{max} = \max_{r \in S}(r.t^{[})$
$t_{med} = (t_{min} + t_{max})/2$
for each dimension x_i **do**
   Find S_i the set of extreme points of projection (x_i, t) of S
   Compute the convex hull H_i of S_i
   Find the edges of H_i that intersect with t_{med}
   Construct $x_i^{[}$ and $x_i^{]}$
end-for

Example 17.1.1   Let us calculate the MBPR of the following parametric rectangles:

ID	X	Y	T
r1	$[7t + 30,\ 7t + 90]$	$[5t + 50,\ 6t + 100]$	$[0,\ 10]$
r12	$[4t + 70,\ 3t + 90]$	$[6t + 45,\ 6t + 55]$	$[2,\ 10]$

Figure 17.4 (left) shows that the projection of r_1 in the (x, t) space already includes that of r_{12}. Hence the MBPR of the two is r_1 in the x dimension.

Figure 17.4 (right) shows the projection of r_1 and r_{12} in the (y, t) space. The dashed line segments AB and BC form the lower half of the convex hull of r_1 and r_{12} in (y, t) space, where A is $(0, 50)$, B is $(2, 57)$, and C is $(10, 100)$. Because the midline crosses BC, the lower bound of the MBPR of r_1 and r_{12} is the extension of BC and the upper bound is the same as the upper bound of r_1 in the y dimension. Note that the line extending BC is $5.375t + 46.25$. Hence the MBPR of r_1 and r_{12} is:

$$([7t + 30,\ 7t + 90], [5.375t + 46.25,\ 6t + 100], [0, 10])$$

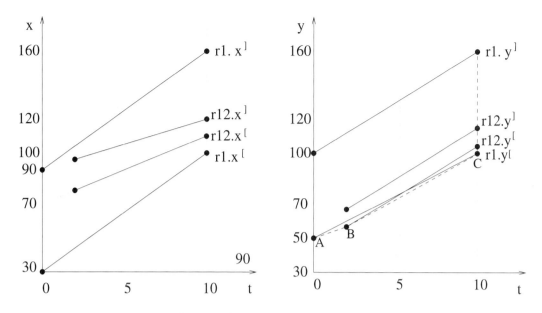

FIGURE 17.4. Find MBPR of r_1 and r_{12}.

Airplane

ID	X	Y	T
r4	$[7t + 30,\ 7t + 50]$	$[6t + 80,\ 6t + 100]$	$[0,\ 10]$
r5	$[12t + 30,\ 12t + 40]$	$[5t + 50,\ 5t + 65]$	$[0,\ 10]$
r6	$[6t + 75,\ 7t + 90]$	$[8t + 70,\ 8t + 80]$	$[2,\ 10]$
r7	$[0,\ 15]$	$[5t + 40,\ 5t + 55]$	$[0,\ 9]$
r8	$[0,\ 12]$	$[4t + 20,\ 4t + 40]$	$[1,\ 10]$
r9	$[30,\ 50]$	$[7t + 10,\ 7t + 20]$	$[0,\ 10]$
r10	$[-5t + 80,\ -5t + 100]$	$[2t,\ 3t + 20]$	$[0,\ 10]$
r11	$[-6t + 60,\ -6t + 70]$	$[-3t + 30,\ -2t + 40]$	$[0,\ 10]$

Example 17.1.2   Relation *Airplane* describes the movement of eight airplanes as parametric rectangles. We can compute using the preceding algorithm that the minimum bounding parametric rectangle for the airplanes r_4, r_5, r_6 is r_1, for the airplanes r_7, r_8, r_9 it is r_2, and for the airplanes r_{10} and r_{11} it is r_3, shown in relation *AirplaneMBPR*.

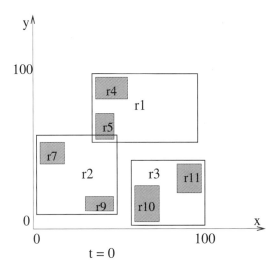

FIGURE 17.5. MBPRs for the airplanes at time $t = 0$.

AirplaneMBPR

ID	X	Y	T
r1	$[7t + 30,\ 7t + 90]$	$[5t + 50,\ 6t + 100]$	$[0,\ 10]$
r2	$[0,\ 50]$	$[5t + 10,\ 5t + 55]$	$[0,\ 10]$
r3	$[-6t + 60,\ -5t + 100]$	$[0,\ t + 40]$	$[0,\ 10]$

Figure 17.5 shows the airplanes (shaded) and their MBPRs at $t = 0$ and Figure 17.6 shows those at $t = 10$. Note that r_6 and r_8 are not shown in Figure 17.5 because they do not exist at $t = 0$. Similarly, r_7 is not shown in Figure 17.6 because it does not exist at $t = 10$.

17.2   The Parametric R-Tree Index Structure

The parametric R-tree (*PR*-tree) is an index structure for parametric rectangles. It is a height-balanced tree in which each node has between $M/2$ and M children, where M is a constant depending on the page size. Each node of a PR-tree is associated with a minimum bounding parametric rectangle.

Example 17.2.1   A PR-tree with $M = 3$ for the Airplanes relation is shown in Figure 17.7.

PR-trees are useful for efficiently *searching* the databases in answering queries of the form *"find all objects that intersect a parametric rectangle A."* PR-trees are also dynamic index structures that allows *insertions* and *deletions* of

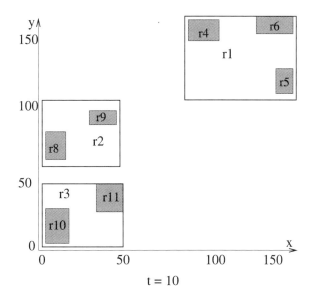

FIGURE 17.6. MBPRs for the airplanes at time $t = 10$.

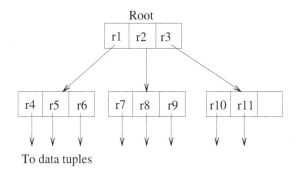

FIGURE 17.7. A PR-tree.

moving objects. The next three sections describe these three operations on PR-trees.

17.2.1 Searching

Given a parametric rectangle R, *searching* a PR-tree returns all the parametric rectangles that intersect with R. The search starts from the root of the PR-tree and moves down to those children that contain an MBPR or parametric rectangle that intersects with R.

By Theorem 14.2.2 it can be checked in $O(d)$ time whether two d-dimensional linear parametric rectangles intersect. If one child is always chosen, then because the PR-tree is always kept balanced, the search can be done in logarithmic time in the number of stored parametric rectangles. In practice, like in several other spatial search structures, there are sometimes several children that intersect R and need to be explored.

17.2.2   Insertion

During *insertion* of a parametric rectangle R into a *PR*-tree, we go down from the root of the PR-tree to find an appropriate leaf node to insert R. At each step we update the current MBPR of the chosen subtree by adding R to it.

If there are any nodes that overflow, i.e., exceed the maximum size bound, then we *split* them and then propagate upward the split while changing accordingly the MBPRs of the affected nodes. The following defines more precisely the criteria for choosing the appropriate subtree and splitting.

Appropriate Subtree: As we saw in the case of searching, a key performance issue is the number of children visited at each node during the search. We would like to keep that number as low as possible. That implies that we should keep the MBPRs as small as possible. Therefore, when inserting a new parametric rectangle, the *insertion* algorithm always tries to add it to the subtree whose associated MBPR needs the least volume enlargement to include it. The least volume enlargement can be defined as follows.

If R is any d-dimensional parametric rectangle, then the *volume* of R, denoted $Vol(R)$, is the volume of the polyhedron P that contains exactly the $(x_1, \ldots, x_d, t)$ points defined by R.

Because for each time instance t' between *from* and *to*, the intersection of P with the plane $t = t'$ is a rectangle with area $\prod_{i=1}^{d}(X_i^] - X_i^[)(t')$, the volume of R is the integral of the area function, that is:

$$Vol(R) = \int_{t^[}^{t^]} \prod_{i=1}^{d}(x_i^] - x_i^[) \, dt \tag{17.1}$$

Example 17.2.2   The volume of r_1 is:

$$\begin{aligned}
Vol(r_1) &= \int_0^{10} ((7t + 90) - (7t + 30))\,((6t + 100) - (5t + 50))\,dt \\
&= \int_0^{10} 60(t + 50)\,dt \\
&= 60(t^2/2 + 50t)\big|_0^{10} \\
&= 60(50 + 500) = 33,000
\end{aligned}$$

Let $V = Vol(FindMBPR(r_1, r_{12}))$, i.e., the MBPR of r_1 and r_{12} of Example 17.1.1. Similarly to the preceding we can calculate the following:

$$V = \int_0^{10} ((7t + 90) - (7t + 30))((6t + 100) - (5.375t + 46.25))\, dt$$

$$= \int_0^{10} 60(0.625t + 53.75)\, dt$$

$$= 60(0.625t^2/2 + 53.75t)|_0^{10}$$

$$= 60(0.625t^2/2 + 53.75t)|_0^{10}$$

$$= 60(568.75) = 34,125$$

Suppose we would like to insert a new parametric rectangle R into one child of an internal node E with children $E_1, \ldots, E_p$. Let M_j be the MBPR of E_j for $1 \le j \le p$. Then we choose the child that needs the least enlargement to include R, that is:

$$\min_j Enlarge(M_j, R) = \min_j (Vol(FindMBPR(M_j, R)) - Vol(M_j))$$

Example 17.2.3 Suppose we would like to add tuple r_{12} of Example 17.1.1 to the *PR*-tree in Example 17.1.2.

We start at the root of the PR-tree and try to add r_{12} to r_1, r_2, or r_3. This requires computation of the enlargement of each of r_1, r_2, and r_3 with r_{12}. We compute, using the results of Example 17.2.2, that:

$$Enlarge(r_1, r_{12}) = Vol(FindMBPR(r_1, r_{12})) - Vol(r_1) = 1125$$

Similarly, we can compute $Enlarge(r_2, r_{12})$ and $Enlarge(r_3, r_{12})$ to find which one needs the least enlargement and is chosen. We leave the rest of the calculations as an exercise.

Node Splitting: When a new entry is added to a node E with M entries an overflow occurs. In this case, it is necessary to split the collection of $M + 1$ entries into two nodes. The splitting is done in a way that results in small MBPRs for the two split halves of the node.

First we find among the $M+1$ entries the two entries that are most undesirable to keep within a node. For those two entries their MBPR has a volume that is large compared to the sum of their volumes. Therefore, we are looking for the pair with the *maximum volume increase*, that is:

$$\max_{r_i, r_j \in E} Vol(FindMBPR(r_i, r_j)) - (Vol(r_i) + Vol(r_j))$$

Once we find r_i and r_j, we know that they are not desirable to keep together. Therefore, we choose r_i and r_j as the first elements of two new groups. Each of the remaining parametric rectangles is inserted into either the group containing r_i or the group containing r_j, depending on which would cause a smaller increase in the current MBPR of the two groups.

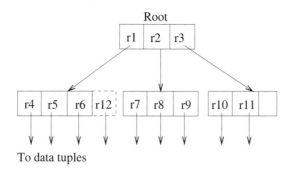

FIGURE 17.8. Inserting r_{12} into r_1.

Example 17.2.4   Let us continue Example 17.2.3. Suppose that the maximum allowed number of children of each node is 3 and the minimum required number of children is 2. In that case, as shown in Figure 17.8, an overflow occurs after the insertion of r_{12} into r_1. Therefore, we need to split r_1 into two new nodes r_{13} and r_{14}.

For each pair of children of r_1, we compute the volume increase of their minimum bounding parametric rectangles. (We leave the details as an exercise.) We find that r_4 and r_{12} are the least desirable to keep together. Therefore, we put r_4 into the new node r_{13} and r_{12} into the new node r_{14}. Next we add r_5 to r_{14}, because $Enlarge\,(r_{14}, r_5)\ <\ Enlarge\,(r_{13}, r_5)$. Then we add r_6 to r_{13}, because $Enlarge\,(r_{13}, r_6) < Enlarge\,(r_{14}, r_6)$.

Finally, we remove r_1 and insert r_{13} and r_{14} into the root as shown in Figure 17.9 (1). This causes the splitting of the root, and the height of the tree increases by 1, as shown in Figure 17.9 (2). The process of the splitting of the root is similar to the splitting of r_1 and is also left as an exercise.

Theorem 17.2.1   The insertion of a parametric rectangle into a PR-tree can be done in $O(dM^2 \log_M n)$ time, where M is the maximum number of children per node, d is the dimension, and n is the number of parametric rectangles.

Proof. As we go down the tree we need at each level to find the appropriate subtree and update the MBPR of the chosen subtree. By Theorem 17.1.1 the computation of the MBPR of two parametric rectangles takes $O(d)$ time. The computation of the volume of a parametric rectangle depends on its dimension and takes $O(d)$ time. There are at most M entries in a node. Hence computing their enlargements and selecting the minimum out of those requires $O(dM)$ time at each level. The height of a PR-tree with n parametric rectangles is $\log_M n$. Therefore, going down the PR-tree to find an appropriate leaf node requires $O(dM \log_M n)$ time.

If we add the new entry to a node that has less than M entries, then splitting is not required and we are done. Otherwise, we need to split the last nonleaf node and then propagate the split upward. Each split requires finding the pair of nodes that are least desirable together. This requires M^2 computations of MBPRs of two parametric rectangles; hence this can be done by Theorem 17.1.1 in $O(dM^2)$

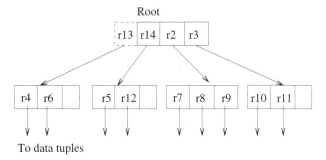

(1) Splitting r_1

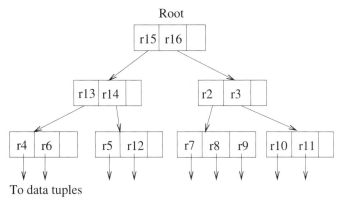

(2) Splitting the root

FIGURE 17.9. Splitting with propagation.

time. To add each of the $M - 2$ other entries to either of the two requires $O(dM)$ time. Because the height of a PR-tree with n parametric rectangles is $\log_M n$, the total time for splitting including propagation upward is $O(dM^2 \log_M n)$.

Finally, note that the PR-tree remains balanced after each insertion because the height of the PR-tree increases only when we split the root node, and that increases each path from the root to a leaf by one. ■

Note that the value of M typically depends on the page size. We can minimize the number of page faults by letting M be the maximum number of entries that can be stored in a page.

17.2.3 Deletion

If we want to enable *deletion* of parametric rectangles, we do the following. We keep the IDs of the parametric rectangles in another search tree in which each entry has a pointer to the parametric rectangle record stored, just like the PR-tree has. After every insertion of a parametric rectangle R with ID i, we insert i and a pointer to R into the second search tree. (Instead of a second search tree we may also use a hashtable.)

To delete a parametric rectangle R with ID i, we first use the second search tree to look up a pointer to R, then delete i from the second search tree, which takes $O(\log_M n)$ time. We also delete R from the PR-tree. Let P be the parent of R. If P has at least $M/2$ children after the deletion, we simply recompute the MBPR of P and propagate this recomputation up to the root. In a PR-tree this takes $O(d \log_M n)$ time. Otherwise, that is, if P has fewer than $M/2$ children, then we delete P and reinsert the remaining children of P into the sub-PR-tree whose root is the parent of P. This takes $O(dM^3 \log_M n)$ time. If the parent of P has fewer than $M/2$ children, then the deletion is propagated upward in a similar manner. Therefore, we have the following.

Theorem 17.2.2   The deletion of a parametric rectangle from a PR-tree can be done in $O(dM^3 \log_M^2 n)$ time, where M is the maximum, $M/2$ is the minimum number of children per node, d is the dimension, and n is the number of parametric rectangles.   ■

Example 17.2.5   Suppose that the current situation is the one shown in part (2) of Figure 17.9 and for some unexpected reason airplane r_{10} makes a forced landing. To reflect this change in the database, we need to delete the parametric rectangle with ID r_{10}. By searching for r_{10} in the second tree we find the pointer to the parametric rectangle whose ID is r_{10}. From there we search in the PR-tree for the parent of r_{10}. In this case it is r_3. Because r_3 contains only one other child, namely, r_{11}, it and r_{11} are deleted and r_{11} is reinserted in the sub-PR-tree with root r_{16}, which is the parent of r_3. We leave further details as an exercise.

17.3   Indexing Constraint Databases

In this chapter we assumed that moving objects are represented by parametric rectangles. However, PR-trees can be also used to index more general objects for which MBPRs can be found. For example, each linear constraint tuple T in d spatial and one temporal dimensions defines a moving object. We can find an MBPR that includes T by first taking the projection of T onto each (x_i, t) space. Then we find the extreme points of the projection and their convex hull in each (x_i, t) space, and from that we calculate as in Section 17.1 the lower and upper bounds of the MBPR in the x_i dimension.

The PR-tree for constraint objects would be like the PR-tree for parametric rectangles. For each constraint object we only store its MBPR and a pointer to the actual object.

Searching can be easily modified in the case of constraint objects. Suppose we want to find all objects that intersect a linear constraint object T. Then we find the MBPR of T; first we do the search as described in Section 17.2.1. The search returns all the intersections of MBPRs. Objects whose MBPRs intersect

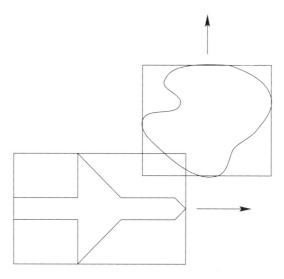

FIGURE 17.10. Example of a false hit.

may not actually intersect. We call such cases *false hits*. Figure 17.10 shows an example of a false hit with one MBPR moving to the right containing an airplane and another MBPR moving upward containing a cloud. In the figure the objects do not intersect, even though their MBPRs intersect.

To eliminate false hits, for each returned MBPR we need to do a more refined check, that is, we have to check whether the conjunction of the constraints in T and the constraint of the object whose MBPR is returned is satisfiable. Then we only report those true hits where this more refined check also succeeds. The use of PR-trees greatly cuts down on the number of times the more refined check, which is computationally more expensive, needs to be performed.

The insertion and deletion operations can be similarly modified for constraint objects.

Bibliographic Notes

Günther [130] Overmars [228], and Samet [279] are books on spatial data structures. R-trees [132], R*-trees [22], and R+-trees [286] are indexing methods for stationary spatial objects. Each of these spatial indexing methods models stationary objects as high-dimensional bounding boxes. It is possible to use these spatial indexing techniques with $(d + 1)$-dimensional bounding boxes to index d-dimensional moving objects. However, that naive approach requires much larger bounding boxes than the MBPRs. Hence that approach also leads to too many false hits.

PR-trees were proposed as an index structure for parametric rectangles in Cai and Revesz [52]. The computation of MBPRs relies on the computation of convex hulls. Efficient algorithms to compute convex hulls are described in Preparata and Shamos [241]. Most of the presentation in this chapter, including Theorems 17.1.1 and 17.2.1 and the examples, are adapted from Cai and Revesz [52].

Most current indexing approaches for moving objects are based on the moving points data model [92, 98, 289], which represents moving objects as a continuous function of time $f(t)$ and updates the database when the parameters of the motion like speed or direction change. Moving points do not represent the spatial extents of the moving objects. Several works including [7, 175, 278, 304] consider the indexing of moving objects.

Agarwal et al. [7] proposes index structures for two-dimensional moving points and shows that it can find all moving points lying in a static rectangle R in $O((N/B)^{1/2+\epsilon} + T/B)$ I/Os. However, it cannot be used to index moving objects with spatial extents and does not consider the queries where R is moving.

Kollios et al. [175] proposes to map the trajectories of a moving point represented by linear functions of the form $y = vt + a$ to a point (v, a) in the dual space and to index them by a regular spatial index structure such as a kd-trees [33]. Kollios et al. [175] also provides a theoretical lower bound on the number of I/Os needed to answer d-dimensional range searching problems. However, [175] assumes the trajectories of the moving objects extend to "infinity." It is not clear how to use this method to index objects with a finite duration.

Saltenis et al. [278] propose an R-tree-like index structure for moving points, which uses a time-parameterized "conservative" bounding rectangle to group moving points together. However, the "conservative" bounding rectangle, of which the lower and upper bounds are set to move with the minimum and maximum speeds of the enclosed points, respectively, is a less tight bound of moving points than MBPRs would be in the case of moving points.

Tayeb et al. [304] uses Quadtree [279] for indexing one-dimensional moving points as line segments in the (x, t) plane. It partitions the time dimension into time intervals of length H and indexes the part of the trajectory of each moving object that falls in the current time interval. This approach introduces substantial data replication in the index because a line segment is usually stored in several nodes.

In general, linear constraint databases cannot be efficiently indexed directly without the use of MBPRs. Some special cases are considered in Bertino et al. [35], Brodsky et al. [43], Goldstein et al. [113], Kanellakis et al. [160], Ramaswamy [245], Ramaswamy and Subramanian [246], and Zhu et al. [339]. Let N/B and T/N be the number of pages required to store N constraint tuples and T retrieved tuples, respectively. Bertino et al. [35] describe a method that can answer half-plane queries for nonmoving 2D linear constraint tuples in $O(log_B N/B + T/B)$ time, assuming that the angular coefficient of the line associated with the half-plane query belongs to a fixed finite set. For spatiotemporal constraint databases no such upper bound is known yet.

Exercises

1. Considering r_2, r_3, and r_{12} of Example 17.2.3, find the following:

   (a) *Vol* (r_2)

   (b) *Vol* (r_3)

   (c) *FindMBPR* $(r_2, \ r_{12})$

   (d) *FindMBPR* $(r_3, \ r_{12})$

   (e) *Enlarge* $(r_2, \ r_{12})$

   (f) *Enlarge* $(r_3, \ r_{12})$

2. Considering Example 17.2.4, find the following:

   (a) Find for each pair of r_4, r_5, r_6, and r_{12} the volume enlargement of their MBPRs.

   (b) Find the MBPRs of r_{13} and r_{14}.

   (c) Find for each pair of r_2, r_3, r_{13}, and r_{14} the volume enlargement of their MBPRs.

   (d) Find the MBPRs of r_{15} and r_{16}.

3. Delete in order the following from the PR-tree in Figure 17.9 (2):

   (a) r_{10}

   (b) r_{11}

18

The MLPQ System

MLPQ, short for *management of linear programming queries*, is a constraint database system for rational linear constraint databases. It allows Datalog queries, minimum and maximum aggregation operators over linear objective functions, and some other operators.

There are two main application areas of the MLPQ system. The first is in operations research when the available data in a database needs to be reformulated by some database query before we can solve a problem by linear programming. In this case, MLPQ provides both the flexibility of database systems in reformulating data and the advantages of linear programming by having linear programming available as one type of aggregation operator.

The second main application area of MLPQ is in dealing with spatial and spatiotemporal data. Spatial data include geographic data, which is also the concern of geographic information systems (GISs). In this case, MLPQ provides the flexibility to go beyond two or three dimensions of mutually constrained data. MLPQ can do computations for high-dimensional constrained data, although some visualization operators are still restricted to two or three dimensions.

Section 18.1 gives an outline of the MLPQ system architecture and describes the functions of its six main modules. Section 18.2 describes the syntax of the MLPQ input files. Section 18.3 describes the graphical user interface (GUI) of the MLPQ system. It gives examples of both Datalog queries and iconic queries that can be called using the tool bar of the GUI. Section 18.4 discusses recursive Datalog queries in MLPQ.

18.1 The MLPQ Database System Architecture

The architecture of the MLPQ system is outlined in Figure 18.1. The architecture consists of six main modules, which can be described as follows:

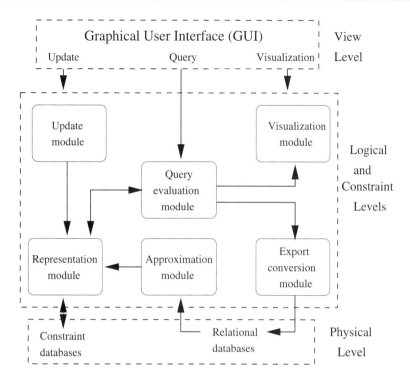

FIGURE 18.1. The MLPQ database system architecture.

Representation: The *representation module* is responsible for the internal representation of constraint databases and queries. This module communicates with the external constraint database storage structures. If it cannot find some needed constraint relation in the constraint database store, then it calls the approximation module that searches its relational database store and provides a converted constraint relation. The representation module provides output to the query evaluation module. The constraint relations of the input files are like those described in Chapter 2.

Query Evaluation: The *query evaluation module* is used to evaluate the queries provided by the user via an input file or graphical user interface (GUI). There are several kinds of constraint query languages, such as relational algebra, SQL, Datalog, and their extensions as described in Chapters 3, 4, and 5. In addition, there are special iconic operators of the graphical user interface that are useful for data visualization or data exporting.

   The output of this module is another constraint relation, which may be added to the database; therefore it may be passed to the data representation module. Alternatively, it may be a relation that is passed to the visualization module, if the query involves query visualization operators. Finally, it could pass the data to the export conversion module, if the query asks for exporting to a relational database. The query evaluation module uses some of the algorithms described in Chapter 12.

Visualization: The *visualization module* shows on the GUI the data that the user asks to see. The visualization module should provide many options. One of the interesting options special to spatiotemporal applications is animation of three-dimensional spatiotemporal data. The input of this module is from the query evaluation module and the output is to the GUI. The visualization module uses some of the algorithms described in Chapter 16.

Approximation: The *approximation module* can be used to convert from relational databases to constraint databases. Typically, the conversion involves a significant data reduction and interpolation of the original relational data. The input is from relational database storage, and the output is to the representation module. The approximation module uses some of the algorithms described in Chapter 15.

Update: The *update module* is responsible for updating the constraint relations as requested by the user. There are several update languages that the user may use to express updates or use iconic operators. There may also be several ways to implement the update requests. The update module uses the algorithm described in Section 15.2.1.

Export Conversion: The *export conversion module* provides conversion from constraint databases to relational databases. The conversion may not always be available, because constraint databases are sometimes equivalent to infinite relational databases, as described in Chapter 1.

18.2   MLPQ Input Files

In the MLPQ system each input file has the following structure:

```
begin %moduleName%
    l₁
    l₂
    ⋮
    lₙ
end %moduleName%
```

where each l_i is a Datalog rule or rational linear constraint tuple, as described in Chapters 4 and 5 with the following differences.

First, each linear constraint has the form:

$$a_1 x_1 + a_2 x_2 + \cdots + a_n x_n \ \theta \ b$$

where each a_i is a constant and each x_i is a variable, and θ_i is a relational operator of the form =, <, >, <=, or >=.

Second, the optional aggregate operator has the form $OP(f)$ where OP is one of the aggregate operators max, min, MAX, MIN, sum_max, or sum_min, and f is a linear function of the variables in the rule. The aggregate operators have the following meanings:

- max gets the maximum value for each constraint tuple.

- sum_max finds the sum of the values returned by max.

- MAX finds the maximum of the values returned by max.

- min, MIN, and sum_min are defined similarly to the preceding.

Third, for negation the symbol ! is used instead of *not*.

The module name controls what type of query evaluation methods will be used. It should be one of the following strings:

- MLPQ—to evaluate *only* nonrecursive Datalog queries.

- RECURSIVE—to evaluate recursive Datalog queries.

- GIS—to evaluate both Datalog and iconic queries.

Next we give a few examples of MLPQ input files. We skip the begin and end keywords and module names.

Example 18.2.1   Suppose relations *Pesticide_A* and *Pesticide_B*, with attributes *id, x,* and *y,* record which land areas were sprayed with pesticide types *A* and *B,* respectively. For example, the following MLPQ constraint tuple represents a part of land area with ID 37 that was sprayed with pesticide *A*:

```
Pesticide_A(37, x, y)   :-   x - y >= -18,
                             2x + 3y <= 104,
                             4x - 7y <= -78,
                             x + 2y <= 48.
```

As the next example shows, we can represent in MLPQ some incomplete spatial information.

Example 18.2.2   There are two planes. The first plane departs from some location between 100 and 200 miles east and between 50 and 150 miles south of location $(0, 0)$, and the second plane departs from some location between 1000 and 1120 miles west and between 690 and 750 miles north of $(0, 0)$. The departure locations of the two planes can be represented in MLPQ as follows:

```
Depart(1, x, y) :- x >=   100,
                   x <=   200,
                   y >=  -150,
                   y <=   -50.

Depart(2, x, y) :- x <= -1000,
                   x >= -1120,
                   y >=   690,
                   y <=   750.
```

Suppose that in one hour the first plane goes east between 490 and 580 miles and north between 400 and 440 miles, and the second plane goes west between 590 and 650 miles and south between 300 and 340 miles. The movement of the two planes within one hour can be represented in MLPQ as follows:

```
Fly(1, x, y) :- x >=  490,
                x <=  580,
                y >=  400,
                y <=  440.

Fly(2, x, y) :- x >= -650,
                x <= -590,
                y >= -340,
                y <= -300.
```

The possible final destinations of the two planes after one hour can be expressed as a Datalog query in MLPQ as follows:

```
Arrive(i, x, y) :- Depart(i, x0, y0),
                   Fly(i, dx, dy),
                   -x + x0 + dx = 0,
                   -y + y0 + dy = 0.
```

Finally, to test whether the two planes could meet at the same location after one hour can be expressed as the following MLPQ Datalog query:

```
Meet(x, y) :- Arrive(1, x, y), Arrive(2, x, y).
```

The next example shows the representation of a spatiotemporal relation.

Example 18.2.3   The ownership information of a piece of land can be stored in an MLPQ relation *Land* with the following attributes: *id*, *x*, *y*, *t*, and *owner*. For example, the fifth piece of land and the information that it belonged to Adam between 1980 and

1990 can be represented by the following:

```
Land(5, x, y, t, 'Adam') :- x >= 0,
                            y >= 0,
                            y <= 5,
                      5x - 3y <= 10,
                      5x + 6y <= 30,
                            t <= 1990,
                            t >= 1980.
```

18.3   The MLPQ Graphical User Interface

When one starts the MLPQ system a window is created. In the top of the window there is a tool bar with several buttons, as shown in Figure 18.2. The second and third lower-left buttons are used to open and store a file.

When an input file is opened all the Datalog rules in it are evaluated, and the defined relations and input relations are all listed on the left-hand side of the graphical user interface, just below the tool bar. The user can right-click on any relation in the list to view the tuples in that relation.

Instead of putting a Datalog query in a file, one can also use the **Datalog Query** icon for querying, which is explained as follows:

Datalog Query: A dialog box comes up, in which the user can type in a new rule to add to the database at run time.

Example 18.3.1   Suppose that information about ownership of a plot of land is stored in the relation *Land* as in Example 18.2.3.

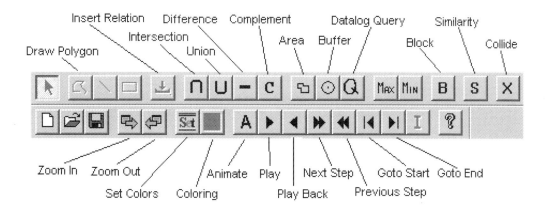

FIGURE 18.2. The MLPQ tool bar.

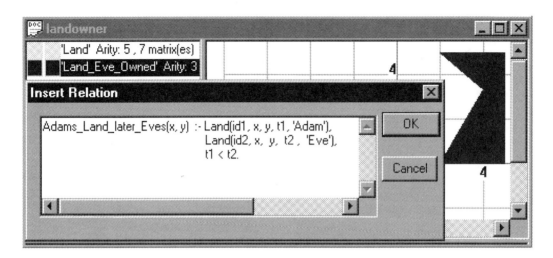

FIGURE 18.3. The land owner problem.

Query: Which parts of the land belonged to Adam and later to Eve?

We click on the **Datalog Query** icon, which brings up a dialog box. Then we enter into the dialog box the Datalog query shown in Figure 18.3.

In addition to Datalog, the MLPQ system supports several GIS and animation operators, which are called by the other icons in the tool bar of the MLPQ graphical user interface.

GIS operators are applied on relations that are of the form $r(id, x, y)$ or $r(id, x, y, z)$ and animation operators to relations of the form $r(id, x, y, t)$, where id is the identification number of an object, x, y, and z are spatial variables, and t is a temporal variable. We call relations in these special forms *2D spatial*, *3D spatial*, and *3D spatiotemporal*. The MLPQ operators on these three types of relations are explained in Sections 18.3.1, 18.3.2, and 18.3.3, respectively.

18.3.1   2D Spatial Operators

Draw Polygon: Open a nonempty database (i.e., a database that already contains at least one relation). Click on the display grid and press the **Draw Polygon** button. The MLPQ system allows the user to draw a polygon in the display grid, with the left mouse button held down. Double-click to complete the drawing. (The buttons for **Draw Rectangle** and **Draw Line** work similarly.)

Insert Polygon: After drawing a polygon, pressing this button will add the polygon to the current (open) MLPQ database. The user will be asked to enter the relation name. The MLPQ system converts each drawing to a linear constraint database representation. For example, the pesticide area of Example 18.2.1 can be entered by drawing the contour of the area instead of entering the linear constraints directly.

Zoom In: The display grid will be zoomed in.

Zoom Out: The display grid will be zoomed out.

Intersection: Select two or more relations (by clicking on them) and press the **Intersection** button. The MLPQ system computes the intersection relation and asks the user to assign a name to it. **Note:** Two 2D spatial constraint tuples intersect only if they have the same ID.

Union: Select two or more relations (by clicking on them) and press the **Union** button. The MLPQ system computes the union relation and asks the user to assign a name to it.

Area: Select a relation and press the **Area** button. For PReSTO databases, the area of the relation will be output on the screen. For MLPQ databases, the user will be asked to enter a left bound, a right bound, and a step size. The result will be a relation containing aggregate information about areas of the different bands specified by the bounds and step size.

Buffer: Select a relation (from an MLPQ database) and press the **Buffer** button. The user will be asked to enter a distance d. A new relation is computed, which contains the surrounding region of the selected relation, up to the distance d. In MLPQ the surrounding region of a point is approximated by a high-degree polygon.

Similarity: For this operation, the user must first open a new database by going to the **File** menu and selecting **New**. Then go to the **File** menu again, and select **Import File**, followed by **Import Line**. This will allow the user to load an image database (extension `.lin`) into the system. Select a relation from the image database and press the **Similarity** button. The MLPQ system computes and displays the similarity of each relation in the database with respect to the selected relation, which is labeled as the *Prototype*. The similarity values are displayed in the relation list.

Next we give some MLPQ queries to illustrate the use of 2D spatial operators.

Example 18.3.2   Suppose we have a database as in Example 18.2.1.

Query: In which locations were both pesticides sprayed?
We implement the query using the GUI interface as shown in Figure 18.4. There we select the relations *pesticide_A* and *pesticide_B* and then click on the

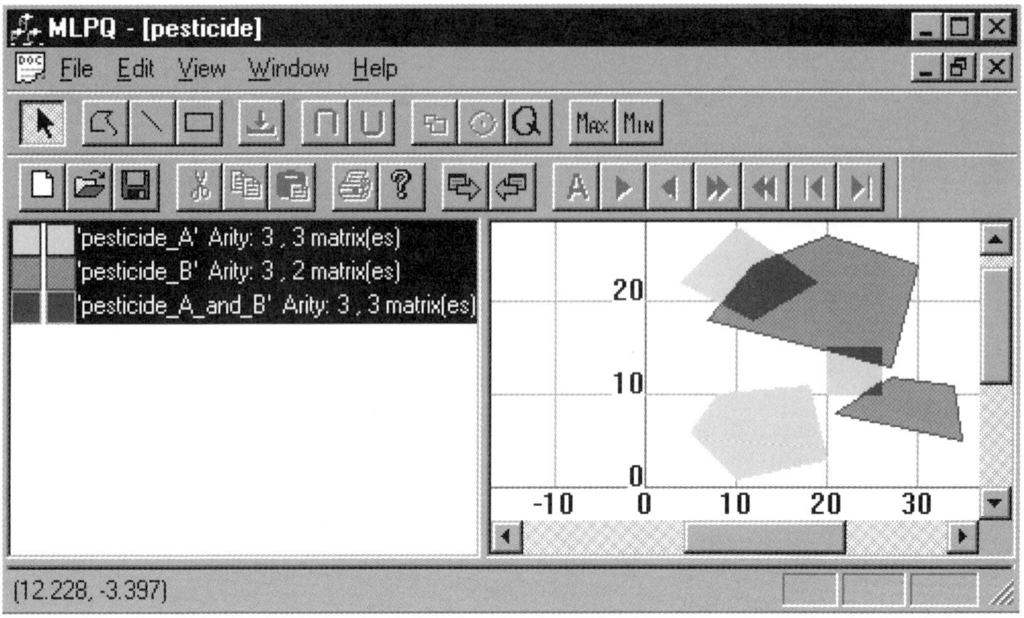

FIGURE 18.4. The pesticide problem.

Intersection icon. A dialog box will appear in which the user can enter the name of the new relation to be generated. By typing in **pesticide_A_and_B**, a new relation with that name is created.

Query: What is the total area in which both pesticides were sprayed?

The area of the region is computed by selecting the relation *pesticide_A_and_B* and then clicking the **Area** icon. Like before, a dialog box pops up in which the name of the new relation is entered. The computed value can be seen by inspecting the new relation generated.

Example 18.3.3 We are given a map of the midwestern United States represented using a linear constraint database. The database also contains information about the route and itinerary of two persons, A and B, who are traveling across the midwest.

Query: When are the two people in the same state at the same time?

To answer this query, we read in the midwestern states one by one and then create a relation called *State* from their union using the **Union** icon. Next, we call a query dialog box and enter a Datalog query as shown in Figure 18.5. This query says to return all (t, i) pairs of time and state such that at time t person A is at

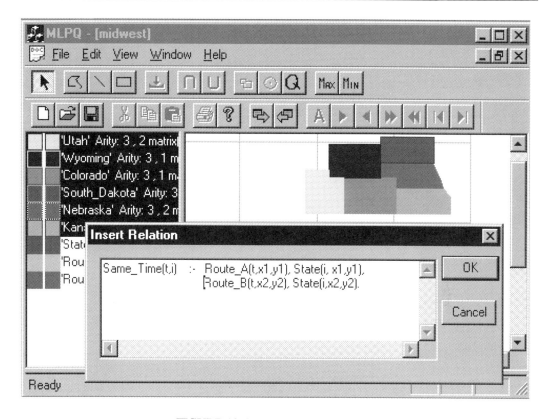

FIGURE 18.5. The Midwest problem.

location $(x1, y1)$ and person B is at location $(x2, y2)$ and both locations are in the same state i.

Example 18.3.4   Suppose person 1 is traveling eastward on an east-west highway as shown in Figure 18.6 and the following relations with attributes Id, x, and y are available in the database:

- *Current_Pos*, which records locations of persons
- *Road*, which records highways
- *Exit*, which records exits from highways
- *Hotel*, which records hotel locations

Query: Which is the closest exit on the highway in his direction?

Since the person is traveling eastward, the nearest exit is the one that intersects the road he is on and has minimum x value. Therefore, the nearest exit can be

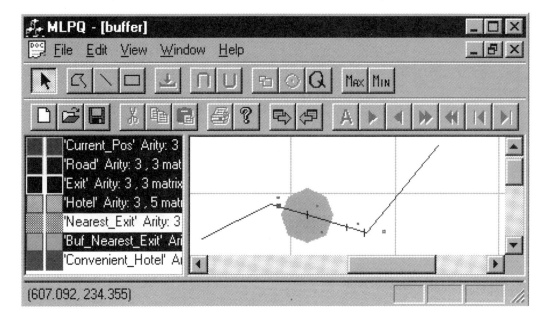

FIGURE 18.6. Finding a convenient hotel.

found using the following Datalog query, again entered into the dialog box of the Datalog query icon:

```
Nearest_X(min(x))    :- Current_Pos(1, x0, y0),
                          Road(i, x0, y0),
                          Road(i, x,  y),
                          Exit(j, x,  y),
                              x >= x0.

Nearest_Exit(j,x,y) :- Nearest_X(x), Exit(j,x,y).
```

Query: Which hotels are within 500 meters of the nearest exit?

For the second query, the **Buffer** icon is used to create relation *Buf_Nearest_Exit*, which contains a 500-meter buffer around the *Nearest_Exit* relation. Then using a Datalog query we find the IDs of those hotels that are located within *Buf_Nearest_Exit*.

18.3.2 3D Spatial Operators

Three-dimensional spatial relations can be displayed in MLPQ as maps with discrete color zones according to the values of the z variable, which can record, for example, elevation, precipitation, or temperature. The following two operators are both needed for such displays:

- **Set Colors:** After opening a BANDS file, pressing this button pops up a dialog box to let the users add, delete, or modify the color ranges for the relation to be loaded.

- **Coloring:** After setting the color ranges of the relation and selecting the relation to be colored, pressing this button displays the relation according to the prescribed color bands.

Example 18.3.5   For example, Figure 16.3 shows an isometric color band map for the total precipitation in the continental United States in 1997.

18.3.3   3D Spatiotemporal Operators

Three-dimensional spatiotemporal relations are visualized in MLPQ using animations. During the animation the color of the objects can change. Note that the relation list has two color boxes to the left of each relation. The left color is the color of the relation at the start of the animation, and the right color is the color at the end of the animation. These colors can be changed by right-clicking on the color boxes. The color changes gradually during the animation from the start color to the end color.

For the color representation, MLPQ uses the RGB format. In that format each color is represented with three basic colors: red, green, and blue. Each color is composed of a shade of these three colors, where the shade ranges from 0 to 255. For example, a pure red color would be represented as $(255, 0, 0)$. A pure green color would be $(0, 255, 0)$. A black color is $(0, 0, 0)$, and a medium gray color would be $(128, 128, 128)$.

Suppose the start color is represented as (r_0, g_0, b_0) and the end color after n time steps is represented as (r_n, g_n, b_n). MLPQ implements a linear change in time for each basic color. That is, for the ith time step the display color will be

$$\left(r_0 + \frac{i(r_n - r_0)}{n}, g_0 + \frac{i(g_n - g_0)}{n}, b_0 + \frac{i(b_n - b_0)}{n} \right)$$

For animating 3D spatiotemporal relations, MLPQ allows the following iconic operators:

- **Animate:** This brings up a dialog box that allows the user to set up the animation parameters such as the start (t_{begin}) and end (t_{end}) times of the animation, the speed of the animation, and the time granularity of the animation, that is, the step size δ. The animation can be specified to be either linear, which is the default, or exponential.

    For the linear animation, MLPQ displays the moving object at times $t_{\text{begin}} + i\delta$ for $i \geq 0$ until $t_{\text{begin}} + i\delta > t_{\text{end}}$. For the exponential animation, MLPQ displays the moving object at times t_{begin} and $t_{\text{begin}} + 2^i \delta$ until $t_{\text{begin}} + 2^i \delta > t_{\text{end}}$.

- **Play:** The system will automatically animate from the start time to the end time, using the animation parameters for the selected relation(s).

- **Play Back:** The system will automatically animate from the end time to the start time, using the animation parameters for the selected relation(s).

- **Next Step:** The system will show the snapshot of the next time point in the animation.

- **Previous Step:** The system will show the snapshot of the previous time point in the animation.

- **Goto Start:** The system will reset the animation back to the start time, that is, the first snapshot.

- **Goto End:** The system will set the animation to the end time, that is, the last snapshot.

The next two examples use the animation features of the MLPQ system.

Example 18.3.6   Figure 16.12 showed two instances of the animation display of the habitat areas of the California Gull bird species. The left area corresponds to 1970 and the right area to 1990.

Example 18.3.7   Suppose several bacterial colonies grow on Petri dish medium. We can approximate the shape of the colonies with polygons. The growth of each bacterial colony can be approximated by the sides of the polygons growing outward. For a good approximation we would need exponential outward growth of the sides, but in MLPQ we have only linear constraints. However, we can approximate by linear constraint input relations the (base two) logarithm of the speed of expansion of the sides of the polygon. When we call the animation operator, we specify the step size to be exponential. Therefore, the bacterial colonies appear to grow exponentially during the animation. Two snapshots are shown in Figure 18.7.

18.4 Recursive Queries

Recursive Datalog queries are entered the same way as nonrecursive queries except that the module name is changed to RECURSIVE. That activates some special evaluation routines that are applicable for recursive queries only. Guaranteeing the safety of the recursive Datalog query is the user's task.

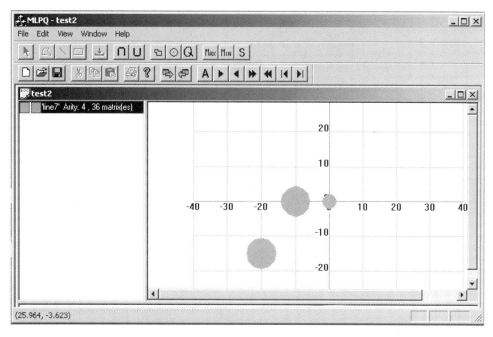

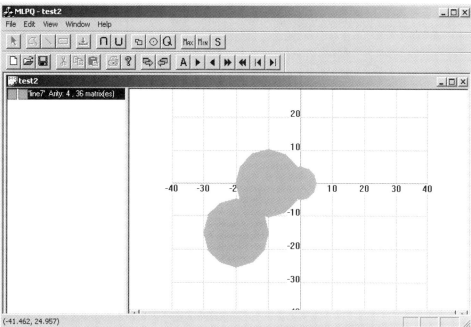

FIGURE 18.7. Bacterial colonies growing into each other.

Example 18.4.1   A housing developer wants to build three types of houses, namely, luxury, family, and town homes.

There are two options for the number of bedrooms and garages. First, the luxury, family, and town houses have 4, 3, and 1 bedroom, and 3, 3, and 1 garage, respectively. Second, the luxury, family, and town houses have 3, 2, and 1 bedroom and 2, 2, and 1 garage, respectively.

The developer also has two choices for the type of floor in the luxury homes, that is, it can be either wood or carpet, while the others can be carpet only. Whatever type of floor is chosen, the three types of homes require 7, 5, and 2 units, respectively, of the floor material.

If wood is used in the luxury homes, then they should have no fireplaces, but the other two type of houses both have 1 fireplace. If carpet is used in the luxury homes, then those can have 2 fireplaces, the family homes 1, and the town homes 0.

There are three choices for swimming pools, both the luxury and the family homes, or the luxury homes only, or none will have swimming pools, with the restriction that if the luxury homes have two fireplaces, then they must have a swimming pool.

Let *bedroom, garage, wood, carpet, fireplace* and *pool* be the constants that represent the number of fireplaces, garages, wood floor units, carpet floor units, and swimming pools available. Let constants *a*, *b*, and *c* be the estimated profit for the luxury, family, and town homes, respectively.

Query: What is the maximum profit the developer could get?

First, let relation *r* represent the set of possible choices. Let *l*, *f*, *t* represent, respectively, the number of luxury, family, and town homes built.

```
R(1,l,f,t)  :- 4l + 3f + t <= bedroom.
R(2,l,f,t)  :- 3l + 2f + t <= bedroom.

R(3,l,f,t)  :- 3l + 3f + t <= garage.     %if 1 chosen
R(4,l,f,t)  :- 2l + 2f + t <= garage      %if 2 chosen

R(5,l,f,t)  :- 7l <= wood,

               5f + 2t <= carpet.
R(6,l,f,t)  :- 7l + 5f + 2t <= carpet.

R(7,l,f,t)  :- f + t <= fireplace.        %if 5 chosen
R(8,l,f,t)  :- 2l + f <= fireplace.       %if 6 chosen

R(9,l,f,t)  :- l + f <= pool.
R(10,l,f,t) :- l <= pool.
R(11,l,f,t).                              %not ok if 8 chosen
```

In this problem we cannot collect all constraints together into one conjunction, because some constraints force a sequential choice of options. For example, intuitively, we should decide on wood floors before deciding on fireplaces. The flow of choices can be represented by relation *Next* as follows.

```
Next(0,1).       %start at 0 and choose either 1 or 2
Next(0,2).

Next(1,3).       %if 1 chosen then 3 must follow
Next(2,4).       %if 2 chosen then 4 must follow

Next(3,5).       %3 and 4 can be both followed by 5 or 6
Next(3,6).
Next(4,5).
Next(4,6).

Next(5,7).       %if 5 chosen then 7 must follow
Next(6,8).       %if 6 chosen then 8 must follow

Next(7,9).       %7 can be followed by 9, 10, or 11
Next(7,10).
Next(7,11).

Next(8,9).       %8 can be followed by 9 or 10 only
Next(8,10).

Next(9,12)       %stop at 12
Next(10,12).
Next(11,12).
```

The following MLPQ recursive Datalog program calculates the answer to the query:

```
Max_Pro(max(p)) :- Profit(12,l,f,t), -p + al + bf + ct = 0.
Profit(j,l,f,t) :- Profit(i,l,f,t), Next(i,j), R(j,l,f,t).
Profit(0,l,f,t).
```

The output will be the maximum profit that the builder could get by building the houses such that all restrictions are satisfied.

Bibliographic Notes

The MLPQ system was built at the University of Nebraska-Lincoln over several years. The first version of the MLPQ system was presented in Revesz and Li [274]. This version included SQL queries and linear programming as a basic function to implement minimum and maximum aggregate operators. The second version of the MLPQ system was presented in Kanjamala et al. [162]. This version included recursive and nonrecursive Datalog queries and a graphical user interface with most of the 2D spatial operators.

The 3D spatial operators are based on the color band display algorithms in Chapter 16. The MLPQ system animation algorithms are based on the description given in Chomicki and Revesz [63] and Chomicki et al. [60], which also contains Example 18.3.6. The animation with exponential increase of time is new. Example 18.3.7 is by Vijay Eadala. A short demo paper of the MLPQ system was presented in Revesz et al. [273].

MLPQ is only one of a growing number of linear constraint database systems that includes the CCUBE system by Brodsky et al. [44, 45] and the DEDALE system by Grumbach et al. [122]. All of these systems use several ideas for query optimization, including efficient implementation of linear constraint database versions of selection, projection, join, union, and intersection operators [41, 112, 121, 122, 266]. Chapter 12 gives more related references on implementation. The MLPQ system is available from the Web page

`http://cse.unl.edu/~revesz/MLPQ`

Exercises

1. Implement in MLPQ the query in Example 18.2.2 and display on the computer screen the area where the two planes may meet.

2. Assume that the planes in Example 18.2.2 travel with a uniform speed. Modify the input relations and queries of Example 18.2.2 accordingly. Test your query in the MLPQ system.

3. Suppose we model a red-hot iron as it cools. Initially, it has a pure red color of $(255, 0, 0)$ and its final color is black $(0, 0, 0)$. What colors will be displayed by an MLPQ animation if we go from time 0 to time 10 with one-unit time steps?

4. Express in Datalog the SQL queries in Examples 15.2.2 and 15.2.3 and implement them in MLPQ, using your own piecewise linear functions for relations *High_Temperature* and *Low_Temperature*. (**Hint:** To express the second query, first create a relation *Temperature*(t, h, l) that contains for each time t the daily high temperature h and low temperature l.)

The DISCO System

DISCO, short for *Datalog with integer set constraints*, is a constraint database system that implements Datalog with *Boolean constraints* on set variables that range over the finite and infinite sets of integers.

Although some deductive database systems allow both Datalog queries and set data types, they do not allow constraints in the input database. This is a problem because often the data that we have is incomplete data that cannot be described precisely but only by using constraints.

Section 19.1 describes the syntax of DISCO queries and gives a few examples. Section 19.2 describes the implementation of the DISCO system, including conversion to relational algebra, and naive and semi-naive evaluation. Section 19.3 describes how the DISCO system can be used and gives some performance results on the sample queries. Section 19.4 talks about extending the DISCO system to other Boolean algebras.

19.1 DISCO Queries

The input file starts with a line that contains 'begin' and ends with a line that contains 'end.' Between these lines is a set of Datalog rules and facts with Boolean constraints as defined in Chapter 4.

The domain of every variable in DISCO is an element of the Boolean algebra B_N in which the zero element is the empty set, the one element is the set of integers, the operator $\wedge$ is interpreted as set intersection, $\vee$ as set union, and $'$ as set complement.

The precedence operator $\leq$, which is defined as $x \leq y$ if and only if $x \wedge y' = 0$, is also allowed in DISCO and is interpreted as the subset-equal relation.

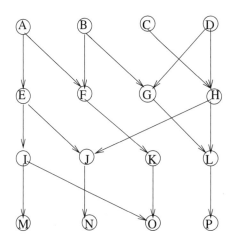

FIGURE 19.1. A packet switching network.

Because the keyboard does not contain symbols like ∧, ∨, and ≤ the DISCO system uses the symbols /\, \/, and <=. Also, DISCO uses @ for the zero element and ! = for the inequality symbol ≠.

Example 19.1.1   Consider the packet switching network in Figure 19.1. In this hierarchical network there are four layers, each with four nodes. Each node represents a router and the directed edges represent connections across which packets can be sent. A set of packets arrive at the top layer and need to be dynamically routed to given nodes of the bottom layer, with some restrictions on the routing in the middle layers.

The connections of the network imply some restrictions, which can be represented by the relation *connect*:

```
/* connections between 1st and 2nd layers */

connect({1},A,B,C,D,E,F,G,H)  :- E <= A,
                                 F <= A \/ B,
                                 G <= B \/ D,
                                 H <= C \/ D.



/* connections between 2nd and 3rd layers */

connect({2},E,F,G,H,I,J,K,L)  :- I <= E,
                                 J <= E \/ H,
                                 K <= F,
                                 L <= G \/ H.
```

```
/* connections between 3rd and 4th layers */

connect({3},I,J,K,L,M,N,O,P) :- M <= I,
                                 N <= J,
                                 O <= I \/ K,
                                 P <= L.
```

Now suppose that some packets are to be sent from the nodes in the top layer to the nodes in the bottom layer. For example, we may have the following set of packets to be routed from and to:

```
from(A,B,C,D) :- A == {1,2,3},
                 B == {4,5},
                 C == {6,7},
                 D == {8,9}.

to(M,N,O,P) :- M == {1},
               N == {2,6,8},
               O == {3,4},
               P == {5,7,9}.
```

To count the number of layers in the network, we define the *next* relation with the following facts:

```
next({1},{2}).
next({2},{3}).
next({3},{4}).
```

The following DISCO query finds to where each packet may be sent:

```
path({1},A,B,C,D) :- from(A,B,C,D).

path(Z,V,W,X,Y) :- path(Z1,Q,R,S,T),
                   connect(Z1,Q,R,S,T,V,W,X,Y),
                   next(Z1,Z).
```

Example 19.1.2   The following query finds which packets should be sent to which nodes in each layer. The query defines the set of packets routed to a layer to be such that each node receives a subset of the packets that can be sent to that layer (hence the *path* relation is used) with the additional constraint that each packet is sent only to one node in each layer, and in particular only the requested packets are to be sent to the bottom layer.

```
route({4},M,N,O,P) :- path({4},M,N,O,P),
                      to(M,N,O,P).
```

```
route(Z,Q,R,S,T) :- path(Z,Q,R,S,T),
                    connect(Z,Q,R,S,T,V,W,X,Y),
                    route(Z1,V,W,X,Y),
                    next(Z,Z1),
                    Q /\ R == @,
                    Q /\ S == @,
                    Q /\ T == @,
                    R /\ S == @,
                    R /\ T == @,
                    S /\ T == @.
```

Example 19.1.3   Now suppose that instead of the requirement that each packet be sent to only one successor, we have the rule that each packet is broadcast, that is, sent to all successors. Then the connections can be represented as follows:

```
/* broadcast connections between 1st and 2nd layers */

connect({1},A,B,C,D,E,F,G,H) :- A <= E, A <= F,
                                B <= F, B <= G,
                                C <= H,
                                D <= G, D <= H.

/* connections between 2nd and 3rd layers */

connect({2},E,F,G,H,I,J,K,L) :- E <= I, E <= J,
                                F <= K,
                                G <= L,
                                H <= J, H <= L.

/* connections between 3rd and 4th layers */

connect({3},I,J,K,L,M,N,O,P) :- I <= M, I <= O,
                                J <= N,
                                K <= O,
                                L <= P.
```

Suppose we know that in the top layer some packet occurs in both nodes B and C:

```
from(A,B,C,D) :- B /\ C != @.
```

What can be said about the nodes in the bottom layer? The same DISCO query for *path* as in Example 19.1.1 can be used.

19.2   Implementation

Section 12.2.4 described a basic Datalog evaluation algorithm. In this section we review some of the concepts and refine them for the case of DISCO queries. In particular, Section 19.2.1 describes the conversion from DISCO Datalog rules to relational algebra formulas, and Section 19.2.2 describes a *naive* and *semi-naive* evaluation of DISCO Datalog queries.

19.2.1   Converting Datalog Rules to Relational Algebra Formulas

DISCO converts each Datalog rule into a relational algebra representation. In the internal relational algebra the following operators are used: join ($\bowtie$), project (π), union ($\cup$), and select (σ). In DISCO the normal cross-product ($\times$) operator is treated as a special case of join. Also, the join and union operators can have more than two arguments.

There are two slightly different functions used for converting Datalog rules to relational algebra rules:

- *EVAL function*—The translation of Datalog to relational algebra is standard, except for the slightly different syntax of the selection operations. Basically, each Datalog rule body is translated as a relational algebra expression that is a join of the relations occurring in the body followed by a sequence of selections, one for each constraint in the body, followed by a projection to the variables that occur in the rule head. If there are several rules for the same relation, then the relational algebra formulas for the individual rules are connected with a union operator.

- *EVAL_INCR function*—This function is similar to the *EVAL* function. The difference is that before conversion each rule is copied as many times as the number of defined relation symbols in its body. In the ith copy a Δ symbol is put before the ith defined relation.

Example 19.2.1   The query in Example 19.1.1 is changed by *EVAL_INCR* into:

```
path({1},A,B,C,D)  :- from(A,B,C,D).

path(Z,V,W,X,Y)  :- Δpath(Z1,Q,R,S,T),
                    connect(Z1,Q,R,S,T,V,W,X,Y),
                    next(Z1,Z).
```

Next this will be translated to relational algebra formulas as follows. The first rule is translated to:

$$\pi_{Z,A,B,C,D}\ (\sigma_{Z=\{1\}}\ From(A, B, C, D) \bowtie Z(Z)$$

where $Z(Z)$ is the relation that contains just the single variable Z without any constraints. The second rule is translated to:

$$\pi_{Z,V,W,X,Y}(\Delta Path\,(Z1,\,Q,\,R,\,S,\,T)$$
$$\bowtie Connect\,(Z1,\,Q,\,R,\,S,\,T,\,V,\,W,\,X,\,Y)$$
$$\bowtie Next\,(Z1,\,Z))$$

The union of the first two expressions will be a relational algebra expression for *Path*.

19.2.2 Naive and Semi-Naive Evaluation Methods

DISCO uses the naive and semi-naive methods for evaluating queries. The naive method repeatedly evaluates the relational algebra formulas that are obtained using the *EVAL* function until the size of the output relations keeps growing. The pseudo code of the naive method is the following:

Naive Method

```
for  := 1 to m do
        P_i := ∅
repeat
        for i:= 1 to m do
                Q_i := P_i
        for i:= 1 to m do
                P_i := EVAL(i, Q_1, ..., Q_m)
until  P_i = Q_i for all i ( 1 ≤ i ≤ m)
```

---

where P_i is the tuples of the ith relation and Q_i is the tuples of the ith relation in the previous step. At the beginning we erase all tuples. Then we repeat the steps of the algorithm until the results of the last two steps are identical. During one step we store the tuples first ($Q_i := P_i$), then calculate the new tuples using the tuples calculated in the previous steps. The calculation is done by the *EVAL* function. In the function, i denotes the index of the current relation and $Q_1, \ldots, Q_m$ denote the tuples of the relations, which can be used by *EVAL*.

Semi-Naive Method

The main disadvantage of the naive method is that it recalculates the same tuples in every iteration. In the previous example during the first step the algorithm calculates the parents; during the second step the parents and the grandparents; during the third and fourth steps the parents, grandparents, and great-grandparents. Therefore the algorithm calculated the parents four times. If the number of the steps is greater—and in a real application it is several times greater—then this disadvantage is also greater. The main idea of the semi-naive method is to omit these recalculations.

If during the calculation we use only old tuples (tuples that were calculated before the previous step), then we only recalculate some older tuples. Therefore if we want to calculate new tuples we should use at least one new tuple that was calculated during the previous step.

Naturally the first step is an exception, because there are no new tuples before the first step; hence the first steps of the semi-naive and naive methods are identical.

The pseudo code of the semi-naive evaluation is the following:

Semi-Naive Method

```
for  := 1 to m do
        ΔPᵢ := EVAL(pᵢ, ∅, ..., ∅)
        Pᵢ := ΔPᵢ
repeat
        for i:= 1 to m do
            ΔQᵢ := ΔPᵢ
        for i:= 1 to m do
        begin
            ΔPᵢ := EVAL_INCR(i, P₁, ..., Pₘ, ΔQ₁, ..., ΔQₘ)
            ΔPᵢ := ΔPᵢ - Pᵢ
        end
        for i:=1 to m do
            Pᵢ := Pᵢ ∪ ΔPᵢ
until ΔPᵢ = ∅ for all i ( 1 ≤ i ≤ m)
```

---

where P_i denotes the tuples of the ith relation, ΔP_i the new tuples in the current relation, and ΔQ_i the new tuples in the previous iteration of the relations. At the first iteration we use the *EVAL* function to calculate the tuples. Then we iterate the algorithm until there are no new tuples derived. In each iteration we first store the new tuples ($\Delta Q_i = \Delta P_i$) and then calculate the new tuples using the *EVAL_INCR* function. After this we check whether the new tuples are really new tuples ($\Delta P_i = \Delta P_i - P_i$). At the end of the iteration we should update the value of P_i ($P_i = P_i + \Delta P_i$). The *EVAL_INCR* function has more parameters than the *EVAL* function, because the *EVAL_INCR* function needs not only all the tuples, but the new tuples as well.

Example 19.2.2   Let's see how Example 19.2.1 is evaluated using DISCO. In the first iteration the algebra expression for the first rule is the only one that will give a tuple:

```
path({1},A,B,C,D)  :- A == {1,2,3},
                      B == {4,5},
                      C == {6,7},
                      D == {8,9}.
```

In the second iteration, the algebra expression for the second rule will give us the tuple, where we use some renamings for greater readability:

```
/* E,F,G,H are renamings for V,W,X,Y */

path({2},E,F,G,H)  :- E <= {1,2,3},
                      F <= {1,2,3,4,5},
                      G <= {4,5,8,9},
                      H <= {6,7,8,9}.
```

Similarly, in the third and fourth iterations, we obtain:

```
/* I,J,K,L are renamings for V,W,X,Y */

path({3},I,J,K,L)  :- I <= {1,2,3},
                      J <= {1,2,3,6,7,8,9},
                      K <= {1,2,3,4,5},
                      L <= {4,5,6,7,8,9}.
```

```
/* M,N,O,P are renamings for V,W,X,Y */

path({4},M,N,O,P)  :- M <= {1,2,3},
                      N <= {1,2,3,6,7,8,9},
                      O <= {1,2,3,4,5},
                      P <= {4,5,6,7,8,9}.
```

For constraint databases and queries that contain only subset or equal to and monotone inequality constraints, DISCO implements the projection operator based on part (2) of the existential quantifier elimination method in Theorem 9.4.5.

Example 19.2.3 It is easy to check that the constraint database in Example 19.1.3 contains only set-order and monotone inequality constraints. When the same *path* query as in Example 19.1.1 is run on this input database, DISCO finds the following tuples:

```
path({1},A,B,C,D)  :- B /\ C != @.
```

```
/* E,F,G,H are renamings for V,W,X,Y */
```

```
path({2},E,F,G,H)  :- F /\ G != @,
                      F /\ H != @,
                      G /\ H != @.



/* I,J,K,L are renamings for V,W,X,Y */

path({3},I,J,K,L)  :- J /\ K != @,
                      J /\ L != @,
                      K /\ L != @.



/* M,N,O,P are renamings for V,W,X,Y */

path({4},M,N,O,P)  :- N /\ O != @,
                      N /\ P != @,
                      O /\ P != @.
```

This is a correct answer because these are the only conclusions that can be drawn from the input fact that B /\ C != @ because O and P are reachable from B, and N and P are reachable from C, and as far as we know the other nodes in the top layer may be empty.

Interactive Semi-Naive Method

The interactive semi-naive evaluation method is like the semi-naive evaluation method except that after each iteration, the user can investigate the new tuples and decide whether to add them to the constraint database. The following is an example of the interactive semi-naive evaluation.

Example 19.2.4   Consider the evaluation of the *route* relation in Example 19.1.2 after the *path* relation of Example 19.1.1 is calculated and added to the constraint database. In interactive mode the first iteration would yield:

```
> route({4},M,N,O,P)  :- M == {1},
                         N == {2,6,8},
                         O == {3,4},
                         P == {5,7,9}.
> accept tuple (Y/N)?
```

Suppose the tuple is accepted. Then the next iteration will give (here variables Q, R, S, T mean I, J, K, L):

```
> route({3},Q,R,S,T)  :- {1} <= Q, Q <= {1,3},
                         {2,6,8} <= R, R <= {2,3,6,8},
```

```
                        {4} <= S, S <= {3,4},
                        T == {5,7,9},
                        Q /\ R = @, Q /\ S = @, R /\ S = @.
```

This tuple shows that while most of the packets have a determined place, packets 3 can be sent to three different places. Suppose the user decides to send packet 3 to *I* by entering:

```
> accept tuple (Y/N)? N
> replace tuple (Y/N)? Y
> replace tuple with:

  route({3},Q,R,S,T)  :- Q == {1,3},
                         R == {2,6,8},
                         S == {4},
                         T == {5,7,9}.
```

Now the interactive evaluation continues, and the following tuple (where variables *Q, R, S, T* mean *E, F, G, H*) is returned:

```
> route({2},Q,R,S,T)  :- Q == {1,2,3},
                         R == {3,4},
                         {5} <= S, S <= {5,9},
                         {6,7,8} <= T, T <= {6,7,8,9},
                         S /\ T = @.
```

There is still some ambiguity about the place of packet 9. The user may choose to send it to *G* by typing:

```
> accept tuple (Y/N)? N
> replace tuple (Y/N)? Y
> replace tuple with:

  route({2},Q,R,S,T)  :- Q == {1,2,3},
                         R == {3,4},
                         S == {5,9},
                         T == {6,7,8}.
```

Finally, the fourth iteration will return the final tuple, where variables *Q, R, S, T* mean *A, B, C, D*, which is accepted:

```
> route({1},Q,R,S,T)  :- Q == {1,2,3},
                         R == {4,5},
                         S == {6,7},
                         T == {8,9}.
> accept tuple (Y/N)? Y
```

The *route* relation calculated with the interactive semi-naive evaluation shows which packages should be sent to which node in each layer.

Although it is not implemented in DISCO, we remark that the interactive method of evaluation can be replaced by a method where the choices are made by some program. For example, a C program may interact with the DISCO system and always make the following choices for each $route(Z, Q, R, S, T)$ tuple:

$$Z = Z$$
$$Q = Q_{max}$$
$$R = R_{max} - Q_{max}$$
$$S = S_{max} - Q_{max} - R_{max}$$
$$T = T_{max} - Q_{max} - R_{max} - S_{max}$$

where subscripts min and max denote the lower and upper bounds of the variable.

19.3 Using the DISCO System

The DISCO system has been implemented in the Java programming language. Hence it can be run on both UNIX and Windows. The program is started by typing in the executable DISCO file name at the operating system prompt. After starting the program a new prompt will appear and the system waits for a user command. After the user enters the command, the system waits for the next command. This process is finished if the user exits from the system.

The most important commands provided in the DISCO system are the following:

- `consult 'filename'`—This command loads an the input file "filename" that should be in the format described in Section 19.1.

- `display ['R'] [onto 'filename']`—When a relation name "R" is given DISCO prints out the rules of the relation. If no "R" is given, then DISCO prints out the names and arities of all the relations. If a file name is specified, then the formula will be printed out to the file, otherwise it will be printed out to the screen.

- `displaydf [onto 'filename']`—This command prints out all the derived facts in the database to the screen or the specified file.

- `memory`—This command displays the total and free memory used by the system.

- `clear`—This command erases all the relations and rules from the database.

- $R(E_1, \ldots, E_n)$?—In this command each E_i can be either a variable or a set of constants. Variables need not be distinct. DISCO will return any derived fact of the relation "R" that can match the input.

- bye—This command exits the program.

The DISCO system also provides several switches that control the evaluation of the system. These on-off switches include time, to display the time used during the evaluation; trace, to display the inner representation of rules; optimize, to use the relational algebra optimization routines; seminaive, to use semi-naive instead of naive evaluation; and interactive, to use interactive (semi)-naive evaluation. To set a switch, one has to type any of the switch names at the command mode switchname on or switchname off. The default for time, trace, and interactive is off and for optimize and seminaive is on.

19.3.1 Experimental Results

We tested the running times of the *path* query in Example 19.1.1, the *route* query in Example 19.1.2, and the *path* query again in Example 19.1.3 with the broadcast network connections. We ran all three queries in non-interactive mode. We measured the results on a Pentium II 267 MHz computer running Windows. The running times are displayed in Figure 19.2, measured in real seconds, not CPU seconds.

19.4 Extensibility of the DISCO System

Although the DISCO system implements a specific Boolean algebra, that is, the Boolean algebra of sets of integers, it is possible to extend the system to deal with other Boolean algebras. Implementing new Boolean algebras enables us to express many more interesting queries.

In changing to a new Boolean algebra, we need to replace only a few of the basic DISCO routines. First, we need to redefine the operators $\wedge$, $\vee$, and $'$. We

Problem	Naive		Semi-Naive	
	Without optimization	With optimization	Without optimization	With optimization
Path	3.746	1.472	2.383	1.261
Broadcast	1.392	0.921	1.131	0.921
Route	35.872	17.966	40.819	18.036

FIGURE 19.2. Test results (Pentium II 267 MHz).

also have to change some of the data storage structures and modify the naive and semi-naive evaluation methods with a new subsumption test. Some of these require some work, but in principle much of the software written for the DISCO system could be reused.

Bibliographic Notes

The DISCO system was developed over several years at the University of Nebraska. The first version of the system implemented only *set-order* and positive *gap-order* constraints and was presented in Byon and Revesz [48]. The quantifier elimination technique of this system was described in Srivastava et al. [293], and the naive evaluation of Datalog queries was considered in Revesz [258, 267]. More details of the evaluation and example queries were given in [262]. This first version was also used to solve some genome assembly problems (see Chapter 22) in Revesz [263]. A shortened earlier version of this chapter appears in Kuper et al. [194].

The second version of DISCO, which we described in this chapter, added to set-order constraints monotone Boolean inequality constraints and Boolean equality constraints over sets of integers [277]. However, general Boolean equality and inequality constraints cannot be used together. For the projection operator two quantifier elimination methods are implemented for the two different additions to set-order constraints. If equality and inequality constraints are found together in a formula before quantifier elimination, then an error message is generated.

The quantifier elimination method for Boolean equality constraints is due to G. Boole, while the one for set-order and monotone Boolean inequality constraints is described in Revesz [265]. More on methods for quantifier elimination in the case of Boolean equality and inequality constraints can be found in Helm et al. [142] and Marriott and Odersky [204].

Examples 19.1.1, 19.1.2, and 19.1.3 are new. The discussion about the relational algebra identities and the naive and semi-naive evaluation are adopted with necessary modifications to include constraints from Ullman [310].

Conjuncto by Gervet [108] is a constraint logic programming system that uses set constraints. The evaluation method is different and its termination is not guaranteed in general for Conjuncto queries.

Exercises

1. Implement in DISCO the street reachability problem in Example 4.4.1.
2. Implement in DISCO the Hamiltonian cycle problem in Example 4.2.1.
3. Implement in DISCO the propositional satisfiability problem in Exercise 4.5.
4. Write a DISCO query that solves the SEND + MORE = MONEY puzzle in Example 7.3.4.

The PReSTO System

PReSTO, short for *parametric rectangle spatiotemporal objects*, is a periodic parametric rectangles spatiotemporal database system. The PReSTO system allows relational algebra queries and several other iconic queries.

Section 20.1 describes the PReSTO input files, including the representation of input relations and queries. Section 20.2 describes the graphical user interface of the PReSTO system and all the iconic queries that are available in PReSTO. Section 20.3 discusses some implementation aspects of the PReSTO system.

20.1 PReSTO Input Files

In the PReSTO system the module name STDB must be used, that is, PReSTO input files have the following structure:

```
begin %STDB%
    r₁
    r₂
    ⋮
    rₙ
end %STDB%
```

where each r_i is a rule or a 2-dimensional periodic parametric rectangle.

Note: The module name STDB, which was not used in the MLPQ system, is important. MLPQ and PReSTO are subparts of a big database system. If the module name STDB is used, then the system expects PReSTO input files and uses

PReSTO query evaluation functions, and if one of the module names MLPQ, RE-CURSIVE, or GIS is specified, then the system expects MLPQ input files and uses the appropriate MLPQ evaluation functions. In this way, the MLPQ and PReSTO systems can share several primitive functions. In addition, this makes data interoperability between the two systems easier.

PReSTO allows each 2-dimensional periodic parametric rectangle of the form:

$$R = (i, \ [a_1t + b_1, \ c_1t + d_1], \ [a_2t + b_2, \ c_2t + d_2], \ [\mathit{from}, \ \mathit{to}]_{m,n})$$

where $i, a_1, b_1, c_1, d_1, a_2, b_2, c_2, d_2, \mathit{from}, \mathit{to}, m$, and n are constants as described in Chapter 13 to be augmented with regular relational attributes $z_1, \ldots, z_k$. The combined tuple can be expressed in a PReSTO input file with the following syntax:

$$
\begin{aligned}
R(z_1, \ldots, z_k) :&- id = i, \\
& x1 - a_1t = b_1, \\
& x2 - c_1t = d_1, \\
& y1 - a_2t = b_2, \\
& y2 - c_2t = d_2, \\
& t >= \mathit{from}, \\
& t <= \mathit{to}, \\
& p = m, \\
& s = n, \\
& z_1 = e_1, \\
& \vdots \\
& z_k = e_k.
\end{aligned}
$$

where the period p and the end time s are both -1 for nonperiodic parametric rectangles. Note that the attributes id, $x1$, $y1$, $x2$, $y2$, t, p, and s are *default attributes* and must always occur in a PReSTO relation. The default attributes are not listed all the time in the argument list of PReSTO relations, but they are assumed to belong there. This convention saves much unnecessary typing. Each z_i can be any variable string. The nondefault attributes must always be listed in the argument list of PReSTO relations. There may also be no nondefault attributes. In that case the argument list is empty.

Example 20.1.1   Suppose that the parametric rectangles

$$\mathit{Ship} = (1, \ [t + 20, \ t + 30], \ [20, \ 30], \ [0, \ 25])$$

and

$$\mathit{Torpedo} = (1, \ [45, \ 48], \ [-t + 45, \ -t + 51], \ [0, \ 25])$$

represent a ship and a torpedo that is fired toward the ship. These can be represented in PReSTO as follows:

```
Ship()  :-       i=1,
                 x1 - t = 20,
                 x2 - t = 30,
                 y1 = 20,
                 y2 = 30,
                 t >= 0,
                 t <= 25,
                 p = -1,
                 s = -1.


Torpedo()  :-    i=1,
                 x1 = 45,
                 x2 = 48,
                 y1 + t = 45,
                 y2 + t = 51,
                 t >= 0,
                 t <= 25,
                 p = -1,
                 s = -1.
```

The next example uses a default attribute.

Example 20.1.2   In Example 13.4.2, the $Clouds(X, Y, T, humidity)$ relation used $humidity$ as a nondefault attribute. The following could be a valid parametric rectangle of this relation in PReSTO:

```
Clouds(h)  :- i=1,
                 x1 - t = 105,
                 x2 - t = 111,
                 y1 - 0.5t = 200,
                 y2 - 0.6t = 205,
                 t >= 0,
                 t <= 300,
                 p = -1,
                 s = -1,
                 h = 90.


Clouds(h)  :- i=1,
                 x1 - t = 230,
                 x2 - t = 420,
                 y1 - 2t = 10,
```

$$y2 - 3t = 50,$$
$$t >= 100,$$
$$t <= 500,$$
$$p = -1,$$
$$s = -1,$$
$$h = 80.$$

This would mean that the humidity is always 90, respectively 80, percent in the area of the 2-dimensional parametric rectangle defined by the default attributes in the first and second tuples.

In the input file queries can also be defined. Currently PReSTO implements a subset of relational algebra queries that are written in a rule style. The projection operation is allowed on any set of the nondefault attributes. The syntax of the projection operation is a Datalog rule, where the attributes in the defined relation list only the projected regular attributes.

Example 20.1.3   We can find the area of the *Clouds*(*X*, *Y*, *T*, *humidity*) relation by the following PReSTO query:

```
Clouds_Area() :- Clouds(h).
```

The selection operation is allowed on the regular attributes and the logical level attributes x, y, and t with the restrictions discussed in Section 13.4.2. The selection operation is indicated by a $ symbol followed by a parenthesized list of conditions.

Example 20.1.4   We can find the cloud areas with a humidity above 75 percent between times 0 and 200 by the following PReSTO query:

```
Clouds(h) :- $(h >= 75, t >= 0, t <= 200) Clouds(h).
```

The intersection operation has the symbol * in PReSTO input files. The operand relations must both be 2-dimensional parametric rectangles.

Example 20.1.5   Let us find using the relations in Example 20.1.1 whether the torpedo hits the ship:

```
Hit() :- Ship() * Torpedo().
```

20.2   The PReSTO Graphical User Interface

When one starts the PReSTO system a window is created. In the top of the window there is a tool bar with several buttons, as shown in Figure 18.2. The second and third lower-left buttons are used to open and store a file. From the tool bar the following iconic operators are available in PReSTO: the iconic operators **Zoom In**, **Zoom Out**, **Intersection**, **Union**, **Area**, and all the iconic operators related to **Animation**. These work as in the MLPQ system.

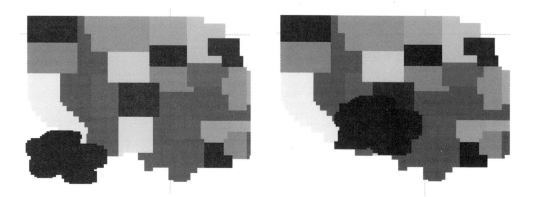

FIGURE 20.1. Clouds at $t = 25$ (left) and $t = 182$ (right).

Example 20.2.1   Let *Clouds* be a set of moving and changing cloud areas, and for each of the continental United States let there be a separate relation, that is, *California, Oregon, Washington*, etc. In PReSTO we can use the **Animation** icon to display the movement of the clouds over the states. First we select all the states by clicking on them. Then we select *Clouds* and press the **Animate** icon. Figure 20.1 shows two snapshots of the PReSTO animation.

Difference: Select two relations (by clicking on them) and press the **Difference** button. The PReSTO system returns a parametric rectangles relation that is equivalent to the relation clicked first minus the relation clicked second.

Complement: Select one relation (by clicking on it) and press the **Complement** button. The PReSTO system returns a parametric rectangles relation that is equivalent to the complement of the selected relation.

Collide: Select two nonperiodic relations (by clicking on them) and press the **Collide** button. The two relations need to have an extra attibute called mass, which has to follow t in the order of the attributes. The PReSTO system returns a parametric rectangles relation that expresses the motion of the objects before and after collision as described in Section 13.4.3.

Block: Select two nonperiodic relations (by clicking on them) and press the **Block** button. A dialog box pops up that asks for a time instance t_k the name of the relation to be created. The PReSTO Block operator returns the points of the first relation at time instance t_k that are not blocked by the second relation at any time before t_k.

Note that the PReSTO Block operator is a single time instant version of the block operator described in Section 13.4.3, which returns for each time t the points of the first relation that are not blocked by the second relation at any time before t.

In other words, if R_1 and R_2 are parametric rectangles relations and t_k is any time instance, then the PReSTO block operator, denoted by $Block(R_1, R_2, t_k)$, is the instantiation at t_k of the set of moving points in R_2 that did not intersect with R_1 any time before or at t_k. More precisely, $Block(R_1, R_2, t_k)$ returns the set of points:

$$\{ ((X(t_k), Y(t_k)) : \exists ([X^[, X^]], [Y^[, Y^]], I) \in R_2, \quad \alpha, \beta \in [0, 1],$$
$$X = \alpha(X^[- X^]) + X^],$$
$$Y = \beta(Y^[- Y^]) + Y^],$$
$$\not\exists\, t' \in I, \ t' \le t_k, \ (X(t'), Y(t'), t') \in sem(R_1)\}$$

In the preceding, X and Y are functions of time that always give the coordinates of the point that is at α and β fractions in the middle of the parametric rectangle. The point instance of these functions at time t_k is returned if its travel is not stopped by any point in R_1 before time t_k.

Example 20.2.2   Suppose that relation *Tornado* represents the movement of a tornado and relation *Mountain* represents the location of a tall mountain range that can stop the tornado.

Query: What is the trajectory of the tornado at time $t = 20$?

This can be answered by clicking on *Tornado* and then *Mountain*. A dialog box pops up and asks for a time instance. We enter **20** and the name of the new relation. The result of the query, evaluated in the PReSTO system, is shown in

FIGURE 20.2. Trajectory of a tornado.

Figure 20.2 superimposed on the map of the continental United States, which covers the *Mountain* relation.

We give further examples of the use of PReSTO and the block operator in Chapter 23.

20.3   Implementation

The implementation of PReSTO in general follows the database system architecture described in Section 18.1. In this section we describe some details related to the PReSTO implementation.

PReSTO computes an approximate result of a block operation by the following recursive algorithm. The algorithm assumes a constant threshold value *max_depth* to guarantee the termination of the recursion.

Block(R_1, R_2, t_k)
input: R_1 and R_2 parametric rectangles relations.
output: An approximate value of $Block(R_1, R_2, t_k)$.
local var d is the current depth of recursion.

   for   each tuple $r_2 \in R_2$ **do**
      $R' = R' \cup Blockrect(R_1, r_2, t_k, 0)$
   return R'

Blockrect (R_1, r_2, t_k, d)
   if $\{r_2\}$ ∩ $R_1 = \emptyset$ **then return** $\{r_2\}$ at t_k
   else if at t_k $\{r_2\} \subseteq R_1$ **then return** $\emptyset$.
   else if $d < max\_depth$ **then**
      partition r_2 into quadrants r_{21}, r_{22}, r_{23}, r_{24}
      return $\bigcup_{1 \leq i \leq 4}$ $Blockrect(R_1, r_{2i}, t_k, d+1)$

Function *Block* calls for each parametric rectangle of R_2 the auxiliary function *Blockrect*. Function *Blockrect* checks tow cases when no further recursion is needed. In the first case, when r_2 and R_1 never intersect, *Blockrect* returns the value of r_2 with variable t instantiated with t_k because none of the points in r_2 are blocked by R_1. In the second case, when at time t_k the parametric rectangle is within R_1 completely, then *Blockrect* returns the empty set because all of the points in r_2 are blocked by R_1. Quite frequently one of the two cases will occur. However, if neither case occurs, then the algorithm breaks the parametric rectangle r_2 into four quadrants and calls *Blockrect* recursively. The union of the returned values will be passed back to the original function call. The depth of the recursion and the precision of the approximation are controlled by the value of *max_depth*.

The following are some results concerning the evaluation of relational algebra queries.

Lemma 20.3.1   Given n different m-degree polynomial functions of time, $f_1(t), \ldots, f_n(t)$, we can find (precisely for $m < 5$, and approximately from $m \geq 5$) a partition of the time dimension into at most $N = O(mn^2)$ intervals $(-\infty, t_1), [t_1, t_2), \ldots, [t_{N-1}, \infty)$ such that within each interval for each time instance the order of the functions is the same.

Proof. The curves that correspond to distinct functions f_j and f_k intersect at most twice because the equation $f_j(t) = f_k(t)$ has at most m roots. Therefore, there are at most $m \times n(n-1)/2$ crossings between the n curves. Let $t_1, \ldots, t_{N-1}$ be the time instances corresponding to the crossings sorted in increasing order. These time instances can be found precisely for $m < 5$ and approximately to any desired precision for larger m. Let $t_0 = -\infty$ and $t_N = \infty$.

Then the corresponding curves of the n functions can intersect in none of the $N \leq (m/2)(n^2 - n) = O(mn^2)$ open intervals (t_{i-1}, t_i) where $1 \leq i \leq N$. We also prove by contradiction that within these N intervals for each time instance the order of the functions is the same. Suppose that this claim is false. Then there must exist within some interval (t_{i-1}, t_i) two different time instances t', t'' such that $f_j(t') < f_k(t')$ and $f_j(t'') \geq f_k(t'')$ for some $1 \leq j, k \leq n$. Then there must be a time instance t''' such that $f_j(t''') = f_k(t''')$, which is a contradiction to the fact that there are no intersections within any interval. This proves the lemma. ■

Let f_1 and f_2 be two functions of time. We say "$f_1 << f_2$" in $[t1, t2]$ if for any time $t \in [t_1, t_2]$, $f_1(t) \leq f_2(t)$.

In the following, we will assume that if the degree $m > 5$, then we are talking about only approximate query evaluation as in the previous lemma.

Lemma 20.3.2   The intersection of two d-dimensional m-degree nonperiodic parametric rectangles relations is a parametric rectangles relation that can be evaluated in PTIME in the size of the relations.

Proof. In this proof, we assume for simplicity that tuples have only spatial and temporal attributes. Let

$$R1 = ([X_{1,1}^{[}, X_{1,1}^{]}], \ldots, [X_{1,d}^{[}, X_{1,d}^{]}], from1, to1)$$

and

$$R2 = ([X_{2,1}^{[}, X_{2,1}^{]}], \ldots, [X_{2,d}^{[}, X_{2,d}^{]}], from2, to2)$$

be two d-dimensional m-degree nonperiodic parametric rectangles. Let

$$from = \max(from1, from2) \quad \text{and} \quad to = \min(to1, to2)$$

For each spatial dimension x_i, by Lemma 20.3.1, there are $O(m) = O(1)$ crossings between bound functions of $R1$ and $R2$. Let S_i be the set of time instances that are between $from$ and to and that correspond to the crossings. This can be computed in $O(1)$ time.

Let $S = \bigcup_{i=1}^{d} S_i$. Let $t_1, \ldots, t_{N-1}$ be the time instances in S sorted in ascending order, and let $t_0 = from$ and $t_N = to$. We can partition the time dimension into $N = O(d)$ intervals using S. Then by Lemma 20.3.1, within each interval $(t_{j-1}, t_j]$ for any time instance the order of the functions of the lower and upper bounds of $R1$ and $R2$ in any dimension is the same. For each time interval $(t_{j-1}, t_j]$, let

$$X_i^[= \begin{cases} X_{1,i}^[& \text{if } X_{2,i}^[<< X_{1,i}^[\text{ in } [t_{j-1},\ t_j] \\ X_{2,i}^[& \text{otherwise} \end{cases}$$

$$X_i^] = \begin{cases} X_{1,i}^] & \text{if } X_{1,i}^] << X_{2,i}^] \text{ in } [t_{j-1},\ t_j] \\ X_{2,i}^[& \text{otherwise} \end{cases}$$

Then the intersection of $R1$ and $R2$ over $(t_{j-1}, t_j]$ is:

$$r_j' = \begin{cases} ([X_1^[, X_1^]], \ldots, [X_d^[, X_d^]], [t_{j-1}, t_j]) & \text{if } \forall i \ X_i^[<< X_i^] \text{ in } [t_{j-1}, t_j] \\ \emptyset \text{ otherwise} \end{cases}$$

The intersection of $R1$ and $R2$ is:

$$R1 \cap R2 = \bigcup_{j=1}^{N} r_j'$$

Because S can be computed and sorted in $O(d + d \log d) = O(d \log d)$ time and computing each r_j' takes $O(d)$ time, thus $r1 \cap r2$ can be computed in $O(d \log(d)) + O(N \cdot d) = O(d^2)$ time. Let $R1$ and $R2$ be two parametric rectangle relations with at most n parametric rectangles in each relation, then:

$$R1 \cap R2 = \bigcup_{r1 \in R1,\ r2 \in R2} (r1 \cap r2)$$

which can be computed in $O(d^2 n^2)$. ■

The union operator is easy to implement because it simply takes the set union of the parametric rectangles in the input relations. The project and selection operators of Section 20.1 are also easy to implement.

Lemma 20.3.3 The complement of a relation R of d-dimensional m-degree nonperiodic parametric rectangles can be evaluated in PTIME in the size of the relation. ■

The difference operator can be expressed using the intersection and complement operators; hence it can also be evaluated. Recall that the definition of cross-product requires that the operand relations have no common attributes. Because each parametric rectangle relation is assumed to contain a T attribute, the cross-product does not apply as an operator. However, the join operator can be easily implemented, by taking for each of the common attributes, including T, the maximum of the lower bounds as the new lower bound and the minimum of the upper bounds as the new upper bound. Therefore, all the basic relational algebra operators that are applicable to parametric rectangles relations can be implemented.

Further, if we restrict the set of period values that may occur in the input database and queries to a fixed finite set, then the operators can also be evaluated in PTIME in the case of periodic parametric rectangles. Therefore, we have the following.

Theorem 20.3.1 For any fixed d dimension, any relational algebra expression (with rename, project, select, union, intersect, difference, complement, and join operators) can be evaluated in PTIME in the size of the input m-degree periodic parametric rectangle database. ∎

In fact, we can note that any fixed database input has only a finite number of different constants. Using this finite number of constants, one can define only a finite number of different parametric rectangles. Therefore, it is also possible to prove the following.

Theorem 20.3.2 For any fixed d dimension, any Datalog query can be evaluated in closed form. ∎

Bibliographic Notes

The PReSTO system was developed at the University of Nebraska-Lincoln. Cai et al. [50] give a short description of the PReSTO system, and Revesz and Cai [271] give more details in the case of periodic parametric rectangles.

The PTIME evaluation of relational algebra operators for nonperiodic parametric rectangles is from Cai et al. [50]. Theorem 20.3.1 on the PTIME evaluation of periodic parametric rectangles is from Revesz and Cai [271, 272]. Further references and comparisons with other systems can be found in Cai [49] and the bibliographic notes of Chapters 13 and 18. The PReSTO system is available from the Web page, http://cse.unl.edu/~revesz/MLPQ.

Exercises

1. Using the PReSTO system and input relations in Example 20.1.1, evaluate the query in Example 20.1.5.

2. Using the PReSTO system do the following:

   (a) Define a parametric rectangles relation *Clouds*(X, Y, T, h) as in Example 20.1.2 but with more tuples.

   (b) Define a parametric rectangles relation *Temperature*(X, Y, T, f) with moving warm and cold regions.

(c) Write a query that finds those areas that are colder than 32 degrees Fahrenheit.

(d) Write a query that finds the areas where it is likely to snow. Assume that it is likely to snow when a cloud area with 80 percent or greater humidity meets an area colder than 32 degrees Fahrenheit.

3. Using the PReSTO system do the following:

(a) Define relations *Weather*($X, Y, T, climate$), which describes the climatic conditions of regions, and *Soil*($X, Y, T, quality$), which describes the type of soil in each region. For climate, the values could be *dry*, *humid*, and *wet* and for soil the values could be *sand*, *clay*, and *rock*, for example.

(b) Write a query that finds those areas that are not suitable for cultivation due to too dry climate or bad soil.

(c) Display the areas that are not suitable for cultivation.

4. Using the PReSTO system do the following:

(a) There is a city located in an area with length [530, 560] and width [410, 420] miles. Represent this by the relation *City*.

(b) Suppose that the shape of a desert at time $t = 0$ is approximately a rectangle with length [0, 500] and width [0, 400] miles. The desert expands 1 mile to the east and 3 miles to the north per year. Represent this by the relation *Desert*.

(c) At time $t = 0$ there is a forest with length [520, 560] and width [405, 410] miles. To protect the city from the desert, people start to expand the forest at the rate of 5 miles per year to the south. Represent this by the relation *Forest*.

(d) Write a query that finds the area of the desert as blocked by the forest ten and twenty years later. Display the desert at these times.

(e) Write a query that finds the area of the city still free from the desert ten and twenty years later. Display the remaining areas of the city.

Computer Vision

Many applications, such as medical diagnosis and military target identification, require the retrieval from a large image database of those images that are similar to a new camera image. This requires the following tasks:

- **Affine-Invariant Similarity Measure:** When a flat object is photographed from different camera angles the photographic images are *affine transformations* of each other. Hence if one image is stored in the image database and another image is seen by the camera, to recognize that both images are showing the same object, there has to be an *affine-invariant similarity measure* between pairs of images.

- **Efficient Indexing:** Efficient indexing is essential when the image database contains a large number of images.

The combination of these two tasks is difficult. In general, computer vision research focuses on the first and neglects the second, while database research focuses on the second and neglects the first.

Computer vision researchers proposed several affine-invariant similarity measures between pairs of pictures, for example, the *minimum Hausdorff distance measure*, the *geometric hashing* technique, and similarity measures based on least squares distance. None of these measures leads to efficient indexing.

Database researchers proposed efficient indexing methods based on the following properties: *shape or contour*, *color* and *color histograms*, *attributed relational graphs*, which represent the spatial relationship between objects by a labeled graph, and various *image compression coefficients*. None of these properties is affine-invariant.

Section 21.1 defines affine invariance using constraint databases. Section 21.2 defines affine-invariant similarity measures and gives several examples that do not lead to efficient indexing. Section 21.3 describes a similarity measure based on *color ratios*. This similarity measure is shown to be affine-invariant and efficiently indexable.

21.1 Affine Invariance

We assume that each image is represented by a set of black points on a white background in the (x, y) plane. The representation can contain all the points in an image or only a special subset of its points. For example, a polygon can be represented by all the points within it or by only its corner vertices.

In either way, we can assume that each picture is described using a constraint relation. Let $A(x, y)$ and $B(x, y)$ be two real constraint relations describing two images. The two are *affine transformations* of each other, denoted $A \sim B$, if and only if the following is true:

$$\exists a, b, c, d, e, f \ \ ad \neq bc \ \ \forall x, y A(x, y) \leftrightarrow B(ax + by + e, cx + dy + f)$$

This is a first-order logical formula with real polynomial constraints and is equivalent to the definition of affine transformation given in Section 13.3. This formula can be evaluated in several different ways. For any fixed real number constants a, b, c, d, e, f such that $ad \neq bc$, we can simplify it and express it as an MLPQ query, which we leave as an exercise.

Example 21.1.1   The two images of a bird shown in Figures 21.1 are affine transformations of each other because we can choose the following values in the formula:

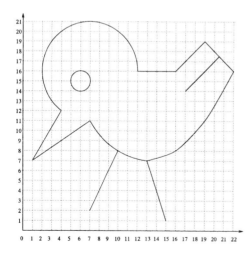
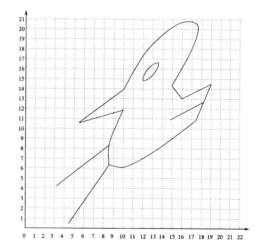

FIGURE 21.1. Two images of a bird.

$$a = \frac{1}{4}, \ b = \frac{3}{4}, \ c = \frac{6}{7}, \ d = \frac{-5}{14}, \ e = 0, \ f = 5$$

A key property of affine transformations is the following.

Lemma 21.1.1 Let A and B be areas that are affine transformations of each other. Then the following holds:

$$Area(B) = |ad - bc| \, Area(A)$$

Proof. We partition the area A into a disjoint set of triangles. Then each triangle in that set is transformed into another triangle that belongs to B. Clearly, if the lemma holds for each pair of triangles, then it holds for A and B. Hence it is enough to prove that the lemma holds for triangles.

Without loss of generality we can assume that the vertices of A are (x_1, y_1), (x_2, y_2), and (x_3, y_3). If these points are collinear then their transformation is also collinear, hence both areas will be zero and the lemma holds. If they are not collinear, then we can calculate the area of A as follows:

$$Area(A) = \frac{(x_1 - x_3)(y_2 - y_3) - (x_2 - x_3)(y_1 - y_3)}{2}$$

For the transformed triangle we can calculate that $Area(B)$ is:

$$\frac{1}{2} \Big[[(ax_1 + by_1) - (ax_3 + by_3)][(cx_2 + dy_2) - (cx_3 + dy_3)] \\ - [(ax_2 + by_2) - (ax_3 + by_3)][(cx_1 + dy_1) - (cx_3 + dy_3)] \Big]$$

Simplifying and taking the ratios we get:

$$\frac{Area(B)}{Area(A)} = \frac{(ad - bc)[(x_1 - x_3)(y_2 - y_3) - (x_2 - x_3)(y_1 - y_3)]}{(x_1 - x_3)(y_2 - y_3) - (x_2 - x_3)(y_1 - y_3)}$$
$$= ad - bc$$

from which the condition of the lemma follows. ∎

In many applications some noise is present, hence the two images are not precise affine transformations of each other. We make the assumption that the noise is at most δ in both the x and y directions. That means that each point (x, y) of A may, due to noise, become some other point (x', y') where $|x' - (ax + by + e)| \leq \delta$ and $|y' - (cx + dy + f)| \leq \delta$. Another type of noise would simply delete the (x, y) point. To account for these possibilities we modify the previous formula as follows:

$$\exists a, b, c, d, e, f \, ad \neq bc \forall x, y \, A(x, y) \rightarrow \exists x', y' (B(x', y') \ and$$
$$|x' - (ax + by + e)| \leq \delta \ and$$
$$|y' - (cx + dy + f)| \leq \delta)$$

21.2 Affine-Invariant Similarity Measures

Let $dist(A, B)$ be any distance measure between pairs of images A and B. Then $dist$ is *affine-invariant* if

$$\forall_{A' \sim A,\ B' \sim B}\ dist(A, B) = dist(A', B') \qquad . \qquad (21.1)$$

Next we give some examples of affine-invariant similarity measures.

Minimum Hausdorff Distance Measure: Let $Euclid(I, J)$ be the Euclidean distance function between two points $I, J \in \mathcal{R}^2$. We define the *directed Hausdorff* distance between A and B as follows:

$$hausdorff(A, B) = \max_{I \in A} \min_{J \in B} Euclid(I, J)$$

The *Hausdorff* distance is defined as:

$$Hausdorff(A, B) = \max(hausdorff(A, B), hausdorff(B, A))$$

The Hausdorff distance measures the mismatch between two sets that are at fixed positions and is not affine-invariant. However, we can define the *minimum Hausdorff* distance between the two sets as follows:

$$m\,Hausdorff(A, B) = \min_{A' \sim A,\ B' \sim B} Hausdorff(A', B')$$

The minimum Hausdorff distance is affine-invariant. However, there is no efficient algorithm to compute the minimum Hausdorff distance. Therefore, the minimum Hausdorff distance cannot be used for efficient indexing.

Geometric Hashing: Geometric hashing stores not the coordinates of the points but their affine-invariant coordinates in a *geometric hash table*. The affine-invariant coordinates can be explained as follows.

Given a triplet of noncollinear points $P_1, P_2, P_3 \in \mathcal{R}^2$ any other point P_4 in an image can be represented as the combination:

$$P_4 = \alpha(P_2 - P_1) + \beta(P_3 - P_1) + P_1$$

After an affine transformation that takes the four points to P_1', P_2', P_3', and P_4', respectively, the condition

$$P_4' = \alpha(P_2' - P_1') + \beta(P_3' - P_1') + P_1'$$

also holds. Therefore, this gives for the point P_4 the affine-invariant representation $(\alpha.\beta)$, which is stored in the geometric hash table.

Suppose that we have made a geometric hash table corresponding to each noncollinear triple of points in the image A. When a new image B is presented, in it some triple (P_1', P_2', P_3') of noncollinear points is chosen and for all the other points in B an affine-invariant representation (α, β) is found using the preceding equation. If B is an affine transformation of A, then there must be a triple of points (P_1, P_2, P_3) in A such that the affine transformation takes that triple to (P_1', P_2', P_3'). Therefore, there must be a geometric hash table associated with (P_1, P_2, P_3) and A such that it contains all the affine-invariant point representations (α, β).

Therefore, we need to test only whether the affine-invariant representations of the points in B are all in one of the geometric hash tables associated with A. If they are, then B and A are affine transformations of each other.

Suppose that there are $O(n)$ points in A and in B. Then there are $O(n)$ affine-invariant representations derived from B. Because there are $O(n^3)$ geometric hash tables associated with A, a naive check of matching the affine-invariant representations with the geometric hash tables would take $O(n^4)$ time. However, a randomized algorithm would just check a constant number of points among the affine-invariant representations against the geometric hash tables. This would give an $O(n^3)$ time randomized algorithm for checking whether A and B are affine transformations of each other. If we have in the database m different images, then the total time would be $O(mn^3)$.

Therefore, the geometric hashing technique does not lead to efficient retrieval when there are a large number of stored images. Moreover, this method is not very robust under noise.

21.3 The Color Ratios Similarity Measure

In this section we assume that each image is represented as a set of colored points. Most pixel-based image representations allow 256 different shades of green, red, and blue. From these a large set of colors can be defined. Suppose we classify each part of an image as having one of n different colors. The following lemma shows that the ratio of the total areas of any pair of colors is *affine-invariant*.

Lemma 21.3.1   Let A_i and A_j be the total areas colored with colors c_i and c_j, respectively, within image A. Let B_i and B_j be the same within an affine transformation B of A. Then

$$\frac{A_i}{A_j} = \frac{B_i}{B_j} \quad \text{if} \quad A_j \neq 0$$

Proof. By Lemma 21.1.1 we have:

$$B_i = |ad - bc| \, A_i$$

and

$$B_j = |ad - bc| \, A_j$$

Hence, by taking the ratio of the first and the second we get the required condition. ∎

Example 21.3.1   Assume that the bird in Figure 21.1 is red except for the eyes, which are black. Then the ratio of black to red areas in both images of Figures 21.1 is the same constant.

Suppose that we have a number of different colors and m possible ratios that are independent of each other. For example, with only the colors *blue, green,* and *red*, we can have only two independent ratios. For example, we may select *blue/red* and *green/red*. Then the *blue/green* ratio can be calculated from those two; hence it is not independent from them.

Given the m independent color ratios, we can describe each image as a vector of m values, where the ith entry corresponds to the value of the ith color ratio. Then the m-dimensional vectors can be indexed using several efficient multidimensional point indexing techniques.

Finally, we can define a color-ratio similarity measure that is robust under noise. Let V_A and V_B be the vectors of the color ratios in images A and B, respectively. Then the distance between A and B is defined as the Eucledian distance between A and B.

Bibliographic Notes

For indexing image databases, *shape or contour* is used, for example, by Jagadish [154] and Mehrotra and Grosky [211]; *color* and *color histograms* are used, for example, by Stricker and Orengo [297] and Swain and Ballard [301]. A combination of color and shape is used by the QBIC system [96] and in Smoliar and Zhang [290]. *Attributed relational graphs*, which represent the spatial relationship between objects by a labeled graph, are used by Petrakis and Faloutsos [238]. *Image compression coefficients*, derived from different methods, are used by the Photobook system [236] and Ravela and Manmatha [247, 248, 249].

In general, these papers hardly even raise the issue of invariance under geometric transformations, except for Ravela and Manmatha [247, 248, 249], whose representation is invariant under translations and rotations, which are only a subset of the affine transformations.

The *minimum Hausdorff distance measure* was proposed by Huttenlocher et al. [146], and the *geometric hashing* technique by Lamdan et al. [195]. An affine-invariant similarity measure based on least squares distance was proposed by Werman and Weinshall [326]. A slight extension of the point representation together with an *absolute difference measure*, which is also affine-invariant, is given by Hagedoorn and Veltkamp [135].

Several other similarity measures require a good knowledge of the shape of the object in the image. These include *Fourier descriptors* used by Arbter et al. [17], *moment invariants* of Wang [321], *curvature scale space* of Mokhtarian et al. [215, 216, 217], and the decomposition approaches of Tsai [307] and Cyganski and Vaz [73]. Ben-Arie and Wang [25] use similar decompositions for small areas of patches identifiable in the picture. The common problem with these approaches is that they are not robust under noise. For example, some of these methods try to identify when the first or second derivative of a contour line is zero. These are difficult to tell with any confidence from a noisy image. Another problem is that the contour of objects used in several of these methods may not be the most important information. For example, the curvature scale space representation [215, 216, 217] is applied to marine creatures, but it cannot be applied for human faces.

Lemma 21.1.1 about the ratio of areas is well known, but Lemma 21.3.1 about affine-invariance of the ratio of colors within an image and its use for efficient indexing are new. Other similarity measures that are not affine-invariant are presented for point sets by Eiter and Mannila [91], for constraint databases by Deng [79] and Revesz [260], and for time series data by Goldin and Kanellakis [111].

Exercises

1. When all the stored images are photographed at a certain angle and we know the current camera angle, then we may calculate the values of a, b, c, d, e, f of the affine transformation between the stored and the new images. For example, a database may contain images of people photographed directly from the front, while the camera may face a door through which people enter at a slight angle.

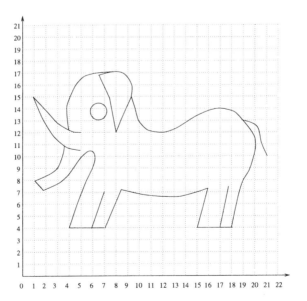

FIGURE 21.2. An elephant.

Write an MLPQ query (see Chapter 18) that tests whether two images are affine transformations of each other, assuming that we know the values of the constants a, b, c, d, e, f and $ab \neq cd$.

2. Show, using a counterexample, that the Hausdorff distance is not affine-invariant.

3. Calculate the black and red areas as specified in Example 21.3.1 for the original and the distorted images of the bird. How close are the ratios of the black and red areas in the two images?

4. Apply the same affine transformation as in Example 21.1.1 to the image of the elephant in Figure 21.2.

Bioinformatics

This chapter describes an application of constraint automata to the *genome map assembly* problem, which is one of the most important problems in bioinformatics.

Section 22.1 gives a brief review of the genome map assembly problem. Section 22.2 presents an abstraction of the genome map assembly problem called the *big-bag matching* problem, which is a problem of building a large string from given substrings. Section 22.3 describes a constraint automaton with Boolean set constraints to solve the big-bag matching problem.

22.1   The Genome Map Assembly Problem

Deoxyribonucleic acid, or DNA, is the genetic material that encodes the blueprint of all living organisms. Each DNA is composed of a string of nucleotides that are adenine (A), thymine (T), cytosine (C), and guanine (G).

Genome biologists use *restriction enzymes* to cut DNA into smaller fragments at specific sites. For example, one restriction enzyme may cut the DNA at each occurrence of the substring GTTAAC (from left to right or right to left; it does not matter for the enzyme) into GTT and AAC. Each different restriction enzyme cuts the nucleotide string at different sites.

Restriction enzymes can be applied together. For example, if a and b are two restriction enzymes, then their union $a \cup b$ can also be used. Their union cuts the DNA at all sites where either a or b cuts it.

After cutting the DNA, all information about the original order of the fragments is lost, because the small fragments just float randomly in the solution. The only exception is the first fragment, which is usually identifiable because it often contains some special sequences of nucleotides.

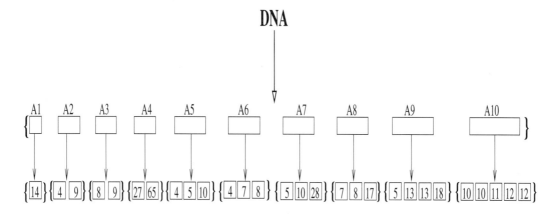

FIGURE 22.1. Cutting by a and then by $b \cup c$.

Genome biologists can use several techniques to measure the lengths of the small DNA fragments. The length of the fragments is measured in the number of nucleotides they contain. Genome biologists can also make multiple copies of the entire DNA or any fragment.

The following is a procedure using three restriction enzymes a, b, and c for obtaining the input data for the genome map assembly problem:

1. Take a copy of the DNA.
2. Apply restriction enzyme a to the copy.
3. Separate the fragments.
4. For each fragment apply restriction enzymes $b \cup c$, cutting the fragment into subfragments.
5. Find the lengths of the subfragments.
6. Repeat steps 1–5 applying b instead of a and $a \cup c$ instead of $b \cup c$.

For example, applying to a certain DNA string steps 1–5 we could obtain Figure 22.1.

Applying to the same DNA string step 6, we could obtain Figure 22.2.

These data serve as the input to the *genome map assembly problem*, which is the task of finding the original order of the fragments generated in step 2. Obviously, knowing the original order allows genome biologists to recover the original DNA string.

22.2 The Big-Bag Matching Problem

In this section we present an abstraction of the genome map assembly problem.

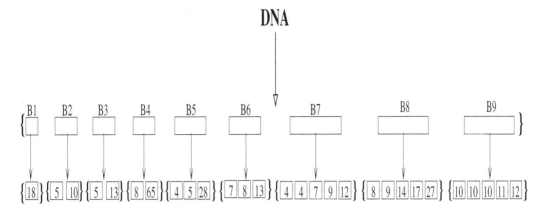

FIGURE 22.2. Cutting by b and then by $a \cup c$.

A *bag* is a multiset, i.e., a generalization of a set in which each element can occur multiple times. A *big-bag* is a multiset whose elements are bags that can occur multiple times.

We call each permutation of the bags and permutation of the elements of each bag within a big-bag a *presentation*. A big-bag can have several different presentations.

For example, $a_1 = [[1, 3], [2, 4], [5, 7, 8]]$ is one presentation of a big-bag A. Similarly, $b_1 = [[1, 2, 4, 8], [3], [5, 7]]$ is a presentation of another big-bag B.

We say that the ith element of a presentation a, written as $a[i]$, is the ith Σ symbol seen when the presentation is read from left to right. For example, in a_1 the third element is 2 and the sixth element is 7, i.e., $a_1[3] = 2$ and $a_1[6] = 7$. The total number of elements, which is independent of any presentation, in A is 7.

We say that two big-bags A and B, both of which have n elements, *match* if there are presentations a for A and b for B such that $a[i] = b[i]$ for $1 \le i \le n$.

For example, A and B match because A can be presented as $a_2 = [[3, 1], [2, 4], [8, 5, 7]]$ and B can be presented as $b_2 = [[3], [1, 2, 4, 8], [5, 7]]$.

The big-bag matching decision problem (BBMD) is the problem of deciding whether two big-bags match. The big-bag matching problem (BBM) is the problem of finding matching presentations for two given big-bags if they match.

22.3 A Constraint-Automata Solution

This section presents an algorithm for solving the big-bag matching problem. The algorithm can be presented using the constraint automaton shown in Figure 22.3. The automaton uses the constraints $\subseteq$ and difference over multisets. The automaton starts in the INIT state and want to reach the HALT state. From the INIT state, we start building a figure like the one shown in Figure 22.4, going from left

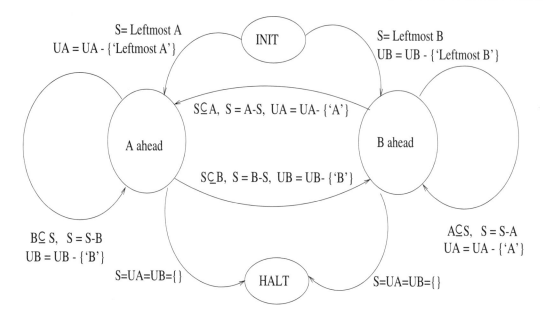

FIGURE 22.3. The automaton.

to right by adding either an A or a B bag. Each bag represents a contiguity constraint for the elements it contains. That is, any valid presentation must contain the elements within a bag next to each other. Therefore, adding a new bag really adds a new contiguity constraint to a set of other such constraints. Only if the set of constraints is solvable (and there could be several solutions) is the automaton allowed to continue with the next transition.

At any point either the list of A bags will be ahead of the list of B bags (and the automaton will be in state "A ahead") or vice versa (and it will be in the state "B ahead") or neither will be ahead, in which case it goes back to the INIT state and starts the matching algorithm again using only the unused A and B bags.

The automaton keeps for each state the following state variables: UA and UB indicating the ID numbers of the unused A and B bags, and S the bag of elements by which either the A list or the B list is currently ahead.

Whenever there are possible alternatives the automaton makes a guess. If the automaton cannot reach the HALT state after a series of guesses, then it will backtrack and try a new guess. We will explain the run of the automaton without backtracking, assuming only correct guesses.

First the automaton guesses the first bag and moves from the INIT state to either the "A ahead" or the "B ahead" state.

If the automaton is in the "A ahead" state then it can guess the next B bag. If the next B bag contains S, which is the set of elements by which A is currently ahead, then the automaton will move to the "B ahead" state and set the value of

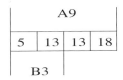

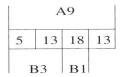

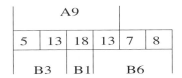

FIGURE 22.4. The first five steps of the constraint automaton.

S to be the value of the new bag minus the current value of S. Otherwise, if the next B bag is contained in S, then the automaton stays in the "A ahead" state but subtracts from S the value of the new bag. In both cases, the elements of S and the new bag are matched as far as possible and the new bag is taken out from UB. The automaton behaves similarly when it is in the "B ahead" state, except that A and B are reversed.

When all the bags are used and UA, UB, and S are empty, then the automaton enters the HALT state and stops.

A9				A8		A3	A1	A4			A6		A2		A10				A7		A5	
5	13	18	13	7	8	17	8	9	14	27	65	8	7	4	9	4	12	11	12	10	10	10	28	5	4	5	10
B3	B1		B6		B8			B4			B7				B9				B5		B2	

FIGURE 22.5. A solution for the big-bags matching problem.

Example 22.3.1 Now we give an example execution of the automaton using the input data shown in Figures 22.1 and 22.2. The first five steps of the constraint automaton are shown in Figure 22.4.

First, the automaton moves from the INIT state to the "B ahead" state after choosing $B3$ as the first bag. We have $S = B3$.

Second, the automaton chooses $A9$ because $S \subseteq A9$, sets $S = A9 - S = \{13, 18\}$ and moves to the "A ahead" state.

Third, the automaton chooses $B1$ because $B1 \subseteq S$, sets $S = S - B1$ and remains in the "A ahead" state.

Fourth, the automaton chooses $B6$ because $S \subseteq B6$, sets $S = B6 - S = \{7, 8\}$ and moves to the "B ahead" state.

Fifth, the automaton chooses $A8$ because $S \subseteq A8$, sets $S = A8 - S = \{17\}$ and moves to the "A ahead" state.

We can continue in this way until we reach a solution like the one shown in Figure 22.5.

Figure 22.6 summarizes each move of the automaton and gives for each transition the name of the new bag added to the figure, the update operation on S, and the values of S, UA and UB.

The correctness of the automaton will be proved in the next theorem.

Theorem 22.3.1 The nondeterministic constraint automaton reaches the HALT state if and only if the two big-bags match.

Proof. We prove by induction on the number of transitions of the automaton the following: After the ith transition, i number of bags in A and B match, and S is a bag that contains those elements of the rightmost bag in A (respectively B) that do not match any of the B (or A) bags if the automaton is in the state "A ahead" (or "B ahead"). (Here the rightmost bag is that bag among those the automaton used that *ends* at the rightmost position. Similarly, the leftmost bag *ends* at the leftmost position.)

Initially, we are given for the value of S the leftmost bag in A and B. The leftmost bag is taken away from one of the big-bags, but nothing is taken from the other big-bag. Hence no bags match yet and the claim is true for $i = 0$.

Now assume that the claim is true for i transitions and prove it for $i + 1$. Because the automaton is symmetric in A and B, we can assume without loss of generality that the automaton is in state "A ahead" after the ith transition. By the

New	S=	S	Unused As	Unused Bs
—	—	—	1, 2, 3, 4, 5, 6, 7, 8, 9, 10	1, 2, 3, 4, 5, 6, 7, 8, 9
B3	B3	5, 13	1, 2, 3, 4, 5, 6, 7, 8, 9, 10	1, 2, 4, 5, 6, 7, 8, 9
A9	A9 - S	13, 18	1, 2, 3, 4, 5, 6, 7, 8, 10	1, 2, 4, 5, 6, 7, 8, 9
B1	S - B1	13	1, 2, 3, 4, 5, 6, 7, 8, 10	2, 4, 5, 6, 7, 8, 9
B6	B6 - S	7, 8	1, 2, 3, 4, 5, 6, 7, 8, 10	2, 4, 5, 7, 8, 9
A8	A8 - S	17	1, 2, 3, 4, 5, 6, 7, 10	2, 4, 5, 7, 8, 9
B8	B8 - S	8, 9, 14, 27	1, 2, 3, 4, 5, 6, 7, 10	2, 4, 5, 7, 9
A3	S - A3	14, 27	1, 2, 4, 5, 6, 7, 10	2, 4, 5, 7, 9
A1	S - A1	27	2, 4, 5, 6, 7, 10	2, 4, 5, 7, 9
A4	A4 - S	65	2, 5, 6, 7, 10	2, 4, 5, 7, 9
B4	B4 - S	8	2, 5, 6, 7, 10	2, 5, 7, 9
A6	A6 - S	4, 7	2, 5, 7, 10	2, 5, 7, 9
B7	B7 - S	4, 9, 12	2, 5, 7, 10	2, 5, 9
A2	S - A2	12	5, 7, 10	2, 5, 9
A10	A10 - S	10, 10, 11, 12	5, 7	2, 5, 9
B9	B9 - S	10	5, 7	2, 5
A7	A7 - S	5, 28	5	2, 5
B5	B5 - S	4	5	2
A5	A5 - S	5, 10	—	2
B2	B2 - S	—	—	—
—	—	—	—	—

FIGURE 22.6. A run of the automaton.

induction hypothesis S is the bag of those elements in the current rightmost A bag that were not yet matched to any elements in B bags. During the $i + 1$st transition the automaton either stays in "A ahead" or moves to "B ahead."

If the automaton stays in "A ahead," then it must find a new B bag whose elements are in S. Hence B can be matched. The transition also updates S by subtracting the elements of B from S. This preserves the condition that S contains the yet unmatched elements of the rightmost A bag. Also, the rightmost bag will remain the same bag in A because S had only a subset of the elements in it and B cannot end later than A because while all of its elements are matched, there may be unmatched elements remaining in S.

If the automaton moves to state "B ahead," then it must find a new B bag that contains S. Therefore all the yet unmatched elements can be matched by the new B bag. Therefore, the rightmost bag will now be the new B bag. Further, the elements in B that are not matched are exactly $B \setminus S$, which is the new value of S. Hence the condition is preserved.

When S is empty and all A and B bags are used, then the automaton moves to the HALT state. Because each transition uses exactly one A or B bag, the only time the automaton could move to the HALT state is on the nth transition, where n is the total number of bags in A and B. Because of the condition, which we proved to be preserved after each transition, all n bags must match. Hence if the automaton reaches the HALT state, then the two big-bags must match. On the other hand, if the two big-bags match, then the automaton can guess correctly the order of the big-bags according to their ending points and use the transition that uses up the next B bag if it is in state "A ahead" or the next B bag if it is in state "B ahead."   ∎

Bibliographic Notes

The abstraction of the genome assembly problem as a big-bag matching problem is new. The big-bag matching problem is studied and shown to be NP-complete in Revesz [269]. Several other variations of the genome map assembly problem are shown to be NP-complete in Karp [164].

A common alternative abstraction to obtain the genome data is to pick random substrings from the DNA as, for example, in Gillett et al. [110], Olson et al. [222], Revesz [263], and Wong et al. [331] (which use restriction enzymes) or in Green and Green [118] and Harley et al. [139] (which use a technique called *hybridization* to test whether two substrings overlap). The random-substrings approach is discussed in Lander and Waterman [196], which gives some estimates about the number of substrings of certain average size required to get good coverage for a DNA of a given size. Unfortunately, the random-substrings approach has the limitation that there could be some gaps on the DNA, that is, regions that are not covered by any randomly picked substring.

In addition, Dix and Yee [82] and Yap [335] considered the following version of the map assembly problem using two restriction-enzymes a and b. For three copies of the same genome the following information is obtained: the set of fragment lengths after complete digestion by enzyme a, the set of fragment lengths after complete digestion by enzyme b, and the set of fragment lengths after complete digestion by both enzymes a and b. Yap [335] shows that this leads to a formulation of the map assembly problem, which is also NP-complete but can be solved in some cases using the CLP(R) system of Jaffar et al. [153]. This method uses only three bags as data, whereas our method uses a separate bag for each substring obtained after step 2. The method in Section 16.11 has more structure and is less likely to lead to a combinatorial explosion during the search.

One other abstraction of the genome map assembly problem, called the probed partial digestion problem, is considered in Tsur et al. [308]. Partial digestion occurs when a restriction enzyme fails to cut all the sites specific to it. The probed partial digestion problem is solved using the LDL deductive database system [309].

Exercises

1. Translate the constraint automaton in Figure 22.3 into Datalog with Boolean set constraints using a DISCO program as in Chapter 19. (**Hint:** You may assume that the bags contain no repetitions of fragment lengths.)

2. Apply your translation in the previous exercise to the following set of values. Find all possible solutions of matching the *A*s and *B*s.

Bag	Fragment Lengths
A1	10, 45
A2	10, 17, 25, 50
A3	15, 17, 50, 60
A4	8, 12, 30, 40, 50
A5	8, 10, 12, 20, 25, 40
A6	5, 8, 10, 15, 25, 30, 35, 45, 50, 60
B1	15,17
B2	8, 25, 45
B3	8, 10, 25
B4	15, 30, 60
B5	10, 12, 40, 50
B6	5, 10, 12, 20, 40
B7	8, 30, 45, 50, 60
B8	10, 17, 25, 35, 45, 50

3. In practice the measurements taken in step 5 of the algorithm in Section 22.1 are subject to error. That is, each fragment length measured can be off by some nucleotides from the actual lengths:

   (a) Modify the constraint automaton in Figure 22.3 to allow a measurement error of at most d nucleotides.

   (b) Write a computer program that implements the modified automaton.

(c) Assume that $d = 1$. Modify the input data in the previous exercise by changing half of the values in A and B by either adding one or subtracting one. Apply your program to the changed data. How well do your programs work on the noisy data?

4. Suppose that you have a set of $2n$ dominos where each domino has a left and a right side with a number of dots between 0 and c, where c is some constant. We divide the dominos into two groups with n dominos each. We give the first set of dominos to one player and the other group to a second player. The two players are trying to build together two parallel rows of dominos with the first player always putting the dominos in the first row and the second player always in the second row such that:

   (i) the two rows are shifted by one-half domino length with respect to each other,

   (ii) in each column the dots match, i.e., the two half-dominos have the same number of dots, and

   (iii) the leftmost and rightmost columns have the same number of dots.

   Find an efficient polynomial time algorithm to find a solution to this domino matching problem. Note that the domino matching problem is a special case of the big-bags matching problem in which each little bag contains exactly two elements. (**Hint:** Reduce this to the Euler circle problem.)

23

Environmental Modeling

Environmental modeling problems occur in many applications, for example, in flood, fire, and pollution control or drought, urban development, and wildlife habitat change monitoring. Environmental modeling systems are used by flood, fire or pollution control emergency response teams, and in agriculture by farmers, insurance companies, crops market analysts, and various government agencies. Each environmental modeling system is specialized for the phenomena of interest and the local conditions and regulations. However, in general one can identify the following three common requirements of environmental modeling systems:

- **Predictive Spread Modeling:** Environmental modeling systems should predict over time intervals the spread of natural phenomena like a flood, a drought, or a forest fire or man-made phenomena like an oil spill or industrial smoke.

- **Visualization:** Environmental modeling systems should provide useful visualization of the modeled phenomena. The goal of the visualization is not prettiness but usefulness to the users. Therefore, the visualization should be fast and safe. For example, the visualization should overpredict rather than underpredict the flooded area at any given time instance.

- **Decision Support:** The visualization may not be enough for users to make valid or fast decisions, especially in emergency situations. In these cases, environmental modeling systems should provide *decision support*, which means the ability to help evaluate the situation and possible responses to it.

It is possible to build, using the spatiotemporal database systems in Chapters 18–20, environmental modeling systems that contain all three features. This chapter describes the process of building an environmental modeling system and illustrates the process by a sample environmental modeling system for monitoring and controling forest fire spread.

Section 23.1 describes predictive spread modeling. Section 23.2 describes the visualization of the fire spread. Finally, Section 23.3 describes a decision support system for the fire control problem.

23.1   Predictive Spread Modeling

Technological advances in remote sensing, global positioning systems (GPS), and high-speed telecommunication make it possible to build a real-time system to track the spread of phenomena like flood, fire, desertification, and smoke. For example, suppose that an airborne or satellite-based sensor sends two successive snapshots of a forest fire at times $t = 1$ and $t = 5$ hours, as shown in Figure 23.1.

We apply the approximation algorithm of Section 15.4 to interpolate between the two snapshots. The algorithm breaks both snapshots into the same number of rectangles and then matches the rectangles in order, as shown in Figure 23.2.

Next, the approximation algorithm builds for each matching pair of rectangles a parametric rectangle. For each pair, the parametric rectangle changes from the rectangle at time $t = 1$ hour into the rectangle at time $t = 5$ hours. Therefore, the set of parametric rectangles gives an interpolation of the spread between times $t = 1$ and $t = 5$ hours.

This interpolation can be easily extended backward in time to estimate the origin of the fire and forward in time to estimate the state of the fire at any given time instance in the future, because it is reasonable to assume that the rate of the fire spread does not change much over a relatively short time. To do this *extrapolation*, we simple change in each parametric rectangle the *from* value to something less than 1 or increase the *to* value to something greater than 5. For example, suppose we change the time interval to [0, 10]. Then at any time between $t = 0$ and

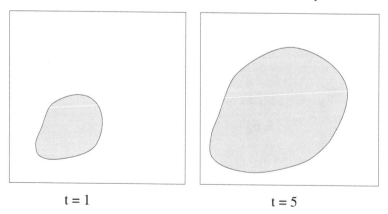

t = 1   t = 5

FIGURE 23.1. Raster snapshots of the fire.

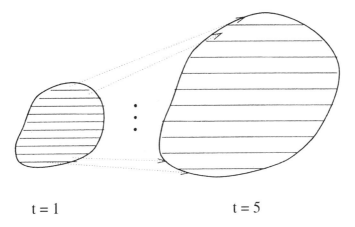

FIGURE 23.2. Interpolation between the snapshots.

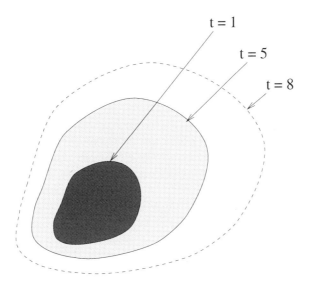

FIGURE 23.3. Predicted spread of the fire.

$t = 10$ we have an estimate for the fire spread. For example, the dashed line in Figure 23.3 shows the predicted fire front at $t = 8$ hours.

The prediction backward in time can be very useful to identify the possible source of the fire, essential information, for example, for insurance companies. The prediction forward in time is useful to enable emergency response to the spreading phenomena. For example, firefighters need to know, to identify the endangered locations, where the fire may spread by $t = 8$ hours.

23.1.1 Interactive Predictive Spread Modeling

The preceding prediction may need some modification when the sensor sends some new information or when there are some blocks in the way of the spreading fire.

The forward prediction can be interactively modified when new data are received. Suppose that the sensor sends a new image every 4 hours. Then when the next image arrives at time $t = 9$ hours, the interpolation can be recomputed based on the latest pair of snapshots, that is, using only the snapshots for the times $t = 5$ and $t = 9$.

In addition, there may be some static blocks of the fire, for example, lakes, rivers, or some rocky or sandy land areas or dynamic blocks of the fire, for example, fire extinguishing foam or water spread by the firefighters. The interaction of the fire and these blocking objects can be modeled using the *Block* operator.

For example, suppose that, as shown in Figure 23.4, a fire starts in one portion of a forest and begins to spread but there is a lake, which acts as a natural block to the fire.

Suppose further that the firefighters can choose, as shown in Figure 23.5, from the following three strategies that determine which way a number of helicopters fly and drop foam in the way of the fire:

1. All fly north.
2. All fly east.
3. Some fly east and some fly west.

We model by a parametric rectangles relation $Strategy(x, y, t, s)$, where the attribute s indicates which strategy is used, the foam dropped by the helicopters.

Let us assume that the current prediction for the spread of the fire is stored in relation *Fire* and the lake area in relation *Lake*. For example, in PReSTO, we can

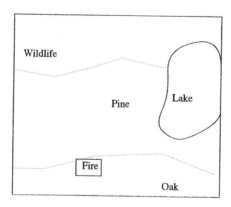

FIGURE 23.4. A fire starts in a forest.

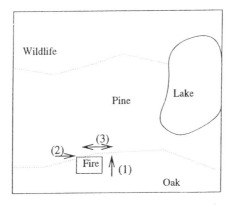

FIGURE 23.5. Three strategies for blocking the fire.

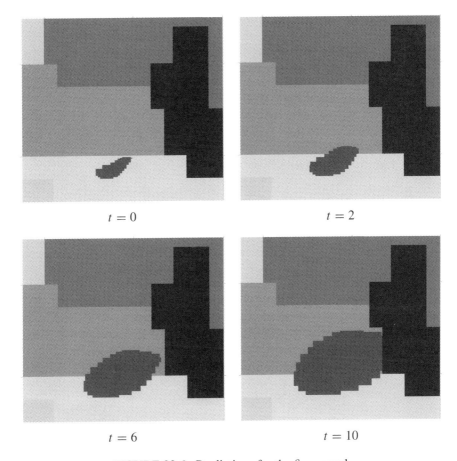

FIGURE 23.6. Predictions for the fire spread.

use the block operator to compute a more refined prediction for the spread of the fire at time 8 hours and in case strategy (1) is used as follows:

$$Fire_{1,8} = Block((Lake \cup (\sigma_{s=1} \, Strategy)), \, Fire, 8)$$

Similarly, we can estimate the spread of the fire at any time and for any strategy.

23.2   Visualization

We can use the PReSTO animation operator to show the spread of the fire and the blocking agents. Figure 23.6 shows an example of using approximation by a set of parametric rectangles to predict the spread of a fire for time instances $t = 6$ and $t = 10$ based on the snapshots at times $t = 0$ and $t = 2$ hours. The images at $t = 0$ and $t = 2$ were simplified from actual satellite images. We see in pictures $t = 6$ and $t = 10$ that the fire spreads to the east and slightly to the north until the lake blocks its spread.

We also created in PReSTO a *Strategy* relation that contained descriptions of the three strategies using parametric rectangles. Figure 23.7 shows the result of the predictions at time instances $t = 6$ and $t = 10$ when both the lake and the foam spread by the firefighters blocks the spread of the fire.

The visualization allows some qualitative assessments. For example, by time $t = 10$ hours, strategy (1) blocks the fire completely in the east and strategy (3) in the north direction. On the other hand, strategy (2) is risky because it leaves a part of the fire escaping to the north of the foam block.

23.3   A Decision Support System

Now we describe a simple decision support system that allows firefighters to choose among the available strategies. Let B_W, B_P, and B_O be the total area burned of the wildlife reserve, the pine forest and the oak forest, respectively. First for each strategy and any time instance of interest, we calculate using the area operator of PReSTO the values of B_W, B_P, and B_O.

Suppose that the three regions have different priorities for protection. For example, the wildlife preserve may be relatively more important than the pine forest per unit area. To reflect these priorities we associate with each region a different damage weight. Let α_W, α_P, and α_O be the damage weights associated with a unit area of wildlife reserve, pine, and oak, respectively. Then the total damage can be estimated by the following formula:

$$Damage = \alpha_W B_W + \alpha_P B_P + \alpha_O B_O$$

The decision support system can quickly compare the estimated damages for a set of possible strategies and find the one with the least damage. For example,

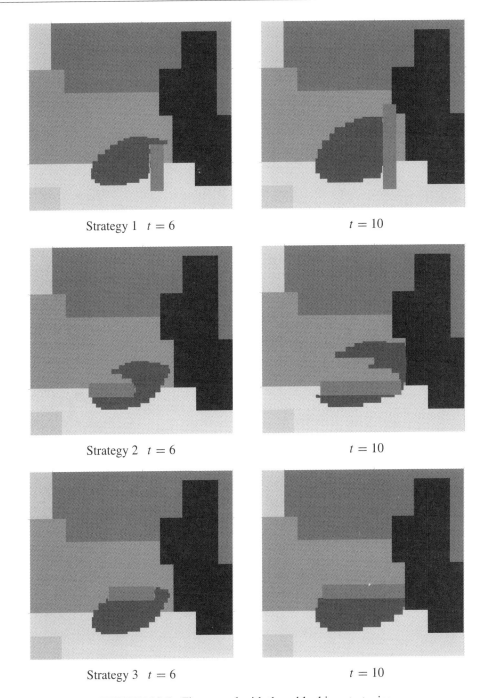

Strategy 1 $t = 6$ $t = 10$

Strategy 2 $t = 6$ $t = 10$

Strategy 3 $t = 6$ $t = 10$

FIGURE 23.7. Fire spread with three blocking strategies.

assuming that $\alpha_W = 3$, $\alpha_P = 2$, and $\alpha_O = 1$, the decision support system would compute the values of the following table:

Strategy	Burned area at $t = 10$			Estimated total
	Wildlife	Pine	Oak	damage
1	0	11203.32	6048.95	28455.59
2	0	6902.92	3292.87	17098.76
3	0	4916.63	6875.0	16708.26

The computation shows that the best of the three strategies is strategy (3) because it leaves the least damage after ten hours.

Bibliographic Notes

Several fire spread models, like BURN by M. Veach et al. [319] and FIREGIS by Goncalves and Diogo [114] use some kind of cellular automata [328], which divide the region into a finite grid of square cells and assume that the fuel, wind, and terrain parameters are uniform in each cell. The rule of how a fire propagates from cell to cell is based on Rothermel's model [276] and related systems like BEHAVE [16], which focus on predicting the local behavior and characteristics of the fires, for example, the spread rate, the flame length, and the intensity.

Other fire spread models, like the FIRE! system [325], represent the fire front using a vector data model and use Huygen's principle [15] and elliptical growth model [275] to expand the fire fronts in two dimensions. Yuan [336, 337] represents time as an independent object linked to the objects in the spatial domain.

None of these models supports modeling the interaction between the fire and the firefighting agents and provides complete decision support for firefighting. The forest fire spread system in this chapter is based on Cai and Revesz [51].

Exercises

1. Suppose that weeds at time $t = 0$ occupy the region $[8, 15] \times [10, 36]$ meters and first spread south with a speed of 2 meters per week until $t = 10$ weeks. Then they spread in all directions (east, west, south, and north) until $t = 30$ weeks with a speed of 3 meters per week.

   (a) Represent the weeds by a PReSTO relation and animate their unchecked growth on the computer screen.

   (b) Suppose that you are allowed to apply a weed killer only at the rate of 9 square meters per week. The weed killer is effective for 5 weeks after being sprayed and a one-meter-wide band can block the spread of the weeds. How would you apply the weed killer? Express your plan in a PReSTO relation, and visualize it at several time instances on the computer screen.

2. Find remote sensing images of any spreading phenomenon at times $t_1, \ldots, t_n$ where $n \geq 5$. Then do the following:

   (a) Apply the approximation algorithm in Section 15.4 for each adjacent pair of images, that is, for each pair of images at times t_i and t_{i+1} for each $1 \leq i \leq n - 1$.

   (b) Use each (t_i, t_{i+1}) pair to estimate the value of the spread at t_{i+2} for each $1 \leq i \leq n - 2$.

   (c) Let A_i be the actual and E_i be the estimated area at time t_i. Find the percent difference in the two areas, that is, find:
   $$\Delta_i = \frac{area(A_i - E_i) + area(E_i - A_i)}{area(A_i)}$$
   How well does the approximation work? What is the average value of Δ_i? What factors may have contributed to the average being large or small?

3. Continuing the previous exercise use the PReSTO system to do the following:

   (a) Enter the approximation between every adjacent time image into a PReSTO relation.

   (b) Define at least two blocking agents that may control the spread. For example, a flood may be blocked by a mountain and water pollution sweeping into the soil may be blocked by rocks. Find the spread in the presence of the blocking agents.

   (c) Visualize at several time instances the spread both with and without the blocking agents. How effective are they in controlling or stopping the spread?

Bibliography

[1] S. Abiteboul, R. Hull, and V. Vianu. *Foundations of Databases*. Addison-Wesley, 1995.

[2] S. Abiteboul, P. Kanellakis, and G. Grahne. On the representation and querying of sets of possible worlds. In *Proc. ACM SIGMOD International Conference on Management of Data*, pages 34–48, 1987.

[3] S. Abiteboul, P. Kanellakis, and G. Grahne. On the representation and querying of sets of possible worlds. *Theoretical Computer Science*, 78(1):159–87, 1991.

[4] N. R. Adam and A. Gangopadhyay. *Database Issues in Geographic Information Systems*. Kluwer, 1997.

[5] F. Afrati, T. Andronikos, and T. Kavalieros. On the expressiveness of first-order constraint languages. In G. Kuper and M. Wallace, editors, *Proc. Workshop on Constraint Databases and Applications*, volume 1034 of *Lecture Notes in Computer Science*, pages 22–39. Springer-Verlag, 1995.

[6] F. Afrati, S. Cosmadakis, S. Grumbach, and G. Kuper. Linear versus polynomial constraints in database query languages. In A. Borning, editor, *Proc. 2nd International Workshop on Principles and Practice of Constraint Programming*, volume 874 of *Lecture Notes in Computer Science*, pages 181–92. Springer-Verlag, 1994.

[7] P. K. Agarwal, L. Arge, and J. Erickson. Indexing mobile points. In *Proc. ACM Symposium on Principles of Database Systems*, pages 175–86, 2000.

[8] P. K. Agarwal and K. R. Varadarajan. Efficient algorithms for approximating polygonal chains. *Journal of Discrete & Computational Geometry*, 23:273–91, 2000.

[9] A. Aiken, D. Kozen, and E. Wimmers. Decidability of systems of set constraints with negative constraints. *Information and Computation*, 122(1):30–44, 1995.

[10] C. E. Alchourrón, P. Gärdenfors, and D. Makinson. On the logic of theory change: Partial meet contraction and revision functions. *Journal of Symbolic Logic*, 50:510–30, 1985.

[11] R. Alur, C. Courcoubetis, and D. L. Dill. Model-checking in dense real-time. *Information and Computation*, 104(1):2–34, 1993.

[12] R. Alur, C. Courcoubetis, N. Halbwachs, T. Henzinger, P.-H. Ho, X. Nicollin, A. Olivero, J. Sifakis, and S. Yovine. The algorithmic analysis of hybrid systems. *Theoretical Computer Science*, 138(1):3–34, 1995.

[13] R. Alur and D. L. Dill. A theory of timed automata. *Theoretical Computer Science*, 126(2):183–235, 1994.

[14] R. Alur and T. A. Henzinger. A really temporal logic. *Journal of the ACM*, 41(1):181–204, 1994.

[15] D. G. Anderson, E. A. Catchpole, N. J. DeMestre, and T. Parkes. Modeling the spread of grass fires. *Journal of Australian Mathematical Society (Ser.B)*, 23:451–66, 1982.

[16] P. Andrews and C. Chase. BEHAVE: Fire behavior prediction and fuel modeling system. In *USDA PMS-439-2, NFES 0277*, 1989.

[17] K. Arbter, W. E. Snyder, H. Burkhardt, and G. Hirzinger. Application of affine-invariant Fourier descriptors to recognition of 3D objects. *IEEE Transactions on Pattern Analysis and Machine Intelligence*, 12(7):640–47, 1990.

[18] M. P. Armstrong. Temporality in spatial databases. In *Proc. URISA Conference on Geographic and Land Information Systems*, volume 2, pages 880–89, 1988.

[19] S. Basu. New results on quantifier elimination over real closed fields and applications to constraint databases. *Journal of the ACM*, 46(4):537–55, 1999.

[20] M. Baudinet, J. Chomicki, and P. Wolper. Constraint-generating dependencies. *Journal of Computer and System Sciences*, 59(1):94–115, 1999.

[21] M. Baudinet, M. Niézette, and P. Wolper. On the representation of infinite temporal data and queries. In *Proc. ACM Symposium on Principles of Database Systems*, 1991.

[22] N. Beckmann, H.-P. Kriegel, R. Schneider, and B. Seeger. The R*-tree: An efficient and robust access method for points and rectangles. In *Proc. ACM SIGMOD International Conference on Management of Data*, 1990.

[23] A. Beller, T. Giblin, K. V. Le, S. Litz, T. Kittel, and D. Schimel. A temporal GIS prototype for global change research. In *Proc. URISA Conference on Geographic and Land Information Systems*, volume 2, pages 752–65, 1991.

[24] A. Belussi, E. Bertino, and B. Catania. Manipulating spatial data in constraint databases. In M. J. Egenhofer and J. R. Herring, editors, *Proc. 5th International Symposium on Spatial Databases*, volume 1262 of *Lecture Notes in Computer Science*, pages 115–41. Springer-Verlag, 1997.

[25] J. Ben-Arie and Z. Wang. Pictorial recognition of objects employing affine invariance in the frequency domain. *IEEE Transactions on Pattern Analysis and Machine Intelligence*, 20(6):604–18, 1998.

[26] M. Ben-Or, D. Kozen, and J. Reif. The complexity of elementary algebra and geometry. *Journal of Computer and System Sciences*, 32(2):251–64, 1986.

[27] A. Benczur, A. Novak, and P. Revesz. Classical and weighted knowledgebase transformations. *Computers and Mathematics*, 32(5):85–98, 1996.

[28] M. Benedikt, G. Dong, L. Libkin, and L. Wong. Relational expressive power of constraint query languages. *Journal of the ACM*, 45(1):1–34, 1998.

[29] M. Benedikt, M. Grohe, L. Libkin, and L. Segoufin. Reachability and connectivity queries in constraint databases. In *Proc. ACM Symposium on Principles of Database Systems*, pages 104–15, 2000.

[30] M. Benedikt and L. Libkin. Relational queries over interpreted structures. *Journal of the ACM*, 47(4):644–80, 2000.

[31] M. Benedikt and L. Libkin. Safe constraint queries. *SIAM Journal of Computing*, 29(5):1652–82, 2000.

[32] F. Benhamou and A. Colmerauer, editors. *Constraint Logic Programming: Selected Research*. MIT Press, 1993.

[33] J. L. Bentley. Multidimensional binary search trees used for associative searching. *Communications of the ACM*, 18(9):509–17, 1975.

[34] E. Bertino, C. Bettini, E. Ferrari, and P. Samarati. An access control model supporting periodicity constraints and temporal reasoning. *ACM Transactions on Database Systems*, 23(3):231–85, 1998.

[35] E. Bertino, B. Catania, and B. Shidlovsky. Towards optimal two-dimensional indexing for constraint databases. *Information Processing Letters*, 64:1–8, 1997.

[36] C. Bettini, X. S. Wang, E. Bertino, and S. Jajodia. Temporal semantic assumptions and their use in databases. *IEEE Transactions on Knowledge and Data Engineering*, 10(2):277–96, 1998.

[37] T. Bittner and A. Frank. On the design of formal theories of geographic space. *Geographical Systems*, 1(3):237–75, 1999.

[38] B. Boigelot, S. Rassart, and P. Wolper. On the expressiveness of real and integer arithmetic automata. In *International Colloquium on Automata, Languages and Programming*, volume 1443 of *Lecture Notes in Computer Science*, pages 152–63. Springer-Verlag, 1998.

[39] B. Boigelot and P. Wolper. Symbolic verification with periodic sets. In *Proc. Conference on Computer-Aided Verification*, pages 55–67, 1994.

[40] Z. Bouziane. A primitive recursive algorithm for the general Petri net reachability problem. In *Proc. IEEE Symposium on Foundations of Computer Science*, pages 130–6, 1998.

[41] A. Brodsky, J. Jaffar, and M. Maher. Towards practical query evaluation for constraint databases. *Constraints*, 2(3–4):279–304, 1997.

[42] A. Brodsky and Y. Kornatzky. The LyriC language: Querying constraint objects. In M. Carey and M. Schneider, editors, *Proc. ACM SIGMOD International Conference on Management of Data*, pages 35–46, 1995.

[43] A. Brodsky, C. Lassez, J. L. Lassez, and M. J. Maher. Separability of polyhedra for optimal filtering of spatial and constraint data. *Journal of Automated Reasoning*, 23(1):83–104, 1999.

[44] A. Brodsky, V. Segal, J. Chen, and P. Exarkhopoulo. The CCUBE constraint object-oriented database system. *Constraints*, 2(3–4):245–77, 1997.

[45] A. Brodsky, V. Segal, J. Chen, and P. Exarkhopoulo. The CCUBE constraint object-oriented database system. In *Proc. ACM SIGMOD International Conference on Management of Data*, pages 577–9, 1999.

[46] S. Burris and H. P. Sankappanavar. *A Course in Universal Algebra*. Springer-Verlag, 1981.

[47] W. Buttner and H. Simonis. Embedding Boolean expressions into logic programming. *Journal of Symbolic Computation*, 4(2):191–205, 1987.

[48] J.-H. Byon and P. Revesz. DISCO: A constraint database system with sets. In G. Kuper and M. Wallace, editors, *Proc. Workshop on Constraint Databases and Applications*, volume 1034 of *Lecture Notes in Computer Science*, pages 68–83. Springer-Verlag, 1995.

[49] M. Cai. *Parametric Rectangles: A Model for Spatiotemporal Databases*. PhD thesis, University of Nebraska-Lincoln, 2000.

[50] M. Cai, D. Keshwani, and P. Revesz. Parametric rectangles: A model for querying and animating spatiotemporal databases. In *Proc. 7th International Conference on Extending Database Technology*, volume 1777 of *Lecture Notes in Computer Science*, pages 430–44. Springer-Verlag, 2000.

[51] M. Cai and P. Revesz. Forest fire modeling in a spatio-temporal database. In *Proc. 4th International Conference on Integrating GIS and Environmental Modeling*, 2000.

[52] M. Cai and P. Revesz. Parametric R-tree: An index structure for moving objects. In *Proc. 10th COMAD International Conference on Management of Data*, pages 57–64. Tata McGraw-Hill, 2000.

[53] B. F. Caviness and J. R. Johnson, editors. *Quantifier Elimination and Cylindrical Algebraic Decomposition*. Springer-Verlag, 1998.

[54] K. Cerans. Deciding properties of integral relational automata. In *International Colloquium on Automata, Languages and Programming*, volume 820 of *Lecture Notes in Computer Science*, pages 35–46. Springer-Verlag, 1994.

[55] R. Chen. *Temporal and Video Constraint Databases*. PhD thesis, University of Nebraska-Lincoln, 2000.

[56] R. Chen, M. Ouyang, and P. Revesz. Approximating data in constraint databases. In *Proc. Symposium on Abstraction, Reformulation and Approximation*, volume 1864 of *Lecture Notes in Computer Science*, pages 124–43. Springer-Verlag, 2000.

[57] J. Chomicki, D. Goldin, and G. Kuper. Variable independence and aggregation closure. In *Proc. ACM Symposium on Principles of Database Systems*, pages 40–8. ACM Press, 1996.

[58] J. Chomicki and T. Imielinski. Finite representation of infinite query answers. *ACM Transactions on Database Systems*, 18(2):181–223, 1993.

[59] J. Chomicki and G. Kuper. Measuring infinite relations. In *Proc. ACM Symposium on Principles of Database Systems*, pages 78–85. ACM Press, 1995.

[60] J. Chomicki, Y. Liu, and P. Revesz. Animating spatiotemporal constraint databases. In *Proc. Workshop on Spatio-Temporal Database Management*, volume 1678 of *Lecture Notes in Computer Science*, pages 224–41. Springer-Verlag, 1999.

[61] J. Chomicki and P. Revesz. Constraint-based interoperability of spatiotemporal databases. In *Proc. 5th International Symposium on Spatial Databases*, volume 1262 of *Lecture Notes in Computer Science*, pages 142–61. Springer-Verlag, 1997.

[62] J. Chomicki and P. Revesz. Constraint-based interoperability of spatiotemporal databases. *Geoinformatica*, 3(3):211–43, 1999.

[63] J. Chomicki and P. Revesz. A geometric framework for specifying spatiotemporal objects. In *Proc. International Workshop on Time Representation and Reasoning*, pages 41–6, 1999.

[64] V. Chvatal. *Linear Programming*. W. H. Freeman, 1983.

[65] A. Cimatti, F. Giunchiglia, and M. Roveri. Abstraction in planning via model checking. In *Proc. Symposium on Abstraction, Reformulation and Approximation*, pages 37–41, 1998.

[66] E. M. Clarke, O. Grumberg, and D. A. Peled. *Model Checking*. MIT Press, 1999.

[67] A. Cobham. On the base-dependence of sets of numbers recognizable by finite automata. *Mathematical Systems Theory*, 3:186–92, 1969.

[68] E. F. Codd. A relational model for large shared data banks. *Communications of the ACM*, 13(6):377–87, 1970.

[69] G. E. Collins. Quantifier elimination for real closed fields by cylindrical algebraic decomposition. In H. Brakhage, editor, *Automata Theory and Formal Languages*, volume 33 of *Lecture Notes in Computer Science*, pages 134–83. Springer-Verlag, 1975.

[70] L. Colussi, E. Marchiori, and M. Marchiori. On termination of constraint logic programs. In U. Montanari and F. Rossi, editors, *Proc. 1st International Conference on Principles and Practice of Constraint Programming*, volume 976 of *Lecture Notes in Computer Science*, pages 431–48. Springer-Verlag, 1995.

[71] J. J. Comuzzi and J. M. Hart. Program slicing using weakest precondition. In *Proc. Industrial Benefit and Advances in Formal Methods*, volume 1051 of *Lecture Notes in Computer Science*. Springer-Verlag, 1996.

[72] J. Cox and K. McAloon. Decision procedures for constraint based extensions of datalog. In *Constraint Logic Programming*, pages 17–32. MIT Press, 1993.

[73] D. Cyganski and R. F. Vaz. A linear signal decomposition approach to affine invariant contour identification. *Pattern Recognition*, 28(12):1845–53, 1995.

[74] G. B. Dantzig. *Linear Programming and Extensions*. Princeton University Press, 1963.

[75] P. J. Davis. *Interpolation and Approximation*. Dover Publications, 1975.

[76] T. Dean and M. Boddy. Reasoning about partially ordered events. *Artificial Intelligence*, 36(3):375–99, 1988.

[77] R. Dechter, I. Meiri, and J. Pearl. Temporal constraint networks. *Artificial Intelligence*, 49(1–3):61–95, 1991.

[78] G. Delzanno and A. Podelski. Model checking in CLP. In *2nd International Conference on Tools and Algorithms for the Construction and Analysis of Systems*, volume 1579 of *Lecture Notes in Computer Science*, pages 74–88. Springer-Verlag, 1999.

[79] Y. Deng. *Similarity Queries for Linear Constraint Databases.* PhD thesis, University of Nebraska-Lincoln, 1999.

[80] B. Dent. *Cartography Thematic Map Design.* McGraw-Hill, 1999.

[81] A. Di Deo and D. Boulanger. A formal background to build constraint objects. In *Proc. 4th International Database Engineering and Applications Symposium*, pages 7–15. IEEE Press, 2000.

[82] T. I. Dix and C. N. Yee. A restriction mapping engine using constraint logic programming. In *Proc. 2nd International Conference on Intelligent Systems for Molecular Biology*, pages 112–20. AAAI Press, 1994.

[83] J. A. Dougenik, N. R. Chrisman, and D. R. Niemeyer. An algorithm to construct continuous area cartograms. *Professional Geographer*, 37(1):75–81, 1985.

[84] F. Dumortier, M. Gyssens, L. Vandeurzen, and D. Van Gucht. On the decidability of semi-linearity for semi-algebraic sets and its implications for spatial databases. *Journal of Computer and System Sciences*, 58(3):535–71, 1999.

[85] F. Dumortier, M. Gyssens, L. Vandeurzen, and D. Van Gucht. On the decidability of semi-linearity for semi-algebraic sets and its implications for spatial databases— Corrigendum. *Journal of Computer and System Sciences*, 59(3):557–62, 1999.

[86] M. Egenhofer. Spatial SQL: A query and presentation language. *IEEE Transactions on Knowledge and Data Engineering*, 6(1):86–95, 1994.

[87] M. Egenhofer and R. Franzosa. Point-set topological spatial relations. *International Journal of Geographical Information Systems*, 5(2):161–74, 1991.

[88] M. Egenhofer and R. Franzosa. On the equivalence of topological relations. *International Journal of Geographical Information Systems*, 9(2):133–52, 1995.

[89] M. Egenhofer and D. Mark. Modeling conceptual neighborhoods of topological line-region relations. *International Journal of Geographical Information Systems*, 9(5):555–65, 1995.

[90] T. Eiter and G. Gottlob. On the complexity of propositional knowledge base revision, updates, and counterfactuals. *Artificial Intelligence*, 57(2–3):227–70, 1992.

[91] T. Eiter and H. Mannila. Distance measures for point sets and their computation. *Acta Informatica*, 34, 1997.

[92] M. Erwig, R. H. Güting, M. M. Schneider, and M. Vazirgiannis. Abstract and discrete modeling of spatio-temporal data types. *Geoinformatica*, 3(3):269–96, 1999.

[93] J. Ferrante and J. R. Geiser. An efficient decision procedure for the theory of rational order. *Theoretical Computer Science*, 4:227–33, 1977.

[94] J. Ferrante and C. Rackoff. A decision procedure for the first order theory of real addition with order. *SIAM Journal of Computing*, 4(1):69–76, 1975.

[95] A. Finkel and Ph. Schnoebelen. Well-structured transition systems everywhere. *Theoretical Computer Science*, 256(1–2):63–92, 2001.

[96] M. Flickner, H. Sawhney, W. Niblack, J. Ashley, Q. Huang, and B. Dom. Query by image and video content: The QBIC system. *IEEE Computer*, 28(9):23–32, 1995.

[97] R. B. Floyd and R. Beigel. *The Language of Machines: An Introduction to Computability and Formal Languages.* Computer Science Press, 1994.

[98] L. Forlizzi, R. H. Güting, E. Nardelli, and M. Schneider. A data model and data structure for moving object databases. In *Proc. ACM SIGMOD International Conference on Management of Data*, pages 319–30, 2000.

[99] J. B. J. Fourier. Solution d'une question particuliére du calcul des inégalités. *Nouveau Bulletin des Sciences par la Société philomathique de Paris*, pages 99–100, 1826.

[100] A. Fournier and D. Y. Montuno. Triangulating simple polygons and equivalent problems. *ACM Transactions on Graphics*, 3:153–74, 1984.

[101] A. Frank, S. Grumbach, and R. Guting et al. Chorochronos: A research network for spatiotemporal database systems. *SIGMOD Record*, 28(3):12–21, 1999.

[102] A. Frank and W. Kuhn. Specifying open GIS with functional languages. *Geomatica*, 49(3):411–36, 1995.

[103] A. U. Frank and M. Wallace. Constraint based modeling in a GIS: Road design as a case study. In *Proc. 12th Auto Carto Conference*, volume 4, pages 177–86, 1995.

[104] U. Frank, I. Campari, and U. Formentini. *Theories and Methods of Spatio-Temporal Reasoning in Geographic Space*. Springer-Verlag, 1992.

[105] L. Fribourg and H. Olsén. A decompositional approach for computing least fixedpoints of datalog programs with Z-counters. *Constraints*, 2(3–4):305–36, 1997.

[106] L. Fribourg and J. D. C. Richardson. Symbolic verification with gap-order constraints. In *Proc. Logic Program Synthesis and Transformation*, volume 1207 of *Lecture Notes in Computer Science*, pages 20–37, 1996.

[107] F. Geerts, B. Kuijpers, and J. Van den Bussche. Topological canonization of planar spatial data and its incremental maintenance. In K.-D. Schewe, editor, *Proc. 7th International Workshop on Foundations of Models and Languages for Data and Objects*. Kluwer, 1998.

[108] C. Gervet. Conjunto: Constraint logic programming with finite set domains. In *Proc. International Logic Programming Symposium*, pages 339–58, 1994.

[109] R. Giacobazzi, S. K. Debray, and G. Levi. Generalized semantics and abstract interpretation for constraint logic programs. *Journal of Logic Programming*, 25(3):191–247, 1995.

[110] W. Gillett, L. Hanks, G. K-S. Wong, J. Yu, R. Lim, and M. V. Olson. Assembly of high-resolution restriction maps based on multiple complete digests of a redundant set of overlapping clones. *Genomics*, 33:389–408, 1996.

[111] D. Goldin and P. C. Kanellakis. On similarity queries for time-series data: Constraint specification and implementation. In U. Montanari and F. Rossi, editors, *Proc. 1st International Conference on Principles and Practice of Constraint Programming*, volume 976 of *Lecture Notes in Computer Science*, pages 137–53. Springer-Verlag, 1995.

[112] D. Goldin and P. C. Kanellakis. Constraint query algebras. *Constraints*, 1:45–83, 1996.

[113] J. Goldstein, R. Ramakrishnan, U. Shaft, and J-B. Yu. Processing queries by linear constraints. In *Proc. ACM Symposium on Principles of Database Systems*, pages 257–67, 1997.

[114] P. P. Goncalves and P. M. Diogo. Geographic information systems and cellular automata: A new approach to forest fire simulation. In *Proc. 5th European Conference and Exhibition on Geographic Information Systems*, pages 702–12, 1994.

[115] S. Graf and H. Saidi. Constructing abstract graphs using PVS. In *Proc. Computer-Aided Verification*, volume 1102 of *Lecture Notes in Computer Science*. Springer-Verlag, 1996.

[116] G. Grahne. *The Problem of Incomplete Information in Relational Databases*, volume 554 of *Lecture Notes in Computer Science*. Springer-Verlag, 1991.

[117] G. Grahne, A. O. Mendelzon, and P. Revesz. Knowledgebase transformations. *Journal of Computer and System Sciences*, 54(1):98–112, 1997.

[118] E. D. Green and P. Green. Sequence-tagged site (STS) content mapping of human chromosomes: Theoretical considerations and early experiences. *PCR Methods and Applications*, 1:77–90, 1991.

[119] M. Grigni, D. Papadias, and C. H. Papadimitriou. Topological inference. In *International Joint Conference on Artificial Intelligence*, pages 901–6, 1995.

[120] S. Grumbach and G. Kuper. Tractable recursion over geometric data. In *International Conference on Constraint Programming*, volume 1330 of *Lecture Notes in Computer Science*, pages 450–62. Springer-Verlag, 1997.

[121] S. Grumbach and Z. Lacroix. Computing queries on linear constraint databases. In *5th International Workshop on Database Programming Languages*, Electronic Workshops in Computing. Springer-Verlag, 1995.

[122] S. Grumbach, P. Rigaux, and L. Segoufin. The DEDALE system for complex spatial queries. In *Proc. ACM SIGMOD International Conference on Management of Data*, pages 213–24, 1998.

[123] S. Grumbach, P. Rigaux, and L. Segoufin. Spatio-temporal data handling with constraints. In *ACM Symposium on Geographic Information Systems*, pages 106–11, 1998.

[124] S. Grumbach, P. Rigaux, and L. Segoufin. Manipulating interpolated data is easier than you thought. In *Proc. IEEE International Conference on Very Large Databases*, pages 156–65, 2000.

[125] S. Grumbach and J. Su. First-order definability over constraint databases. In U. Montanari and F. Rossi, editors, *Proc. 1st International Conference on Principles and Practice of Constraint Programming*, volume 976 of *Lecture Notes in Computer Science*, pages 121–36. Springer-Verlag, 1995.

[126] S. Grumbach and J. Su. Finitely representable databases. *Journal of Computer and System Sciences*, 55(2):273–98, 1997.

[127] S. Grumbach and J. Su. Queries with arithmetical constraints. *Theoretical Computer Science*, 173(1):151–81, 1997.

[128] S. Grumbach, J. Su, and C. Tollu. Linear constraint query languages: Expressive power and complexity. In D. Leivant, editor, *Logic and Computational Complexity*, volume 960 of *Lecture Notes in Computer Science*, pages 426–46. Springer, 1995.

[129] P. Gundavarapu. Implementation of a refinement query system. Master's thesis, University of Nebraska-Lincoln, August 1998.

[130] O. Günther. *Efficient Structures for Geometric Data Management*, volume 337 of *Lecture Notes in Computer Science*. Springer-Verlag, Berlin, 1988.

[131] S. M. Gusein-Zade and V. S. Tikunov. A new technique for constructing continuous cartograms. *Geography and Geographic Information Systems*, 20(3):167–73, 1993.

[132] A. Guttman. R-trees: A dynamic index structure for spatial searching. In *Proc. ACM-SIGMOD Conference on Management of Data*, pages 47–57, 1984.

[133] M. Gyssens, J. Van den Bussche, and D. Van Gucht. Complete geometric query languages. *Journal of Computer and System Sciences*, 58(3):483–511, 1999.

[134] S. Haesevoets and B. Kuijpers. Closure properties of classes of spatio-temporal objects under Boolean set operations. In *Proc. International Workshop on Time Representation and Reasoning*, pages 79–86, 2000.

[135] M. Hagedoorn and R. C. Veltkamp. Reliable and efficient pattern matching using an affine invariant metric. *International Journal of Computer Vision*, 31:203–25, 1999.

[136] S. L. Hakimi and E. F. Schmeichel. Fitting polygonal functions to a set of points in the plane. *Computer Vision, Graphics, and Image Processing*, 52(2):132–6, 1991.

[137] N. Halbwachs. Delay analysis in synchronous programs. In *Proc. Conference on Computer-Aided Verification*, pages 333–46, 1993.

[138] P. Halmos. *Lectures on Boolean Algebras*. Springer-Verlag, 1974.

[139] E. Harley, A. Bonner, and N. Goodman. Good maps are straight. In *Proc. 4th International Conference on Intelligent Systems for Molecular Biology*, pages 88–97, 1996.

[140] W. Harvey and P. Stuckey. A unit two variable per inequality integer constraint solver for constraint logic programming. In *Proc. Australian Computer Science Conference (Australian Computer Science Communications)*, pages 102–11, 1997.

[141] N. Heintze and J. Jaffar. Set constraints and set-based analysis. In A. Borning, editor, *Proc. 2nd International Workshop on Principles and Practice of Constraint Programming*, volume 874 of *Lecture Notes in Computer Science*, pages 1–17. Springer-Verlag, 1994.

[142] R. Helm, K. Marriott, and M. Odersky. Spatial query optimization: From Boolean constraints to range queries. *Journal of Computer and System Sciences*, 51(2):197–201, 1995.

[143] T. A. Henzinger, P.-H. Ho, and H. Wong-Toi. HyTech: A model checker for hybrid systems. In *Proc. Conference Computer-Aided Verification*, number 1254 in Lecture Notes in Computer Science, pages 460–63. Springer-Verlag, 1997.

[144] D. S. Hochbaum and J. Naor. Simple and fast algorithms for linear and integer programs with two variables per inequality. *SIAM Journal of Computing*, 23(6):1179–92, 1994.

[145] D. H. House and C. J. Kocmoud. Continuous cartogram construction. In D. Ebert, H. Hagen, and H. Rushmeier, editors, *Proc. IEEE Visualization Conference*, pages 197–204. IEEE Press, 1998.

[146] D. P. Huttenlocher, G. A. Klauderman, and W. J. Rucklidge. Comparing images using the Hausdorff-distance. *IEEE Transactions on Pattern Analysis and Machine Intelligence*, 15:850–63, 1993.

[147] O. H. Ibarra and J. Su. On the containment and equivalence of database queries with linear constraints. In *Proc. ACM Symposium on Principles of Database Systems*, pages 32–43, 1997.

[148] T. Imielinski. Incomplete information in logical databases. *Data Engineering*, 12(2):29–39, 1989.

[149] T. Imielinski and W. Lipski. Incomplete information in relational databases. *Journal of ACM*, 31(4):761–91, 1984.

[150] N. Immerman. Relational queries computable in polynomial time. *Information and Control*, 68:86–104, 1986.

[151] J. Jaffar and J. L. Lassez. Constraint logic programming. In *Proc. 14th ACM Symposium on Principles of Programming Languages*, pages 111–9, 1987.

[152] J. Jaffar, M. J. Maher, P. Stuckey, and R. H. Yap. Beyond finite domains. In A. Borning, editor, *Proc. 2nd International Workshop on Principles and Practice of Constraint Programming*, volume 874 of *Lecture Notes in Computer Science*, pages 86–94. Springer-Verlag, 1994.

[153] J. Jaffar, S. Michaylov, P. J. Stuckey, and R. H. Yap. The CLP(R) language and system. *ACM Transactions on Programming Languages and Systems*, 14(3):339–95, 1992.

[154] H. V. Jagadish. A retrieval technique for similar shapes. In *Proc. ACM SIGMOD International Conference on Management of Data*, pages 208–17, 1991.

[155] P. Jeavons, D. Cohen, and M. Gyssens. How to determine the expressive power of constraints. *Constraints*, 4(2):113–31, 1999.

[156] C. S. Jensen, M. D. Soo, and R. T. Snodgrass. Unification of temporal data models. In *IEEE International Conference on Data Engineering*, pages 262–71, 1993.

[157] F. Kabanza, J.-M. Stevenne, and P. Wolper. Handling infinite temporal data. *Journal of Computer and System Sciences*, 51(1):1–25, 1995.

[158] P. C. Kanellakis, G. M. Kuper, and P. Revesz. Constraint query languages. In *Proc. ACM Symposium on Principles of Database Systems*, pages 299–313, 1990.

[159] P. C. Kanellakis, G. M. Kuper, and P. Revesz. Constraint query languages. *Journal of Computer and System Sciences*, 51(1):26–52, 1995.

[160] P. C. Kanellakis, S. Ramaswamy, D. E. Vengroff, and J. S. Vitter. Indexing for data models with constraints and classes. *Journal of Computer and System Sciences*, 52(3):589–612, 1996.

[161] P. C. Kanellakis and P. Revesz. On the relationship of congruence closure and unification. *Journal of Symbolic Computation*, 7(3-4):427–44, 1996.

[162] P. Kanjamala, P. Revesz, and Y. Wang. MLPQ/GIS: A GIS using linear constraint databases. In C. S. R. Prabhu, editor, *Proc. 9th COMAD International Conference on Management of Data*, pages 389–93, 1998.

[163] N. K. Karmarkar. A new polynomial-time algorithm for linear programming. *Combinatorica*, 4:373–95, 1984.

[164] R. M. Karp. Mapping the genome: Some combinatorial problems arising in molecular biology. In *Proc. 25th ACM Symposium on Theory of Computing*, pages 278–85. ACM Press, 1993.

[165] H. Katsuno and A. O. Mendelzon. A unified view of propositional knowledge base updates. In *Proc. 11th International Joint Conference on Artificial Intelligence*, pages 1413–19, 1989.

[166] H. Katsuno and A. O. Mendelzon. On the difference between updating a knowledge base and revising it. In *Proc. 2nd International Conference on Principles of Knowledge Representation and Reasoning*, pages 387–94, 1991.

[167] H. Katsuno and A. O. Mendelzon. Propositional knowledge base revision and minimal change. *Artificial Intelligence*, 52:263–94, 1991.

[168] H. Katsuno and A. O. Mendelzon. On the difference between updating a knowledge base and revising it. In *Belief Revision*, pages 183–203. Cambridge University Press, 1992.

[169] A. Kemper and M. Wallrath. An analysis of geometric modeling in database systems. *ACM Computing Surveys*, 19(1):47–91, 1987.

[170] A. Kerbrat. Reachable state space analysis of lotos specifications. In *Proc. 7th International Conference on Formal Description Techniques*, pages 161–76, 1994.

[171] L. G. Khachiyan. A polynomial algorithm in linear programming. *Doklady Akademii Nauk SSR*, 20:191–4, 1979.

[172] W. Kim, I. Choi, S. Gala, and M. Scheevel. On resolving semantic heterogeneity in multidatabase systems. In W. Kim, editor, *Modern Database Systems: The Object Model, Interoperability, and Beyond*, pages 521–50. ACM Press, 1995.

[173] P. Kolaitis and C. H. Papadimitriou. Why not negation by fixpoint? *Journal of Computer and System Sciences*, 43(1):125–44, 1991.

[174] P. Kolaitis and M. Vardi. Conjunctive-query containment and constraint satisfaction. *Journal of Computer and System Sciences*, 61(2):302–32, 2000.

[175] G. Kollios, D. Gunopulos, and V. J. Tsotras. On indexing mobile objects. In *Proc. ACM Symposium on Principles of Database Systems*, pages 261–72, 1999.

[176] C. P. Kolovson, M-A. Neimat, and S. Potamianos. Interoperability of spatial and attribute data managers: A case study. In *International Symposium on Large Spatial Databases*, pages 239–64, 1993.

[177] R. Kosaraju. Decidability of reachability in vector addition systems. In *Proc. 14th Annual ACM Symposium on Theory of Computing*, pages 267–80, 1982.

[178] M. Koubarakis. Representation and querying in temporal databases: The power of temporal constraints. In *Proc. 9th International Conference on Data Engineering*, pages 327–34, 1993.

[179] M. Koubarakis. Complexity results for first-order theories of temporal constraints. In *Principles of Knowledge Representation and Reasoning: Proc. 4th International Conference*, pages 379–90. Morgan Kaufmann, 1994.

[180] M. Koubarakis. Database models for infinite and indefinite temporal information. *Information Systems*, 19(2):141–73, 1994.

[181] M. Koubarakis. Foundations of indefinite constraint databases. In A. Borning, editor, *Proc. 2nd International Workshop on the Principles and Practice of Constraint Programming*, volume 874 of *Lecture Notes in Computer Science*, pages 266–80. Springer-Verlag, 1994.

[182] M. Koubarakis. The complexity of query evaluation in indefinite temporal constraint databases. *Theoretical Computer Science*, 171(1–2):25–60, 1997.

[183] M. Koubarakis. From local to global consistency in temporal constraint networks. *Theoretical Computer Science*, 173:89–112, February 1997.

[184] M. Koubarakis and S. Skiadopoulos. Querying temporal and spatial constraint networks in PTIME. *Artificial Intelligence*, 123(1–2):223–63, 2000.

[185] D. Kozen. Complexity of Boolean algebras. *Theoretical Computer Science*, 10:221–47, 1980.

[186] S. Kreutzer. Fixed-point query languages for linear constraint database. In *Proc. ACM Symposium on Principles of Database Systems*, pages 116–25, 2000.

[187] S. Kreutzer. Query languages for constraint databases: First-order logic, fixed-points, and convex hulls. In *International Conference on Database Theory*, volume 1973 of *Lecture Notes in Computer Science*, pages 248–62, 2001.

[188] B. Kuijpers. *Topological Properties of Spatial Databases in the Polynomial Constraint Model*. PhD thesis, University of Antwerp, 1998.

[189] B. Kuijpers and J. Van den Bussche. On capturing first-order topological properties of planar spatial databases. In C. Beeri and P. Buneman, editors, *International Conference on Database Theory*, volume 1540 of *Lecture Notes in Computer Science*, pages 187–98. Springer-Verlag, 1999.

[190] B. Kuijpers, J. Paredaens, M. Smits, and J. Van den Bussche. Termination properties of spatial datalog programs. In D. Pedreschi and C. Zaniolo, editors, *Proc. Logic in Databases*, volume 1154 of *Lecture Notes in Computer Science*, pages 101–16. Springer-Verlag, 1996.

[191] B. Kuijpers and M. Smits. On expressing topological connectivity in spatial datalog. In V. Gaede, A. Brodsky, O. Gunter, D. Srivastava, V. Vianu, and M. Wallace, editors, *Proc. Workshop on Constraint Databases and Their Applications*, volume 1191 of *Lecture Notes in Computer Science*, pages 116–33. Springer-Verlag, 1997.

[192] G. M. Kuper. On the expressive power of the relational calculus with arithmetic constraints. In *International Conference on Database Theory*, volume 470 of *Lecture Notes in Computer Science*, pages 202–14. Springer-Verlag, 1990.

[193] G. M. Kuper. Aggregation in constraint databases. In *Proc. Workshop on Principles and Practice of Constraint Programming*, pages 161–72, 1993.

[194] G. M. Kuper, L. Libkin, and J. Paredaens, editors. *Constraint Databases*. Springer-Verlag, 2000.

[195] Y. Lamdan, J. T. Schwartz, and H. J. Wolfson. Affine invariant model-based object recognition. *IEEE Journal of Robotics and Automation*, 6:578–89, 1990.

[196] E. S. Lander and M. S. Waterman. Genomic mapping by fingerprinting random clones: A mathematical analysis. *Genomics*, 2:231–9, 1988.

[197] G. Langran and R. N Chrisman. A framework for temporal geographic information. *Cartographica*, 25(3):1–14, 1988.

[198] C. Lassez and J-L. Lassez. Quantifier elimination for conjunctions of linear constraints via a convex hull algorithm. In *Symbolic and Numerical Computation for Artificial Intelligence*, pages 103–19. Academic Press, 1992.

[199] J-L. Lassez, T. Huynh, and K. McAloon. Simplification and elimination of redundant linear arithmetic constraints. In *Proc. North American Conference on Logic Programming*, pages 35–51, Cleveland, 1989.

[200] J-L. Lassez and M. Maher. On Fourier's algorithm for linear constraints. *Journal of Automated Reasoning*, 9(3):373–9, 1992.

[201] R. Laurini and D. Thompson. *Fundamentals of Spatial Information Systems*. Academic Press, 1992.

[202] H. J. Levesque. Foundations of a functional approach to knowledge representation. *Artificial Intelligence*, 23:155–212, 1984.

[203] M. Lowry and M. Subramaniam. Abstraction for analytic verification of concurrent software systems. In *Proc. Symposium on Abstraction, Reformulation and Approximation*, pages 85–94, 1998.

[204] K. Marriott and M. Odersky. Negative Boolean constraints. *Theoretical Computer Science*, 160(1–2):365–80, 1996.

[205] K. Marriott and P. J. Stuckey. *Programming with Constraints: An Introduction*. MIT Press, 1998.

[206] U. Martin and T. Nipkow. Boolean unification—The story so far. *Journal of Symbolic Computation*, 7:275–93, 1989.

[207] Y. Matiyasevich. Enumerable sets are diophantine. *Doklady Akademii Nauk SSR*, 191:279–82, 1970.

[208] E. Mayr. An algorithm for the general Petri net reachability problem. *SIAM Journal of Computing*, 13(3):441–60, 1984.

[209] K. McMillan. *Symbolic Model Checking*. Kluwer, 1993.

[210] N. Megiddo. Linear programming in linear time when the dimension is fixed. *Journal of the ACM*, 31(1):114–27, 1984.

[211] R. Mehrotra and W. I. Grosky. Shape matching utilizing indexed hypotheses generation and testing. *IEEE Transactions on Robotics and Automation*, 5(1):70–7, 1989.

[212] S. Michaylov. *Design and Implementation of Practical Constraint Programming Systems*. PhD thesis, Carnegie-Mellon University, 1992.

[213] M. L. Minsky. Recursive unsolvability of Post's problem of "tag" and other topics in the theory of Turing machines. *Annals of Mathematics*, 74(3):437–55, 1961.

[214] M. L. Minsky. *Computation: Finite and Infinite Machines*. Prentice Hall, 1967.

[215] F. Mokhtarian and S. Abbasi. Retrieval of similar shapes under affine transformations. In *Proc. International Conference on Visual Information Systems*, pages 566–74, 1999.

[216] F. Mokhtarian, S. Abbasi, and J. Kittler. Efficient and robust retrieval by shape content through curvature scale space. In *Proc. International Workshop on Image Databases and MultiMedia Search*, pages 35–42, 1996.

[217] F. Mokhtarian, S. Abbasi, and J. Kittler. Robust and efficient shape indexing through curvature scale space. In *Proc. British Machine Vision Conference*, pages 53–62, 1996.

[218] B. Momjian. *PostgreSQL: Introduction and Concepts*. Addison-Wesley, 2000.

[219] S. Morehouse. ARC/INFO: A geo-relational model for spatial information. In *Proc. International Symposium on Computer Assisted Cartography*, pages 388–97, 1985.

[220] S. Morehouse. The architecture of ARC/INFO. In *Proc. 9th Auto Carto Conference*, pages 266–77, 1989.

[221] J. R. Norris. *Markov Chains*. Cambridge University Press, 1997.

[222] M. V. Olson, J. E. Dutchik, M. Y. Graham, G. M. Brodeur, C. Helms, M. Frank, M. MacCollin, R. Scheinman, and T. Frank. Random-clone strategy for genomic restriction mapping in yeast. *Genomics*, 83:7826–30, 1986.

[223] P. O'Neil. *Database—Principles, Programming, and Performance*. Morgan Kaufmann, 1994.

[224] B. C. Ooi. *Efficient Query Processing in a Geographic Information System*, volume 471 of *Lecture Notes in Computer Science*. Springer-Verlag, 1990.

[225] M. Otto and J. Van den Bussche. First-order queries on databases embedded in an infinite structure. *Information Processing Letters*, 60:37–41, 1996.

[226] M. Ouyang. *Efficient Visualization and Querying of Geographic Databases*. PhD thesis, University of Nebraska-Lincoln, 2000.

[227] M. Ouyang and P. Revesz. Algorithms for cartogram animation. In *Proc. 4th International Database Engineering and Applications Symposium*, pages 231–5. IEEE Press, 2000.

[228] Mark H. Overmars. *The Design of Dynamic Data Structures*, volume 156 of *Lecture Notes in Computer Science*. Springer-Verlag, 1983.

[229] A. Paoluzzi, F. Bernardini, C. Cattani, and V. Ferrucci. Dimension-independent modeling with simplicial complexes. *ACM Transactions on Graphics*, 12:56–102, 1993.

[230] C. H. Papadimitriou. *Computational Complexity*. Addison-Wesley, 1994.

[231] C. H. Papadimitriou, D. Suciu, and V. Vianu. Topological queries in spatial databases. *Journal of Computer and System Sciences*, 58(1):29–53, 1999.

[232] J. Paredaens, J. Van den Bussche, and D. Van Gucht. Towards a theory of spatial database queries. In *Proc. ACM Symposium on Principles of Database Systems*, pages 279–88. ACM Press, 1994.

[233] J. Paredaens, J. Van den Bussche, and D. Van Gucht. First-order queries on finite structures over the reals. *SIAM Journal of Computing*, 27(6):1747–63, 1998.

[234] J. Paredaens, B. Kuijpers, and J. Van den Bussche. On topological elementary equivalence of spatial databases. In *International Conference on Database Theory*, volume 1186 of *Lecture Notes in Computer Science*, pages 432–46. Springer-Verlag, 1997.

[235] J. Paredaens, B. Kuijpers, G. Kuper, and L. Vandeurzen. Euclid, Tarski and Engeler encompassed. In S. Cluet and R. Hull, editors, *Proc. 6th International Workshop on Database Programming Languages*, volume 1369 of *Lecture Notes in Computer Science*, pages 1–24, 1998.

[236] A. Pentland, R. Picard, and S. Sclaroff. Photobook: Content-based manipulation of image databases. *International Journal of Computer Vision*, 18(3):233–54, 1996.

[237] J. Peterson. *Petri Net Theory and Modeling of Systems*. Prentice-Hall, 1981.

[238] E. G. M. Petrakis and C. Faloutsos. Similarity searching in large image databases. *IEEE Transactions on Knowledge and Data Engineering*, 9(3):435–47, 1997.

[239] D. J. Peuquet and N. Duan. An event-based spatiotemporal data model (ESTDM) for temporal analysis of geographical data. *International Journal of Geographical Information Systems*, 9(1):7–24, 1995.

[240] D. J. Peuquet and D. F. Marble. ARC/INFO: An example of a contemporary geographic information system. In D. J. Peuquet and D. F. Marble, editors, *Introductory Readings in Geographic Information Systems*. Taylor & Francis, 1990.

[241] F. P. Preparata and M. I. Shamos. *Computational Geometry: An Introduction*. Springer-Verlag, 1985.

[242] X. Qian and T. F. Lunt. A semantic framework of the multilevel secure relational model. *IEEE Transactions on Knowledge and Data Engineering*, 9(2):292–301, 1997.

[243] R. Ramakrishnan. *Database Management Systems*. McGraw-Hill, 1998.

[244] R. Ramakrishnan and D. Srivastava. Pushing constraint selections. *Journal of Logic Programming*, 16(3&4):361–414, 1993.

[245] S. Ramaswamy. Efficient indexing for constraint and temporal databases. In *International Conference on Database Theory*, volume 1186 of *Lecture Notes in Computer Science*, pages 419–31. Springer-Verlag, 1997.

[246] S. Ramaswamy and S. Subramanian. Path caching: A technique for optimal external searching. In *Proc. ACM Symposium on Principles of Database Systems*, pages 25–35, 1994.

[247] S. Ravela and R. Manmatha. Retrieving images by similarity of visual appearance. In *IEEE Workshop on Content-Based Access of Image Databases*, pages 311–47, 1997.

[248] S. Ravela and R. Manmatha. On computing global similarity in images. In *4th IEEE Workshop on Applications of Computer Vision*, pages 82–7. IEEE Press, 1998.

[249] S. Ravela and R. Manmatha. Retrieving images by appearance. In *IEEE International Conference on Computer Vision*, 1998.

[250] W. Reisig. *Petri Nets: An Introduction*. Springer-Verlag, 1985.

[251] R. Reiter. Towards a logical reconstruction of relational database theory. In M. Brodie, J. Mylopoulos, and J. Schmidt, editors, *On Conceptual Modelling: Perspectives from Artificial Intelligence, Databases and Programming Languages*, pages 191–233. Springer-Verlag, 1984.

[252] R. Reiter. A sound and sometimes complete query evaluation algorithm for relational databases with null values. *Journal of the ACM*, 33(2):349–70, 1986.

[253] R. Reiter. On specifying database updates. In *Proc. 3rd International Conference on Extending Database Technology*, 1992.

[254] J. Renegar. On the computational complexity and geometry of the first-order theory of the reals. *Journal of Symbolic Computation*, 13(3):255–352, 1992.

[255] P. Revesz. A closed form for Datalog queries with integer order. In *International Conference on Database Theory*, volume 470 of *Lecture Notes in Computer Science*, pages 187–201. Springer-Verlag, 1990.

[256] P. Revesz. *Constraint Query Languages*. PhD thesis, Brown University, May 1991.

[257] P. Revesz. A closed-form evaluation for Datalog queries with integer (gap)-order constraints. *Theoretical Computer Science*, 116(1):117–49, 1993.

[258] P. Revesz. Datalog queries of set constraint databases. In G. Gottlob and M. Y. Vardi, editors, *International Conference on Database Theory*, volume 893 of *Lecture Notes in Computer Science*, pages 425–38. Springer-Verlag, 1995.

[259] P. Revesz. Safe stratified Datalog with integer order programs. In U. Montanari and F. Rossi, editors, *Proc. 1st International Conference on Principles and Practice of Constraint Programming*, volume 976 of *Lecture Notes in Computer Science*, pages 154–69. Springer-Verlag, 1995.

[260] P. Revesz. Model-theoretic minimal change operators for constraint databases. In F. Afrati and Ph. Kolaitis, editors, *International Conference on Database Theory*, volume 1186 of *Lecture Notes in Computer Science*, pages 447–60. Springer-Verlag, 1997.

[261] P. Revesz. On the semantics of arbitration. *International Journal of Algebra and Computation*, 7(2):133–60, 1997.

[262] P. Revesz. Problem solving in the DISCO constraint database system. In V. Gaede, A. Brodsky, O. Gunter, D. Srivastava, V. Vianu, and M. Wallace, editors, *Proc. Constraint Databases and Applications*, volume 1191 of *Lecture Notes in Computer Science*, pages 302–15. Springer-Verlag, 1997.

[263] P. Revesz. Refining restriction enzyme genome maps. *Constraints*, 2(3–4):361–75, 1997.

[264] P. Revesz. Constraint databases: A survey. In L. Libkin and B. Thalheim, editors, *Semantics in Databases*, volume 1358 of *Lecture Notes in Computer Science*, pages 209–46. Springer-Verlag, 1998.

[265] P. Revesz. The evaluation and the computational complexity of Datalog queries of Boolean constraint databases. *International Journal of Algebra and Computation*, 8(5):472–98, 1998.

[266] P. Revesz. Safe Datalog queries with linear constraints. In M. Maher and J.-F. Puget, editors, *Proc. 4th International Conference on Principles and Practice of Constraint Programming*, volume 1520 of *Lecture Notes in Computer Science*, pages 355–69. Springer-Verlag, 1998.

[267] P. Revesz. Safe query languages for constraint databases. *ACM Transactions on Database Systems*, 23(1):58–99, 1998.

[268] P. Revesz. Datalog programs with difference constraints. In *Proc. 12th International Conference on Applications of Prolog*, pages 69–76, 1999.

[269] P. Revesz. The dominating cycle problem in 2-connected graphs and the matching problem for bag of bags are NP-complete. In *Proc. International Conference on Paul Erdős and His Mathematics*, pages 221–5, 1999.

[270] P. Revesz. Reformulation and approximation in model checking. In B. Choueiry and T. Walsh, editors, *Proc. 4th International Symposium on Abstraction, Reformulation, and Approximation*, volume 1864 of *Lecture Notes in Computer Science*, pages 124–43. Springer-Verlag, 2000.

[271] P. Revesz and M. Cai. Efficient querying of periodic spatiotemporal objects. In *Proc. 6th International Conference on Principles and Practice of Constraint Programming*, volume 1894 of *Lecture Notes in Computer Science*, pages 396–410. Springer-Verlag, 2000.

[272] P. Revesz and M. Cai. Efficient querying of periodic spatio-temporal databases. *Annals of Mathematics and Artificial Intelligence*, to appear, 2001.

[273] P. Revesz, R. Chen, P. Kanjamala, Y. Li, Y. Liu, and Y. Wang. The MLPQ/GIS constraint database system. In *Proc. ACM SIGMOD International Conference on Management of Data*, 2000.

[274] P. Revesz and Y. Li. MLPQ: A linear constraint database system with aggregate operators. In *Proc. 1st International Database Engineering and Applications Symposium*, pages 132–7. IEEE Press, 1997.

[275] G. D. Richards. An elliptical growth model of forest fire fronts and its numerical solution. *International Journal of Numerical Methods Engineering*, 30:1163–79, 1990.

[276] R. Rothermel. Modelling fire behavior. In *Proc. International Conference on Forest Fire Research*, pages 1–19. Coimbra, 1990.

[277] A. Salamon. Implementation of a database system with Boolean algebra constraints. Master's thesis, University of Nebraska-Lincoln, May 1998.

[278] S. Saltenis, C. S. Jensen, S. T. Leutenegger, and M. A. Lopez. Indexing the positions of continuously moving objects. In *Proc. ACM SIGMOD International Conference on Management of Data*, pages 331–42, 2000.

[279] H. Samet. *The Design and Analysis of Spatial Data Structures*. Addison-Wesley, 1990.

[280] V. Saraswat. *Concurrent Programming Languages*. PhD thesis, Carnegie-Mellon University, 1989.

[281] H. J. Scheck and A. Wolf. From extensible databases to interoperability between multiple databases and GIS applications. In *International Symposium on Large Spatial Databases*, pages 207–38, Singapore, 1993.

[282] H. Schneider and G. P. Barker. *Matrices and Linear Algebra (Second Edition)*. Dover Publications, 1973.

[283] M. Scholl and A. Voisard. Object-oriented database systems for geographic applications: An experiment with O2. In F. Bancilhon, C. Delobel, and P. C. Kanellakis, editors, *The O2 Book*, pages 585–618. Morgan Kaufmann, 1992.

[284] A. Schrijver. *Theory of Linear and Integer Programming*. John Wiley and Sons, 1986.

[285] L. Segoufin and V. Vianu. Querying spatial databases via topological invariants. *Journal of Computer and System Sciences*, 61(2):270–301, 2000.

[286] T. Sellis, N. Roussopoulos, and C. Faloutsos. The R^+-tree: A dynamic index for multi-dimensional objects. In *Proc. IEEE International Conference on Very Large Databases*, pages 507–18, 1987.

[287] J. Sharma. Oracle8i spatial: Experiences with extensible databases. In *An Oracle Technical White Paper*, May 1999.

[288] A. Silberschatz, H. Korth, and S. Sudarshan. *Database System Concepts*. McGraw-Hill, 1998.

[289] A. P. Sistla, O. Wolfson, S. Chamberlain, and S. Dao. Modeling and querying moving objects. In *Proc. 13th IEEE International Conference on Data Engineering*, pages 422–32, 1997.

[290] S. Smoliar and H. Zhang. Content-based video indexing and retrieval. *IEEE Multimedia Magazine*, 1(2):62–72, 1994.

[291] R. T. Snodgrass, editor. *The TSQL2 Temporal Query Language*. Kluwer, 1995.

[292] D. Srivastava. Subsumption and indexing in constraint query languages with linear arithmetic constraints. *Annals of Mathematics and Artificial Intelligence*, 8(3–4):315–43, 1993.

[293] D. Srivastava, R. Ramakrishnan, and P. Revesz. Constraint objects. In A. Borning, editor, *Proc. 2nd International Workshop on Principles and Practice of Constraint Programming*, volume 874 of *Lecture Notes in Computer Science*, pages 218–28. Springer-Verlag, 1994.

[294] J. Star and J. Estes. *Geographic Information Systems: An Introduction*. Prentice-Hall, 1989.

[295] A. P. Stolboushkin and M. A. Taitslin. Safe stratified Datalog with integer order does not have syntax. *ACM Transactions on Database Systems*, 23(1):100–9, 1998.

[296] G. Strang. *Linear Algebra and Its Applications*. Academic Press, 1976.

[297] M. Stricker and M. Orengo. Similarity of color images. In *Proc. SPIE Conference on Storage and Retrieval for Image and Video Databases III*, volume 2420, pages 381–92, 1995.

[298] P. J. Stuckey and S. Sudarshan. Compiling query constraints. In *Proc. ACM Symposium on Principles of Database Systems*, pages 56–68, 1994.

[299] S. Sudarshan, D. Srivastava, R. Ramakrishnan, and C. Beeri. Extending the well-founded and valid model semantics for aggregation. In *International Logic Programming Symposium*, pages 114–26, 1993.

[300] P. Svensson and H. Zhexue. Geo-sal: a query language for spatial data analysis. In *Proc. Advances in Spatial Databases*, volume 525 of *Lecture Notes in Computer Science*, pages 119–40. Springer-Verlag, 1991.

[301] M. Swain and D. Ballard. Color indexing. *International Journal of Computer Vision*, 7(1):11–32, 1991.

[302] A. Tansel, J. Clifford, S. Gadia, S. Jajodia, A. Segev, and R. T. Snodgrass, editors. *Temporal Databases: Theory, Design, and Implementation*. Benjamin/Cummings, 1993.

[303] A. Tarski. *A Decision Method for Elementary Algebra and Geometry*. University of California Press, Berkeley, 1951.

[304] J. Tayeb, O. Ulusoy, and O. Wolfson. A quadtree-based dynamic attribute indexing method. *The Computer Journal*, 41(3):185–200, 1998.

[305] D. Toman. *Foundations of Temporal Query Languages*. PhD thesis, Kansas State University, 1995.

[306] D. Toman and J. Chomicki. Datalog with integer periodicity constraints. *Journal of Logic Programming*, 35(3):263–90, 1998.

[307] F. C. D. Tsai. Robust affine invariant matching with application to line features. In *Proc. IEEE Conference on Computer Vision and Pattern Recognition*, pages 393–9, 1993.

[308] S. Tsur, F. Olken, and D. Naor. Deductive databases for genome mapping. In *Proc. NACLP Workshop on Deductive Databases*, 1993.

[309] S. Tsur and C. Zaniolo. LDL: A logic-based data-language. In *Proc. IEEE International Conference on Very Large Databases*, pages 33–41, 1986.

[310] J. D. Ullman. *Principles of Database and Knowledge-Base Systems*. Computer Science Press, 1989.

[311] K. Vadaparty. On the power of rule-based query languages for nested data models. *Journal of Logic Programming*, 21(3):155–75, 1994.

[312] L. Van Den Dries. Alfred Tarski's elimination theory for real closed fields. *Journal of Symbolic Logic*, 53:7–19, 1988.

[313] R. van der Meyden. Recursively indefinite databases. *Theoretical Computer Science*, 116(1):151–94, 1993.

[314] R. van der Meyden. The complexity of querying indefinite data about linearly ordered domains. *Journal of Computer and System Sciences*, 54(1):113–35, 1997.

[315] A. Van Gelder. The well-founded semantics of aggregation. In *Proc. ACM Symposium on Principles of Database Systems*, pages 127–38, 1992.

[316] A. Van Gelder, K. A. Ross, and J. S. Schlipf. The well-founded semantics for general logic programs. *Journal of the ACM*, 38(3):620–50, 1991.

[317] P. Van Hentenryck. *Constraint Satisfaction in Logic Programming*. MIT Press, 1989.

[318] M. Vardi. The complexity of relational query languages. In *Proc. 14th ACM Symposium on the Theory of Computing*, pages 137–45, 1982.

[319] M. Veach, P. Coddington, and G. C. Cox. BURN: A simulation of forest fire propagation. In *Project Report for the Northeast Parallel Architectures Center*, 1994.

[320] M. B. Vilain and H. Kautz. Constraint propagation algorithms for temporal reasoning. In *Proc. National Conference on Artificial Intelligence*, 1986.

[321] K. Wang. *Affine-Invariant Moment Method of Three-Dimensional Object Identification*. PhD thesis, Syracuse University, 1977.

[322] X. S. Wang, S. Jajodia, and V. S. Subrahmanian. Temporal modules: An approach toward federated temporal databases. In *Proc. ACM SIGMOD International Conference on Management of Data*, pages 227–36, 1993.

[323] J. Warmer and A. Kleppe. *The Object Constraint Language: Precise Modeling with UML*. ACM Press, 1998.

[324] T. C. Waugh and R. G. Healey. The GEOVIEW design: A relational database approach to geographical data handling. *International Journal of Geographic Information Systems*, 1(2):101–18, 1987.

[325] D. Weinstein, K. Green, J. Campbell, and M. Finney. Fire growth modeling in an integrated GIS environment. In *Proc. Environmental System Research Institute User Conference*, 1995.

[326] M. Werman and D. Weinshall. Similarity and affine invariant distances between 2D point sets. *IEEE Transactions on Pattern Analysis and Machine Intelligence*, 17:810–14, 1995.

[327] H. P. Williams. Fourier-Motzkin elimination extension to integer programming problems. *Journal of Combinatorial Theory (A)*, 21:118–23, 1976.

[328] S. Wolfram. Cellular automata as models of complexity. *Nature*, 311:419–24, 1984.

[329] O. Wolfson, A. Sistla, B. Xu, J. Zhou, and S. Chamberlain. DOMINO: Databases for moving objects tracking. In *Proc. ACM SIGMOD International Conference on Management of Data*, pages 547–9, 1999.

[330] P. Wolper and B. Boigelot. An automata-theoretic approach to Presburger arithmetic constraints. In *Proc. Static Analysis Symposium*, volume 983 of *Lecture Notes in Computer Science*, pages 21–32. Springer-Verlag, 1995.

[331] G. K-S. Wong, J. Yu, E. C. Thayer, and M. V. Olson. Multiple-complete-digest restriction fragment mapping: Generating sequence-ready maps for large-scale DNA sequencing. In *Proc. National Academy of Sciences, USA*, pages 5225–30, 1997.

[332] M. F. Worboys. A unified model for spatial and temporal information. *Computer Journal*, 37(1):26–34, 1994.

[333] M. F. Worboys. *GIS: A Computing Perspective*. Taylor & Francis, 1995.

[334] M. Yannakakis. Expressing combinatorial optimization problems by linear programs. In *Proc. ACM Symposium on Theory of Computation*, pages 223–8, 1988.

[335] R. H. C. Yap. A constraint logic programming framework for constructing DNA restriction maps. *Artificial Intelligence in Medicine*, 5:447–64, 1993.

[336] M. Yuan. Wildfire conceptual modeling for building GIS space-time models. In *Proc. URISA Conference on Geographic and Land Information Systems*, pages 859–68, 1994.

[337] M. Yuan. Modeling semantical, temporal and spatial information in geographic information systems. In *Geographic Information Research: Bridging the Atlantic*, pages 334–7. Taylor & Francis, 1996.

[338] X. Zhang and M. Ozsoyoglu. On efficient reasoning with implication constraints. In *International Conference on Deductive and Object-Oriented Databases*, volume 760 of *Lecture Notes in Computer Science*, pages 236–52. Springer-Verlag, 1993.

[339] H. Zhu, J. Su, and O. H. Ibarra. An index structure for spatial joins in linear constraint databases. In *IEEE International Conference on Data Engineering*, pages 636–43, 1999.

Index

TEXTS IN COMPUTER SCIENCE

(continued from page ii)

Merritt and Stix, Migrating from Pascal to C++

Munakata, Fundamentals of the New Artificial Intelligence

Nerode and Shore, Logic for Applications, Second Edition

Pearce, Programming and Meta-Programming in Scheme

Peled, Software Reliability Methods

Revesz, Introduction to Constraint Databases

Schneider, On Concurrent Programming

Smith, A Recursive Introduction to the Theory of Computation

Socher-Ambrosius and Johann, Deduction Systems

Stirling, Modal and Temporal Properties of Processes

Zeigler, Objects and Systems